Homosexual Behavior

HOMOSEXUAL BEHAVIOR

A MODERN REAPPRAISAL

EDITED BY

JUDD MARMOR

Basic Books, Inc., Publishers   *New York*

Library of Congress Cataloging in Publication Data

Main entry under title:
Homosexual behavior.

Includes bibliographies and index
1. Homosexuality—Addresses, essays, lectures.
I. Marmor, Judd. [DNLM: 1. Homosexuality. WM615
H7623]
HQ76.25.H673   306.7′6   78–24659
ISBN: 0–465–03045–9

To Katherine

CONTENTS

PART I
The View of the Biological Sciences

PART II
The View of the Social Sciences

PART III
The View of the Clinician

FOREWORD

Although there is a plethora of books on homosexuality, none of them can be compared with this one in the breadth and depth of its presentation of the many faceted aspects of this controversial subject. We are all greatly indebted to Dr. Marmor and the other contributors for this excellently balanced presentation of the most recent (as well as earlier) theories and research findings from the biological and social sciences, and from varied clinicians' viewpoints and experiences. From each of these sources, hitherto unpublished new conceptualizations and new research findings are presented. The book is, indeed, a cornucopia of riches.

The pervasive theme of the book (which is admirably presented in Dr. Marmor's "Overview on the Multiple Roots of Homosexuality") is that biological, social-psychological and cultural variables must all be taken into consideration if we are to understand the complex phenomena encompassed by the term homosexuality. For example, the inclusion of excellent chapters on cross-cultural data, the Gay Liberation Movement, legal issues and religion, among others, provides evidence that the forms and expressions of homosexuality cannot be understood apart from the norms and values of the larger society and, similarly, apart from the many minority subcultures or worlds that lesbians and homosexuals themselves develop.

For those who seek a balanced and comprehensive picture of homosexuality and lesbianism, and a presentation based on the theory and research now available, this book will help fill that need most admirably. It should appeal to a wide audience, not only of scientists and professionals who seek to keep abreast of the latest developments in this area, but also to laymen in many walks of life who have interests in and concerns about homosexuality: judges, legislators, the clergy, parents of lesbians and homosexuals, as well as homosexuals and lesbians themselves.

Evelyn Hooker, Ph.D.

PREFACE

This book attempts to bring to the reader a compendium of the most advanced knowledge and thinking that presently exists on the subject of homosexual reactions and behaviors in both men and women. A previous volume, *Sexual Inversion: The Multiple Roots of Homosexuality,* published in 1965, represented a similar effort. In the intervening years, however, there have been considerable advances in our understanding of the phenomenon of homosexual experience—biologically, sociologically, and clinically—so that the previous volume, a landmark in its time, must now be considered to be in large part outdated. Consequently, although a few of the articles from the former book have been revised and retained, by far the greater part of the present volume consists of articles that are completely new and written specially for it.

My basic orientation to the subject continues to be a multifactorial one. It is my firm conviction that the complex issues surrounding the phenomenon of same-sex object-choice cannot be understood in terms of any unitary cause whether it be biological, psychological, or sociological. Thus I have again attempted to assemble relevant information from every sector of biological and social science that can be helpful—history, comparative zoology, genetics, endocrinology, sociology, anthropology, law, psychology, and psychiatry. In addition, however, because recent historical developments have brought religious and social action issues to the fore, I have solicited new chapters in these two areas. The result, I believe, is a comprehensive and objective presentation of the multifaceted aspects of our knowledge and understanding of homosexual behavior and experience in this latter part of the twentieth century.

ACKNOWLEDGMENTS

The bringing of a volume of original papers to fruition is always a complex task that requires the cooperation of many people. I am grateful to the many contributors to this volume who went to great lengths to collate the latest knowledge in their respective areas. I am also indebted to the staff of Basic Books for their careful and judicious editing. Finally, I cannot begin to express my appreciation to my Administrative Assistant, Mrs. Leona H. Light, for her dedicated, creative helpfulness throughout the preparation of the manuscript.

CONTRIBUTORS

LEE BIRK, M.D. Associate Clinical Professor of Psychiatry, Harvard Medical School; Director, Learning Therapies, Inc.

J. M. CARRIER, Member, Gender Research Clinic, University of California School of Medicine, Los Angeles, California.

R. H. DENNISTON, II, Ph.D. Senior Professor of Zoology and Physiology, The University of Wyoming.

RICHARD GREEN, M.D. Professor, Departments of Psychiatry and Behavioral Science, and Psychology, State University of New York at Stony Brook, Stony Brook, New York.

SEWARD HILTNER, Ph.D., D.D. Professor of Theology and Personality, Princeton Theological Seminary, Princeton, New Jersey

EVELYN HOOKER, Ph.D. Research Professor of Psychology, retired, UCLA, Los Angeles, California; Chairman of Task Force on Homosexuality of the Institute of Mental Health.

LAUD HUMPHREYS, Ph.D. Professor of Sociology, Pitzer College; Professor of Government, Claremont Graduate School, Claremont, California; Private Psychotherapy Practice, Los Angeles, California.

ARNO KARLEN, Ph.D. formerly Associate Professor of English, Pennsylvania State University, State College, Pennsylvania; author of *Sexuality and Homosexuality* (Norton, 1971).

JAMES KELLY, Ph.D. Associate Professor, California State University at Long Beach and San Diego State University; Consultant, Department of Psychiatry, UCLA School of Medicine/Sepulveda Veterans' Administration Medical Center.

MARTHA KIRKPATRICK, M.D. Associate Clinical Professor of Psychiatry, UCLA; Member, Los Angeles Society for Psychoanalysis.

JUDD MARMOR, M.D. Franz Alexander Professor of Psychiatry, University of Southern California School of Medicine, Los Angeles.

BRIAN MILLER, Ph.D. Candidate, Department of Sociology, University of Alberta, Edmonton, Canada; Private Psychotherapy Practice, Los Angeles, California.

JOHN MONEY, M.D. Professor of Medical Psychology; Associate Professor of Pediatrics and Director, Psychohormonal Reasearch Unit, The Johns Hopkins University and Hospital, Baltimore, Maryland.

CAROLE MORGAN, Doctoral Candidate, Wright Institute of Los Angeles; Psychology Intern, Di Di Hirsh Community Mental Health Association, Culver City, California.

LIONEL OVESEY, M.D. Clinical Professor of Psychiatry, Center for Psychoanalytic Training and Research, College of Physicians and Surgeons, Columbia University.

BARBARA PONSE, Ph.D. Psychotherapist in private practice in the greater Los Angeles area; formerly Assistant Professor of Sociology at Washington University, St. Louis, Missouri.

BERNARD F. REISS, Ph.D. Professor of Professional Psychology, New School for Social Research, N.Y.C.; Director, Housatonic Mental Health Center, Lakeville, Connecticut.

ELI ROBINS, M.D. Wallace Renard, Professor of Psychiatry, Washington University School of Medicine, St. Louis, Missouri.

MARCEL T. SAGHIR, M.D. Associate Professor of Clinical Psychiatry, Washington University School of Medicine, St. Louis, Missouri.

LEON SALZMAN, M.D. Clinical Professor of Psychiatry, Georgetown University Medical School, Washington, D.C.; Faculty and Board of Directors, Washington School of Psychiatry, Washington, D.C.

DAVID S. SANDERS, M.D. Associate Clinical Professor of Psychiatry, University of California, Los Angeles; Attending Psychiatrist, Cedars–Sinai Medical Center, Los Angeles, California.

RALPH SLOVENKO, LL.B, Ph.D. Professor of Law and Psychiatry, Wayne State University School of Law, Detroit, Michigan.

GARFIELD TOURNEY, M.D. Professor of Psychiatry and Director of Residency Training, Department of Psychiatry and Human Behavior, University of Mississippi School of Medicine.

BRUCE VOELLER, Ph.D. President, The Mariposa Education and Research Foundation; Founder, The National Gay Task Force.

CAROL WARREN, Associate Professor, Department of Sociology, Univeristy of Southern California; Senior Research Associate, Social Science Research Institute, University of Southern California, Los Angeles.

Homosexual Behavior

Overview:
The Multiple Roots
of Homosexual Behavior

JUDD MARMOR

The Problem of Definition

A major difficulty underlying any discussion of the phenomenon of homosexual experience is that of definition. What exactly is meant when the term "homosexuality" is used? Is it a state of mind or a form of behavior? Must it be conscious or can it be unconscious? Is it a universal ontogenetic aspect of all human behavior, or is it a reflection of a specific type of psychopathology? Is it an outgrowth of individual family disturbances, broad sociocultural influences, or biological or genetic factors?

A search of the literature reveals a wide spectrum of opinion on these and other questions, with passionate proponents of each point of view. Historically, the most influential theory of causation has been that of Sigmund Freud (1905), who believed that homosexuality stems from a biologically rooted bisexual predisposition and is the expression of a universal human trend. In accordance with the strong Darwinian cast in his thinking, Freud believed that all persons go through an inevitable "homoerotic" developmental phase in the process of achieving heterosexuality. Certain kinds of life experience can arrest this evolutionary process, and the individual then remains "fixated" at a homosexual level. Even if development proceeds normally, certain vestiges of homosexuality remain as permanent aspects of the personality; these universal "latent homosexual" tendencies are reflected in "sublimated" expressions of friendship for members of one's own sex and in patterns of behavior or interest that are presumably more appropriate to the opposite sex—for example, artistic, culinary, or other "passive" interests in males, and athletic, professional, or similar "aggressive" tendencies in females.

Putting aside for the moment the theoretical validity or invalidity of these ideas, it is important to note that the definition of homosexuality in Freud's theoretical system is not linked to overt sexual behavior per se, but to a conglomerate system of feelings, attitudes, and reactions that exists in varying degrees in everyone, although it is most evident in persons whose behavior is overtly homosexual. Despite the fact that there is nothing inherently illogical in such a definition, it raises an important practical question. At what point, on this basis, is one justified in designating a person as "homosexual"? Is it a quantitative or qualitative matter? In terms of Freud's views, it is essentially a quantitative one: inasmuch as homosexual patterns are present in the unconscious of all people, the clinical problem of homosexuality becomes one of the *degree* to which these patterns are manifested in thought or behavior. Such a line of demarcation is inevitably vague and indefinite.

I believe it is possible to arrive at a more precise *qualitative* definition of homosexuality, although, as we shall see, quantitative factors are also involved. Some authors define it in purely behavioral terms, i.e., a homosexual is one who, in adult life, engages repeatedly in overt sexual relations with a member or members of the same sex. Such a characterization, however, does not do justice to the complex variables involved; a definition based on overt behavior alone fails to make a distinction between those who indulge in homosexual behavior out of an intense sexual attraction to members of the same sex and those who engage in such behavior for a variety of other reasons.

Sexual behavior, no less than other human reactions, is remarkably adaptive. In the absence of heterosexual objects, many humans (as well as lower animals—see Denniston, chapter 1, this volume) will ultimately seek gratification from same-sex individuals. An example of this is the homosexual behavior that takes place among prisoners or sailors as a consequence of prolonged sexual deprivation. Indeed, in the absence of any available human object, sexual release may be sought not merely in autoerotic practices, but occasionally with animals or even through the medium of inanimate objects.

Homosexual behavior may also be a reflection of some impairment of an individual's inner controls—a malfunction of what psychoanalysts call the "superego." When such inner controls are weak or absent, an individual may indulge in homosexual behavior for a wide variety of motives which have nothing to do with erotic preference— e.g., for money, for adventure, from boredom, from curiosity, from a need to please, or from hostility to or rebellion against parental or societal standards. Reiss (1961) has described a group of delinquent heterosexual youths who go through a period, sometimes of several years, of allowing themselves to be used, for money, by adult fellators, yet who do not define themselves as homosexuals and who totally discontinue their "homosexual" relationships as they move into adulthood. Homosexual behavior may also be the expression of transitory and exploratory sexual interest among adolescents and preadolescents in a society that places obstacles in the way of the heterosexual explorations that most of them would prefer. It can even have ideological roots, as in the deliberate lesbian activity of some radical women's liberationists (see Ponse, chapter 8, and Kirkpatrick and Morgan, chapter 20, this volume).

A psychodynamic definition of homosexuality, therefore, cannot ignore the element of motivation. To be *meaningful* as a distinct psychosexual phenomenon, homosexuality should imply the same kind of strong and spontaneous capacity to be erotically aroused by a member of one's own sex as heterosexuality implies in relation to members of the opposite sex. I would characterize the homosexual person, therefore, as one *who is motivated in adult life by a definite preferential erotic attraction to members of the same sex and who usually (but not necessarily) engages in overt sexual relations with them.* [1]

Such a definition still encompasses and retains wide quantitative variations, but is essentially qualitative in nature. It excludes the transitory, opportunistic homosexual patterns of delinquents, and also does away with the ambiguous, essentially meaningless, and nonoperational concept of "latent homosexuality" (see Salzman, chapter 17, this volume). It also excludes patterns of homosexual behavior that are not motivated by specific, preferential erotic desire, patterns like the incidental homosexual behavior of adolescents or the situational homosexual reactions of heterosexually-deprived persons. It does *not,* however, exclude those who are involved in fantasies of intense sexual longing for members of the same sex, yet are prohibited by fears or moral considerations from actually indulging in overt homosexual activity; such individuals are simply the homosexual analogues of inhibited or repressed heterosexuals.

To further complicate the definition, it also must be noted that the presence of homosexual erotic motivation does *not* exclude the capacity for heterosexual arousal. Homosexual and heterosexual responsiveness in human beings are not always clearly differentiated patterns. As Kinsey and his associates (1948) have demonstrated, these levels of responsiveness are points on a continuum that ranges from exclusive heterosexual reactivity to exclusive homosexual reactivity with various

---

1. The presence of such a basic homoerotic motivation does not preclude the possibility that other motivations (power, dependency, hostility, etc.) may also be involved just as they can be in heterosexual behavior (see Ovesey and Woods, chapter 18, this volume).

gradations in between. Kinsey has suggested a seven-point scale for this continuum based on both overt experience and inner psychological reactions: 0 on the scale denotes being exclusively heterosexual; 1, predominantly heterosexual, only incidentally homosexual; 2, predominantly heterosexual, but more than incidentally homosexual; 3, equally heterosexual and homosexual; 4, predominantly homosexual, but more than incidentally heterosexual; 5, predominantly homosexual, only incidentally heterosexual; and 6, exclusively homosexual. Individuals in the 5 and 6 categories are often referred to as obligatory homosexuals. The term "bisexual" should be reserved for those who rate 2, 3 or 4 on the Kinsey scale. In the remarks that follow, unless otherwise indicated, the term "homosexual" will be used to refer to individuals who are either 5 or 6 on the Kinsey scale.

Incidence

Homosexual behavior has probably existed since time immemorial. Records of its presence can be found in prehistoric art as well as in the pictographs and hieroglyphs of ancient cultures. It is probable that homosexual activities of some kind occur in most if not all societies, but the attitudes of societies toward such practices vary widely. In a study of seventy-six societies other than our own, Ford and Beach (1952) found that in 64 percent of them, homosexual activities were considered either normal or socially acceptable, at least for certain members of the community. In some societies (Keraki of New Guinea, Aranda of Australia, and Siwans of North Africa), male homosexual activities were universal, although such activity did not preclude the more predominant heterosexual relationships. Devereux (1937) has pointed out that among the Mojave Indians there was a recognized class of exclusively homosexual women.

Ford and Beach note that even among the 36 percent of societies in which homosexual practices were either condemned or prohibited, there was evidence, at least in some, that such practices continued to take place secretly. It is clear that in these latter societies, as in our own, efforts to study the prevalence of homosexuality encounter profound difficulties. Actual numbers are almost impossible to ascertain because of the opprobrium and/or shame with which such inclinations are regarded. It seems fair to assume that actual incidence figures in such societies are probably higher than most studies report.

In most Western cultures homosexual behavior can be encountered in all walks of life, at all socioeconomic levels, among all racial and

ethnic groups, and in rural as well as urban areas. Kinsey and his associates (1948), in their survey of more than 5,000 white American males,
found that 10 percent were more or less exclusively homosexual for at
least three years between the ages of sixteen and fifty-five, and 4 percent were exclusively homosexual throughout their lives. In an analogous survey of American women (1953), the Kinsey group found that
between 2 and 6 percent of the unmarried women in the sample, but
less than 1 percent of the married ones, had been more or less exclusively homosexual between the ages of twenty and thirty-five.

The Kinsey reports represent the most thorough and extensive surveys done to date. A number of smaller studies have been made in
Europe, and all are in approximate agreement with the Kinsey findings
(Romer, 1906; Hirschfeld, 1920; Friedeberg, 1953; and Schofield, 1965).
On the basis of these various studies it is fair to conclude, conservatively,
that the incidence of more or less exclusively homosexual behavior in
Western culture ranges from 5 to 10 percent for adult males and from
3 to 5 percent for adult females. If bisexual behavior is included, the
incidence may well be twice these figures. It is clear, therefore, that the
propensity for homosexual reactivity is a widespread one even in societies such as ours which strongly discourage it. The psychiatrically intriguing question is why so many millions of men and women become
motivated towards such behavior despite the powerful cultural taboos
against it. Although innumerable explanations can be found in psychiatric and psychoanalytic literature for the origins of specific instances of
homosexual reactivity, no single determinant has as yet been uncovered that adequately explains all homosexual patterns. Clearly we are
dealing with a syndrome that has multiple and diverse roots. In the
pages that follow I shall review the evidence from the biological, psychological, and sociocultural points of view for various factors that seem
to be relevant.

Biological Factors

To what extent does the nature of the organism itself—the biological
factor—play a role in the genesis of homosexuality? Is there a genetic
predisposition for such behavior? Kallman (1952) studied eighty-five
pairs of twins in which at least one of each pair was overtly homosexual
—5 or 6 on the Kinsey scale. Forty-five were members of dizygotic pairs
(nonidentical twins), and the concordance rates for overt homosexuality
in them were somewhat—but not markedly—higher than those reported by Kinsey for the total male population. On the other hand, for

the forty subjects who were members of monozygotic pairs (identical twins), Kallman reported the extraordinary finding of 100 percent concordance in overt behavior. This finding would suggest the presence of a decisive genetic factor in homosexuality, except that Kallman's results have not been replicated by other investigators. For example, Kolb (1963) has described seven monozygotic twin pairs in which there was no concordance between the homosexual member of the pair and his twin sibling. It should also be pointed out that, given the higher degree of mutual identification in identical twins, and other possible facilitating familial and environmental circumstances, it is conceivable that there may be nongenetic reasons for a greater tendency in them toward concordance in homosexual behavior. Nevertheless, the consistently higher incidence of such concordance in monozygotic twins as compared to dizygotic ones does suggest the possibility that there may be a hidden genetic predisposition that interacts with subsequent environmental factors. Kallman considered homosexuality to be analogous to left-handedness, which is genetically controlled but the manifestations of which can be masked or precluded by conditioning in a predominantly right-handed world.

Some recent studies by Dörner (1967) raise a strong possibility that the predisposing factors in at least some obligatory homosexuals may be due to intrauterine or early postnatal influences. Dörner believes that the male hormone, at a critical point of prenatal ontogenesis, organizes the developing hypothalamic centers of the brain in such a way as to mediate masculine behavior postnatally. Conversely, a deficiency of such androgenization predisposes the individual to effeminate patterns of behavior. This theory evolved from a significant experiment in which Dörner demonstrated that geno- and phenotypically normal rats who were castrated on the first day of life, when treated with androgens after they had achieved maturity, manifested female sexual behavior even though they developed normal masculine physiques. If, however, after such castration, they were given a single small injection of testosterone on the third day of life, the same androgen treatment in adulthood led to perfectly normal heterosexual behavior. Dörner postulates that a similar absolute or relative androgen deficiency in the human male fetus at a critical period of differentiation (between the fourth and seventh month of intrauterine development, he suggests) may create a "neuroendocrine predisposition for homosexuality" in the adult male even though there is subsequent normal testosterone production and normal secondary sexual characteristics.

Later studies done by Dörner and his associates (1975) have lent credence to this hypothesis. When intravenous injections of estrogens were administered to group 6 homosexuals, it was found that the plasma luteinizing hormone (LH) levels in these subjects followed a response pattern more characteristic of women than of men; that is to say, there was a decrease in LH followed by a positive rebound above the baseline. In contrast, the heterosexual male controls showed a similar initial decrease but no rebound. Dörner considers this difference between the homosexual and heterosexual subjects to be a confirmation of differences in hypothalamic sensitization during prenatal development.

No chromosomal differences have been found between homosexual subjects and heterosexual controls (Pare, 1965; and Money, chapter 3, this volume). Recent technological advances in hormone assay methods, however, have begun to turn up some intriguing findings with regard to possible hormonal differences. As Tourney (chapter 2, this volume) points out, a number of recent studies have reported abnormally low twenty-four-hour urinary testosterone levels in exclusively homosexual males as well as variations in their plasma testosterone levels. As he indicates, however, these findings are by no means consistent and there may be extraneous reasons for them. Plasma and urinary testosterone levels are sensitive to a number of other variables such as general health, diet, drug use, cigarette smoking, sexual activity, use of marijuana, and physical and emotional stress, which must be ruled out in each instance.

Nevertheless, these studies, like those of Dörner, point to the possibility that at least some group 6 homosexuals, most likely those with clearly "effeminate" characteristics, may be born with what Money calls "a hidden predisposition, perhaps lurking in the neurohumoral system of the brain, that makes [them] more vulnerable to differentiate a psychosexual identity as a homosexual—not in any automatic or mechanistic sense, but only if the social environment happens to provide the right confluence of circumstances" (Money, 1967, p. 47).

It is worth noting also that biological factors may be relevant to the development of homosexuality in other respects as well. Insofar as a particular kind of bodily appearance, build, or physical incoordination may affect parental or sibling reactions to a child or his or her ability to participate in peer activities, it may play a significant part either in the gender role assigned to the child by others or in the child's ability to identify with his or her own sexual group. This may act as a facilitating factor for an ultimate homosexual object choice. This is by no means inevitable, however, for as has often been noted, constitutionally "effeminate" boys or "masculine" girls *can* develop normal heterosexual object relationships when their family environments and their opportunities for appropriate gender-role identification are favorable.

Slater (1962) found that the birth order of 401 male homosexuals whom he studied showed a significant shift to the right, i.e., they were born later in the sibship than would be theoretically expected. Pare (1965) speculated that the later maternal ages that this shift implied might possibly result in some kind of chromosomal abnormality analogous to that in Down's syndrome, in which late maternal age seems also to be a factor. This, of course, is possible, but in the absence of any demonstrable chromosomal abnormality, it seems more plausible to assume that mothers are apt to be more emotionally involved with children born late in their lives. The younger child in the family is more apt to be "babied" or to develop feelings of inadequacy in relation to older siblings. The younger or youngest child is also more apt to become the prime target of an older mother's affectional needs if her husband's interest in her has begun to diminish. Only if these and similar environmental concomitants of the "shift to the right" can be ruled out would it be justifiable to hypothesize some unknown chromosomal abnormality in the genesis of homosexuality.

Family Background

The most prevalent theory concerning the etiology of homosexuality is that which attributes its development to a pathogenic family background. Bieber and his associates (1962), in a study of 106 male homosexual patients who had been in psychoanalytic treatment with 77 cooperating psychoanalysts, conclude that the most significant factor in the genesis of homosexuality is the parental constellation of a detached, hostile father and a close-binding, seductive mother who dominates the husband and diminishes his stature.

That such parental constellations are frequently found in the background of homosexual men has long been known. Shortly after the turn of the century, Freud (1905) observed that men with weak or absent fathers and frustrating mothers are apt to become homosexual. The common denominator in a host of clinical studies appears to be a poor relationship with a father figure which results in a failure to form a satisfactory masculine identification, and a close but ambivalent relationship with a mother figure which presumably results in strong, unconscious fears or hatred of women. The difficulty with this as a *specific* cause of homosexuality, however, is that dominating and seductive mothers and weak, hostile, or detached fathers, as well as variations of this constellation, abound in the histories of countless heterosexual individuals also. I do not mean to imply that such family constellations are irrelevant to the etiology of homosexuality. There does seem to be a reasonable amount of evidence that boys exposed to this kind of family background have a greater than average likelihood of becoming homosexual. But since cases of homosexuality can and do occur with quite varied family histories, the family background described by the Bieber group—although an important and relevant factor—is not specifically etiological in the sense that the tubercle bacillus is specific for tuberculosis. Homosexuals can also come from families with distant or hostile mothers and overly close fathers, from families with ambivalent relationships with older brothers, from homes with absent mothers, absent fathers, idealized fathers, and from a variety of broken homes. Hatterer (1970) lists over fifty variables in maternal, paternal, sibling, and familial patterns that he has found to be relevant in the homosexual development of his male patients. These encompass a wide range of factors, most of which can also be found in many heterosexual patients. Indeed, as Evans (1969) and Siegelman (1974) have demonstrated, group 6 homosexuals who are not effeminate and those who tend to be less neurotic and socially and psychologically better adjusted are more likely to come from relatively "normal" family backgrounds. Bieber et al. (1962) assert that a truly loving father absolutely precludes the development of homosexuality in a son even though a homosexually inductive mother may be present. Clinical evidence, however, demonstrates that this generalization does not always hold true. Over the years I have seen a number of homosexuals who had close relationships with affectionate and caring fathers. Evans and Siegelman report similar findings.

Moreover, if the strong-mother/weak-or-absent-father constellation were a determining factor, one would expect to find a much higher incidence of male homosexuality among urban blacks, since life in the black ghetto has for decades produced a large number of broken homes in which the mother was the mainstay of family life. However, there is no evidence that the incidence of homosexuality is any greater in black men than in white men. This highlights the fact that there are other acculturating factors that probably play a significant role in the genesis of homosexual behavior. For example, as Harlow and Harlow (1965) have shown, good peer relationships can often override the negative effect of a poor mother relationship. The numerous, readily available peer relationships of ghetto life may present compensating models for masculine identification that make up for the absence of such models within the family. In addition, the mores of ghetto life do not usually reflect the sexual puritanism and antiheterosexual bias that so often characterizes the background of middle-class homosexuals, both male and female.

Social and Cultural Factors

Most discussions concerning the etiological background of homosexual behavior tend to emphasize either the biological factors or familial and developmental ones, but social and cultural factors tend to be minimized. Nevertheless, there is reason to believe that the social and cultural contexts of human development are relevant in the genesis of some homosexual behavior (see Warren, chapter 6, and Humphreys and Miller, chapter 7, this volume). As Opler indicates (1965), experimental work points to the significance of social conditions in patterns of sexual behavior even among such lower mammals as rhesus monkeys and Norway rats. Konrad Lorenz's observations (1959) of graylag geese show similar findings: under conditions of crowding analogous to human slum conditions, there was a breakdown of "normal" heterosexual behavior patterns and an associated formation of male homosexual pairs. Caution should be exercised, however, in transferring such conclusions to the infinitely more complex patterns of human interrelationships.

One of the problems attendant on cross-cultural studies of primitive peoples, as Mead (1961) points out, is that statements on the absence of homosexual behavior can be accepted only with great caution because of such factors as language barriers, unbreakable cultural taboos, needs for personal privacy, distrust of Caucasian investigators, retrospective falsification, and even, in some nonliterate societies, conventions of courtesy that demand telling a questioner what he presumably wants to hear! Opler (1965) cautions that there may also be wide differences in investigators' definitions of homosexuality—from the incidental and exploratory same-sex play of adolescents to highly institutionalized gender-role changes that may be essentially religious in their significance to genuine adult homoerotic practices. Nevertheless, bearing all these reservations in mind, there is no doubt that there are widespread cultural variations both in the incidence of homosexuality and in the degree of social sanction it receives.

Gender-role patterns—what is considered "masculine" or "feminine" behavior—vary markedly among different cultures, despite the common assumption that our Western concepts of masculinity and feminity are rooted in the biological difference between the sexes. Opler (1965) points to some striking variations from our own gender-role concepts among the Navajo, the Andaman Islanders, the Cubeo, and the upper-class Tuareg. Mead (1961) calls attention to other significant variations among the Manus, the Iatmul, and others. Constitutional patterns of physique or temperament may also be linked to varying gender-role concepts in different cultures. In some cultures, for example, mesomorphic females are thought masculine and endomorphic or ectomorphic males are considered feminine. Mead also points out that in American culture, height is regarded as a significant factor: small men and tall women are considered somehow less male and less female, respectively, than their opposites.

These socially determined values may and probably do play a significant part in many cultures in "pushing" people toward inverted gender roles. Among those American Indian tribes that gave social sanction to the careers of *berdaches* or transvestite males, male children were observed and tested from an early age to determine whether they were "braves" or "women." Once the elders made the choice, the expected patterns were reinforced by elaborate institutionalized prescriptions. In our society, the unathletic or poorly coordinated boy and the unattractive or "masculine looking" girl are sometimes similarly "pushed" into inverted gender roles, not only by the reactions of people on the outside, but also by distortion of their own self-concepts, which are similarly dependent on the dominant social values of their environments. Even such nonphysiological personality attributes as mathematical ability in a girl or artistic talent in a boy may be endowed by a culture with values that then tend to push such children toward distorted self-concepts and inverted gender roles. It is important to recognize that such value orientations do not necessarily always take place explicitly or overtly. Quite frequently, perhaps even most of the time, they operate through subtle, covert, nonverbal patterns of behavior and interaction—patterns of which the participants themselves may be totally unaware.

Social and cultural factors also have an important bearing on attitudes toward homosexuality among males and females. In some societies, adoption of cross-gender roles, including transvestism, is open only to one sex or the other (Taylor, 1965). In modern Western society, male attire on females has a degree of acceptance that is absent for female attire on males. As Clara Thompson has pointed out (Green, 1964, pp. 6–7), "Women in general are permitted greater physical intimacy with each other [in our culture] without social disapproval than is the case with men. Kissing and hugging are acceptable forms of friendly expression between women. . . . Two overt homosexual women may live together in complete intimacy in many communities without social disapproval. . . . Two men attempting the same thing are likely to encounter marked hostility."

There are probably other broad social or cultural factors that are also relevant to the genesis of homosexuality. Fisher (1965) suggests that, in ancient Greece at least, there was a relationship between the rise of homosexuality and the degraded status of women, although Karlen (chapter 4, this volume) asserts that the evidence for this assumption is by no means conclusive. Taylor (1965) hypothesizes that in societies that conceive of their deities as mother-figures, incest is the major taboo, while homosexuality is treated as of little importance; and conversely, that in societies that have father-figure deities, homosexuality is regarded as an "overwhelming danger," while incest, although also taboo, "falls far behind homosexuality in importance." Westermarck (1921) related male homosexuality to the absence of eligible women (too few or too chaste). Homosexuality as part of the warrior's code among primi-

tive peoples may have been associated with this factor. Westermarck
also remarks that homosexual behavior appears to increase at periods
of high civilization.

Economic factors probably play a part also, even in relatively simple
societies. As Opler (1965) points out, the large amount of male homosexual behavior among the Chukchee seems to be related to the difficulties
that a young man has in that highly patriarchal culture in accumulating
enough wealth to acquire a wife. Kardiner (1954) has suggested that the
growing complexity of our Western civilization renders the achievement of masculine identity increasingly difficult for the adolescent male
and enhances the desire to flee the demands and responsibilities of the
masculine role. In more recent years, the feminine revolution, the
emerging assertive tendencies of many American women, and the diminishing importance of the paternal role in the home have become
significant sociological factors which may reverberate in intrafamilial
relations and have a bearing on the development of gender-role patterns in both sexes.

Latent Homosexuality

The concept of latent homosexuality derives from Freud's theory of
psychic bisexuality, a theory upon which modern sex research has cast
considerable doubt. Freud assumed that vestiges of an original homosexual phase of development continued to be manifested in all persons
in the sublimated form of tender or affectionate feelings toward members of one's own sex and in gender-role behavioral patterns that Freud
considered as appropriate to the opposite sex. Passive or esthetic tendencies in men and aggressive or athletic tendencies in women were
believed to fall into this category.

Rado (1940, p. 464) pointed out that, biologically speaking, "there is
no such thing as bisexuality either in man or in any other of the higher
vertebrates," except for developmental disturbances that are clearly
recognizable as "inconsistencies of sex differentiation." Even more important, he pointed out that there is no justification for assuming that
so-called masculine and feminine psychological manifestations are the
direct expression of a constitutional component.

As we have seen, gender-role patterns vary widely not only in different cultures but also in different historical periods. They evolve under
the influence of acculturation processes that infants encounter in the
first several years of their lives. Although it is true that in the aggregate,
males tend to be constitutionally more aggressive and more physically

active than females, the distribution of these behavioral traits in males and females falls into overlapping curves. Many perfectly normal female infants are constitutionally more aggressive and vigorous than some perfectly normal male infants. Subsequent environmental experiences can profoundly alter these initial differences, however, either accentuating or negating them.

Apart from its questionable theoretical basis, the concept of latent homosexuality carries with it some dubious and potentially harmful clinical inferences, as indicated by Salzman and by Ovesey and Woods (chapters 17 and 18, this volume). In Freudian theory it is widely assumed that the syndrome of homosexual panic, for example, is due to life situations that have unduly stimulated the "latent homosexuality" of a person to the point at which his ego has become overwhelmed by fear that these homosexual impulses may emerge. It is true that in occasional instances this kind of mechanism may be operative, but it would be more correct to consider this a manifestation of *repressed* homosexuality rather than *latent* homosexuality. Some men may have strong erotic interests in other men that they have repressed—witness the 13 per cent of American males (Kinsey, 1948) who report reacting erotically to other men even though they have never had any overt homosexual contacts.

In most cases of homosexual panic, however, the issue is not one of homosexual anxiety but rather of what Ovesey (1955) has called "pseudohomosexual anxiety." In cultures such as ours, where homosexuality is identified with weakness and effeminacy in men, many men who are insecure about their masculinity express this insecurity in the form of fears that they are really homosexual or will be so regarded by others. Most often it will be found that such anxieties are not related to repressed homoerotic tendencies but rather to profound feelings of masculine inadequacy. Psychotherapeutic interpretations along these lines will prove to be more fruitful and effective.

Female Homosexuality

Although phenomenologically homosexuality in females parallels that in males, in actuality there are significant differences in its patterning. A number of studies in recent years, most notably those of Hedblom (1973), Gagnon and Simon (1967), and Schafer (1977), Bell and Weinberg (1978), and Saghir and Robins (chapter 15, this volume) all underline the fact that "the patterns of overt sexual behavior on the part of homosexual females tend to resemble closely those of heterosexual females and to differ radically from the sexual activity patterns of both heterosexual and homosexual males" (Gagnon and Simon, 1967, p. 180).

Lesbians, like other women, tend to become aware of their sexual needs and to express them at a somewhat later age than men, and like other women, they tend to seek and hold to more stable and faithful partnerships than do men. They are much less promiscuous than their male counterparts, although they have a slightly greater tendency to shift partners than do heterosexual females. As Schafer (1977) puts it, "lesbian women . . . have internalized the sociosexual norms of combining love and sexuality equally as much as heterosexual women" (p. 362), and "being a woman tends to influence the sexual behavior of women more than being a homosexual" (p. 355).

Western civilization does not attach the same degree of stigmatization to sexual intimacies between women as it does to men. Women can kiss, embrace, and hold hands in public without arousing public censure or shock as would the same acts between men. Two women can live together without arousing suspicion of sexual deviancy; men under similar circumstances tend to be suspect.

Even our culture's attitude toward "deviant" gender identity differs with regard to men and women. The girl "tomboy" is often an object of admiration, the boy "sissy," of disdain. Women in male attire, so long as their mannerisms are not too "butch," are taken for granted; men who dress or behave effeminately are suspect.

In practical terms this means that lesbians in general are not apt to suffer the same degree of injury to their self-esteem in the course of growing up as are male homosexuals, nor are they as subject to threats of blackmail or the consequences of exposure. Not unexpectedly, therefore, lesbians tend to be less prone to difficulty in accepting their homosexuality than are male homosexuals (Bell and Weinberg, 1978).

Why, in spite of all this, is the incidence of female homosexuality, from all available figures, only about half that for men? There are a number of probable reasons.

First, in terms of conventional gender identity, the achievement of a feminine identity is less difficult in contemporary society than is that of a masculine identity; dependency patterns are more easily achieved than the patterns of competitiveness, vocational accomplishment, and self-reliance that are traditionally required of men. It is important to note, however, that these gender-role patterns are gradually changing. As women become more and more involved in life patterns previously denied them—in the business world, in professions, and in politics, with all the assertive and competitive responsibilities that accompany such roles—it is possible that we shall witness a gradual increase in the incidence of homosexual behavior among them. The increased acceptance of patterns of bisexuality as well as lesbianism among members of the women's liberation movement may be indicative of such a trend.

Second, the adaptation to the heterosexual patterns demanded by the sexual mores of our culture is easier for women who may have homosexual inclinations than it is for their male counterparts. It is much less difficult for a woman to simulate competence in the sex act than it is for a man. Thus it is not surprising to find that most surveys indicate that from 70 to 80 percent of group 5 and 6 lesbians have experienced some heterosexual intercourse during their adult lives, in contrast to only 20 to 25 percent of group 5 or 6 homosexual men.

Third, women who for various psychodynamic reasons have fears, inhibitions, or aversions to heterosexual relations have an acceptable option open to them in our culture that is not as available to men, psychologically speaking. As demonstrated by the Kinsey survey (1953), 14 to 19 percent of unmarried women and 5 to 8 percent of previously married ones have been so sexually repressed in the course of their acculturation that they have never had any sociosexual responses throughout their adult years, and live totally asexual lives. The double standard of sexuality in our culture is quite accepting of such an adjustment in women, but not in men; in the latter, functioning sexually is considered a necessary aspect of masculinity, as seen in Friedenberg's amusing essay (1978) on the shocked reactions of his friends to his life-long virginity—"the rarest of perversions" in men. Thus, men who are heterosexually inhibited may be more apt to move toward a homosexual adaptation than are women in similar circumstances.

The etiology of female homosexuality is no less complex than that of male homosexuality, and multiple factors are undoubtedly also involved. The family backgrounds of lesbians are equally diverse, and often indistinguishable from those of heterosexual women. Some have had domineering, hostile mothers and detached, unloving or unassertive fathers, similar to those seen in the background of many male homosexuals. Others, however, have had fathers who were overly close and seductive, with mothers who were withdrawn and narcissistic. In still others, there appears to have been intense rivalry with male siblings, or feelings that the male siblings were favored, with resultant hostility to men. Others have grown up feeling that their femininity was a disappointment to their parents who would have preferred them to have been boys. A common finding in the backgrounds both of lesbians and male homosexuals is a strong antiheterosexual puritanism, stemming from either or both parents, that tends to color heterosexual relationships with feelings of guilt or anxiety. In these women, during their developing years, physical contacts with boys were strongly discouraged, while "crushes" on girls were disregarded or covertly encouraged.

Sociological factors are relevant to the etiology of lesbianism as well as to male homosexuality. It is probable that at least some women choose homosexual relationships because they feel deprived of access to heterosexual affection or intimacy—for reasons of shyness, feelings of inadequacy, fears of rejection, or lack of available men. The latter factor may become increasingly important in societies where the surplus of women, particularly in the middle- and older-age groups, continues to grow. Another significant sociological factor in recent decades has been the growing strength of the women's liberation movement, and the resentment that it has generated among some of its members against male chauvinism and the use of sex as a "political" instrument (Millett, 1970). Thus there has been a tendency among more radical women's liberationists, as a kind of political statement, to reject heterosexuality and turn to their own sex for libidinal gratification. At the very least, patterns of bisexuality in women have become more widespread and acceptable as a consequence.

Homophobia and Its Derivations

The legal, moral, and stigmatizing aspects of the issue of homosexuality are so closely intertwined as to be almost inseparable. The laws of a society, in matters such as these, are simply encoded reflections of its moral values (see Slovenko, chapter 10, this volume). In Western culture in general, the prevailing attitudes toward homosexuality derive from Judeo-Christian tradition. Hiltner (chapter 11, this volume) reviews this in a balanced and judicious manner, as do Jones (1966), Pittinger (1970), and McNeil (1976). It is an interesting reflection of the emotions that surround this issue to see fundamentalists quoting passages about the "sin" of homosexuality from Leviticus and from Paul's Epistles to the Romans and Corinthians to justify their passionate intolerance of homosexuals, while at the same time maintaining a remarkable Christian tolerance toward the presumably equally sinful acts (according to the Bible) of alcoholism and adultery. Leviticus contains a host of other "legal" pronunciamentos concerning clean and unclean food, menstruation, ritual sacrifice, etc., all of which are conveniently overlooked by pious religionists, even though these passages, too, presumably represent the "word of God."

Yet, primarily on the basis of these religious teachings, homosexuals have been subjected to legal discrimination and persecution throughout Western culture for almost two millennia, at times in proportions bordering on genocide. As Crompton (1978) has pointed out, homosexuals were extensively brutalized and murdered, first by the ancient Hebrews around 550 B.C. and then about 850 years later when Christianity came to power in Western Europe. Genocidal laws against homosexuals remained in the criminal codes in France until 1791, in England until 1861, and in Scotland as late as 1889. Both male and female homosexuals were subject to capital punishment in a number of the American colonies, but the death penalty was gradually revoked after the revolution. The most recent episode of genocide of homosexuals was in Hitler's Germany when more than 50,000 of them in Germany alone were arrested and sent to perish in concentration camps. When those seized by the Nazis in occupied countries are added, estimates of the number of homosexuals who died from illness, neglect, medical experiments, and the gas chamber range from 100,000 to more than 400,000 (Crompton, 1978).

Clearly, behind this selective focus on the "unnatural sin" of homosexuality lie deep-seated fears and anxieties—fears that have recently come to be subsumed under the concept of *homophobia*. Homophobia in its most intense forms represents a pathological fear of homosexuality, usually based on one or more of the following factors: (1) a deep-seated insecurity concerning one's own sexuality and gender identity, (2) a strong religious indoctrination, or (3) simple ignorance about homosexuals.

Men and women who are genuinely secure about their gender identity and/or heterosexuality are less apt to be threatened by homosexuality than are those who are less secure. Similarly, people who are more liberal in their religious convictions or who have no religious affiliations are generally less homophobic than are fundamentalists of all faiths. Perhaps the most important source of homophobic reactions, however, is the widespread ignorance that exists in the general public about what makes people homosexual. Many people still tend to think of homosexuality either as a pattern that is freely chosen by a conscious act of will, or as something that is "caught" from others, either as a result of seduction or by an "infectious" imitation or "modeling" of oneself after homosexuals to whom one has been exposed. These latter myths have played a powerful role in the recent "backlash" taking place in a number of states with regard to the legal rights of homosexual teachers.

Understandably, most parents in our culture have fears with regard to their children becoming homosexual. These fears are easily stimulated by ignorant or malicious assertions that children exposed to homosexual teachers (particularly if these teachers are popular and likeable) are in danger of modeling themselves after such teachers and thus becoming homosexual themselves. Yet there is not an iota of evidence for such assertions! As we have seen, the etiology of homosexuality is affected by many factors, some possibly genetic or constitutional, others dependent on early familial relationships, still others deriving from sociocultural elements. People do not "choose" to be homosexual any more than they "choose" to be heterosexual. In almost all instances, the basic factors that lead to a homosexual propensity are established before the age of six, well before the school years even begin (see Green, chapter 13, this volume). That modeling is not a relevant factor, in any event, is indicated by the fact that all homosexuals come from hetero-sexual families, and that the overwhelming majority of the "models" they are exposed to in our culture are heterosexual.

Thus the "model" of a popular homosexual teacher can never "cause" homosexuality to develop in any child of either sex whose programming, both biologically and developmentally, is proceeding along heterosexual lines. The only effect that exposure to homosexual teachers can have on heterosexual children (assuming the teachers' sexual orientations become known) is to create more tolerance and understanding toward homosexuals as people, and to dispel the wide-spread prejudicial myths about them, thus reducing potential homo-phobia. As for that small percentage of children who for prior develop-mental reasons are already struggling with homosexual feelings, with all the guilt and self-hatred attendant upon such feelings in our culture (see Miller, 1971), a role-model with whom they can identify in a positive way can only help them to feel better about themselves and thus contribute to their mental health (see Voeller, chapter 12, this volume). In both instances, the basic effect is a positive one rather than a negative one.

There is no doubt that ultimately an enlightened and civilized soci-ety must rid itself of its homophobic fears and prejudices. The vast majority of homosexual men and women ask only to be accepted as human beings and allowed to live their own lives free of persecution or discrimination. To the extent that they are permitted to do so, we can anticipate that many of the defensive excesses and bizarre "acting out" behaviors that characterize some of the more extreme gay liberationists will disappear from our cultural scene. In any event, legal sanctions against homosexual behavior, as Slovenko points out (chapter 10, this volume) have no effect on the incidence of homosexuality; there is no evidence that its frequency is any higher in countries like France, Sweden and the Netherlands, where it has been decriminalized, than in the United States, where it has not.

Recognizing this fact, there is an increasing trend in the Western world, despite an occasional backlash, to legalize homosexual behavior between consenting adults in private, and also to outlaw discrimination against homosexuals in employment, housing, public accommodation and licensing. It should be emphasized that, contrary to homophobic propaganda, such legislation does not mean the condoning of the seduc-tion of minors or the violation of reasonable standards of public de-cency; such behavior, *whether by homosexuals or heterosexuals,* will remain illegal. But the legalization of homosexual behavior between consenting adults and the outlawing of discriminatory practices against homosexuals is a first and necessary step in making it possible for the millions of men and women whose early life experiences, through no fault of their own, have rendered them erotically responsive to their own sex to live lives of dignity and self-respect. This is a mental health issue of the first magnitude, one with important and widespread implications for homosexuals and heterosexuals alike (see also Marmor, Epilogue, this volume).

REFERENCES

Bell, A. P., and Weinberg, M. S. 1978. *Homosexualities.* New York: Simon & Schuster.

Bieber, J. et al. 1962. *Homosexuality: A psychoanalytic study.* New York: Basic Books.

Crompton, L. 1978. Gay genocide from Leviticus to Hitler. In L. Crew, ed. *The gay academic* (Palm Springs, Calif.: ETC Publications), pp. 67–91.

Devereux, G. 1937. Institutionalized homosexuality of the Mohave Indians. *Human Biology* 9:498.

Dörner, G. 1967. Tierexperimentalle untersuchungen zur frage einer hormonellen pathogenese der homosexualitet. *Acta Biologica et Medica Germanica* 19:569–84.

Dörner, G. et al. 1975. A neuroendocrine predisposition for homosexuality in men. *Archives of Sexual Behavior* 4:1–8.

Evans, R. B. 1969. Childhood parental relationships of homosexual men. *Journal of Consulting and Clinical Psychology* 33:129–35.

Fisher, S. 1965. A note on male homosexuality and the role of women in ancient Greece. In J. Marmor, ed. *Sexual inversion: The multiple roots of homosexuality* (New York: Basic Books), pp. 165–74.

Ford, C. S., and Beach, F. A. 1951. *Patterns of sexual behavior.* New York: Harper & Bros.

Freud, S. 1905. Three essays on the theory of sexuality. In J. Strachey, ed., *The standard edition of the complete psychological works of Sigmund Freud,* vol. 7 (London: Hogarth Press, 1953–74), pp. 125–243.

Friedeberg, L. v. 1953. Die umfrage in der intimsphäre. *Beitraege zur Sexualforschung,* vol. 4.

Friedenberg, E. Z. 1978. Gaiety and the laity. In L. Crew, ed. *The Gay Academic* (Palm Springs, Calif.: ETC Publications), pp. 49–56.

Gagnon, J., and Simon W., 1967. The lesbian, a preliminary overview. In J. Gagnon and W. Simon, eds. *Sexual deviance.* New York: Harper & Row, pp. 247–82.

Green, M. R., ed. 1964. *Interpersonal psychoanalysis: The selected papers of Clara M. Thompson.* New York: Basic Books.

Harlow, H. F., and Harlow, M. F. 1965. The affectional systems. In A. M. Schrier; H. F. Harlow; and F. Stollwitz, eds. *Behavior of nonhuman primates,* vol. 2 (New York: Academic Press), p. 287.

Hatterer, L. 1970. *Changing homosexuality in the male.* New York: McGraw-Hill.

Hedblom, J. H. 1973. Dimensions of lesbian sexual experience. *Archives of Sexual Behavior* 2:329–42.

Hirschfeld, M. 1920. *Die homosexualität des mannes und des weibes.* Berlin: L. Marcus.

Jones, H. K. 1966. *Toward a christian understanding of the homosexual.* New York: Associated Press.

Kallman, F. J. 1952. A comparative twin study on the genetic aspects of male homosexuality. *Journal of Nervous and Mental Disease* 115:283.

Kardiner, A. 1954. *Sex and morality.* Indianapolis: Bobbs-Merrill.

Kinsey, A. C.; Pomeroy, W. B.; and Martin, C. E. 1948. *Sexual behavior in the human male.* Philadelphia: W. B. Saunders.

Kinsey, A. C. et al. 1953. *Sexual behavior in the human female.* Philadelphia: W. B. Saunders.

Kolb, L. 1963. Therapy of homosexuality. In J. Masserman, ed. *Current psychiatric therapies,* vol. 3 (New York: Grune & Stratton), p. 131.

Lorenz, K. 1959. The role of aggression in group formation. In B. Schaffner, ed. *Group processes,* vol. 4. (New York: Macy Foundation), pp. 181–251.

McNeil, J. 1976. *The church and the homosexual.* Kansas City: Sheed Andrews & McMeel.

Mead, M. 1961. Cultural determinants of sexual behavior. In W. C. Young, ed. *Sex and Internal Secretions,* 3rd. ed., vol. 2 (Baltimore: Williams & Wilkins), pp. 1433–79.

Miller, M. 1971. *On being different: What it means to be a homosexual.* New York: Random House.

Millett, K. 1970. *Sexual politics.* New York: Doubleday & Co.

Money, J. 1967. Sexual dimorphism and homosexual gender identity. Working paper prepared for the NIMH Task Force on Homosexuality.

Opler, M. K. 1965. Anthropological and cross-cultural aspects of homosexuality. In J. Marmor, ed. *Sexual inversion:* the multiple roots of homosexuality (New York: Basic Books), pp. 108–23.

Ovesey, L. 1955. The pseudohomosexual anxiety. *Psychiatry* 18:17–25.

Pare, C. M. B. 1965. Etiology of homosexuality: Genetic and chromosomal aspects. In J. Marmor, ed. *Sexual inversion: The multiple roots of homosexuality* (New York: Basic Books), pp. 70–80.

Pittinger, N. 1970. *Time for consent: A christian's approach to homosexuality,* 2d ed. London: SCM Press.

Rado, S. 1940. A critical examination of the concept of bisexuality. *Psychosomatic Medicine* 2:459–67.

Reiss, A. J., Jr. 1961. The social integration of queers and peers. *Social Problems* 9:-102–20.

Romer, L. v. 1906. Die uranische familie. *Beitraege zur Erkentniss des Uranismus.* vol. 1.

Schafer, S. 1977. Sociosexual behavior in male and female homosexuals: A study in sex differences. *Archives of sexual behavior* 6:355–64.

Schofield, M. 1965. *The sexual behavior of young people.* Boston: Little, Brown.

Siegelman, M. 1974. Parental background of male homosexuals and heterosexuals. *Archives of sexual behavior* 3:3–18.

Slater, E. 1962. Birth order and maternal age of homosexuals. *Lancet* 1:69–71.

Taylor, G. R. 1965. Historical and mythological aspects of homosexuality. In J. Marmor, ed. *Sexual inversion: The multiple roots of homosexuality.* New York: Basic Books.

Westermarck, E. 1921. *The history of human marriage,* 5th ed. London: Macmillan.

PART I

The View of the

Biological Sciences

1 / Ambisexuality in Animals

R. H. DENNISTON

The problem of homosexual behavior—or better, of ambisexual behavior—in lower animals presents several intriguing theoretical facets that have implications for human beings. The general problem involves the relationship between sex drive and sex behavior. Is sex drive specific to sex, that is, is there a male sex drive and a female sex drive, each resulting in its own appropriate behavior? Or is there a general sex drive that expresses itself in behavior appropriate to the anatomy, endocrine balance, conditioning, and present stimulus? If the drive is sex-limited, is it one drive or, as Beach (1958) and Denniston (1954) have suggested, is there a progressive series of drives creating the components of courtship and mating behavior?

There is no question that sex behavior represents a chained response series or that both positive and negative feedbacks play their roles at all levels of its organization. For this response chain to occur, certain prerequisites must be present in the organism and in the environment. The organism must be in a normal nutritional, maturational, and endocrine situation and must have had whatever experience is necessary for the given sex and taxonomic level. The response chain then proceeds somewhat as follows:

1. A generalized tendency toward intraspecies gregariousness is aroused by visual, olfactory, auditory, or other distant cues from a potential partner. The tendency and the stimulus combine to produce approach behavior toward the source of the stimuli.

2. The approach behavior leads to contact or near contact if the pertinent cues continue to be positive or to afford positive feedback. When contact has been established, the approach tendency is satisfied temporarily, and an investigatory tendency takes its place.

3. If investigatory behavior leads to the appropriate positive stimu-

lus-producing responses (or possibly simply to the absence of negative ones) from the partner, sexual arousal begins. The rate of interaction increases with each partner's stimulation of the other and with positive feedback into the arousal mechanisms. When arousal is sufficient, appropriate genital contact is established, and a new set of interactions begins. The passive partner is stimulated to adopt the typical receptive posture. (In many species, this posture is almost identical to the submissive posture in an aggressive situation.)

4. If the stimuli provided by the receptive partner are adequate, seminal emission takes place, and the ejaculatory drive is reduced for a variable time during the postejaculatory period. Each step in the chain is caused by appropriate stimuli interacting with the psychobiological condition of the organism. The response to each step leads to a change from one set of stimuli to another: from distant to near contact, then to special receptor contact, and finally to genital contact. At each step, a tendency is satisfied, and another is aroused. As is typical of positive feedback situations, the activities accelerate to climax.

Before going further, we might well attempt to provide operative definitions of some terms from the psychobiological point of view (see Beach, 1958; Verplanck, 1957; or Wilson, 1975): aggression = threat and attack behavior; ambisexuality (bisexuality) = sexual behavior with either sex; dominance-subordination heirarchy = pecking order; drive = an organism's tendency to change the rate and direction of its behavior in relation to certain categories of stimulus complexes (the general effect of such behavior is a return to homeostatic balance; the behavior is referred to as a response to the stimuli in question); hermaphroditic (monoecious) = referring to an individual organism that contains both male and female reproductive systems; homosexuality = sexual behavior with a member of the organism's own sex; instincts = sets of responses characteristic of a species, preceded by definite stimuli and drives and demonstrable under conditions calculated to preclude learning; estrus = behavioral female sex receptivity; reinforcement = a stimulus previously demonstrated to strengthen the probability of the response which precedes it; sex receptivity = behavior of a female animal that permits or encourages copulation.

One of the interesting problems in homosexual behavior is its relationship to the relative dominance positions of the active and passive partners in the social group. Much male courtship behavior is indistinguishable from aggressive dominance behavior per se, and only by considering the environs and consequences of such behavior can it be categorized. That such socially conditioned homosexual behavior is almost universal among animals is one of our themes.

Within the last few years another theme has been developing in the observations and theoretical constructions of sociobiologists such as Wilson (1975) and Trivers (1971). This theme is the possible adaptiveness of homosexuality. Above usefulness to the individual, the retention within a species of a genetically influenced trait depends on some manner of general usefulness to that species. How could a nonreproducing sub-group such as homosexuals pass on any trait?

One answer is found in the kin selection concept. If the nonrepro-ducers provide help to closely related individuals, they are favoring the passing on of many of their own genes, possibly including those favoring homosexual behavior. Help provided to a parent or to a full sib (as with yearling birds helping to care for nestling sibs) would have the same effect as if the individual himself were to mate. Although many animals show altruistic kin selection at some step in their lives, few such helpers show homosexual behavior.

Certainly homosexual behavior itself may be adaptive in other ways. Hutchinson (1959) has suggested that genes for homosexual tendencies could be advantageous in the heterozygous condition. A strong tend-ency for some family members to make pseudosexual presentations to more dominant forms could lower the intrafamilial level of harmful aggression. The wild goats and sheep described by Geist (1974) are an interesting example.

In similar cases of limited access to receptive females, male homosex-ual behavior could lower a sort of conflict which could seriously inter-fere with heterosexual mating. In those species where polygamous mat-ing is adaptive, homosexual behavior in the nonbreeding male population could be an important tension-lowering device. Kirsch and Rodman (1977) have summarized some data and present some ideas on the possible genetic adaptiveness of homosexual behavior in man from an evolutionary point of view.

A related problem is the evolutionary or phylogenetic progression of sex specific behavior. Some primitive animals tend to be monoecious or functionally bisexual, producing both eggs and sperm. In the very com-mon cases—as in the earthworm—of mutual cross-fertilization, it would be most interesting to analyze the involved behavior patterns in a careful and systematic way. In those organisms that are functionally male when young and functionally female when older, what are the behavior patterns in the male, transitional, and female stages?

According to Coe (1940), in the marine snail *(Crepidula)* all young are functional males and change to functional females as they grow older. There are two types of young male. The one that has more primary ovocytes in the ovotestes shows less masculine behavior and is always more passive (femalelike). Association of the young with females pro-longs the male phase of life. Coe speculates that this prolongation of maleness is due to stimuli received from the female. Sometimes the transitional phase from male to female is prolonged and accompanied by appearance and behavior of an intergrade type. In other varieties, there seems to be a dedifferentiation toward a neuter type before femaleness starts to develop. Chaetopod annelids of the genus *Ophryo-trocha* show a similar protandrous development, except that under certain unfavorable circumstances a re-reversal from female back to male may take place. When two females are confined together, the more vigorous may obtain a mate by biting the other female in two or by eating all the available food. As the female is somewhat exhausted by the egg-laying process, the male may grow once again, change into a female, and bite his "wife" in two, thus reversing the roles. Coe concludes that more or less numerous representatives of nearly every phylum of invertebrates and of every phylum of plants are functionally hermaphroditic (1940).

In the vertebrates, apparent homosexual behavior increases as we ascent the taxonomic tree toward mammals. A word of caution should be entered here. There are at least two possible reasons why such an apparent increase in homosexual behavior may not be real. First, there has been far less objective and well-controlled study of the behavior of lower vertebrates than of the higher ones; second, investigations of lower vertebrates have been more difficult to interpret on sex-recognition and empathetic grounds.

Before discussing the data on chordates, it is well to consider possible causal factors in animal homosexual behavior, so that we may apply "Occam's razor" to anthropomimetic explanations of such acts.[1]

1. One such factor could be failure to discriminate the true sex of the partner. In forms that lack distinct sexual dimorphism, such as the common grass frog, indiscriminate sexual approaches may be the rule, with behavioral warning or lack of receptivity comprising the pertinent discriminating factor.

2. A second and frequently confusing situation involves dominance-subordination behavior, in either sex, that closely resembles aggression-submission. Domestic chickens illustrate this phenomenon.

3. Finally, the "play" activities of juvenile organisms may include sex-type mounts and may be quite indiscriminate as to the sex of the participants—as seems to be true of almost all mammals.

In fish, sex discrimination may be quite poor in strange situations and may be established only in terms of responses to courtship approaches. This writer has observed male guppies courting each other for weeks while confined in a one-sex group. This behavior included the S–curve dance, nipping of the genital area, and gonapodial[2] swinging. Areas in which fish have been accustomed to breed or in which there has been chemical conditioning of the water by ripe females are likely sites for the induction of homosexual behavior by the utilization of suitable

1. Morris (1952) lists the first two of these factors.
2. A gonapodium is an anal fin that transfers sperm.

hormones, either applied directly to the fish or dissolved in the aquarium water.

Desmond Morris (1952) reports a well-controlled series of experiments on male sexual behavior in the ten-spined stickleback in response to crowding. Among these fish, the males make nests of water weeds glued together with their own secretions. Only the dominant males are able to build and maintain such nests under crowded conditions. Such males are black, whereas subordinate males are parti-colored. Having built a nest and established a territory, which implies the repeated vanquishment of subordinate males, a dominant male dances head down before a female, attempting to lead her to the nest and to have her enter it and deposit eggs. Although subordinate males may not establish territories or build nests, they are very highly motivated. They dance for the females, produce "glue," bore into weeds as though they were nests and seem to try to show females such imaginary nests. Homosexual courting behavior is shown by the dominant male in cases in which females have previously been present. Usually, courted males will not follow the dominant one and therefore are bitten and chased by him. Sometimes, however, a subordinate male will push aside a female from the nest entrance and pass through the nest in her stead. We shall refer to such behavior as "feminine male homosexual" (FMH). The dominant male shivers along the pseudofemale's tail once it is in the nest, just as if it were a true female, thus showing "masculine male homosexuality" (MMH). Once homosexual behavior has started in the nest, the pseudofemale shows all aspects of normal female behavior except actual egg-laying. Morris indicates some possible ways homosexual behavior functions under such crowded conditions: as an outlet relieving sexual frustration and as a device limiting the production of fertilized eggs, thereby cutting the population density. That endocrine abnormalities are not involved in these fish is demonstrated by the fact that the pseudofemale will behave in a normal manner within seconds after his homosexual behavior, if given the opportunity.

Morris' classification of the possible reasons for this example of homosexuality (slightly modified by the present writer) is of interest.

I. Sensory (MMH) Active
    A. Lack of sex discrimination
    B. Sufficiency of suboptimal stimulus; possible adequate identification of sex but overriding stimulated motivation
    C. Preference for own sex as a partner (conditioned and strong habit for IA or IB)
II. Motor (FMH) Passive
    A. Inversion of behavior pattern in response to patterns listed under I (frustration in subordinate males)
    B. Preference for inversion in spite of available heterosexual outlets (conditioned IIA)

It is interesting that none of these categories involves hormonal abnormality or subnormality.

In a later paper, Morris (1955) performed the reciprocal experiment. Crowded females in the absence of males showed male-type dancing (MFH). Other females sometimes followed such dancing (FFH).

Morris lists four possible general causes of homosexual behavior, although they are not related directly to the data presented in the paper: hormonal or structural abnormality, reversal of male-female dominance-subordination roles, frustrated sexual motivation, and some appropriate female-associated stimuli shown by a male or vice versa.

Another set of initials used by Morris distinguishes the relative strengths of tendencies to flee (F), attack (A), and mate (M); and FMH would show FaM (high tendencies to *f*lee and *m*ate, low *a*ttack tendency).

Tavolga published data in 1955 showing that castration of gobioid fish did not immediately reduce courtship but rendered it indiscriminate as to object. Such castrates will court equally other males, gravid females, and unripe females.

The toads and frogs appear to have almost no sex recognition at a distance. A. P. Blair describes the breeding behavior of the American toad as almost entirely nocturnal, which inhibits utilization of visual cues. Males usually call in chorus; the call of one stimulates others to call. If a male sees another moving toad, he quickly approaches and clasps this toad. If the toad clasped is a male, he at once begins chirping and is usually released forthwith. If the toad clasped is a female, there is no chirping; the male maintains his grip, and oviposition and fertilization follow (Blair, 1942).

In addition to the warning chirp, other contact discriminating factors are the slenderness of the male or spent female and the vibration of the male body when clasped. That this vibration, rather than the other factors, is of paramount importance in sex discrimination has been demonstrated by well-controlled experiments (Aronson, 1944). Among these animals, then, courtship—if it can be called that—is completely indiscriminate, and the contact cue of the clasped male's warning croak or vibration is the first effective indication to the active male that his behavior has been homosexual rather than heterosexual. Sexually active males attempt to clasp members of a pair in amplexus. As the male of the pair is on top, he is clasped 97 percent of the time and is often dislodged.

The mating behavior of lizards and their methods of sexual recognition are much better understood than seems to be the case with snakes and turtles. An early paper by Noble and Bradley (1933) describes the mating behavior of various genera of lizards. Among the *Teiidae,* the active male masturbates by rubbing the genital area on the substratum of the pond and then seeks a mate of either sex. As the active male pokes at the neck of the partner, the latter's cloacal lips erect. He rubs the partner's opposite flank, reaching across to do so, then bites and grasps the rubbed area, swings his tail under the partner's, everts the hemipenes, and inserts the near one into the partner's cloaca. This whole process can be carried out equally well with a passive male or with a female. Homosexual copulation stimulates the passive male, so that he may change roles with the previously active male and complete a copulation in turn. These lizards may pile up three deep in copulation. Among the *Iguanidae,* ten of twenty-one observed copulations were male homosexual. The weaker or smaller males fall automatically into the passive homosexual role, as active males fight or threaten on sexual approach and smaller males and females do not.

In a group of lizards with well-developed male bluffing behavior, much less homosexual activity is seen. In another group, in which the female has a characteristic humpbacked posture, males not showing such a posture may nevertheless be courted.

According to Greenberg and Noble (1944), the American chameleon, *Anolis,* may be one of the few lizards in which female homosexual behavior appears. One of their females showed indiscriminate malelike mounting combined with fairly severe biting, instead of the usual grip used by the male in mounting. Both MFH and FFH behavior were induced in female *Anolis* by implantation of testosterone propionate. Six of eight females showed both types of homosexual behavior. Certain testosterone-implanted females tended to be dominant in their cages. They were defeated and then copulated with by aggressive, sexually active males but not by other treated females. These dominant, treated females were the most active in aggression and also in malelike copulatory performance. Among males, testosterone-treated castrates were more aggressive, courted more, and copulated more than the control castrates. Such treated animals might show either the complete male or female copulatory pattern, depending on relative dominance positions.

Among nocturnal American geckos (Greenberg and Noble, 1944), active males must depend on contact cues for sex recognition. As in nocturnal amphibia, the preliminary stages of courtship are necessarily carried on indiscriminately. Usually a male approached by another male shows fight before much contact is made. The locomotor postures of the sexes are different. Anesthetized males may be courted, and males with female tails attached may have the tails courted.

Collared lizards are diurnal, establish territories and show well-developed dominance-subordination behavior. Dominant males fight other males that show the conspicuous yellow throat patch. If subordinate males do not show the patch, they may be courted, especially if the dominant male approaches the subordinate from the rear. Since copulation among these lizards, as among the geckos, calls for considerable cooperation by the partner playing the feminine role, homosexual mating seems to be rare.

Birds show components of the sex-behavior patterns of reptiles, as might be expected of a class so closely related. The typical locomotion and posture of the courting male, the submissive-receptive crouch of the female, the male's neck grip, and even his treading action have their counterparts in lizards, the most generalized of present-day reptiles. Some pioneers in modern animal behavior studies have used birds as their principal experimental form. Schjelderup-Ebbe and Allee, who made famous the "peck order" or social hierarchy, and Lorenz and his imprinted geese and ducks are a few who come to mind. The early work of the Chicago group—Koch, Gallagher, Domm, and their associates—is notable (Koch, 1939). They studied the effects of hormonal treatment of chick embryos and newborn chicks on their subsequent sex behavior.

Early in their studies of the pecking order, Allee and his group showed that one social-dominance system held for males and another for females, but that any normal mature male was dominant over any female. High social rank among the males carried with it breeding rights (a kind of droit du seigneur), whereas high-ranking hens showed rather little breeding activity. Crucial male sex recognition or releaser cues were provided by facing the active rooster and erecting the hackles, whereas a female turned the other way and squatted. If a male happened to be in such a position while taking a dust bath or if he gave a crouching response to the wing-dragging courting waltz of a rooster, he might be mounted by the active male. Males low in the pecking order may be driven and trodden upon to such an extent that they are killed or mutilated (Guhl, 1953).

Guhl also reports the conditions under which female homosexual behavior may appear in a flock of hens (1948). Five of forty-two hens observed took the male role in such behavior with twenty-seven passive hens. The active hens did not crow or waltz. In 173 of 181 homosexual matings, the mounting female was socially dominant to the one mounted. The passive female was either resting on the floor or dusting when the mating transpired. When cocks were present, they trod the active homosexual hens as females. The size of the combs of such active hens was no greater than average, and the hens themselves were in active laying condition at the time the observations were made, which suggests no unusually high androgen titer.

Hale (1955) reports similar findings for sexually aroused turkey hens, which were able to bring passive females to "orgasm" and subsequent temporary reduction in sex motivation. Hale does not indicate whether the sex drive of the active hen was similarly reduced.

Many annually breeding wild birds show rather little homosexual behavior, perhaps because copulation normally occurs only between well-established partners and because establishment of such a pair takes a considerable length of time and a complex interaction of courtship behaviors. An intruding male may show female-submissive behavior in the presence of the holder of a territory. This behavior seemed evident in the finches studied by Hinde (1955).

In the zebra finch, as described by Morris (1954), a frustrated male shows female receptive behavior after thwarted copulation attempts and long, intense courtship. In several pairs, the males were mounted by their mates following such display. This display was not typical of the submissive display when one male is beaten by another, nor was it a typical juvenile pattern. Morris believes that the pseudofemale display may inhibit the female's tendency to flee when she is not ready to respond to courtship, or it may be a result of the male's tendency to flee in such a situation. He says that this pattern differs from that among the stickleback fish, in which pseudofemale behavior is the result of conflict between tendencies to attack and to mate.

A recent paper by Hunt and Hunt (1977) reports one of the few cases of female homosexuality in free-living birds. In Western gulls pairs of females that remain together for a season or more are associated with abnormally large clutch sizes. Intervals between the laying of eggs in such clutches are shorter than normal, indicating that both females in the pair layed eggs in the clutch. Further, most of these eggs are infertile. In heterosexually mated birds the average clutch size is three, with 81 percent fertility. Clutch sizes of five and six eggs from homosexual female pairs showed 14.8[3] and 0 percent fertility respectively. Members of homosexual pairs showed all courtship and territorial behavior used by heterosexually mated birds, except heavy courtship feeding, mounting, and copulation, which were unusual but not absent. In the few cases where female-female pairs raised chicks, they did so successfully.

Hormonally induced homosexual behavior in the fowl has been rather thoroughly studied. The normal cock is high in aggressiveness and sex behavior measures compared with the capon. The position in the pecking order and the amount of sexual behavior seem to be positively correlated, although they are probably not independent variables. A classical experiment was performed by Davis and Domm in 1943. They injected androgen into capons, or castrated cocks, and into poulards, or spayed hens, and estrogen into capons, poulards, and cocks. The complete male behavior pattern could be induced in capons by androgen but only with difficulty in poulards, which never reached copulation with the relatively small amounts of hormone used, although they did so in later experiments. Capons receiving estrogen showed the courtship wing flutter and copulated listlessly but did not crow. Pou-

---

3. Where fertility occurs in such homosexual pairs, it is due to some promiscuous heterosexual copulation which may occur in gulls even though they are paired (occurs in heterosexual pairs also).

lards receiving estrogen lost aggression and crouched to receive the cock. Precocial development of male sex-behavior components can be induced in chicks by androgen treatment and increases directly in accord with dosage used. Estrogen introduced into four-day eggs led to the development of structural and behavioral intersex conditions in genetic males. Degree of maleness correlated positively with position in the pecking order. The behavioral range of the intersexes did not seem to include any part of the female pattern but extended from neuter to normal male type.

Frequent homosexual activity has been described for all species of mammals of which careful observations have been made. This behavior is so common in domestic stock as to attract little notice from the husbandman, unless he chooses to use it for some specific purpose. Cows in heat so frequently mount other cows that the behavior is considered diagnostic of the estrous condition. Young bulls or steers are often used as "teasers" to arouse mature bulls in preparation for the collection of ejaculates for use in artificial insemination. As a matter of fact, if a heifer has been used several times as a "teaser" for a bull, the bull will then react more readily to a "teaser" of his own sex than to a female. A. F. Fraser, reporting in Fox (1968), describes nymphomaniacal cows which would mount other cows or would stand for the bull at any time. Heifers coming in heat have been observed to mount an estrous mare and ass. Mares occasionally show nymphomania. Geist (1974) in his mountain sheep demonstrates that male-male mounting is a "normal" part of dominance behavior and happens frequently in this context. Dominant rams court and mount the estrous ewe as they do the subordinate ram. Eighty-eight percent of male-male mounts were by the dominant male. An estrous ewe will evidence lordosis; so do subordinate rams. If a ewe is not in heat she simply walks away. Smaller rams do not do this. The dominant ram has the right to produce horn displays and to court subadults and adults of either sex. As for many ungulates, a part of a dominant ram's courtship consists of licking and sniffing the genital area of his sex object. This behavior is followed by flehmen—a peculiar lip curl with the head elevated. Dominant rams among Stone sheep, when courting subordinates, will take the subordinate's penis in the mouth and follow this by the lip curl.

When a dominant ram is courting and copulating with an estrous ewe, the subordinate males become excited and mount each other indiscriminately. Geist counted sixty-nine male homosexual mounts out of one hundred encounters in such a situation. Feral goats show the same behavior. Rams may ejaculate at any time during the year in homosexual interaction. It is interesting that the estrous ewe's courtship pattern contains elements of a male challenge to combat, followed by a short flight. In this courtship she may horn the dominant ram, which subordinate males may also do. In sheep and in feral goats as reported by Shank (1972), dominance fights end with the victor mounting the vanquished. Wilson (1975) reports that Hamadryas baboon males present colored rumps in appeasement to the dominant. Females have colored sex skin when in estrous. Both are mounted by the dominant male.

So, in many well-organized, polygamous mammalian societies, subordinate males are mounted by the dominant or may occasionally mount each other. This expression of the social hierarchy is well recognized and prevents interference with mating by the fittest (most dominant) male in the group.

Young (1961) describes estrous mounting in twelve species of animals ranging from the shrew to the chimpanzee. Many workers believe that high levels of estrogen predispose females to homosexual mounting. Beach (1958) has presented data to show that such mounting in the rat is more probably influenced by androgen than by estrogen. It is possible that in other species the excess estrogens or progesterone present at the time of estrous mounting are partly converted into androgenic metabolites. Other workers believe that androgens of adrenal origin are responsible for the hormonal background of this behavior. Young (1961, p. 1194) indicates that malelike mounting behavior by estrous females is only one of eight possible categories of behavioral effects of gonadal hormones. In each sex there are thus two possible effects of the two types of sex hormone (or $2^3 = 8$). Those categories pertinent to our present subject include feminine behavior induced in the male under either androgenic or estrogenic hormone influence and the reciprocal situation in the female.

The first such category is Young's Number Three (feminine behavior shown by a male under androgen influence). The instances of this (FMH) behavior in rodents apparently occur in the presence of supraphysiological doses of androgen. In other cases of this behavior, the social conditioning of the dominance hierarchy seems to be the predominant influence. I have noted occurrences of such behavior involving both the extrinsic androgen treatment and the social-dominance factors in the intact squirrel monkey.

Young's Category Number Four is FMH under estrogen influence. This behavior is notably difficult to obtain and often requires enormous dosages of estrogens in mammals. Some birds show such behavior more readily.

Young's Category Number Seven (MFH), masculine behavior shown by females under the influence of estrogens, has previously been discussed. That similar behavior (Young's Category Number Eight, also MFH) may be elicited under the influence of androgen is perhaps less surprising. It is the easiest of homosexual behaviors to obtain under hormonal influences. Female rabbits show this behavior with females but return to the feminine role in the presence of males. Such behavior has been induced in sheep, cattle, and rats. It evidently requires more androgen, however, than the amount needed to restore normal male behavior in male castrates. In addition, this behavior in the female seems to be of lower incidence and strength than in the male.

Young and his co-workers have shown an "organizing" effect of prenatally administered androgens on female guinea pig reproductive structures and subsequent behavior. These pretreated intersexes could be easily induced to assume the male behavior pattern. Evidence from neonatally gonadectomized rodents, however, tends to demonstrate that the homologous hormone is not necessary for such organization. Such early deprived animals are as capable of showing the homologous sex pattern as much later castrates. Furthermore, female guinea pigs of a genetic strain that does not show malelike mounting cannot be induced to show homosexual behavior, no matter what the hormone treatment. Relative size, innervation, and sensitivity of the clitoris in androgen-treated females have been too little studied in lower forms.

Most endocrinologists have failed to take into account the factors of both genetic predisposition for tissue reactivity and experimential factors of a psychological nature. Central among reactive structures must be the nervous system. That different centers and circuitry are involved in male and female behavior is in some ways an attractive assumption. Beach's work on the importance of the cerebral cortex for male behavior (1940), its lack of importance for the female (1944), and the reciprocal dependence of female behavior on hormone levels and balance are to the point. It must be kept in mind that both neural mechanisms are present in both sexes. Certain central structures like the hippocampus appear to be involved in both. Those di- and mesencephalic structures and pathways involved in penile erection in the male squirrel monkey (MacLean, Denniston, and Dua, 1961) may well be involved in clitoridean erection in the female.

At the present stage in our knowledge, little consideration has been given to the problems of what, when, and how intermediary structures are affected by gonad hormones and how these structures in turn affect behavior. The intermediary complex is called "soma or substrate" (Young, 1961, p. 1913). It is considered to be organized either innately (e.g., in the male rat—Beach, 1940) or through experience (e.g., in the guinea pig—Young, 1961). Hormones are regarded as nondirective activators of the otherwise organized system. The difference between the effects of male hormones on female and male reactive somas is simply one of threshold, not of heterologous or homologous directive effects.

Directive factors seem to include the genetic constitution of the soma and—increasingly as we ascend the taxonomic tree—the amount of contact with other animals, including types of early sex experience. Another factor suggested by Ford and Beach (1951, p. 140) is the "degree of need" or "strength of drive." This factor is particularly strong in a male that has been intensely aroused by a female but has not reached orgasm. When mating behavior in rodents is studied with arbitrarily determined observation periods, the male is often returned to a holding cage with other males after a test during which he has failed to reach orgasm. On return to the male cage, he will mount and be mounted by his fellow males. Under similar circumstances, females show similar homosexual activity but with lower incidence and intensity. The receptive females of many species will show malelike mounting of males that are sluggish or partly inadequate in courtship behavior. This behavior is, of course, reversible inversion, not homosexuality.

Morris (1970) reports a case of irreversible sexual abnormality in a pair of male orangutans which were caged together. Both animals were young but sexually mature. Their play activities included sexual mounts with anal intercourse. When at a later time one of the now more mature males was placed with a mature female, he persistently performed anal intercourse with her and was never seen to perform a normal copulation. Although the female did not become pregnant under these circumstances, she did with another male.

The dolphin has recently received attention because of its large and highly convoluted cerebral cortex. We might expect this interesting animal to show a corresponding variety of responses, including those of a sexual nature. According to McBride and Hebb (1948) and other observers, such is indeed the case. The mature male dolphin has perhaps as broad an array of self-stimulating methods as has the mature human male. The males show evidence of sexual excitation throughout the year. Much of this evidence is in the area of homosexual behavior. The male dominance hierarchy is closely related to size. Two sorts of homosexual activity were frequently observed among the larger males. There were apparent attempts at masturbation against the flanks of smaller, less dominant males and incipient intromission with such males. Such activity frequently follows arousal without climax in heterosexual activity.

Animals with highly developed and convoluted cortexes—the porpoises, monkeys, and apes—constitute a separate category in terms of their sex behavior. Homosexual relations are established fairly readily without overwhelming drive either of hormonal or immediate stimulus source. Both male and female homosexual behaviors are shown in the primates, but the former is more obvious and may go to apparent climax per anum (evidently rectal smears have not been made under these circumstances). This writer has frequently observed such activity in a colony of squirrel monkeys. The behavior was of two sorts. The commonest was between a mature male and a much smaller but also mature male. Both males were living with a colony of mature females. Often the dominant riding of the smaller male by the larger led to a sexual clasp and pelvic thrusting by the latter. No penetration was observed.

Another homosexual situation was sometimes observed between two mature males of nearly equal dominance status after a standard erection presentation situation. In the squirrel monkey, dominance status may be established and maintained when the more dominant male presents his erect penis for inspection by the subordinate male. Ford and Beach (1951) report many instances of male homosexuality among such social primates as the baboons. The relationship is usually established between a mature male and a juvenile, with the latter being protected by the adult. Mutual genital manipulation during the mount is described, as is handling of the submissive male's penis by the dominant male or by himself. The adoption of the feminine receptive posture, as in fish and lizards, may be a means of preventing aggression or of obtaining the satisfaction of other biological needs like food.

Female primate homosexual behavior seems to take the form of mutual grooming, including oral contacts with the external genitalia and occasional mounts. Such activity almost never includes pelvic thrusting.

Cow elephants in one-sexed groups spend much time masturbating each other with their trunks (Morris, 1970).

Within the last ten years several changes have become apparent in the field of animal ambisexuality. Animal examples and theory built on ethology have been used as explanation of human homosexual behavior, as in Kirsch and Rodman (1977). The adaptive or useful possibilities of homosexual behavior have been more thoroughly explored by Hamilton (1970), Trivers (1971), and Wilson (1975). These range from the fairly obvious advantages of cutting down population growth to allowing the fittest to breed (the dominant male) and still maintaining a good-sized population of males for territorial defense, predation defense, and a reservoir of new dominants. It is interesting that Andre Gide (1925) in *Corydon* was able to cite many examples of animal homosexual behavior which he used to support his contention that such behavior is "natural." His thesis was that there is a superabundance of males and semen in many animal groups and that homosexual behavior is the "natural" way of relieving the pressures of such superabundance. He cited examples from Darwin and Fabre, as well as from other less well-known naturalists. Since Coe's (1940) excellent paper including data on invertebrate homosexuality, a small but significant group of papers on invertebrate aberrant behavior has been accumulating.

This survey of homosexual activity among lower animals should serve to explode several widely held misconceptions. First, it certainly is not a uniquely human practice. It occurs in every type of animal that has been carefully studied. Second, it has little relation to hormonal or structural abnormality. Even as lowly an organism as the fish shows homosexuality related to social dominance-subordination conditioning rather than to endocrine aberrations. It is behavioral preconditioning that is directive, with hormones playing a permissive or generalized activating role.

REFERENCES

Aronson, L. R. 1944. The sexual behavior of Anura. *Natural history* novitiate, 6 (1250), 1–15.

Beach, F. A. 1940. Effects of cortical lesions upon the copulatory behavior of male rats. *J. Comparative and Physiological Psychology* 29:193–244.

———. 1944. Effects of injury to the cerebral cortex upon sexual receptive behavior in the female rat. *Psychosomatic Medicine* 6:40–55.

———. 1958. *Hormones and behavior.* New York: Harper & Bros.

Blair, A. P. 1942. Isolating mechanisms in a complex of four species of toads. *Biological. Symposia.* 6:235–49.

Coe, W. R. 1940. Divergent pathways in sexual development. *Science* 91:175–82.

Davis, D. E., and Domm, L. V. 1943. The influence of hormones on sexual behavior in the domestic fowl. In D. E. Davis, ed., *Essays in biology in honor of H. E. Evans* (Berkeley: University of California Press) pp. 171–80.

Denniston, R. H. 1954. Quantification and comparison of sex drives in terms of a learned response. *Journal of Comparative and Physiological Psychology* 47:437–40.

Ford, C. S., and Beach, F. A. 1951. *Patterns of sexual behavior.* New York: Harper & Bros.

Fox, M. W. 1968. *Abnormal behavior in animals.* Philadelphia: W. B. Saunders.

Geist, V. 1974. *Mountain sheep.* Chicago: University of Chicago Press.

Gide, A. 1925. *Corydon.* Paris, France: Librairie Gallimard,

Greenberg, B., and Noble, G. K. 1944. Social behavior of the western banded gecko. *Physiological Zoology* 16:110–22.

Guhl, A. M. 1948. Unisexual mating in a flock of white Leghorn hens. *Transactions of the Kansas Acadamy of Science,* 5:107–11.

———. 1953. Social behavior of the domestic fowl. *Technical Bulletin of the Agricultural Experiment Sta.* Kansas: Kansas State Univ. 73:1–48.

Hale, E. B. 1955. Defects in sexual behavior as factors affecting fertility in turkeys. *Poultry Science* 34:1059–67.

Hamilton, W. D. 1970. Selfish and spiteful behavior in an evolutionary model. *Nature* 228:1218–20.

Hinde, R. A. 1955. A comparative study of the courtship of certain finches. *Ibis* 97:-706–45; 98:1–23.

Hunt, G. L., and Hunt, M. W. 1977 Female pairing in Western gulls (Larus occidentalis) in Southern California. *Science* 196:1466–67.

Hutchinson, G. E. 1959. *American Naturalist* 93, 81.

Kirsch, J. A. W. and Rodman, J. E. 1977. The natural history of homosexuality. *Yale Scientific Magazine* 51(3):7–13.

Koch, F. C. 1939. The biochemistry of androgens. In E. Allan, ed., *Sex and internal secretions,* 2nd ed. (Baltimore: Williams & Wilkins), pp. 807–45.

McBride, A. F., and Hebb, D. O. 1948. Behavior of the captive bottle-nose dolphin. *Journal of Comparative and Physiological Psychology* 41:111–23.

MacLean, P. D.; Denniston, R. H.; and Dua, S. 1961. Di-and mesencephalon loci involved in penile erection and seminal discharge. *Federation Proceedings* 20:331 C. (Abstract.)

Morris, D. 1952. Homosexuality in the ten-spined stickleback. *Behaviorism* 4(4):233–61.

————. 1954 Reproductive behavior in the zebra finch with special reference to pseudo-female behavior and displacement activities. *Behavior* 6:271–322

————. 1955 The causation of pseudo-female and pseudo-male behavior; a further comment. *Behavior* 8:46–56

————. 1970 *Patterns of reproductive behavior.* New York: McGraw-Hill.

Noble, G. K., and Bradley, H. T. 1933. The mating behavior of lizards; its bearing on the theory of sexual selection. *Annals of New York Academy of Sciences* 35:25–100.

Shank, C. C. 1972. Some aspects of social behaviour in a population of feral goats. *Zeitschrift fur Tierpsychologie* 30:488.

Tavolga, W. N. 1955. Effects of gonadectomy and hypophysectomy on pre-spawning behavior in males of the gobioid fish, Bathygobious soporator. *Physiological Zoology* 28:218–33.

Trivers, R. L. 1971. The evolution of reciprocal altruism. *Quarterly Review of Biology* 46:35–57.

Verplanck, W. S. 1957. A glossary of some terms for use in the objective science of behavior. *Psychol Review Supplement* 64:1.

Wilson, E. O. 1975. *Sobiobiology.* Cambridge, Mass.: Harvard Univ. Press.

Young, W. C. 1961 The hormones and mating behavior. In W. C. Young, ed., *Sex and Internal Secretions,* 3rd. ed., vol 2 (Baltimore: Williams & Wilkins), pp. 1173–1239.

2 / Hormones and Homosexuality

GARFIELD TOURNEY

Introduction

For many years homosexual behavior was considered the result of genetic, constitutional, and biological factors rather than of psychological experiences. This was the belief of Havelock Ellis, who pioneered the scientific study of homosexuality with his work, *Sexual Inversion* (Ellis, 1898, 1936). Such an interpretation, emphasizing the inborn nature of the disturbance, considered homosexuality to be largely untreatable. With the discovery of the glands of internal secretion, their function and various hormones, homosexuality came to be considered a matter of endocrine imbalance (Forel, 1924). Later investigators, such as Kinsey, even concluded that constitutional factors played a role in the development of homosexuality, establishing it as an early, fixed, non-modifiable pattern of behavior that became manifest as a result of early conditioning experiences (Kinsey, Pomeroy, and Martin, 1948).

Perloff (1965) emphasized the lack of definite evidence for hormonal factors in homosexual behavior. An early belief of investigators, as he noted, was that significant correlations of sexual hormones would occur with sexual behavior. To some extent this is true of lower species, but with the primates, the hormonal theory of sexual regulation, particularly in terms of orientation toward the sexual object, lacks evidence. This is seen even with gross endocrinological problems such as pituitary eunuchism and Turner's syndrome where there may be "normal" sexual desires of a heterosexual nature (Money and Mazur, 1977). Menopausal women with a deficiency in estrogens can actually have an increase in libido (Van Keep and Gregory, 1977). A definite correlation between levels of testosterone and frequency of sexual behavior in the male has not been demonstrated (Eik-Nex, Molen, and Brownie, 1967). The hormones largely have their effect on end organ sensitivity while the libidinal urge or sexual drive may be largely psychological.

Perloff (1965) concluded that hormonal disturbances were not evident in homosexual subjects. He admitted the limitations in determining the levels of hormones through the then current techniques of bioassay. The hormones function primarily in developing the organs needed for the sexual act and increasing their sensitivity to stimulation, but the psychological factor essentially controls the choice of the sexual object and the intensity of the sexual emotions. He pointed out that estrogens administered to normal men decrease their libido, but in no sense alter their sexual orientation. The administration of large doses of androgens to normal women may intensify their sexual desires, but does not cause them to assume male sexual roles. There is no evidence of value in the treatment of male homosexual patients with male hormones. He also pointed out that so-called "sexual mannerisms" and aggressive behavior as well as impotence and frigidity cannot ordinarily be related to any hormonal disturbance. These "sexual mannerisms" cannot be influenced by the administration of exogenous hormones, and it is not possible to deduce the type and level of hormones produced in a patient by observing his behavior. Hence, the problem of homosexuality was largely regarded as a disturbance in psychosexual development reflecting purely psychological problems.

During the past twelve years a tremendous amount of new information has been accumulated regarding steroid metabolism, the identification of steroid hormones, the methods of determining levels of these hormones, the circadian rhythms and the episodic release of hormones producing a characteristic diurnal variation and periodicity over longer periods of time.

Steroid hormones including the various androgens and estrogens have been identified and can be analyzed accurately in small amounts of plasma. The early studies were largely concerned with the excretory products, particularly the 17-ketosteroids, which were metabolic end-products of a number of steroids as well as of sex hormones. Now accurate measures with the aid of gas chromatography (Lipsett, 1965), competitive protein binding (Odell and Daughaday, 1971), and radioimmunoassay (Abraham, 1977) allow for accurate determinations of a number of hormones directly from plasma. No longer do investigators have to rely primarily on using urine consisting of the metabolic breakdown products of the hormones. Frequently such studies on urine may reflect more the functional capacity of these organs involved in metabolic breakdown than the actual level of the hormones in the bloodstream. The new, sophisticated methodologies allow for a careful examination of a number of hormonal hypotheses related to sexual behavior including homosexuality. Numerous studies have been done on the circulating levels and excretory products of the hormones.

In addition to these methodological developments, a number of interesting hypotheses regarding homosexuality based on animal work have been raised. Sex hormones apparently act during intrauterine life and influence the functioning and, at times, the morphology of fetal development. There appears to be a critical period at which the developing fetus is particularly sensitive to androgens and estrogens, and, depending on the sex of the fetus, subsequent behavior may be altered (Money and Ehrhardt, 1972). A proper hormonal balance in fetal development can be upset by developmental malfunction or disease. It is the impression of some investigators, like Money, that the most likely source of hormonal differences between homosexual, bisexual, and heterosexual individuals would occur not during puberty, adolescence or adulthood, but prenatally (Money, 1972). At the present time, of course, prenatal hormonal differences between these three patterns of sexual behavior, if they in fact exist, are not known. Nevertheless, there is much interesting investigation on the effect of prenatal drugs which counteract prenatal hormones, and the need exists to understand many commonly used drugs that may have a neuroendocrine effect, particularly at a critical phase of fetal development (Money, 1972). Stress within the pregnant mother herself may also trigger some hormonal imbalance that would have an impact on the fetus. This has been demonstrated in stressed pregnant rats, whose male offspring were rendered deficient in masculine behavior in adulthood, presumably through hormonal mediation (Ward, 1972).

In the review which follows, some of the recent knowledge about neuroendocrinology as it applies to sexual functioning, some of the recent studies on hormones in homosexuality, and some of the experimental work largely derived from studies on subprimates will be reviewed for their relevance to homosexuality.

Physiology of Neuroendocrine Mechanisms in Sexuality

Great strides have been made in understanding the role of the gonads, the pituitary, and central nervous system (CNS) mechanisms with regard to sexual behavior. Figure 2.1 schematizes male reproductive endocrinology, emphasizing higher level central nervous system activity, including the influence on the hypothalamus of stress and patterns of social dominance. The hypothalamus, through its venous connections with the anterior pituitary, affects the latter through the follicle stimu-

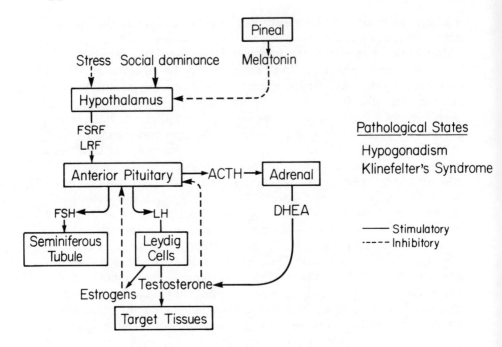

Figure 2.1
Male Reproductive Endocrinology

lating releasing factor (FSRF) and the luteinizing releasing factor (LRF).
The anterior pituitary in turn has influence on the male gonads' production of spermatazoa via the follicle stimulating hormone (FSH), while
the luteinizing hormone (LH) influences the Leydig cells to produce
primarily testosterone but also small amounts of estrogens. Upon stimulation by ACTH from the anterior pituitary, the adrenal produces the
androgen dehydroepiandrosterone (DHEA). Recent work indicates
some degree of inhibition of hypothalamic hormones via the release of
melatonin by the pineal gland.

Figure 2.2 illustrates female reproductive endocrinology. Factors
similar to those in the male affect the relationship between the higher
central nervous system and the influence of stress on the hypothalamus.
The hypothalamus releases oxytocin which acts directly on the target
organs, breast and uterus. Other hypothalamic hormones which act via
the pituitary include the follicle stimulating releasing factor, the luteinizing hormone releasing factor, and the prolactin releasing factor
(PRF). From the pituitary prolactin is released, which directly stimulates milk production by the breasts. The follicle stimulating hormone
is important in the ripening and release of the ova as well as in the
regulation of progesterone production. The luteinizing hormone, sim-

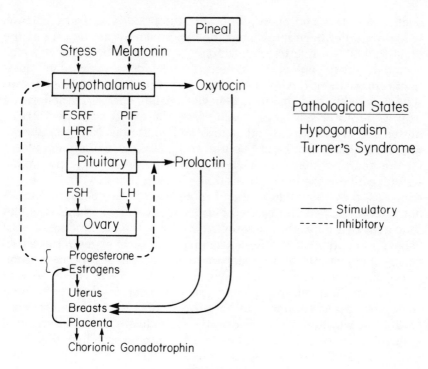

Figure 2.2
Female Reproductive Endocrinology

ply stated, plays a major role in the production of estrogens. The placenta in the pregnant female releases a number of chorionic gonadotrophins which in turn have a feedback influence on estrogen and hypothalamic releasing factors.

The usual pathological states associated with the male reproductive organs are hypogonadism and Klinefelter's syndrome. These are in no way related to homosexual behavior. Hypogonadism in the female, including Turner's syndrome, is also not related to homosexuality.

Figure 2.3 is a schematic representation of steroid hormone metabolism in the male. The steroids and their metabolic products as investigated in most of the studies to be discussed are derivative of both adrenocortical and gonadal functions. Plasma testosterone is a measure of testes function, while dehydroepiandrosterone (DHEA) and androstenedione give indications of overall gonadal and adrenal cortical function. Both DHEA and its 11-hydroxy derivatives are secreted in adrenals in only small amounts, and form the precursors for the testosterone levels in females. The testes also forms estradiol and estrone in small amounts. Androsterone and etiocholanolone are the principal metabolic breakdown products of plasma androgens that are found in the urine. The 17-ketosteroids represent not only the breakdown products from the androgens, but also those derived from cortisol.

Many studies have implicated the hypothalamus as one area of the brain that is sensitive to sex hormones, and it may be a site at which hormones act to control sexual behavior (Davidson, 1972). Many questions remain about the link forged between hormones, central nervous system activity, and, in turn, behavior—a link forged by actions on neurotransmitter substances, particularly the monoamine neurotransmitter activity in the hypothalamus and midbrain. Norepinephrine, serotonin, and dopamine are neurotransmitters particularly significant for the neurohormonal interactions. Other components of the limbic system contain these neurotransmitters and, along with the hypothalamus, they may influence and modulate sexual behavior. Everitt (1977) has reviewed and carried out pertinent studies in this area and concludes that depressing serotonin activity in the CNS induces sexual behavior in both male and female animals, but no changes in the sexual choice of object. Elevation of dopamine levels in males and depression of dopamine levels in females have a similar effect. The actions of epinephrine and norepinephrine are less clear in their behavioral consequences. As yet one does not have evidence that the amines underline the way in which hormones act to modulate nerve activity and, in turn, induce sexual activity, but studies based on such hypotheses are continuing and seem to suggest a positive relationship.

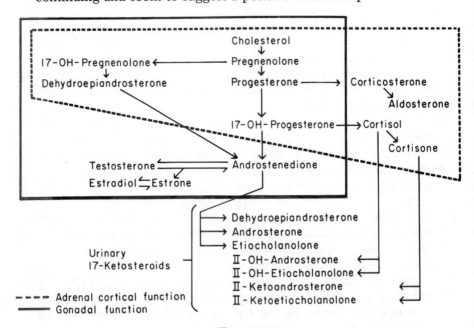

Figure 2.3

Schematic Representation of Steroid Hormome Metabolism (Males)

Recent Hormonal Studies on Homosexual Subjects

Since 1969 a series of studies on steroid hormones using modern sophisticated techniques have been carried out by a number of investigators.
These studies are summarized in Table 2.1. As can be observed, relatively few subjects have been studied, and most of these are males. Most
studies have been limited to the identification of several hormones, and
do not represent a comprehensive survey of pituitary and sex hormones
in plasma and urine. Many studies have included homosexuals with
psychiatric problems, such as depressions and psychoneuroses, while
others have studied homosexuals relatively free of any psychiatric
symptoms. Other studies are poorly controlled for age, body build, use
of medication, alcohol, marijuana, and physical illness, all of which may
have some impact on hormonal levels. Definitions of homosexuality
have varied, and some studies have used subjects who are bisexual in
orientation, while others have limited the subjects to Kinsey class 5 and
6 homosexuals. These various studies will now be reviewed and evaluated in detail.

Dewhurst (1969) investigated a male homosexual subject (Kinsey rating 6) to see if he would exhibit cyclical hormonal excretion patterns
analogous to the female rhythms of ovulation and menstruation. Urinary steroid patterns for estrogen, 17-oxysteroids, and 17-hydroxyster-
oids in an overt homosexual male and four heterosexual males showed
recurring excretion cycles of 9 ± 1 days' duration. This suggests a
periodic pattern of hormone production in the males, but no evidence
of any difference between heterosexual and homosexual subjects. Loraine et al. (1970) reported on serial assays of hormones and their
metabolites in the urine of three male and four female homosexuals.
Abnormalities were reported in all but one of these cases. Two males,
exclusively homosexual, had abnormally low testosterone levels, and
the third, who was bisexual, had a normal level. In the women, where
assays were performed throughout the menstrual cycle, the pattern of
excretion was ovulatory for three and questionably ovulatory for one.
Levels of testosterone and luteinizing hormones were elevated, while
estrogens were lower for the homosexual women as compared with the
heterosexual female controls. Follicle stimulating hormones and pregnanediol demonstrated no differences between the homosexual and the
heterosexual female subjects. The authors conclude that their studies
give credence to the hypothesis that abnormalities in endocrine function, along with psychological factors, may be of significance in the
genesis of homosexuality. Further investigation (Loraine et al., 1971)
carried out with a large number of control subjects confirmed their
impressions, although no new homosexual subjects were involved. This

TABLE 2-1

Steroid Studies on Homosexual Subjects

Investigator	Ss	Cs	Plasma Determinations						Urine Determinations							
			LH	FSH	T	AD	DHEA	ES	LH	FSH	T	AS	ET	A/E	ES	17-Keto
Dewhurst (69)	1	4													o	o
Loraine (70, 71)	3	7–21							o		−				−	
	4F	7–23F							+	o	+					
Margolese (70)	15	15			−							−	o	−		o
Kolodny (71)	15	50	+	+												
Evans (72)	44	111										o	o	−	o	o
Kolodny (72)	13	50			o											
Doerr (73)	32	46			o			+								
Margolese (73)	23	24	o	o	o							o	o			o
Tourney (73, 75)	14	11	o	o	o	o	o					o	o	o		o
Brodie (74)	19	20	o	o	+	o	o									
Parks (74)	6	6	o	o	o											
Pillard (74)	28	36			−?											
Griffiths (74)	36F	0			+						o				o	o
Doerr (76)	26	26	+	+	o			+								
Newmark (77)	4	4	o	+	+			+								
Gaitwell (77)	21F	19F			+											

Ss=Subjects, Cs=Controls, LH=luteinizing hormone, FSH=follicle stimulating hormone, T=testosterone, AD=androstenedione, DHEA=dehydroepiandrosterone, ES=estrogen, AS=androsterone, ET= etiocholanolone, A/E=androsterone/etiocholanolone ratio, 17-Keto=17-ketosteroids, o=no change, −=reduction, +=increase. All subjects are male unless number is designated by an F for female.

remains one of the few studies on female homosexuality in which all (four) subjects demonstrated a gross distortion of the pattern of testosterone, estrogen and luteinizing hormone output. The findings are interpreted as possibly reflecting the infringement of psychological factors upon the hypothalamus.

In 1970, Margolese made a well-publicized report in which he claimed that two important breakdown products of testosterone in the urine, etiocholanolone and androsterone, existed in an abnormal ratio in homosexuals. He pointed out that the female has a relatively lower androsterone than etiocholanolone excretion quotient (reduced A/E ratio) and that the metabolic condition which results in a relatively high androsterone value was possibly the cause of sexual preference for females by either sex. He stated furthermore that a relatively low androsterone value would be associated with sexual preference for males by either sex. He admitted to the limitations of the data, but was hopeful that he had established a somatic correlate for homosexuality. Kolodny et al. (1971) published a study of a group of healthy homosexuals living in a university community that revealed a diminished plasma testosterone concentration and impaired spermatogenesis in members of the group who were 5 or 6 on the Kinsey scale. Nine of these fifteen subjects also showed impaired spermatogenesis. The authors indicated that their results suggested a possible testicular, pituitary, or hypothalamic disturbance. The work of Margolese and of Kolodny's group provided considerable stimulation for further investigation and a need for clarification in the issue of hormonal disturbances in homosexuality.

Constitutional as well as hormonal factors in male homosexuals were investigated by Evans (1972). The androsterone/etiocholanolone ratio was found to be reduced for the homosexual subjects, giving support to Margolese's thesis. He also reported higher levels of urinary 11-keto-etiocholanolone and 11-hydroxy-etiocholanolone. Cortisone was higher in the homosexual subjects, which may indicate a higher level of anxiety in this group. No significant differences were found in the estrogen excretion between the homosexual and control subjects. The author concluded that the most likely hypothesis to account for various differences in physical characteristics and in biochemical factors between homosexuals and heterosexuals is of an unidentified common factor that underlies both the physical and the personality characteristics of homosexuality. Meanwhile, Margolese and Janiger (1973) repeated Margolese's 1970 study on a large sample of subjects, and the data supported the initial findings of the reduced A/E ratio in homosexuals. They believe that this is further evidence for their hypothesis of an abnormal metabolic pathway for testosterone existing in homosexual subjects.

In several reports (Tourney and Hatfield, 1973; Tourney, Petrilli, and Hatfield, 1975), Tourney could find no evidence of any alteration in the gonadotrophins, plasma androgens including testosterone, or the androgen excreting products in homosexual subjects. The reduced testosterone levels reported by Kolodny and the lower urinary androsterone/etiocholanolone ratios found by Margolese and by Evans were not supported by Tourney's work. He did note that in Kolodny's report, a number of subjects were active in the use of marijuana, and that Margolese's subjects showed greater age variability than his own. The changes in androgen metabolism with age and the effects of the use of many drugs, including alcohol, need to be clarified.

Doerr et al. (1973) studied plasma testosterone and estradiol along with semen analysis in thirty-two homosexuals and forty-six normal adult controls. They were not able to confirm Kolodny's findings of a reduced testosterone level or a reduced sperm count, but found the homosexual group to have a highly significant elevation of plasma estradiol concentrations. They point out that the experimental subjects, therefore, do have a different endocrine status, but they are not ready to postulate its exact meaning for homosexuality.

To further confuse the issue, Brodie et al. (1974) reported significantly *higher* levels of testosterone in homosexual men. Multiple samples (three) were drawn from each experimental subject, and they emphasize that they had a larger number of Kinsey 6 subjects than Kolodny or Tourney's investigations. This only adds to the inconsistency of the results and makes it more difficult to reach any conclusions. The work of Parks et al. (1974) emphasized the need for more than single determinations of hormones in carrying out any comparative study. They investigated six young, male homosexuals and six young, male heterosexuals, matched for both age and pubertal stage, with twenty-eight consecutive daily determinations of follicular stimulating hormone, luteinizing hormone, and testosterone. All subjects were in the same daily institutionalized regime. The hormonal values did not differ significantly between the two groups, although there was great variation in the day-to-day levels in both the homosexuals and the controls, indicating that single determinations do not necessarily give a clear picture of the pituitary-gonadal axis. Pillard, Rose, and Sherwood (1974) reported findings suggestive of a lowered plasma testosterone mean for homosexual men, but there was considerable variability in both groups of subjects with much overlap. Testosterone level was not related to relative masculinity or femininity or to any other measured psychological variable.

As an extension to their earlier (1971) work on plasma-testosterone levels and impaired spermatogenesis, Kolodny et al. (1972) studied plasma gonadotrophins and prolactin levels in the same university group of male homosexuals. With regard to plasma gonadotrophins, four of the thirteen men with low plasma testosterone levels and sperm counts had raised levels of luteinizing hormone and follicle stimulating hormone. A central mechanism seems apparent in that the other nine subjects with low testosterone levels had low luteinizing hormone levels. None of the subjects fulfilled the criteria for a diagnosis of Klinefelter's syndrome. All the Kinsey group 6 subjects within the group had increased plasma levels of prolactin. The authors conclude, "Our studies support the idea of a direct reciprocal relationship between spermatogenesis and plasma-gonadotrophin levels and emphasize that endocrine dysfunction must be considered in association with homosexuality. Available data do not allow a conclusion to be drawn relating endocrine disturbances in homosexuality to either cause or effect. Endocrine dysfunction is unlikely to be found in most men with a history of homosexual involvement; whereas in men with a predominantly or exclusively homosexual behavior pattern, such dysfunction may be quite common" (Kolodny, p. 20).

A subsequent study by Doerr et al. (1976) elaborated on his previous methodology, and the results for the homosexual group demonstrated significant increases in plasma estradiol, estrone, dehydrotestosterone, percentage free (nonprotein bound testosterone) and luteinizing hormone. Considerable overlapping in the findings occurs. The increased luteinizing hormone could account for the increase in estradiol, estrone, dehydrotestosterone and percent free testosterone. It is not clear whether the increased levels of luteinizing hormone are due to a relative insensitivity of the hypothalamus to gonadol hormones or are a result of increased hypothalamic stimulation via higher neuronal circuits. This study also indicates the necessity of observing a spectrum of interrelated hormones, rather than a single hormone like testosterone, when searching for an endocrine correlative of homosexuality.

The episodic or pulsatile secretion of pituitary gonadotrophins, testosterone and estradiol, illustrates the limitations in the use of a single blood sample in order to arrive at an accurate picture of hypothalamic-pituitary-testes activity. The tremendous variability reported in blood samples is often related to the single sampling method. Newmark et al. (1976) have recently presented data using a multiple sampling technique for several hours to determine the gonadotrophin-testosterone-estradiol profile in homosexual and heterosexual subjects. Because of the vast amount of laboratory work necessary, only four subjects in each group were studied. Their preliminary findings displayed elevated estradiol levels and decreased follicular stimulating hormone levels for the homosexual group, while testosterone and luteinizing hormone levels were the same for the two groups. Further studies are necessary on additional subjects, but these results strongly suggest that some homosexuals differ in their levels of gonadotrophins, estradiol, and testosterone.

Several recent studies have examined hormonal patterns in homosexual females. Griffiths et al. (1974) studied thirty-six members of a lesbian organization. Urinary levels of estrone, estradiol, estriol, pregnanediol, 17-oxosteroids, 17-hydroxycorticosteroids, testosterone, and epitestosterone were determined, and no consistent pattern of hormonal abnormality occurred. Control subjects were not used, but the data from the experimental subjects were compared with the published normal readings for these substances. Gaitwell, Loriaux, and Chase (1977) examined plasma testosterone levels in homosexual and heterosexual women which revealed that testosterone concentrations averaged 38 percent higher in homosexual than heterosexual subjects, although the two groups overlapped considerably. Samples were collected in the resting state on the first, second and third days of the menstrual cycle. The authors do not attempt to interpret the significance of their data, and point out that this might either reflect a primary mechanism or a secondary response to a particular sexual orientation.

Having reviewed the literature on the subject over the past twelve years, one becomes aware of the increasing complexity of the matter under investigation, and of the fact that much of the data collected continues to present a confusing picture, as illustrated in Table 2.1. In male subjects the findings were as follows: (1) With the major androgen, testosterone, two investigators report that homosexual subjects have a decrease in testosterone levels, one a questionable decrease, five investigators report no change, and four investigators report an increase. (2) In the five investigations made of estrogens, all report an increase in the levels of certain estrogenic hormones in the plasma, and one reports a decrease in the urine. (3) Examination of the gonadotrophins presents conflicting data. For the luteinizing hormone, four investigators report no change and three investigators an increase, and for the follicle stimulating hormone, two studies show an increase, while three report no changes. In female subjects, only three studies have been done with the following findings: Increased urinary testosterone, increased luteinizing hormone and decreased estrogens for one study; increased plasma testosterone for another study; and no changes in urinary estrogens and testosterone in a third study. This again reflects the conflicting nature of the data and the difficulties involved in interpreting the meaning of the findings.

At present one cannot merely dispose of the role of hormonal mechanisms in some aspect of homosexuality. Investigations over the past twelve years have been suggestive, but far from definitive, regarding some possible hormonal disturbance in homosexuality, or at least certain groups of homosexuals. The methods for careful investigation are now available, and one can establish adequate criteria for selection of subjects, biochemical determinations, and the avoidance of extraneous factors that might possibly influence hormonal measurements. Homosexual subjects undergoing investigation should fall clearly into Kinsey category 6, that is, subjects with a chronically fixed pattern of homosexual behavior. Control subjects need to be matched with the experimental subjects for age, sex, height, weight, education, intelligence, drug use, and freedom from disease. Experimental subjects and controls need to be free of psychiatric disorders other than mild anxiety. Sexual inventories should be carried out as to psychosexual history, frequency of sexual activity, orgasmic response, and other factors. An analysis of a number of androgens, estrogens, and gonadotrophins needs to be carried out, primarily in the plasma rather than the urine. Female homosexuals need to be studied by taking into account the menstrual cycle and related hormonal changes. Repeated sampling methods are needed to take into account the episodic secretion patterns, circadian variation, and ultradian[1] variation. Such comprehensive studies should do much to clarify what has become an increasingly confused collection of conflicting reports regarding the relationship of hormones to homosexuality.

Neuroendocrine Factors in the Development of Homosexuality: A Series of Hypotheses

During the past fifteen years increasing attention has been devoted to the study of sex hormones, brain development, and brain function. A major focus of these studies has been the relationship of prenatal hormones to the central nervous system. In their review, Money and Ehrhardt (1972) report that there is no relationship between postpubertal androgen or estrogen levels and homosexuality, bisexuality, or heterosexuality. Injections of hormones in therapeutic trials do not modify the object choice. Androgens, within limits, increase the libido in both sexes, while estrogens inhibit the libido in males. They believe that if hormonal patterns play a role in the genesis of homosexuality, bisexuality, and heterosexuality, that these effects will not likely be found to occur at puberty, but prenatally. Hormonal factors of endogenous or exogenous origin, drugs, and stress of the pregnant mother have all been postulated as resulting in some basic hormonal imbalance that affects sexual differentiation at the level of the brain.

Based on numerous observations that the developing brain is more vulnerable to change within the internal and external environment than is the adult brain, it has been postulated that during certain "critical periods," the exposure of the brain to certain types of hormonal

1. Ultradian cycles are biological rhythms of less than twenty-four-hour duration, in contrast to circadian cycles which are twenty-four-hour rhythms.

patterns will result in an imprinting process on certain regulatory nuclei and circuits, so that both behavior and endocrine function may be
modified in adult life. Regulation involves humoral factors within the
brain or pituitary: the gonadotrophic hormones of the pituitary, the
releasing hormones or factors from the hypothalamus which regulate
pituitary function, and the classic neurotransmitters, namely, acetyl-
choline, the catecholamines, and serotonin. Drugs acting on these
neurotransmitters are known to alert the luteinizing hormone releasing
factor and the follicle stimulating releasing factor in the hypothalamus.

On the basis of animal studies, it has become well accepted that fetal
sexual differentiation is dependent upon androgens (Harris, 1964).
Dörner (1976, 1977) and his colleagues in East Germany have investigated the subject extensively and have arrived at a hypothetical model
for the development of homosexuality. In work with rats, Dörner believes that he has located a male mating center in the preoptic hypothalamic area, and a female center in the ventromedial nucleus region
of the hypothalamus. Sex hormone implants to these areas would stimulate male or female sexual behavior, and destructive lesions would inhibit such behavior. Other work has been supportive of these inferences, and Dörner has concluded that different neuronal reflexes are
responsible for male and female sexual behavior. An androgen-sensitive
control center of a neuron reflex circuit responsible for male behavior
is located in the preoptic anterior hypothalamic area. The ventromedial
nucleus region includes a sex hormone-sensitive center of a neuronal
reflex circuit which regulates female sexual behavior.

The significance of the androgen level during a critical phase of
development has been reported in early studies and subsequently
confirmed. Phoenix et al. (1959) prenatally androgenized female guinea
pigs, and during adulthood these females demonstrated increased male
sexual behavior when given androgens, and decreased female behavior
with estrogens. One sees here a prenatal organizational period and a
postpubertal activation period with respect to sexual behavior for
guinea pigs. In the first phase, the hypothalamus becomes physiologically organized, depending on the androgen level, and during the second phase, puberty, the hypothalamus is activated by either androgens
or estrogens. Harris (1964) reported that male rats castrated shortly
after birth showed especially strong female behavior when given estrogens as adults. The administration of an antiandrogen to fetal male rats
resulted in similar effects (Neumann et al., 1967). Work in Dörner's
laboratory pursued these studies further and his findings can be out-
lined as follows:

1. Genetic males showing a temporary androgen deficiency during the
   hypothalamic developmental period, but with normal androgen levels
   in adulthood, were sexually aroused preferentially by partners of the
   same sex. Such studies were carried out on rats and hamsters.

2. This neuroendocrine-conditioned male homosexuality could be prevented by administering androgens during the critical hypothalamic differentiation period.

3. The higher the androgen level during the hypothalamic differentiation phase, the stronger the male and the weaker the female behavior during adulthood, irrespective of the genetic sex. A complete revision of sexual behavior could be seen in androgen deficient males or androgen overdosed females. From these findings, he hypothesizes a neuroendocrine predisposition for primary hyposexuality, bisexuality, or homosexuality based on different degrees of androgen deficiency in males and overdoses in females during sex-specific brain differentiation.

4. Morphologically, the higher the androgen level during the critical hypothalamic differentiation period, the larger the nuclear volumes of neurons in the arcuate and neutral premammillary nuclei (male mating center) and the smaller the nuclear volumes of neurons in the preoptic anterior hypothalamic area and in the ventromedial nuclei (female mating center) of the adult rats.

5. Male rats castrated after birth have a positive estrogen feedback effect similar to that induced in normal females.

6. In male homosexuals, the positive estrogen feedback mechanism occurs. Thus in homosexual men, an injection of conjugated estrogens produces a primary decrease of plasma luteinizing hormone levels. Heterosexual and bisexual men did not have the rise above the resting level of luteinizing hormone that occurs in homosexuals and females. This suggests to Dörner that male homosexuals may have a predominantly female-differentiated brain.

7. In female rats, high androgens and/or estrogens administered during the critical hypothalamic differentiation phase caused anovulatory sterility and/or a neuroendocrine predisposition for female hyposexuality, bisexuality, and homosexuality. With combined prenatal and postnatal androgen treatments, a complete masculinization of sexual behavior in female rats occurred.

8. In both male and female rats, very high androgen and/or estrogen levels during the hypothalamic differentiation phase led to hypogonadism.

For humans, Dörner believes that this critical hypothalamic differentiation phase may occur between the fourth and seventh months.

Dörner et al. (1975) have also studied twenty-four-hour urinary excretion of unconjugated testosterone in homosexuals, and have found these to be within normal limits. These homosexual men did have a positive estrogen feedback test as described above. This test was not positive in the heterosexual controls. He concludes that these findings suggest that homosexual men possess a predominantly female-differentiated brain which may be activated to a homosexual orientation by normal or approximately normal androgen levels in adulthood. This predominantly female differentiation of the brain would be caused by an absolute or relative androgen deficiency during the critical hypothalamic organizational phase in early life.

An excellent review of neuroendocrine research and hypotheses was recently made by Meyer-Bahlburg (1977). He emphasizes that the Dörner findings on the positive estrogen feedback effect in homosexual males are in striking contrast with the lack of correlation of homosexuality with other hormonal or somatic abnormalities. Such findings need further study, and, if replicated, would support the hypothesis of temporary deficiencies in prenatal hormone production as well as of changes in central target organ sensitivities to normal levels of circulating androgen. Such temporary deficiencies in androgenization must occur relatively late in prenatal development so as not to interfere with peripheral differentiation, since homosexuals are not characterized by genital intersexuality. The condition must also be reversible, since the postnatal hormone production of homosexuals appears usually to be normal. However, many of Dörner's concepts are extrapolated from studies on the rat and applied directly to the human. He has also maintained a strict biological interpretation of homosexuality, and has largely disregarded the data based on psychodynamic and learning theory approaches. In fact, Dörner (1976) even advocates a plan for preventing homosexuality by fetal hormone treatment. Such a program does not seem justified at present, since Dörner's own studies have not been replicated. Even if such replication were to occur, the degree to which the alleged prenatal hormonal deficiency actually contributes to the development of homosexuality would still need much fuller exploration. Such factors may only predispose one to homosexuality, not causate it, and they would operate in conjunction with a various patterns of life experiences in order to result in homosexuality.

Conclusions

During the past decade there has been rapid development within the field of psychoneuroendocrinology. These developments have encouraged the formulation of hypotheses about the relationship between hormones and the pathophysiology and etiology of homosexuality. Accurate and resistive determinations of the steroids have been established by radioimmunoassay. Other developments include the isolation and synthesis of hypothalamic releasing factors, autoradiographic localization of sex hormones in the brain, the study of the role of neurotransmitters in limbic system and hypothalamic regulation, the chemical analysis and identification of sex pheromones in mammals, and the demonstration of the influence of behavior on sex-hormone levels. None of the studies on homosexuality in humans has taken into account the degree of methodological sophistication now available to the investigator. The studies of sex hormone measurements in homosexual subjects have produced complicated data needing further experimental clarification. Hypotheses of some hidden predisposition to homosexuality, somehow lurking in the brain, and perchance based upon androgen deficiency or other altered hormonal states during a critical phase of fetal development, are challenging. This may contribute the factor that would result in the tendency to differentiate a psychosexual identity as a homosexual. This would occur providing that the social environment, particularly the early relationships within the family, provides the dynamic circumstances which result in overt homosexuality.

REFERENCES

Abraham, G. E. 1977. *Handbook of radioimmunoassay.* New York: Marcel Dekker.

Brodie, H. K.; Gaitwell, N.; Doering, C.; and Rhue, T. 1974. Plasma testosterone levels in heterosexual men. *American journal of psychiatry* 131:82–83.

Davidson, J. M. 1972. Hormones and reproductive behavior. In H. Babin, and S. Glasser, eds. *Reproductive biology* (Amsterdam: Excerpta Medica [Elsevier]).

Dewhurst, K. 1969. Sexual activity and urinary steroids in man with special reference to male homosexuality. *British journal of psychiatry* 115:1413–15.

Doerr, P.; Kockott, G.; Vogt, H. J.; Pirke, K. M.; and Dittmor, F. 1973. Plasma testosterone, estradiol and semen analysis in male homosexuals. *Archives of general psychiatry* 29:829–33.

Doerr, P.; Pirke, K. M.; Kockott, G.; and Dittmor, F. 1976. Further studies on sex hormones in male homosexuals. *Archives of general psychiatry* 33:611–14.

Dörner, G. 1976. *Hormones and Brain Differentiation.* Amsterdam: Elsevier Scientific.

———. 1977. Sex-Hormone-Dependent Brain Differentiation and Reproduction. In J., Money, and H. Musaph, eds. *Handbook of Sexology* (New York: Excerpta Medica [Elsevier]), pp. 227–43.

Dörner, G., et al. 1975. A neuroendocrine predisposition for homosexuality in men. *Archives of sexual behavior* 4:1–8.

Eik-Nex, N. B.; Molen, H. F. van der; and Brownie, A. C. 1967. Testosterone. In H. Garstensen, ed. *Steroid Hormone Analysis* (New York: Marcel Dekker), pp. 319–65.

Ellis, H. 1936 (orig. 1898). Sexual Inversion. Republished in Ellis, H. *Studies in the Psychology of Sex* vol. 2 (New York: Random House). Part II, pp. 1–388

Evans, R. B. 1972. Physical and biochemical characteristics of homosexual men. *Journal Consulting and Clinical Psychology* 39:140–47.

Everitt, B. J. 1977. Central monoamines and sexual behavior. In J. Money and H. Muspah, eds., *Handbook of sexology.* New York: Excerpta Medica (Elsevier).

Forel, A. 1924. *The sexual question.* New York: Physicians and Surgeons Book Co.

Freud, S. 1905. Three essays on the theory of sexuality. In J. Strachey, ed., *The standard edition of the complete psychological works of Sigmund Freud,* vol. 7 (London: Hogarth Press, 1953).

Gaitwell, N. W.; Loriaux, D. L.; and Chase, T. N. 1977. Plasma testosterone in homosexual and heterosexual women. *American Journal of Psychiatry* 134:1117–119.

Griffiths, P. D., et al. 1974. Homosexual women: An endocrine and psychological study. *Journal of Endocrinology* 63:549–56.

Harris, G. W. 1964. Sex hormones, brain development and brain function. *Endocrinology* 75:627–48.

Kinsey, A. C.; Pomeroy, W. B.; and Martin, C.E. 1948. *Sexual behavior in the human male.* Philadelphia: W. B. Saunders.

Kolodny, R. C., et al. 1971. Plasma testosterone and semen analysis in male homosexuals. *New England Journal of Medicine* 285:1170–74.

———. 1972. Plasma gonadotrophins and prolactin in male homosexuals. *Lancet* 2:-18–20.

Lipsett, M. B., ed. 1965. *Gas chromatography of steroids in biological fluids.* New York: Plenum Press.

Loraine, J. A., et al. 1970. Endocrine function in male and female homosexuals. *British Medical Journal* 4:406–8.

———. 1971. Patterns of hormone excretion in male and female homosexuals. *Nature* 234:552–54.

Margolese, M. S. 1970. Homosexuality: A new endocrine correlate. *Hormones and Behavior* 1:151–55.

Margolese, M. S., and Janiger, O. 1973. Androsterone etiocholanolone ratios in male homosexuals. *British medical journal* 3:207–10.

Meyer-Bahlburg, H. F. L. 1977. Sex hormones and male homosexuality in comparative perspective. *Archives of Sexual Behavior* 6:297–325.

Money, J. 1972. Sexual dimorphism and homosexual gender identity. In J. M. Livingood, ed. *National institute of mental health task force on homosexuality* (Rockville, Md.: National Institute of Health), pp. 42–54.

Money, J., and Ehrhardt, A. A. 1972. *Man and woman, Boy and girl:* Differentiation and dimorphism of gender identity from conception to maturity. Baltimore: Johns Hopkins Press.

Money, J., and Mazur, T. 1977. Endocrine abnormalities and sexual behavior in man. In J. Money, and H. Musaph, eds. *Handbook of sexology* (New York: Excerpta Medica [Elsevier]), pp. 485–92.

Neumann, F.; Elger, W.; and von Berswordt-Wallrabe, R. 1967. Intersexualitat mannlicher feten und hemmung androgenabhangiger funktionen bei erwachsenen tieren durch testosteron blocker. *Deutsche Medizinische Wochenschrift* 92:360–66.

Newmark, S. R., et al. 1976. Gonadotrophin, estradiol, and testosterone profiles in homosexual males. Paper read at the Southern Section, American Federation for Clinical Research, New Orleans, 26 January 1976.

Odell, W. D., and Daughaday, A., eds. 1971. *Competitive protein binding assays.* Philadelphia: W. B. Saunders.

Parks, G. A., et al. 1974. Variation in pituitary-gonadal functions in adolescent male homosexuals and heterosexuals. *Journal of Clinical Endocrinology and Metabolism* 39:-796–801.

Perloff, W. H. 1965. Hormones and homosexuality. In J. Marmor, ed. *Sexual Inversion: The Multiple Roots of Homosexuality* (New York: Basic Books), pp. 44–70.

Phoenix, C. H., et al. 1959. Organizing action of prenatally administered testosterone propionate on the tissues mediating mating behavior in the female guinea pig. *Endocrinology* 65:369–82.

Pillard, R. C.; Rose, R. M.; and Sherwood, M. 1974. Plasma testosterone levels in homosexual men. *Archives of Sexual Behavior* 3:453–58.

Tourney, G., and Hatfield, L. M. 1973. Androgen metabolism in schizophrenics, homosexuals and normal controls. *Biological Psychiatry* 6:23–36.

Tourney, G.; Petrilli, A. J., and Hatfield, L. M. 1975. Hormonal relationships in homosexual men. *American Journal of Psychiatry* 123:288–90.

Van Keep, P. A., and Gregory, A. 1977. Sexual relations in the aging female. In J. Money, and H. Musaph, eds. *Handbook of Sexology* (New York: Excerpta Medica [Elsevier]), pp. 839–46.

Ward, I. 1972. Prenatal stress feminizes and demasculinizes the behavior of males. *Science* 175:82–84.

3 / Genetic and Chromosomal Aspects of Homosexual Etiology

Hereditary Concepts of Homosexuality in History

In the era of the Inquisition and before, heredity played a role in thinking about homosexuality only by way of the belief that the sins of the fathers might be visited on the children. According to the official dogma of the era, homosexuality was fully explained as a form of demonic possession, and was part of a trilogy that included heresy and treason. The individual was deemed responsible for being the demonic host, and so was tortured and killed for the good of his own soul.

By the eighteenth century, the theory of demonic possession lost much of its credibility. With respect to human sexuality, its place was taken by degeneracy theory, highly respected in the medicine of its day as the ultimate etiology of all diagnostic conditions not otherwise explainable. Masturbation was posited somewhat contradictorily as both the cause of degeneracy and as a sign of a degenerate pedigree. It was believed that a degenerate pedigree would manifest itself by producing many syndromes of degeneracy, ranging from tuberculosis to epilepsy, mental deficiency, insanity, delinquency, and crime. Homosexuality was also included. Degeneracy theory was nihilistic. Apart from exhorting individuals to desist from masturbation, it held no therapeutic promise. Thus it led the way to the segregation or punishment of the afflicted and in the nineteenth century to their eradication by preventing them from breeding, according to the doctrine of eugenics. Hitler carried hereditary degeneracy theory to its apex of absurdity. Homosexuals were among those consigned to the gas ovens, along with Jews and dwarfs.

Although degeneracy theory is still not completely dead (witness the term, sexual degenerates), in most of medicine it had lost its vogue by the end of the nineteenth century. This was the period of the beginnings of modern sexology. Early sexologists gave up the idea of homosexuality as a manifestation of degeneracy. They placated a hostile academic and lay society by qualifying homosexuality as a perversion and an abomination while at the same time classifying it as a syndrome of psychopathology.

It became the new vogue to subdivide homosexuality into two forms, hereditary and acquired. The acquired form would today be better named situational homosexuality. It is found, for example, in adolescents and adults who are forcibly segregated from the other sex and who use a member of their own sex as a surrogate to approximate as closely as possible the opposite sex. Thus, a male might use a youth in anal intercourse as if he were having sex with a female. Such a male should more accurately be called partially bisexual, rather than homosexual, because his primary erotic interest remains with females as soon as he is no longer segregated. In the older terminology, now known to be oversimplified, such a male was classified as an active homosexual because his erotic performance with a male followed closely the stereotype of how a man should perform with a woman, and there were no stereotypic effeminacies in other, nonerotic aspects of his gender identity and role.

The partner of the active homosexual might also have been classified as having the acquired form, in which case the enforced penetration of his anus, or his mouth, would have represented a form of rape. Alternatively, he might have been classified as a passive homosexual, in which case he would have solicited the sexual attention of his partner, would have avoided a partnership with a woman and, most likely, would have manifested stereotypic effeminacies in other, nonerotic aspects of his gender and identity role. This is the type of person whom sexologists of the turn of the century would have considered to have been a candidate for what they considered to be the hereditary form of homosexuality.

For everything in the foregoing referred to in the masculine gender, there is a counterpart in the female gender. Homosexuality and bisexuality in females, however, have always been of far less concern to the church, to law, to medicine, and to research than have their male counterparts.

It was still common in early twentieth century medicine to classify syndromes into hereditary, innate, congenital, or idiopathic, on the one hand, and acquired on the other. The basis for this dichotomization was chronological rather than causal. That is to say, the acquired syndromes were of postnatal onset, whereas the nonacquired ones were present at or before birth. If not overtly obvious at birth, then the etiology was prenatally ascribed, with first symptoms delayed in onset. So-called hereditary homosexuality fell into this category. Obviously a baby cannot manifest itself as homosexual. In later infancy and childhood, however, it is possible for a child to show the signs of a transposition of gender role and identity in such a way as to reach adolescence and adulthood as a homosexual.

A homosexual characterized by an extreme form of female impersonation is known in today's street argot as a drag queen. There is no agreed upon professional terminology for such a condition, unless it be that it constitutes a forme fruste of transsexualism, without the episodic alternations so typical of another allied condition, transvestism.

Feminization of behavior and mentality is pervasive in the homosexual drag queen, just as it is in the transsexual and in the cross-dressed transvestite. In early times these three conditions were not well differentiated. Some of all three were probably included in the category of hereditary homosexuality hypothesized by early sexologists.

The hypothesis of a hereditary class of homosexuals was not a sophisticated one. It could not be authenticated on the basis of an unusual prevalence of homosexuality in selected pedigrees, for such did not exist. It could not be tested by loosely allying homosexuality with various other conditions formerly attributed, en masse, to a common hereditary degeneracy or weakness: the etiological triumphs of germ theory had put an end to such untenable mixing of syndromes.

The hypothesis of hereditary homosexuality could exist at all only because of the impact on medicine of the new science of genetics, following the rediscovery and confirmation of Mendel's principle of genetically recessive inheritance. R. B. Goldschmidt's hybridization of fruit flies so as to produce strains that would have intersexed progeny gave further impetus to the idea that homosexuality may be a covert form of genetic intersexuality—not visible in the gross anatomy of sex, but only in behavior and the mind. This idea linked up with an earlier idea proposed by Krafft-Ebing, namely, that there are different brain centers for sexuality in males and females, from which is derived the hypothesis that male homosexuals are endowed with a female brain center, and vice versa for lesbians.

Statistical Genetics

So much for the speculative genetics of homosexuality. It was not until the mid-twentieth century that attempts at empirical verification began to appear. The methodology was statistical, and the investigative design pertained to the sex ratio, ordinal birth position, and twin concordance.

In sex-ratio studies, the male:female ratio in the sibships of male homosexuals was compared with the expected ratio of 106:100 (Darke, 1948; Jensch, 1941a, 1941b; Kallmann, 1952; Lang, 1940; Slater, 1958). Each study turned up a different ratio, some with and some without statistical significance, ranging from 106:100 in Darke's small sample to 125:100 in Kallmann's twin study. The most often quoted study is that of Lang, based on 1,015 cases. His ratio was 121:100, which could be subdivided to 128:100 for those cases over the age of twenty-five, and to 113:100 for the younger age group. It is possible that the results of all these studies have no more significance than if the figures had been drawn from a random numbers table, a procedure which sometimes chances to yield statistically significant differences. On the other hand, the results may reflect a tendency for homosexual men to have more brothers in the family than expected. In this case, the findings may signify not a genetic predisposition to homosexuality, but a tendency for an effeminate gender identity to develop more easily in boys whose families have a shortage of sisters and daughters. From this latter point of view, it is provocative that Slater found a brother:sister ratio in the families of male exhibitionists of 109:144—an excess of female sibs to form an audience for their show-off brother!

Extending his observations from family constellation to ordinal position of siblings, Martensen-Larsen (1957) somewhat casually reported findings on a sample of sixty-three homosexuals which not only confirmed a preponderance of brothers over sisters but also showed the homosexuals to have a predominance of ordinal position in the lowest third of the sibship. There was also a preponderance of brothers in the families of the forty-two fathers and twenty-one grandfathers studied, whereas the twenty-five grandmothers and forty-five mothers had a preponderance of sisters. In the forty-four homosexual women and the thirty-nine of their mothers and sixteen maternal grandmothers studied, sisters predominated in the sibships with no data reported for the fathers. The homosexual women came from the upper and lower thirds of the sibship more often than the middle.

In the matter of ordinal position, Slater's data (1958, 1962) showed that compared with exhibitionists, homosexuals tended to be born late in the sibship and of older mothers.

Another type of study purporting to implicate a genetic mechanism for homosexuality is that of Kallmann (1952) on homosexual twins. Kallmann reported a high degree of concordance for homosexuality in each of thirty-seven pairs of identical, monozygotic twins. The figure for fraternal, dizygotic twins was quite different. There were twenty-six such pairs of twin brothers studied, with the index case known to be overtly homosexual; 58 percent of the dizygotic co-twins revealed no evidence of homosexual experience after the age of adolescence, whereas the remaining 42 percent ranged over the full scale of 1 to 6 on the Kinsey homosexuality ratings. Only 11.5 percent of the co-twins (three of the twenty-six) were homosexual enough to get a rating as high as 5 or 6 (which requires a high or exclusive degree of homosexuality for at least three years between the ages of sixteen and thirty-five). Kinsey's corresponding percentage for ratings of 5 or 6 in the general male population was 10 percent.

Kallmann's identical twins were not reared apart. Their concordance for homosexuality may, therefore, represent a tendency in monozygotic twins to be replicas of one another while growing up and to respond similarly to their shared life experiences. In this case, their homosexuality would not be a primary genetic unfolding, but secondary to the unison in which the pair encountered life's transactions.

A further word of caution, applicable not only to homosexual but to all twin studies, is very much in order; namely, identical twins are not necessarily cytogenetically identical. That is to say, twins who qualify as identical by all the usual criteria (including blood type, dermatoglyphics, and skin transplant) may not have the same number of chromosomes. This surprising finding has emerged from the study of mongolism (trisomy-21) and Turner's syndrome, when identical and apparently monozygous twins proved to be cytogenetically discordant (Bruins et al., 1963; Lejeune et al., 1962; Ross, Tjio, and Lipsett, 1969; Russell et al., 1966; Turpin et al., 1961). These findings may require a rather extensive revision of current concepts of perfect genetic identity in monozygous twins, since they may be identical for all but one chromosome or one pool of genes. The missing (or added) part of the genetic code may be the very part that makes all the difference with respect to the trait, like homosexuality, which is the subject of behavioral interest in a twin study. There are cases of monazygatic twins discordant for homosexuality.

Cytogenetics: The Sex Chromosomes

The discovery that a difference between the sexes is visible in individual cells of the body dates from as recently as 1949. It was then
that Barr and Bertram at London, Ontario, discovered the sex-
chromatin spot (Moore, 1966), since known as the Barr body, present
in the nucleus of cells from female mammals but not in those from
males. Subsequently, it was discovered that the cells of certain mor-
phologic-appearing males, namely those with Klinefelter's syndrome,
have a Barr body in them. The significance of this finding remained
obscure until after 1956, at which time it first became possible actually to visualize and count the chromosomes in a single cell (see review by Bartalos and Baramki, 1967). The chromosome count of a
phenotypic male with Klinefelter's syndrome shows him to have a
supernumerary X chromosome. Instead of the normal male count of
44+XY chromosomes, or the normal female count of 44+XX, the
Klinefelter male has 44+XXY (47,XXY). In some cases, there is
more than one supernumerary X chromosome. To the extra X chromosome is attributed responsibility for the stigmata of the syndrome: a tendency to eunuchoidism of body build; late onset of puberty; weak pubertal virilization with possible breast development,
as in a female; small penis, small sterile testes; and subnormal subjective experience of libido or sexual drive. The central nervous system seems also to be involved, witness an elevated frequency of the
occurrence of mental deficiency and of various forms of psychopathology. Homosexuality and the related conditions of transsexualism
and transvestism have been recorded in Klinefelter's syndrome, al-
beit infrequently (Money, 1963; Money and Pollitt, 1964; Nielsen,
1969).

The coexistence of the two conditions, cytogenetic and psychosexual,
is important not for its prevalence, which is sparse, but for the relative
rarity of both—especially in the case of transsexualism. Such rarity
forces a consideration of what the relationship between the two, if not
purely coincidental, may be.

It cannot be said that the extra X chromosome of Klinefelter's syndrome induces a degree of psychic femininity in all affected individuals, but only that the incidence of effeminacy is increased. Many individuals escape entirely. The best way to make sense of this state of
affairs is to postulate a genetically determined condition of vulnerability to error in psychosexual differentiation. The developmental period
of greatest risk would appear to be postnatal, during the preschool
years, which is when psychosexual differentiation chiefly is accomplished (Money, Hampson, and Hampson, 1955, 1957). At this time all

development is susceptible to influence from the social environment —like, for example, the acquisition of a native language. That the differentiation of a gender identity is also powerfully influenced by social experience can be clearly demonstrated in matched-paired cases of hermaphroditism. As in the case of a native language, however, the process of psychosexual differentiation is clearly one of interaction between brain and social stimulus. The child with injury to language centers of the dominant hemisphere may be defective in language acquisition. One cannot be very specific about the human brain in matters of psychosexual identity, except to note that psychosexual changes may, in rare instances, be associated with temporal lobe malfunction or injury; and that these changes sometimes are reversed as a consequence of successful brain surgery (Blumer, 1969; Epstein, 1961, 1969). Such cases have not been reported in Klinefelter's syndrome, though an elevated incidence of electroencephalographic abnormality has been observed (Hambert, 1966).

Other syndromes in which the sex chromosomes are implicated are the female triple-X syndrome, Turner's syndrome, and the XYY syndrome in males (Bartalos and Baramki, 1967; Gardner, 1975; Wilkins, 1965). Triple-X females are morphologically and psychosexually unremarkable.

Patients with Turner's syndrome are morphologic females who are dwarfed, without gonads, and subject to a variety of other birth defects. The chromosomal error is most typically an absence of one of the pair of X chromosomes (45,X). Girls with this condition need hormonal replacement therapy at the age of puberty in order to mature sexually. Psychosexually they represent virtually the obverse of homosexuality, which is conspicuous by its absence in this syndrome. The girls not only conform to the style of femininity idealized in our cultural definition of femininity, but, long before they know the prognosis of their condition, they are maternal in their childhood play and adult aspirations. This very complete feminine gender identity and absence of homosexual traits may have its origins in a total absence of gonadal hormones during fetal development, so that there is no malelike hormonal effect on the sex-regulating centers of the developing brain (Money and Mittenthal, 1970).

The XYY karyotype was first identified in 1961 (Sandberg et al.). It soon became the vogue to correlate XYY chromosomal status with criminal violence and tall stature, for the first surveys for XYY were conducted among tall men in maximum security institutions. Before screening surveys in the population at large could be adequately completed, they were suppressed by the protests of antiscientific political radicals. Thus there are no acceptable statistics regarding the prevalence of behavioral variability in the XYY syndrome. There is clinical evidence, however, to suggest an increased prevalence of poorly regulated or impulsive behavior, sexual behavior included (Money, Gaskin, and Hull, 1970; Money et al., 1975). The prevalence of bisexuality in XYY men appears to be elevated. It may occur among XYY men who are not institutionalized, but is most likely to manifest itself as situational homosexuality among those who are institutionalized, followed by heterosexuality upon release.

Nuclear sex-chromatin surveys of homosexuals, transsexuals and transvestites have disclosed no consistent discrepancies between them and control groups of heterosexual males (Bleuler and Wiedemann, 1956; Pare, 1956; Raboch and Nedoma, 1958). Likewise, karyotyping surveys (Pritchard, 1962) in which the chromosomes are actually visualized and counted have revealed no consistent discrepancies between male homosexuals (or transsexuals and transvestites) and heterosexuals. The greater cytogenetic detail made possible by the newer techniques of chromosome banding and fluorescence has not required a revision of the earlier findings of no cytogenetic difference between homosexuals and heterosexuals. Cytogenetic surveys of lesbians and female-to-male transsexuals are conspicuous by their absence, which is in keeping with the widespread neglect of lesbian research. However, on the basis of clinical rather than survey sampling, there is no reason to suspect that lesbians differ cytogenetically from heterosexual women.

On the basis of present knowledge, there is no basis on which to justify an hypothesis that homosexuals or bisexuals of any degree or type are chromosomally discrepant from heterosexuals. On the basis of cytogenetic techniques currently available, however, there is no way of implicating a peculiarity of the genetic code on one or more of the chromosomes instead of a gross chromosomal anomaly. There is, as yet, no technique for visualizing, counting, or otherwise directly implicating the genetic code in the etiology of psychosexual status. Such an implication must always be by inference, and no such inference is yet possible with respect to psychosexual behavior genetics.

Matched-Pair Studies in Intersexuality

Cases of human intersexuality or hermaphroditism are highly relevant to the genetics of psychosexuality, insofar as individuals born with the same syndrome and belonging to the same chromosomal sex may be matched in pairs, one assigned in gender and living as a female, the other as a male (Lewis and Money, 1977; Money, 1968a, 1970; Money and Dalery, 1976; Money and Ehrhardt, 1972; Money and Ogunro, 1974).

Comparison of such pairs shows that the female-assigned member of a matched pair typically grows up to have a feminine gender identity and role, and the male member develops the masculine counterpart, including the psychosexual, erotic component. This phenomenon occurs irrespective of chromosomal sex (46,XX or 46,XY) and irrespective of the etiology of the intersexual condition and its prenatal developmental history. It is capable of occurring also in those cases of postnatal mismanagement in which the genitalia are not surgically corrected in early infancy, as ideally they should be, and in which the regulation of the hormonal status of puberty is not endocrinologically regulated soon enough so as to prevent early adolescent bodily development discordant with the sex or rearing.

In addition to cases of intersexuality, there are also other cases of birth defects of the genitalia, namely agenesis of the penis or micropenis in chromosomal (46,XY) males, in which the medical habilitative plan is to assign the baby as a girl, with appropriate surgical correction and, in time, hormonal feminization. In such cases, the postnatal differentiation of gender identity and role follows the same route as in parallel cases of intersexuality. That is, it is dictated not by the chromosomal sex, nor the other prenatal components of sexual differentiation, but is dependent on postnatal determinants, particularly stimuli from the social environment.

The matched pair method of comparison in cases of intersexuality is particularly effective in cases of female (46,XX) hermaphroditism associated with the adrenogenital syndrome; matched pairs shed light on the relative unimportance of the sex chromosomes as determinants of homosexuality. In extreme cases, 46,XX babies with the adrenogenital syndrome are born with a phallic organ that, instead of being a clitoris, has differentiated into an anatomically normal penis, accompanied by a normal-appearing, though empty, scrotum. The internal reproductive structures are female, and the gonads are normally placed ovaries. The adrenogenital syndrome has its origin in a recessive genetic defect. When two parents happen to be hidden carriers, so-called, of the recessive gene, then there is a 25 percent chance at each conception that the baby will get the recessive gene from each parent and become an open carrier, affected with the syndrome. The pathway whereby the genetic defect produces a masculinization of the external genitalia is by way of the fetal adrenocortical glands. These adrenocortices, instead of secreting their proper hormone, cortisol, secrete instead a precursor product which is androgenic in biochemical structure and in physiologic action (it is easy for the body to interchange adrenocortical, testicular, and ovarian hormones, for they are all steroids and closely related to one another).

Confronted with a sufficiency of masculinizing hormone, regardless of its source, the fetus conforms to what may be called the "Adam principle." That is to say, it masculinizes, even if it is chromosomally 46,XX. In the case of the adrenogenital syndrome, the Adam principle takes effect after the internal reproductive structures have differentiated as female, at a time when only the external genital anatomy is still undifferentiated and capable, therefore, of becoming differentiated as masculine. This contradictory state of affairs may pass undiagnosed at birth, in which case adrenocortical malfunction continues its masculinizing course, producing an early, masculinizing puberty. In such a case, correct case management is to allow the child to continue living as a boy, with surgical and hormonal rehabilitation adjusted as appropriate for a boy. The correctness of this procedure is dictated by the fact that an infant's gender identity and role become differentiated between the ages of one and a half and four and a half to five and a half years, after which they cannot be eradicated or changed by edict.

There are some adrenogenital babies whose condition is diagnosed at birth because it is associated with a deficiency in the adrenal salt-regulating hormone, aldosterone. Uncorrected, this deficiency is lethal. Establishment of the diagnosis in the neonate usually leads to a decision to feminize the external genitals surgically, to reannounce the sex of the baby as female, and to regulate adrenocortical function from birth onward (by hormonal treatment with synthetic cortisol) so that teenage puberty will be feminizing. With this type of medical biography, an adrenogenital baby grows up to differentiate a girl's gender identity and role, but one that is tinged with what may metaphorically be called the hue or flavor of tomboyism. According to the most recent evidence (Money and Schwartz, 1977), in her teens she is late, maybe very late, as compared with control age-mates, in reaching the romantic stage of dating and boyfriends. There is a greater than average chance that she will experience bisexual imagery in fantasy and dreams, the actualization of which will most likely be suppressed, though in some cases will lead to a lesbian love affair. In other cases, a heterosexual love affair is established, followed by marriage and motherhood.

There are three cases of the 46,XX adrenogenital syndrome in which the baby, born with a penis, was reared as a boy and is now an adult man (Money and Daléry, 1976). In all three cases, these boys as teenagers reached the romantic stage of dating girls and falling in love in synchrony with their male age-mates. They experienced no disposition toward bisexuality. As males, they were exclusively heterosexual in their reported imagery and actual behavior.

Heterosexuality in these three cases obviously cannot be attributed to their 46,XX chromosomal status. Nor can it be attributed exclusively to their sex of assignment and rearing, for that would entail a total absence of bisexuality or lesbianism in counterpart cases reared as girls. It may possibly be attributed to their postnatal, postpubertal masculine hormonal status, though that possibility is unlikely in view of other evidence that pubertal hormones discordant with assigned sex and psychosexual status do not change the latter. The most likely hypothesis, therefore, is that the same prenatal hormonal influences which masculinized the external genitalia had a parallel effect on the fetal brain pathways (notably in the hypothalamus and the nearby limbic system) that mediate sexual dimorphism of behavior and imagery (see Dörner et al., 1975). This hypothesis is supported by the evidence of other types of hermaphroditism—for example, the obverse of the adrenogenital syndrome, namely the androgen-insensitivity or testicular-feminizing syndrome (Money, 1968b) in which a 46,XY individual is born with the external anatomy of a female. Above all, it is supported by an extensive body of animal experimentation (see, for example, Dörner, 1976; Ward, 1977; and review by Money and Ehrhardt, 1972).

Conclusion

According to currently available evidence, the sex chromosomes do not directly determine or program psychosexual status as heterosexual, bisexual, or homosexual. The sex chromosomes complete their contribution to psychosexual differentiation when they program the undifferentiated embryonic gonads to differentiate as testes or ovaries. The principle involved is conveniently known as the Adam principle, by which it is meant that something must be added to permit an embryo or fetus to differentiate as a male, for nature's primal disposition is always to differentiate a female, regardless of chromosomal genetics. In the first instance, the Adam principle is effected by way of H-Y antigen, a masculine-programming substance that adheres to the Y chromosome. After the Y chromosome programs the differentiation of a testis, hormonal secretion from the testis, chiefly androgen, continues the programming of the reproductive anatomy as male. At the same time, androgen also exerts a programming effect on the brain, the details of which have been definitively mapped in lower animals. They apply to brain pathways that ultimately regulate hormonal secretions of the pituitary gland in concert with other pathways that regulate correlative behavioral functioning. The hormones of puberty do not change the basic psychosexuality of a person. They simply activate and intensify it.

In future research, the most likely hypotheses concerning a

prenatal determinant of homosexuality will pertain not to genetics per se, but to prenatal hormonal influences on the brain. It remains to be seen whether an as-yet-undetected genetic (genic, not chromosomal) origin will be found for anomalies of prenatal hormonal functioning that ultimately program psychosexuality as heterosexual, bisexual, or homosexual. Meantime, available evidence supports a nongenetic hypothesis for the origin not only of homosexuality, but of psychosexual differences and variations of all types. Prenatal hormonal determinants probably do no more than create a predisposition on which the postnatal superstructure of psychosexual status differentiates, primarily, like native language, under the programming of social interaction.

REFERENCES

Bartalos, M., and Baramki, T. A. 1967. *Medical cytogenetics.* Baltimore: Williams & Wilkins.

Bleuler, M., and Wiedemann, H. R. 1956. Chromosomengeschlecht und psychosexualitaet. *Archiv fuer Psychiatrie und Zeitschrift Neurologie* 195:14–19.

Blumer, D. 1969. Transsexualism, sexual dysfunction and temporal lobe disorder. In R. Green and J. Money, eds., *Transsexualism and Sex Reassignment* (Baltimore: Johns Hopkins Press).

Bruins, J. W., et al. 1963. Discordant mongolism in monozygotic twins? *Genetics Today. Proceedings of the XI International Congress of Genetics, The Hague, Netherlands,* vol. 1 (abstract 16.26). New York: Macmillan.

Darke, R. A. 1948. Heredity as an etiological factor in homosexuality. *Journal of Nervous and Mental Disease* 107:251–68.

Dörner, G. 1976. *Hormones and brain differentiation.* Amsterdam and New York: Elsevier.

Dörner, G., et al. 1975. A neuroendocrine predisposition for homosexuality in men. *Archives of Sexual Behavior* 4:1–8.

Epstein, A. 1961 Relationship of fetishism and transvestism to brain and particularly to temporal lobe dysfunction. *Journal of Nervous and Mental Disease* 133:247–54.

———. 1969. Disordered human sexual behavior associated with temporal lobe dysfunction. *Medical Aspects of Human Sexuality* 3:62–68.

Gardner, L. I. ed. 1975. *Endocrine and genetic diseases of childhood and adolescence,* 2nd ed. Philadelphia: W.B. Saunders.

Hambert, G. 1966. *Males with positive sex chromatin.* Göteborg: Akademiförlaget-Gumperts.

Jensch, K. 1941a. Zur genealogie der homosexualitaet. *Archiv für Psychiatrie und Nervenkrankheiten* 112:527–40.

———. 1941b. Weiterer beitrag zur genealogie der homosexualität. *Archiv für Psychiatrie und Nervenkrankheiten* 112:679–96.

Kallmann, F. J. 1952. Comparative twin study on the genetic aspects of male homosexuality. *Journal of Nervous and Mental Disease* 115:283–98.

Lang, T. 1940. Studies on the genetic determination of homosexuality. *Journal of Nervous and Mental Disease* 92:55–64.

Lejeune, J., et al. 1962. Monozygotisme hétérocaryote: Jumeau normal et jumeau trisomique 21. *Comptes Rendus de l'Académie des Sciences* 254:4404–6.

Lewis, V. G., 1978. Vaginal atresia in the 46,XY androgen insensitivity (testicular feminizing) Syndrome and the 46XX Rokitansky Syndrome: Female Gender Identity/Role Compared. Ph.D. dissertation. Loyola College.

Martensen-Larsen, O. 1957. The family constellation and homosexualism. *Acta Genetica et Statistica Medica* 7:445–46.

Money, J. 1963. Cytogenetic and psychosexual incongruities with a note on spaceform blindness. *American Journal of Psychiatry* 119:820–27.

————. 1968a. *Sex errors of the body: dilemmas, education and counseling.* Baltimore: Johns Hopkins Press.

————. 1968b. Psychologic approach to psychosexual misidentity with elective mutism: Sex reassignment in two cases of hyperadrenocortical hermaphroditism. *Clinical pediatrics* 7:331–39.

————. 1970. Matched pairs of hermaphrodites: Behavioral biology of sexual differentiation from chromosomes to gender identity. *Engineering and Science* (California Institute of Technology; special issue: *Biological bases of human behavior*) 33:34–39.

Money, J., and Daléry, J. 1976. Iatrogenic homosexuality: Gender identity in seven 46,XX chromosomal females with hyperadrenocortical hermaphroditism born with a penis, three reared as boys, four reared as girls. *Journal of homosexuality* 1:357–71.

Money, J., and Ehrhardt, A. A. 1972. *Man and woman, boy and girl: Differentiation and dimorphism of gender identity from conception to maturity.* Baltimore: Johns Hopkins Press.

Money, J.; Gaskin, R. J.; and Hull, H. 1970. Impulse, aggression and sexuality in the XYY syndrome. *St. John's Law Review* 44:220–35.

Money, J.; Hampson, J. G.; and Hampson, J.L. 1955. Hermaphroditism: Recommendations concerning assignment of sex, change of sex, and psychologic management. *Johns Hopkins Hospital Bulletin* 97:284–300.

————. 1957. Imprinting and the establishment of gender role. *Archives of Neurology and Psychiatry* 77:333–36.

Money, J., and Mittenthal, S. 1970. Lack of personality pathology in Turner's syndrome: Relation to cytogenetics, hormones and physique. *Behavior Genetics* 1:43–56.

Money, J., and Ogunro, C. 1974. Behavioral sexology: Ten cases of genetic male intersexuality with impaired prenatal and pubertal androgenization. *Archives of Sexual Behavior* 3:181–205.

Money, J., and Pollitt, E. 1964. Cytogenetic and psychosexual ambiguity: Klinefelter's syndrome and transvestism compared. *Archives of General Psychiatry* 11:589–95.

Money, J., and Schwartz, M. 1977. Dating, romantic and nonromantic friendships, and sexuality in 17 early-treated adrenogenital females, aged 16–25. In P. A. Lee, L. P. Plotnick, A. A. Kowarski, and C. J. Migeon, eds., *Congenital Adrenal Hyperplasia* (Baltimore: University Park Press).

Money, J., et al. 1975. 47,XYY and 46,XY males with antisocial and/or sex-offending behavior: Antiandrogen therapy plus counseling. *Psychoneuroendocrinology* 1:165–78.

Moore, K. L., ed. 1966. *The Sex Chromatin.* Philadelphia: W. B. Saunders.

Nielsen, J. 1969. *Klinefelter's syndrome and the XYY syndrome: A genetical, endocrinological and psychiatric-psychological study of 33 hypogonadal male patients and 2 patients with karyotype 47,XYY.* Copenhagen: Munksgaard.

Pare, C. M. B. 1956. Homosexuality and chromosomal sex. *Journal of Psychosomatic Research* 1: 247–51.

Pritchard, M. 1962. Homosexuality and genetic sex. *Journal of Mental Science* 108:-616–23.

Raboch, J., and Nedoma, K. 1958. Sex chromatin and sexual behavior. A study of 36 men with female nuclear pattern and of 194 homosexuals. *Psychosomatic Medicine* 20:55–59.

Ross, G. T.; Tjio, J. H.; and Lipsett, M.B. 1969. Cytogenetic studies of presumptive monozygotic twin girls discordant for gonadal dysgenesis. *Journal of Clinical Endocrinology and Metabolism* 29:440–45.

Russell, A., et al. 1966 Gonadal dysgenesis and its unilateral variant with testis in monozygous twins: Related to discordance in sex chromosomal status. *Journal of Clinical Endocrinology and Metabolism* 26:1282–92.

Sandberg, A. A., et al. 1961. An XYY human male. *Lancet* 2:488–89.

Slater, E. 1958. The sibs and children of homosexuals. In D. R. Smith, and W. A. Davidson, eds., *Symposium on Nuclear Sex* (New York: Interscience Publishers).

————. 1962. Birth order and maternal age of homosexuals. *Lancet* 1:69–71.

Turpin et al. 1961. Présomption de monozygotisme en dépit d'un dimorphisme sexuel: sujet masculin XY et sujet neutro, Haplo X. *Comptes Rendus de l'Académie des Sciences* 252:2945–46.

Ward, I. L. 1977. Exogenous androgen activates female behavior in noncopulating, prenatally stressed male rats. *Journal of Comparative and Physiological Psychology* 91:465–71.

Wilkins, L. 1965. *The diagnosis and treatment of endocrine disorders in childhood and adolescence,* 3rd ed. Springfield, Ill.: Charles C Thomas.

PART II

The View of the

Social Sciences

4 / Homosexuality in History

ARNO KARLEN

Many writers on homosexuality refer to its occurrence in history. Usually it is to prove a point or justify a view of the present. Has homosexuality existed in all times, places, and social classes? If so, perhaps desiring either sex is as natural as liking Gruyère or Gorgonzola. Does it increase with urbanization, prosperity, or permissiveness? Then perhaps it accounts for the fall of Rome or the ills of our century. Is it related to creativity? Perhaps it explains the Renaissance or the modern American theater. Is it more common where sex roles are rigid or flexible? Perhaps we should change our laws and customs and raise children differently.

When so many people turn to the past for ammunition, the historian must try to establish the evidence.

Methods and Evidence

Unfortunately, scholars have paid more attention to the forms of human economy and polity than to those of human sexuality. The handful who do study sexuality with the tools of modern history and of interdisciplinary sex research find their sources surprisingly slim. Most historical material consists not of data but of opinion, gossip, and easily misused documents. Some chroniclers are accurate, others polemical or self-serving. And written sources reflect a tiny literate minority through most of Western history.

Sex behavior rises from the interplay of myriad biological, social, family, and individual factors. To understand an era's sexual life, we should know its sex behavior, overt and covert mores, family structure, and child-rearing practices, all in a biological and cross-cultural perspective. Otherwise we have only isolated facts, anecdotes, and hints. That is just what we are stuck with in studying the history of all sex behaviors.

If I begin with caution, it is because we must try to reconstruct a complex design from scattered fragments of a nearly vanished mosaic —a task often attempted with passion or irresponsibility. I have sketched elsewhere (Karlen, 1971a) an overview of homosexuality in our past. In this chapter I can only touch certain periods, each of which raises questions about homosexuality today.

The Pre-Christian "Paradise": Evolutionary Theories

The scientific study of sex began with the anti-Victorian movement of the late nineteenth century. It has often contained open or implied bias against many traditional values, variously called Victorian, Puritan, or Judeo-Christian. All three terms are misleading, for they imply a golden age of pagan permissiveness that probably never existed. The idea of "Judeo-Christian restrictiveness" is often related to evolutionary theories of history and to the homosexual "temple prostitution" banned by the ancient Hebrews but practiced by many of their neighbors.

First we must note that virtually all societies have the institutions of marriage and the family and discourage as *predominant adult* sex behavior anything but heterosexual intercourse (Murdock, 1949; Ford and Beach, 1951; Gebhard, 1971; Davenport, 1977; Karlen, 1971a). Some societies permit homosexuality, chastity, sodomy, incest, and other nonmarital, nonreproductive behaviors for certain people at certain times of life, but nowhere for most adults most of the time.

The ancient Hebrews had a positive attitude toward marital coitus; they saw no value in chastity for its own sake (Patai, 1959; Cole, 1960). In this they were less restrictive than many other peoples in Western history. They forbade homosexual acts by law, as did the Egyptians and Assyrians (Bullough, 1976).

According to Herodotus (1942) and other ancient writers, many peoples of the ancient Near East and eastern Mediterranean worshiped a goddess—variously known as Artemis, Astarte, Isis, and Cybele—whose rites included heterosexual or homosexual intercourse with priests, priestesses, or "temple prostitutes" of both sexes.

In some places the male priests or prostitutes might be eunuchs, transvestites, or both.

These practices have been interpreted as ordinary prostitution, mystical rites, or a mixture of the two (Patai, 1959; Taylor, 1958; Karlen, 1971a). Actually we know almost nothing about them; I use quotation marks to emphasize that "temple prostitution" may or may not have been religious in the usual modern sense or prostitution in the usual sense. How many people performed these acts? On certain occasions or whenever they wished? Could one choose between a same-sex and an opposite-sex partner? Could either partner take the insertor role in homosexual acts? Did people feel such acts inside the temple were different from the same acts outside the temple? Were they obligatory, neutral, or only tolerated? About all these things, as about most people's daily sex lives, we know almost nothing.

Homosexuality was one of the Hebrews' most ancient shalt-nots (Leviticus 20), but first without reference to temple prostitution. But in later Old Testament books (Deuteronomy, Kings I and II, Hosea), the word translated as "sodomite" or the "harlot" in the King James version is a specific reference to the male and female servants and the Great Mother. Apparently the Great Mother cults sprang up sporadically within Hebrew lands. Hosea (4) complained that men "sacrifice with cult prostitutes." This caused periodic purges of temple and town. Temple prostitution may have resulted from the growth of foreign enclaves or from conversions to neighboring people's religions. In the mid-nineteenth century, Bachofen (1967) have speculated that the Hebrews themselves originally worshiped the Great Mother and tolerated homosexuality, and that the change to worshiping a male god brought a ban on temple prostitution and homosexuality. In fact, Bachofen claimed that all societies began in a state of promiscuity, martiarchy, communism, and goddess-worship; they evolved to monogamy, partiarchy, private property, and god-worship.

Some still claim that Great Mother cults, and their alleged matriarchies, were emotionally and erotically permissive; Hebrew patriarchy, they say, plunged the West into an over-control of sex and emotion, "laws of sexual property," and horrified vengefulness toward homosexuality.

The chief objection to the theory is that no matriarchy exists or to our knowledge, ever has (Westermarck, 1917; Murdock, 1949; Goode, 1964; Friedll, 1975). Another is that no society or even higher species is pansexually permissive (Beach, 1977).

Ancient Greece: The Modern Myth

The commonest reference to homosexuality in our past is to the alleged acceptance of homosexuality or bisexuality in ancient Greece.[1] The idea that Greek society approved of homosexuality rises from three successive rewritings of history; one was in Greece itself, one during the Renaissance, the third in the late nineteenth century. The Mycenaean Greeks of Homer's epics, more than three millennia ago, left no record of homosexuality (Karlen, 1971a). If it was present or important in their society, their surviving literature does not say so. The protagonists of Homer's *Iliad* (1966) and *Odyssey* (1946) praised marriage and family; today Hector and Andromache are still used as examples of marital love and commitment. Homer's society was a warrior culture, and he praised the loyal love of comrades in arms, such as Achilles and Patroclus, but none of Homer's heroes went to bed together. One can always infer latent or hidden homosexuality if one wishes, but we are hardly the first to say that people of the same sex can love each other without erotic desire.

The Mycenaeans were eventually displaced by militaristic Dorian invaders, and there followed centuries of social change that left no record. When the record does resume, around the seventh century B.C., the value placed on male comradeship had been joined by angry and mistrustful contempt of women and by certain forms of homosexual behavior (Brinton, 1959; Finley, 1954; Hesiod, 1959; Flacelière, 1962; Karlen, 1971a). Some writers conclude that the new misogyny and homosexuality were related (Flacelière, 1962; Hunt, 1959; Symonds, 1931). Others ascribe the homosexuality to Dorian traditions. But there have been other times and cultures in which misogyny and an elite military caste did not coexist with widespread homosexuality (Karlen, 1971a). Furthermore, homosexuality seems to have become more open and perhaps more common in the Greco-Roman world as women's social position improved (Seltman, 1962). In any case, modern clinical knowledge and research both caution against seeking a single cause for homosexual behavior in an individual or in a society. We can only dimly guess what fosters sociosexual change in our own culture, let alone in ancient Greece. And we must remember that we know very little about the Greeks' sexual attitudes and

---

1. I use the term bisexuality throughout these pages with reluctance. It tends to imply a dual physical or instinctual system that produces attraction to both males and females, an idea that has been ably argued against (e.g., Rado, 1940). And few people in our society maintain equal amounts of desire for, sexual activity with and satisfaction from partners of both sexes over a long period. It clarifies nothing to call bisexual or homosexual those who are various 10 percent, 50 percent, and 90 percent homosexual or heterosexual in desire and behavior. But no better term is in common use.

behavior except through the writings of a tiny leisured upper class.

Whatever the reasons, homosexuality was increasingly referred to in Greek literature and depicted in Greek art from the sixth century B.C. on—in the poetry of Sappho and Anacreon, the prose of Plato, the plays of Aeschylus. In fact, Greece was rewriting ancient Mycenaean myth at this time to fit its very different sensibility. Hercules, Zeus, and Poseidon were given homosexual escapades; Aeschylus retold the story of Achilles and Patroclus, making them lovers (Licht, 1963). Even many writers who spoke scathingly of homosexuality, such as Lucian (1913), adopted to some degree the new literary convention of adding homosexuality to ancient myth.

Some Greek literature and art portrayed sexual relations between two women or two men, but the vast majority showed men and *ephebi,* or pubescent boys (Karlen, 1971a). Poets praised "a beardless, tender and beautiful youth"; Solon (Flacelière, 1962), who created Athens' democratic constitution, wrote, "Boys in the flower of their youth are loved; the smoothness of their thighs and soft lips is adored." The descriptions and metaphors evoke a slender sapling or an almost androgynous creature, coquettish yet naive, or a fuzzy little peach. Poets and philosophers debated whether a youth was most beautiful before he had a beard, when down started to appear on his face, or a bit later. Hair on the legs and chest usually meant the end of the affair. Now the young man was supposed to have intercourse with women and with males younger than himself. But sexual relations between two grown men was no subject of rhapsody.

In fact, homosexuality was now commonly called pederasty, or love of children, and erotic writings gushed about *ta paidika,* or childish qualities. Writers justified sex with boys by the Dorian tradition of male comradeship and the Cretan ideal of pedagogical relationships between men and youths in the military class. Such pederasty was supposed to transmit manly virtues of mind and body from nobleman to young lover (Vangaard, 1972). We do not know to what extent this was a real or an ideal view; there were varied opinions even in Ancient Greece. But some Greek writers began attributing everything virtuous and desirable to homosexuality (Morrow, 1956).

Plato gathered all this and more in his dialogue *The Symposium* (1948). Its basic argument was this: the beautiful is the good; love is love of the good and beautiful; men are better and more beautiful than women; hence love of men is the highest love. Socrates added that now, in his philosophic late years, he realized that the most important beauty is not physical but moral. This point was later lost on the early Stoics, who openly equated physical and moral beauty. For instance, Ariston (Flacelière, 1962) wrote, "A virtuous and noble mind may be discerned in the bloom and grace of a body, just as a well-made shoe reveals the beauty of a foot."

The Symposium professes to defend homosexuality to the many who do not grasp its virtues. This hardly suggests vast social acceptance. Aristophanes, whom Plato used as a mouthpiece to explain homosexuality in *The Symposium,* had in reality mocked homosexuality as harshly in his plays as any twentieth century burlesque comedian. It was he, not Plato, who spoke for the majority of Greeks. Plutarch, Lucian, Herodotus, Aristotle, and many later Stocis and Cynics spoke of homosexuality in tones from disapproving to scathing (Hunt, 1959; Karlen, 1971a).

Flacelière (1962) concludes that homosexuality was never prevalent "except in one class of society and over a limited period, and that there is no evidence that homosexuality met with any social approval. . . . The Greeks never 'canonized' the physical act of sodomy" (p. 217). Apparently some upper-class Greek men did switch back and forth between women and boys without suffering the crises of heterosexual and masculine identity that would commonly occur today. This resembles a pattern which exists in part of the Mediterranean world, some prisons, and some non-Western societies (Karlen, 1971a). Homosexuality is defined as a sexual act between adult males or adult females, but women and boys (those penetrated) are considered "not-men," as are effeminate males. In such cultures, a man is not labeled homosexual by others or by himself if he penetrates defined nonmen occasionally or as a substitute for coitus.

Apparently some people, a minority even in the Greek upper classes, encouraged, approved, or easily tolerated homosexuality, but clearly heterosexuality was the encouraged norm, as it has been in every society past and present (Diamond and Karlen, 1980).

Today ancient Greece's "acceptance" of homosexuality or of "natural bisexuality" remains common knowledge—to all who have not read the primary sources.

Rome: Sex versus Civilization

Rome has traditionally been associated with the words "decadence" and "orgy." From Gibbon (1957–62) through von Ranke (1909) to Toynbee (1964), opponents of sexual permissiveness have pointed to the fall of Rome as a lesson for the twentieth century. From Juvenal to Freud to many recent texts on history and sex (Bullough, 1972), it has been said that civilization is built on repression, or at the least on controlled heterosexuality, and that sexual "excess" brings an increase in deviance, a decline in the family, the arts, society, and statecraft.

Over a few centuries, the small Italian tribe called Latins became the world's greatest power. Then, ruling a far-flung, cosmopolitan empire, they looked at their past with nostalgia, bewailing the loss of old-fashioned rural virtues. Seneca, Cato, and Tacitus complained that impiety, adultery, effeminacy, and homosexuality were corrupting and destroying Rome from within. They sound much like present-day conservatives evoking small-town nineteenth century life as they imagine it.

It is true that early Roman laws and values reflected a striving for dignity, simplicity, and straightforwardness. But only myth tells us that they were really more sober, abstemious, and straightforward than their descendants; despite later writers' retrospective piety, we know very little about their sex behavior and about whether homosexuality existed among them.

In our century, urbanization and changes in family structure and sex role have occurred along with changes in sex behavior (Kinsey et al., 1948, 1953). To some extent this probably happened in Rome as it grew as well (Carcopino, 1940). People cast off the traditions of provincial villages and entered the life of the empire's cities. Suetonius (1957) and many others present a startling panorama of psychosexual disorders, from transvestism to sadism. The *Satires* of Juvenal (1958) portray male and female homosexuals in detail, and in the ninth satire a male homosexual prostitute is described. For perhaps the first time in history, Juvenal recorded such matters as a drag queen's cosmetics and the secret relations between male prostitutes and homosexual men with marriages as social fronts.

The poets Catullus (1956) and Martial (1961) made it clear that among the upper class and some of the uprooted urban poor, a number of men who identified as heterosexuals sometimes had sexual relations with boys; like the Greeks, they equated masculine heterosexuality with aggression, dominance, and being the sexual penetrator, but scorned predominant homosexuality and other failures of the traditional masculine role. Martial, who could refer flippantly to buggering a boy on occasion, would verbally flay anyone effeminate or predominantly homosexual. He mocked lesbians harshly. And like many writers of his time, he feared that society's leaders were indulging in indiscriminate hedonism, leaving the empire to drift like an unpiloted ship toward calamity.

Nevertheless, we do not know for sure that homosexuality increased at this time. Complaints that homosexuality is increasing have been heard in virtually every generation in Western history, and obviously have been wrong more often than not. Urbanization brought some changes in sexual attitudes, and it was accompanied by a relaxation of traditional ideas of sex roles, marriage, divorce, and child-rearing, but the relationship of any of these to the incidence of homosexuality remains unknown. Kinsey et al. (1948, 1953) showed that despite the massive changes in sexual attitudes and behavior in the period between

1890 and 1950, there was no significant increase in homosexual behavior, exploratory or temporary or long-term, male or female. Despite another wave of permissiveness in the 1960s and 1970s, no reliable studies show any significant increase in homosexuality in that period either (Karlen, 1978). Although we cannot draw a sure and direct inference about the past from twentieth century America, the evidence of our day cautions against assuming there was a massive increase in homosexuality in ancient Rome.

Furthermore, we do not know that sexual behavior in urban and cosmopolitan societies is necessarily greater in amount or variety than in rural or tribal societies. Some nontechnological societies have far more homosexual behavior than ours, and others have far less (Ford and Beach, 1951; Davenport, 1977). Kinsey et al. did find (1948, 1953) a small but significant urban–rural difference, in many sex behaviors in the United States, but these findings may or may not apply to other times and places.

Obviously cities offer more potential partners and more opportunities for anonymous encounters. Furthermore, they may contain enough sexual deviants of many kinds for visible subsocieties to develop; we do not know whether these actually induce more people to become deviant or merely make deviance more apparent. It is now a commonplace among all but the most zealous biological determinists and social determinists that homosexuality results from the interplay of many biological, social, and psychological factors. The presence of a visible homosexual subculture is only one factor, and it may or may not be an important one. The same caution is called for in response to theories that homosexuality increased in Rome along with the emancipation of women (Churchill, 1967) or that Rome fell with a crisis of family life (Zimmerman, (1947). Bullough (1972) quite properly comments that some such one-cause theories suffer from improper methods. Others contain inaccuracies that would discredit an undergraduate term paper.

Many people today, like moralists of the Roman empire, fear that if people have as much sex as they want, they are heading into a moral trough, and society is going to hell in a handbasket (Karlen, 1980). Yet the Roman empire prospered for centuries after Senecan moralizings had become clichés. Not all Romans were devoted to ambisexual orgies. Doubtless many or most were busy working and raising families and had little time, money, opportunity, or even inclination for the doings of a Nero or a Caligula. Roman cries of "degeneracy" were succeeded by centuries of artistic, civic, technological, and managerial accomplishment. And there were large parts of the empire where vast numbers of people continued to live traditionally in villages and small towns. We do not know how happy or satisfied any of these people were, but there have been permissive cultures in which individuals' psyches and social institutions are not visibly damaged by lack of sexual frustration (Ford and Beach, 1951; Devereux, 1963; Karlen, 1980; Marshall and Suggs, 1971).

Finally, we do not know that sexual deviance increased much or at all through the history of the Roman empire, that deviance bred further deviance, nor that deviance or sexual permissiveness in general harmed society or weakened the empire. It is a logical inference from modern research that massive social change, including urbanization, *may* have brought a small increase in homosexual activity; this remains an inference, not a fact. If Rome does have a lesson for the twentieth century, it is that a society can continue more or less efficiently despite the alarm of outraged moralists who equate nonmarital sexual expression with disaster.

The Church: Deviance as Sin

It is widely believed today that strictures on homosexuality in the West rise from "Judeo-Christian repressiveness." We have already seen that ancient Judaism was not uniformly antisexual, and that most or all ancient Western cultures we know about were like Christianity in forbidding homosexuality. Furthermore, Western religious ideals cannot correctly be seen as a tyranny enforced from above by a handful of zealots. Sexual regulation is basic to all human society—or as anthropologist Claude Lévi-Strauss once put it, in the realm of sexuality, one may not do entirely as one pleases.

Religion is only one of many traditions and institutions that mold and limit human sexuality. Civil law, ethical values, folkways, humor, art, all express and reinforce a society's sexual values. Today formal religion is not the most authoritative influence on sex behavior to many Westerners; that power has passed largely to custom, science, and civil law. But through most of Western history, the church was the chief reflection and instrument of sociosexual values, and it was not necessarily out of harmony with widespread values and other institutions. Certainly our society remains restrictive through secular attitudes and institutions.

Christianity arose as a syncretic religion; many of its beliefs had long been common in the ancient world—baptism, blood communion with a deity, a dualistic view of pleasure and impulse battling self-denial and otherworldliness (Cole, 1960; Brinton, 1959). Some of the Great Mother cults called for chastity or for castration of clerics. Such philosophies as Stoicism, Epicureanism, and Pythagoreanism offered salvation through conquering the flesh and desire. Obviously Christianity did not have to battle a sea of pagan hedonism, only the behavior of some areas and some parts of society. In fact, in waging a polemical campaign for their faith, some church fathers pointed to nonbelievers as examples of abstemious rigor. Saint Salvian praised the Vandals for their morals as Tacitus had praised the Germans, to shame the "indulgent" among his own people.

We have only fragments of gossip and anecdote about whether there was homosexual behavior among the Vikings, Visigoths, Celts, Vandals, and other peoples of the Dark Ages. Certainly none we know of approved homosexuality, and some punished it ferociously. Visigoth law, like fourth-century Roman law, condemned homosexuals to be burned at the stake; revision in the early Middle Ages reduced this to castration (Bullough, 1976). The Byzantine legal code of the Emperor Justinian, in the sixth century, ordered that homosexuals be tortured, mutilated, paraded in public, and executed (Procopius, 1935). It depends on which chronicler or preacher one believes whether the Visigoths and Vandals were ruttish or ascetic, and we do not know how often or how harshly they enforced their laws, but clearly Christianity did not have to put a repressive heel on their necks to make them condemn homosexuality.

The formal rationale for the church's condemnation of homosexuality flowed from the writings of St. Augustine and Thomas Aquinas, but these were not new in spirit. Tertullian (1899–1900), in the second century, said succinctly, "So far as sex is concerned, the Christian is content with a woman." In 305 A.D., the Council of Elvira denied communion to homosexuals and prostitutes even when they were dying (Karlen, 1971a). Around the end of that century, St. Augustine (1957) set this traditional view in a theological framework.

Augustine equated reason, virtue, and impulse control; to these he opposed impulse, sex, and sin. It would be best, he said, if men and women lived without sex; if they could not, they should copulate only for procreation, never for pleasure. They must, of course, be married, and when motherhood was not the aim of sex, the wife became, in God's eyes, a mistress. Oral-genital intercourse, sodomy, masturbation, coitus when conception was impossible or unlikely (after menopause or during menstruation), could only be for pleasure, so they were sins. Obviously homosexuality was a sin as well.

In the thirteenth century, Thomas Aquinas (1969) expanded and further systematized these ideas, and the results became church doctrine. Acts that could not lead to conception were unnatural and sinful. In increasing unnaturalness, these were masturbation (which omits the partner), heterosexual oral and anal intercourse (joining the right sexes but the wrong apertures), homosexual acts (joining the wrong sexes), and bestiality (joining the wrong species).

This was theory; we know almost nothing about sex behavior during the so-called Dark Ages. We have some hints from penitential handbooks, which were used by priests from Ireland to the Near East as a guide in assigning penance for sins admitted in confession. Various ones (Karlen, 1971a) called for seven years penance for coitus *a tergo* (from behind), excommunication and lifelong fasting for sodomy with one's wife, and various other penance for men who saw their wives naked, had intercourse on Sunday, had nocturnal emissions, or loitered around churches after midnight. The penances for homosexuality and effeminacy were usually greater than those for fornication, adultery, sometimes even incest, and might be lifelong.

We have no idea whether these formulas in penitential handbooks reflected widely held values inside or outside the church or whether they were put into use. For instance, Bishop Burchard of Worms (Cleugh, 1964), in the early eleventh century, said clergymen should question women in confession to make sure they had not used "a certain engine or mechanical device in the form of the male sexual organ, the dimensions being calculated to give you pleasure, and binding it to your own or another women's pudenda, and have you thus committed fornication with other evilly disposed women or they, using the same or some other apparatus, with yourself" (p. 283). Burchard may have encountered such behavior in life or heard about it, but because of his language one cannot help wondering whether he was repeating a sin he had read about in synopses of classical works.

We can only be fairly sure that churchmen and the newly converted "barbarian" tribes shared pretty much the same formal values about homosexuality, inherited from common ancestors. Church law and civil law were not far apart. Just as the rise of Christianity did not create but only perpetuated hostility to homosexuality, so the waning of religious authority of the past several centuries apparently has not made homosexuality more common or more accepted. Furthermore, the punitive Christian attitude was only part of a broader restrictive view of all sexuality: homosexuality was punished along with—and according to a similar rationale as—premarital coitus, adultery, oral-genital intercourse, and other defined sex offenses. Those seeking to explain the nature of formal sanctions against homosexual behavior in the West must look not only at the church but beyond it, to the social fabric of which it is only one thread.

Evil Outsiders: The Infection Theory

Between about A.D. 1000 and 1500, as Europe began to reurbanize, there appeared a growing record of homosexuality. Late in the twelfth century, Marie de France (1944) said that any man who ignored a woman's advances ran the risk of being suspected of homosexuality. In 1230, Jacques de Vitry (Durant, 1944) complained that in Paris "prostitutes dragged passing clerics to brothels almost [sic] by force, and openly through the streets; if the clerics refused to enter, the whores called them sodomites. . . . That abominable vice sodomy so filled the city that it was held a sign of honor if a man kept one or more concubines." There were probably at least two or three homosexual popes, and allegedly a cardinal, with a fine blend of presumption and whimsy, successfully petitioned one of them (Sixtus IV) for an indulgence to commit sodomy during the warm months of the year (Lea, 1887–88). There are many records of people being burned at the stake for homosexuality and of rising complaints by moralists (Ellis, 1936).

One of the most common explanations was (and still is) the "infection" theory, which blames homosexuality, effeminacy, and other sexual deviance on foreign influence, especially from the evil East. Some Romans blamed the Greeks for increasing homosexuality, some Greeks blamed Persians and other Near Eastern peoples, and in the Middle Ages it was said that crusaders had trafficked with and been corrupted by Muslims instead of exterminating them (Karlen, 1971a). This reminds one of the English calling syphilis the French disease, the French calling it the Italian disease, and the Russians calling it the Polish disease. However, homosexuality is not contagious, and the burden of proof is on those who say that a people who historically abhorred it would adopt it from enemies or aliens, like children grabbing sweets.

A good example of the infection theory is the argument that homosexuality increased in England after the Norman invasion, like syrup stirred into a glass of water. After the Norman conquest in 1066, homosexuality did seem to some writers to become more common or more visible, first among Normans and then Anglo-Saxons. For instance, Ordericus Vitalis, a Norman-English chronicler, wrote in the mid-twelfth century that the Normans had become effeminate, and homosexuality was open and common throughout England (Ellis, 1936). William the Conqueror's son and successor, William Rufus, was probably homosexual, as was Edward II (Bullough, 1976). Havelock Ellis (1936) concluded that "among the Normans, everywhere, homosexuality was markedly prevalent; the spread of sodomy in France about the eleventh century is attributed to the Normans and their coming to England seems to have rendered it at times almost fashionable, at all events at court" (p. 40).

If only there had been a Kinsey in Normandy! Were Norman homosexuals 2 or 10 or 20 percent of the population? How did they so quickly turn to homosexuality? They were descendants of Vikings who had settled not long before in France, where they adapted to a Celtic culture. The Celts and Vikings were hardly notorious for effeminacy or homosexuality. And how did those transformed Normans so quickly seduce what was allegedly a staunchly straight Anglo-Saxon nation?

In truth, we have no idea of the extent or nature of homosexuality among any of these peoples. Rural Anglo-Saxon England may have had little or much of it, as may the Normans, Celts, and Vikings. We said earlier that both Roman and early Christian writers tended to portray the Germanic tribes, of which the Anglo-Saxons were one, as hardy proto-Boy Scouts; they may have been accurate or may have been using the Germans as a polemical foil. There is a similar problem in assessing the accusers of the Normans; many of them were outraged clerics.

Another problem is the medieval passion for paraphrasing revered authors of the past. For instance, in 1159, John of Salisbury (1938) spoke in his *Polycraticus* of men pandering for their wives and daughters, even pimping off their sons to homosexuals. John gave details about the homosexual's "elaborately frizzled and curled" hair, his hand "encased in a glove to protect it from the sun and keep it soft for the voluptuary's purpose. . . ." This apparently precise account is actually a pastiche of quotations and paraphrases of Juvenal, St. Jerome, and other ancient writers, even to details of hairdo. John's talk of the emperor's homosexual minions paraphrases accusations against the Byzantine ruler Justinian, dead for six centuries. We may never know whether John used classical sources to accurately describe his world, regurgitated classics by reflex, or indulged in slimly justified outrage.

The Normans, rooted in a northern European warrior culture, had recently become more urban and prosperous. The Anglo-Saxons saw them as sophisticated and hedonistic, and the Normans lived in courts and cities where prostitution and homosexuality, if not more common than in the countryside, were probably more conspicuous. In Rome two thousand years ago, in Norman England, and in Peoria today, people have claimed that foppish, cunning, oversexed Fancy Dans from cities to the east have been corrupting the pure locals. Both big-city and small-town folks have tended to believe this; it remains to be seen whether it has been true. The recent reporting of extensive homosexual cruising and organized homosexual prostitution in such provincial towns as Dayton and Xenia, Ohio (Karlen, 1971a), and Boise, Idaho (Gerassi, 1966), give one pause.

The impression in much of the late Middle Ages of increased homosexuality may have reflected reality or it may have resulted from urbanization, with its rather small increase in most sex behaviors and its visible deviant subcultures. Or perhaps there were sociosexual changes of which we have no record or with which we still do not make significant correlations. Perhaps, indeed, the Normans did experience a higher rate of homosexuality and this did influence the rest of Great Britain. But the usual analogy to infection, then and in other ages, should arouse skepticism. I suggest that infection theories have kept reappearing through Western history for three possible reasons. One is that to many people homosexuality seems socially alien and ego alien, so much so that it must be ascribed to people unlike oneself, and its appearance in one's own milieu ascribed to alien influence. Another is that deviance is often thought of as a social ill, and the metaphor of infection follows naturally. And, finally, there has often been a tendency to ascribe to people who are different in one major way still other differences. This we shall examine in more depth in the late-medieval equation of homosexuality with heresy and treason.

The Homosexual Heresy: Sexual Treason

Through much of Western history, if a person seemed to reject any of society's treasured norms or values—sexual, religious, or political—he was suspected of rejecting the others (Karlen, 1971b). The ancient Hebrews equated homosexuality with idolatry and treason; Roman law demanded the death penalty for treason, sacrilege, and sodomy; the church fathers associated sexual deviance with paganism. In the recent past, we saw a national obsession with the homosexual as a security risk, loyal to godless communism. A classic example of this linking of deviances was the ferocious prosecution of heretics in the Middle Ages on the grounds of homosexuality.

In the eleventh and twelfth centuries, religious splinter sects began to spring up in many parts of Europe, and many people were declared to be heretics and destroyed by fire and sword. One of the most important of these were the Cathars, or Albigensians (Rougemont, 1956). They preached nonviolence, the end of private property, and spiritual (chaste) marriage. As the movement grew, especially in southern France, it drew the angry attention of Inquisitors. Opponents claimed that in order to maintain chastity, the Cathars sodomized their wives; in this they were said to be like the heretical Bogomile sect of Bulgaria. The French word *bougre* came into use for sodomite, a corruption of the Latin *bulgaris*. It passed into English as "bugger." Today the commonest English word for anal intercourse, used synonymously with homosexuality, is an old word for heretic.

Pope Innocent II launched a crusade of a half million men, who slaughtered the Cathars throughout Provence. Other heretical sects were accused of sexual deviance and destroyed. The Adamites, Hussites, Brethren of the Free Spirit, and Waldensians were variously accused of sodomy, incest, bestiality and orgy (Brinton, 1959; Lea, 1887–88; Legman, 1966; Karlen, 1971a).

Many of the accusers probably believed what they were saying. However, Philip IV of France and Pope Clement V were apparently quite ruthless in defaming and destroying the Order of the Knights Templars as sodomites and heretics in the early fourteenth century in order to seize their treasury (Legman, 1966; Simon, 1959; Lea, 1887–88). Inquisitors got Templars to admit under torture (Martin, 1929) that they had been required to spit on the cross, enter a pact with the Muslims, and commit sodomy with any Templar who demanded it. This formula of charges—heresy, treason, and homosexuality—became routine in heresy and witchcraft trials.

The confessions of heretics and witches were often alike; they had been exacted under torture from prepared sets of questions. Their tales of spitting on the cross, being buggered by Satan, and orgying together sound like fantasies of acting out the forbidden, a vision of Christianity systematically reversed or violated. There apparently grew up in the late Middle Ages a picture of a radical antisocial conspiracy, with sexual and nonsexual elements, rather like that used to justify anti-Semitism.

The radical deviant of any kind is often seen as betraying his community by ignoring its self-defining principles and deep loyalties (Karlen, 1971a, 1971b); he is seen as part of a conspiracy to control or destroy society. He may be called a heretic, homosexual, security risk, traitor, or any combination of these. Witch-hunts and persecutions may follow, and there are ferocious punishments that at other times seem out of proportion to the offense. Crusades against sexual deviants also seem to start when fears arise that they are proselytizing or trying to influence youth. This has recently been an issue in many cities where there have been controversies about the right of homosexuals to work as teachers or to counsel teenagers.

Therefore, accusing a person of any major deviance has long been a good way to get him in trouble for other deviances. Procopius (1935), in his history of the Byzantine empire, told of a wave of accusations of homosexuality under the emperor Justinian, whose legal code required that homosexuals be tortured, mutilated, paraded in public, and executed. Procopius said that "not in all cases, however, was this punishment inflicted in the beginning, but only upon those reputed to be Greens [a political faction] or to be possessed of great wealth or those who in some way chanced to have offended the rulers" (p. 144). Gibbon (1957–62) commented more than a thousand years later that "pederasty became the crime of those to whom no crime could be imputed" (p. 94). In recent times, homosexuality has remained a common charge against people whose social, class, or political characteristics arouse antagonism (Karlen, 1971a).

The Renaissance: Creativity, Femininity, and Culture

The Renaissance, like ancient Greece, has been called a time of exploratory gusto in art, science, philosophy, public life, and sexuality. There are clichés that both cultures owe their brilliance in part to exuberant bisexuality, and that homosexuality and perhaps feminimity are related to creativity. Actually, the Renaissance was a loose adaptation of Greco-Roman culture by Europe's upper classes. The so-called Renaissance man, educated in Latin and Greek, tried in a serious or dilettantish way to emulate the art, philosophy, rhetoric, and statecraft of the classical world. In that past culture he saw praise for a way of life that did not sharply separate the cerebral and artistic, the aggressive and contemplative, the logical and emotional. Later, in the nineteenth century, scholars would look at the Renaissance and see similar virtues there. Actually, even in ancient Greece there was often an assumption that intellectual, artistic, and other sedentary pursuits were less masculine than aggressive, physical ones, but the separation was not always as sharp as in Renaissance Europe or some later periods (Brinton, 1959; Karlen, 1971a).

One important reason for the modern belief in homosexuality during the Renaissance is that era's neo-Platonic philosophy and art. A great deal of it, in imitation of Greek models, was addressed by men to other men. Shakespeare, for instance, referred to his dead friends as "my lovers gone," and Ben Jonson signed a letter to a male friend "your true lover" and dedicated his eulogy to Shakespeare "to the memory of my beloved." Historians and editors had to tell readers only a few generations later that such speech and poetry had been a literary convention, not necessarily an expression of homosexuality (Karlen, 1971a).

It is difficult or impossible today to know whether the motive for certain Renaissance poems and essays on friendship was emulation of the classics, male friendship, or homosexuality. One must decide in each case whether to take internal literary evidence or even autobiography at face value. When the Roman poet Catullus spoke mostly of heterosexual love and eroticism but bragged occasionally of a fling with a boy when angry at women, it seems safe to take his word. But when Sir Thomas Browne (1964) wrote, "I could be content that we might procreate like trees without . . . this trivial and vulgar way of union," one must remember that he had children and assume he was striking a literary pose. Shakespeare wrote the sonnet in which he called himself a leafless old tree when he was about thirty (Rowse, 1963). And Sir Francis Bacon, who wrote scathingly of homosexuality (1924), was notorious for keeping young Welsh boys in his house as bed partners (Ellis, 1936).

We should assume that a writer is homosexual only on the grounds of reliable witnesses or firsthand statements, supported by knowledge of the period and milieu. According to such standards of evidence, the number of homosexuals among the great creative figures of the Renaissance is strikingly small. For instance, consider Italy. Aretino and Cellini have been written of as "bisexual." It seems that Aretino was predominantly heterosexual but pursued boys on occasion, at least in later life (Karlen, 1971a). Cellini (1924) said in his autobiography that twice in his life detractors unjustly accused him of homosexuality; there is no further reliable mention of the subject. Michelangelo wrote some Platonic love poems to young men; we know of no lovers in his life, male or female (Bullough, 1976). Da Vinci spent two months in jail, accused of relations with a male model with a tarnished local reputation; the charges were dropped, and he was freed, but a second charge was made later in his life (Bullough, 1976). Aside from these facts, there is virtually no evidence on the matter. Freud (1964) concluded that da Vinci was probably sexually inactive most of his life. Of all the major painters of the Italian Renaissance, only one was surely an active homosexual, Giovanni Bazzi, popularly known as Sodoma (Vasari, 1906). Two great scholars, Strozzi and Politian, were perhaps suspected of being homosexual by Dante (1961–62).

A list of all the great artists and scholars of the Italian Renaissance would fill this page. Of them all, Sodoma was homosexual, Strozzi and Politian and da Vinci perhaps homosexual; Aretino probably had some homosexual episodes. Descriptions of Italian cities in the fifteenth and sixteenth centuries give the impression that homosexuality was visible and far from rare; Venice and Florence even had special courts empowered to discover and try homosexuals (Ellis, 1936; Bullough, 1976). If anything, there seem to have been fewer known homosexuals among the creative figures of the Renaissance than in the urban population at large.

Only two first-rank English artists of the time were surely homosexual, playwright Nicholas Udall and Sir Francis Bacon (Karlen, 1971a). Homosexuality or bisexuality has been imputed to both Shakespeare and Marlowe. The allegation about Marlowe arose after his death, as part of a politically motivated attempt at character assassination (Bakeless, 1942). The theory that Shakespeare was homosexual was first put forth in 1889 by Oscar Wilde (Hubler, 1962). The novelist Samuel Butler agreed; Butler also said, on the basis of stylistic analysis, that Homer was a woman. But the direct and inferential evidence that Shakespeare was heterosexual is overwhelming. The only alleged evidence to the contrary is the series of sonnets he wrote to a man or youth with the initials W. H., in conventional neo-Platonic style (Hubler, 1962; Pearson, 1949).

"Latent homosexuality" and a "homosexual temperament" have also been ascribed to Erasmus, Montaigne, and others on equally slim grounds (Karlen, 1971a). The idea of a great wave of bisexual creative figures in the Renaissance became popular through hopeful homosexual-hunting late in the nineteenth century. Homosexual apologists and others trying to destigmatize homosexuality combed literature and history, seizing on even the smallest possible inference of deviance.

For instance, Havelock Ellis (1936) helped disseminate the idea of homosexuals' artistic and moral equality, even superiority. He claimed, in effect, that any affection for a person of the same sex showed at least a "bisexual temperament." Although he himself had discovered the document indicating that the allegations of homosexuality against Marlowe were false, he concluded through internal literary analysis that Marlowe had had a "bisexual temperament." He said that Shakespeare "narrowly escapes inclusion in the list of distinguished inverts" (p. 44) —an odd way to dissociate him from homosexuality. In a similar vein, he listed allegedly homosexual kings in history and commented that "kings, indeed, seemed particularly inclined to homosexuality" (p. 35). He suggested that musical and dramatic talents might spring from the same "abnormal" streak in the constitution as did homosexuality. He added that "distinguished women in all ages and in all fields . . . have frequently displayed some masculine traits" (p. 196).

This sort of pseudohistory was taken up by minds far less distinguished than Ellis's. It could not be widely accepted were it not for two traditional Western assumptions. One, stretching back at least to the Greco-Roman world, is that men who perform sedentary pursuits are less masculine. The other is that creative people possess special sensitivity, which is thought of as feminine. Typically, the eminent Shakespeare scholar J. Wilson Knight (1959) wrote that "our greatest writers all have this share of supersexual understanding." It is arguable that sensitivity is synonymous with creativity or that either is a feminine characteristic; most of the world's great creative work has been done by men. Oddly, creative women are often characterized as masculine by the same people who call creativity feminine. The idea that creativity contains any homosexual element is probably, in e.e. cummings' words (1954), an idea definitely not to be resharpened (p. 168).

Puritans and Anti-Puritans: Permission and Repression

Some people, looking through history, claim that sexual deviance flourishes when societies are sexually restrictive. Others say the opposite, that deviation increases when sexual controls loosen. Proponents of both views have claimed that the Puritans and anti-Puritans of the seventeenth and eighteenth centuries prove their arguments.

From the late sixteenth to early nineteenth centuries, the record of sexual deviation kept rising in England and France—for instance, in the writings of Brantôme, d'Aubigné, Restif de la Bretonne, Rousseau, Rochester, Otway, Smollett, and Fielding (Karlen, 1971a). In the upper class, this was the time of the rake, *galant,* and libertine, of sex as trophy hunting. Lesbianism, transvestism, and sadomasochism were apparently common knowledge to readers and playgoers. In Smollett's *Roderick Random* (1927), Earl Strutwell declared that homosexuality was growing so quickly in England that it would probably in a short time become "a more fashionable vice than simple fornication." It is difficult now to know whether many such statements were fact, gossip, or easy jokes, but the accumulated weight of references is convincing. Certain deviations were becoming institutionalized—served by specialized brothels and, in an age of growing literacy, by specialized pornography (Karlen, 1971a; Lewinsohn, 1964). In England, from the Restoration on, upper-class adult delinquents formed clubs notorious for assault, rape, drinking, and whoring. One, the Mollies, consisted of homosexuals; there were inns that catered to effeminate and homosexual prostitutes, called Molly houses (Ward, 1927). Eighteenth century London had an extensive homosexual world complete with brothels, pickup points, and cruising grounds (Ellis, 1936).

There were social critics who carried on like Arnold Toynbee at an orgy, proclaiming the death of morality, heterosexuality, the family, civilization itself. And society at large still did not take homosexuality lightly. There were police drives against it (Ellis, 1936); even attempted homosexual acts might be punished by years in prison and time in the pillory, where missiles thrown by mobs might injure or kill (Taylor, 1958). During a homosexual prostitution scandal in Paris in 1702, prominent men were arrested; some were burned and others cut their throats (Karlen, 1971a).

Just as harsh laws apparently did not prevent homosexuality, lenient laws did not foster it. At the turn of the nineteenth century, Napoleon's civil code decriminalized consenting adult homosexual acts, secularized marriage, and permitted divorce. Many people predicted gay orgies in the streets and the death of the family. They were, of course, disappointed. Homosexuality did not become noticeably more common or more open. Divorces occurred, but not a vast number. Despite the code, police continued to harass homosexuals (Ellis, 1936; Karlen, 1971a); where formal sanctions left off, informal ones took over. Customs, attitudes, and individual behavior are strongly shaped in early life; traditional values are internalized and felt to be one's own. The idea that social permissiveness opens the door to untrammeled sex behavior of all kinds underestimates cultural continuity, childhood socialization, and perhaps biosocial forces promoting heterosexuality, childbearing, and the family.

The contrary idea, that restrictiveness creates deviance because blocked sexuality takes twisted substitutive forms, is also short of proof. For instance, the Puritans are commonly portrayed today as authoritarian hypocrites who tried to deny their own sexuality and to crush that of others, and this is said to have caused widespread psychosexual problems. A look at the origin and nature of puritanism raises doubts.

Puritanism's roots lay in the Reformation's angry reaction to the Catholic church's negative position on sex and marriage. Luther, Calvin, and others claimed that the church's call for celibacy was a snare of the devil. Sexual desire, they said, is so strong and deep that resisting it only invites the sins of fornication, adultery, and homosexuality (Cole, 1966). They put a new emphasis on earthly love and on sex within marriage. It is true that they tried to set up theocracies with elaborate sexual controls, but they were no harsher in theory or practice than Roman Catholic clerics and laymen of their own and preceding centuries. Pillories, ducking stools, and branding were common punishments for sexual offenses in the Catholic Middle Ages, and the Puritan record for burning witches and sexual offenders pales beside that of the Inquisition (Taylor, 1954; Karlen, 1971a). The controls were not always effective anyway. Calvin's Genevan system lasted only a century, and its rules were widely violated (Brinton, 1959); the city had many forced marriages and bastards, and Calvin's own daughter and sister-in-law were caught at adultery. In New World Puritan colonies, premarital coitus and adultery were common (Morgan, 1966); and there, as in Old World Puritan communities, sexual passion within marriage was highly valued (Miller, 1953).

Despite the extreme moralizing of every aspect of life by many Puritans, and the occurrence of some sexually tinged witchcraft crazes, there is no evidence that they had a higher rate of psychosexual dysfunction than other religious groups. Cases of homosexuality came before the law in some Puritan colonies, but this occurred in non-Puritan ones as well, such as New York, and brought such extreme penalties as burning at the stake (Karlen, 1971a; Brinton, 1959). Finally, no relationship has been clearly established between sexual restrictiveness and neurosis, psychosis, or sexual deviance in any broad historical or cross-cultural comparison (Karlen, 1971a). It has been suggested that quite permissive societies contain a lower incidence of paraphilias and dysfunctions (Gadpaille, in press), but this remains only informed speculation because of the paucity of data.

Victorians: Attitudes and Behavior

Victorianism was in force long before Queen Victoria took the throne in 1847, and it was on its way out in the upper and upper-middle classes well before she died in 1901 (Taylor, 1954). It extended beyond England, to the United States and Europe. There was nothing basically new in it—viewing marital coitus as the only legitimate sex activity, restraining all sexuality and impulsiveness, and setting the basis for this by limiting childhood sexuality (Karlen, 1971a). Its distinguishing details were putting as much emphasis on society's eye as God's (that is, secularizing Puritan values) and making sexuality an almost exclusively male attribute (Marcus, 1964). According to one popular view, it did not really affect the incidence of homosexuality and other paraphilias.

Brinton (1959) and Lewinsohn (1964) , for instance, say that although attitudes became more restrictive, sex behavior probably changed very little—in Brinton's words, "the usual difference of a few percentage points." In other words, change in sexual attitudes does not change sexual behavior. This implies that the liberalizing of sexual attitudes in the post-Victorian period has had equally little effect. Opposed to this view are the beliefs that blocking heterosexual expression causes an increase in other, "substitute" forms of sexuality; that greater permissiveness reduces sexual deviation. All of these views have been defended by using Victorianism as a case in point.

In fact, it is easy to defend almost any view by pointing to the Victorians, because we simply do not know what they did in bed. If the most common post-Victorian opinion is true, Victorian sexuality was tense, hurried, shameful, and as infrequent as possible. Data from the older subjects in the research of Kinsey et al. (1948, 1953) suggests that certain sex behaviors (oral sexuality, premarital coitus) were less common in the late nineteenth century than today. But those data also suggest that homosexual behavior was no more common, and that some heterosexual behaviors (e.g., marital coitus) were more frequent. And for every notorious case of Victorian inhibition, one can cite a convention-defying love affair or a secret or notorious sexual deviant (Marcus, 1964). Davenport (convincingly argues that sex behavior is rooted relatively weakly to biological forces (e.g., oral sex) change most under social influences; those with strong biological roots (e.g., male orgasmic drive) change least. The findings of Kinsey et al. show that sometimes very many percentage points can be involved. But one must recall that some basic and powerful cultural forces may have changed little for millenia.

A wide variety of sources suggest that homosexuality and other deviations were abundant in the Victorian era (Marcus, 1964; Taylor, 1958; Ellis, 1936; Karlen, 1971a). New York, London, Paris, and Berlin had great numbers of homosexual scandals, clubs, cruising grounds, and prostitutes. An erotic periodical of 1822 listed twenty-five sexual deviations, most known to modern psychiatry (Taylor, 1958). If one uses erotic advertisements, pornography, and mentions of brothels and scandals as guides, sadomasochism, both homosexual and heterosexual, seems to have been more common and more open than it is today, as does fetishism. I have speculated (Karlen, 1971a) that sadism and angry ambisexuality seem particularly visible in the late seventeenth and early eighteenth centuries, as do masochism and homosexuality in the eighteenth and nineteenth centuries, perhaps because of changing patterns of family life and child-rearing. Still, we do not know that homosexuality or any other sex behavior was more or less common in the Victorian world than in the twelfth or twentieth century. We can only make some tentative inferences from our own century's sex research.

Certain figures produced by Kinsey et al. have been criticized as too high or too low, especially those about homosexuality. Still, they are the best figures we have for statistically significant populations, and many subsequent studies more or less agree with them. They reveal that from before 1900 until almost 1950, a great attitudinal leap toward heterosexual permissiveness was followed by a moderate step in behavior, especially during the sexual revolution of the twenties. Yet through the entire period, there was virtually no change in the incidence of homosexual behavior, from experimental and situational to lifelong and exclusive. Numerous small studies since 1950 suggest another great wave of permissiveness in attitudes and, again, a more modest increase in certain heterosexual behaviors and a lower age of initial sexual activity; and again, despite rhetoric about increasing homosexuality and bisexuality, there is no comparable increase—perhaps no significant increase at all—in homosexual behavior (Karlen, 1978). In an era in which many people have an emotional stake in the idea of sociosexual change, this continuity in homosexual and in some heterosexual behaviors has been systematically ignored or denied. Since some people have always claimed that sexual "excess" and deviance are increasing, the idea calls for reflex skepticism, and the most reliable data bear out such doubt.

So far, no pattern of sexual attitudes or behavior has been proven to invariably correlate with an increase or decrease in homosexuality. No single factor or even group of factors can yet explain the very different incidences of style of homosexual behavior in a broad range of cultural milieu.

Conclusion

It is not our task here to describe homosexuality today (for an overview, see Karlen, 1978). We have picked a few historical periods and questions of special interest. Doing so has shown that each generation repaints according to its own preoccupations, in order to assess the present and think toward future. Especially in such emotion-laden matters as sexuality, the tools of history are therefore sometimes curved mirrors instead of searchlights. During much of the nineteenth century, history was often used to reinforce traditional ideas about chastity, monogamy, and sexual conformism. More recently, it has been used to destigmatize behavior once considered sickness or sin. At the worst extremes, writers have tried to make the past prove various sexual patterns either cancers in the social body or ornaments upon it.

It is not only inevitable but useful to keep reexamining the past and seeking more from it. But such efforts must always stay rooted in fact and probability. This is difficult if one feels that the integrity of society is threatened. It is equally difficult when concern for public opinion and civil rights tempt one to smudge the line between the world as it is and the world as one would like to see it.

Sexual history is rather new. It still draws on modern interdisciplinary sexology too rarely, and sometimes it has little patience for honestly leaving questions unresolved. But it is inevitably part of the study of sex, and as more scholars give it better effort, it will cast more light for the benefit of other disciplines seeking to understand sexuality.

REFERENCES

Aquinas 1969. *Summa theologicae*, 2 vols. ed. Thomas Gilby. Garden City, N.Y.: Image Books.
Augustine. 1957. *The city of God.* Trans. George E. McCracken. Cambridge, Mass.: Harvard University Press.
Bachofen, J. 1967. *Myth, religion, and mother right*. Trans. Ralph Manheim. Princeton: Princeton University Press.
Bacon, F. 1924. *New Atlantis.* Ed. Alfred B. Gough. Oxford: Clarendon Press.
Bakeless, J. 1942. *The tragicall history of Christopher Marlowe.* Cambridge, Mass.: Harvard University Press.
Brinton, C. 1959. *A history of western morals.* New York: Harcourt, Brace & World.
Browne, Sir T. 1964. *Works.* ed. Geoffrey Keynes. Chicago: University of Chicago Press.
Bullough, V. 1972. Sex in history: A virgin field. *Journal of Sex Research* 8: 101–16.
———. 1976. *Sexual variance in society and history.* New York: John Wiley.
Carcopino, J. 1940. *Daily life in Ancient Rome.* New Haven: Yale University Press.

Catullus. 1956. *The poems of Catullus.* Trans. H. Gregory. New York: Grove Press.

Cellini, B. 1924. *The life of Benvenuto Cellini.* Trans. J. A. Symonds. London: Macmillan.

Churchill, W. 1967. *Homosexual behavior among males.* New York: Hawthorne Books.

Cleugh, J. 1964. *Love locked out.* New York: Crown Publishers.

Cole, W. G. 1960. *Sex and love in the bible.* New York: Association Press.

———. 1966. *Sex in Christianity and Psychoanalysis.* New York. Oxford University Press.

cummings, e.e. 1954. *Poems 1923–1954.* New York: Harcourt, Brace.

Dante. 1961–62. *The divine comedy.* Trans. John Ciardi. New York: New American Library.

Davenport, W. H. 1977. Sex in cross-cultural perspective. In F. A. Beach, ed., *Human sexuality in four perspectives* (Baltimore: Johns Hopkins University Press).

Devereux, G. 1963. Institutionalized homosexuality of the Mohave Indians. In H. Ruitenbeck, ed., *The problem of homosexuality in modern society* (New York: E. P. Dutton).

Diamond, M., and Karlen, A. 1980. *Sexual decisions.* Boston: Little, Brown.

Durant, W., and A. 1944. *Caesar and Christ.* New York: Simon & Shuster.

Ellis, H. 1936. *Studies in the psychology of sex,* Vol. 2, Pt. 2. New York: Random House.

Finley, M. 1954. *The world of Odysseus.* New York: Viking Press.

Flacelière, R. 1962. *Love in ancient Greece.* Trans. James Cleugh. New York: Crown Publishers.

Ford, C. S., and Beach, F. A., 1951. *Patterns of sexual behavior.* New York: Ace Books.

Freud, S. 1964. *Leonardo da Vinci and a memory of his childhood.* New York: W. W. Norton.

Friedll, E. 1975. *Women and men: An anthropologist's view.* New York: Holt, Rinehart, and Winston. ·

Gadpaille, W. Psychosexual developmental tasks imposed by pathologically delayed childhood: a cultural dilemma. In press.

Gebhard, P. 1971. Human sexual behavior. In D.S. Marshall and R. Suggs, eds. *Human Sexual Behavior* (New York: Basic Books).

Gerassi, J. 1966. *The Boys of Boise.* New York: Macmillan.

Gibbon, E. 1957–62. *The decline and fall of the Roman empire.* 6 vols. New York: E. P. Dutton.

Goode, W. 1964. *The family.* Englewood Cliffs, N.J.: Prentice–Hall.

Greek anthology, poems from the. 1912–1926. Trans W. R. Paton. 5 vols. Cambridge, Mass.: Harvard University Press.

Herodotus. 1942. In R.B. Francis, ed., *The Greek historians,* vol. 1, trans. G. Rawlinson (New York: Random House).

Hesiod. 1959. *The works and days: Theogony; The shield of Herakles.* Trans. R. Lattimore. Ann Arbor: University of Michigan Press.

Homer. 1966. *The Iliad.* Trans. E. V. Rieu. Baltimore: Penguin Books.

———. 1946. *The Odyssey.* Trans. E. V. Rieu. Baltimore: Penguin Books.

Hubler, E. 1962. *The riddle of Shakespeare's sonnets,* 1st ed. New York: Basic Books.

Hunt, M. 1959. *The natural history of love.* New York: Alfred A. Knopf.

John of Salisbury. 1938. *Frivolities of courtiers and footprints of philosophers.* Trans. G. B. Pike. Minneapolis: University of Minneapolis Press.

Juvenal. 1958. *The Satires.* Trans. R. Humphries. Bloomington: Indiana University Press.

Karlen, A. 1971a. *Sexuality and homosexuality: A new view.* New York: W. W. Norton.

———. 1971b. The homosexual heresy. *The Chaucer Review* 6:44–63.

———. 1978. Homosexuality: The scene and its students. In J. Henslin, and E. Sagarin, eds., *The Sociology of Sex* (New York: Schocken Books).

———. 1980. The soiled pinafore: A sexual theme in psychiatric history. In T. B. Karasu, and Socarides, C. W., eds., *Contemporary sexuality: Contributions from psychoanalysis* (New York: International Universities Press).

Kinsey, A. C.; Pomeroy, W.; and Martin, C. 1948. *Sexual behavior in the human male.* Philadelphia: W.B. Saunders.

Kinsey, A., et al. 1953. *Sexual behavior in the human female.* Philadelphia: W.B. Saunders.

Knight, G. W. 1959. *The wheel of fire*, 4th rev. ed. London: Methuen.

Lea, H. C. 1887–88 *History of the inquisition in the middle ages.* 3 vols. New York: Harper & Bros.

Legman, G. 1966. *The Guilt of the templars.* New York: Basic Books.

Lewinsohn, R. 1964. *A history of sexual customs.* Trans. A. Layce. New York: Fawcett World Library.

Licht, H. 1963. *Sexual life in ancient Greece.* L. H. Dawson, ed. Trans. J. H. Freese. New York: Barnes & Noble.

Lucian. *Collected Works.* 8 vols. Trans. by A. M. Harmon and M. D. MacLoed. Vols. 1–2, New York: Macmillan, 1913–15. Vols. 3–4, New York: G.P. Putnam's, 1921–25. Vols. 5–7, Cambridge, Mass.: Harvard University Press, 1936–61. Vol. 8, New York: Macmillan, 1967.

MacNamara, D. E. J., and Sagarin, E. 1977. *Sex, crime, and the law.* New York: Free Press.

Marcus, S. 1964. *The other Victorians.* New York: Basic Books.

Marie de France. 1944. *Lais.* A. Ewart, ed. Oxford: Blackwell.

Marshall, D. S., and Suggs, R. C., eds. 1971. *Human sexual behavior.* New York: Basic Books.

Martial. 1961. *Epigrams.* Trans. Walter C.A. Ker. 2 vols. Cambridge, Mass.: Harvard University Press.

Martin, E. J. *The trial of the templars.* London: George Allen & Unwin, 1929.

Miller, P. 1953. *The New England mind: from colony to province.* Cambridge, Mass.: Harvard University Press.

Morgan, E. S. 1966. *The Puritan family.* New York: Harper & Row.

Murdock, G. P. 1949. *Social structure.* New York: Macmillan.

Patai, R. 1959. *Sex and family in the bible and the middle east.* Garden City, N.Y.: Doubleday.

Pearson, H. 1949. *A life of Shakespeare.* London: Carroll & Nicholson.

Plato. 1948. *The Portable Plato.* S. Buchanan, ed. New York: Viking Press.

Procopius. 1935. *Works.* vol. 6. Cambridge, Mass.: Harvard University Press.

Ranke, L. v. 1909. *History of the latin and teutonic nations, 1494–1514.* Rev. trans. by G. R. Dennis. London: George Bell.

Rougemont, Denis de. 1956. *Love in the western world.* Rev. ed. trans. by M. Belgion. New York: Fawcett Books.

Rowse, A. K. 1963. *William Shakespeare: A biography.* New York: Harper & Row.

Seltman, C. 1962. *Women in antiquity.* New York: Collier Books.

Simon, E. 1959. *The piebald standard: A biography of the knights templars.* London: Cassell.

Smollett, T. 1927. *Roderick Random.* New York: E. P. Dutton.

Stoller, R. J. 1975. *Perversion.* New York: Dell Publishing.

Suetonius. 1957. *The twelve caesars.* Trans. R. Graves. Baltimore: Penguin Books.

Symonds, J. A. 1931. *Studies in sexual inversion.* Privately printed.

Taylor, G. R. 1954. *Sex in history.* New York: Vanguard Press.

———. 1958. *The angel makers.* London: Heinemann.

Tertullian. 1899–1900. *To His Wife.* In A. Roberts, and J. Donaldson, eds., *The Ante Nicene Fathers,* vol. 4 (New York: Scribner's).

Toynbee, A. 1964. Why I dislike Western civilization. *New York Times Magazine,* 18 May.

Vangaard, T. 1972. *Phállos: A symbol and its history in the male world.* Trans. by the author. New York: International Universities Press.

Vasari, G. 1906. *Stories of the Italian artists from Vasari.* Trans. E. L. Seeley. London: Chatto & Windus; New York: E. P. Dutton.

Ward, N. (Edward). 1927. *The London spy.* A. Hayward, ed. New York: George H. Doran Co.

Westermarck, E. 1917. *Origin and development of the moral ideas.* 2nd ed., 2 vols. London: Macmillan.

———. 1939. *Christianity and morals.* London: Paul, Trench, Trubner.

Zimmerman, C. C. 1947. *Family and civilization.* New York: Harper & Bros.

5 / Homosexual Behavior in Cross-Cultural Perspective

Introduction

The available cross-cultural data clearly show that the ways in which individuals organize their sexual behavior varies considerably between societies (Westermarck, 1908; Ford and Beach, 1951; and Broude and Greene, 1976). Although biological and psychological factors help explain variations of sexual behavior between individuals within a given society, intercultural variations in patterns of human sexual behavior are mainly related to social and cultural differences occurring between societies around the world. The purpose of this chapter is to consider what kinds of variations in homosexual behavior occur between societies, and to determine which sociocultural factors appear to account for the variance of the behavior cross-culturally.[1]

---

1. Homosexual behavior or activity will be used here to describe sexual behavior between individuals of the same sex; and it may have nothing to do with sexual object choice or sexual orientation of the individuals involved. Additionally, the terms "sex role" and "gender role" will be used to describe different behavioral phenomena. As Hooker (1965) points out, they "are often used interchangeably, and with resulting confusion." Following her suggestion, the term "sex role," when homosexual practices are described, will refer to typical sexual performance only. "The gender connotations (M-F) of these performances need not then be implicitly assumed." The term gender role will refer to the expected attitudes and behavior that distinguish males from females.

The author is particularly indebted to Evelyn Hooker for her invaluable comments and criticisms; and to the Gender Identity Research Group at UCLA for an early critique of the ideas presented in this paper.

The Cross-Cultural Data

Data available on homosexual behavior in most of the world's societies, past or present, are meager. Much is known about the dominant middle-class white populations of the United States, England, and northern European countries where most scientific research on human sexual behavior has been done, but very little is known about homosexual behavior in the rest of the world. The lack of knowledge stems from the irrational fear and prejudice surrounding the study of human sexual behavior, and from the difficulties associated with the collection of information on a topic that is so personal and highly regulated in most societies.

Most of the cross-cultural information on sexual behavior has been gathered by Western anthropologists. The quality of the information collected and published, however, varies considerably. Based on a survey of the literature, Marshall and Suggs (1971) report that: "Sexual behavior is occasionally touched upon in anthropological publications but is seldom the topic of either articles or monographs by anthropologists." Broude and Greene (1976), after coding the sexual attitudes and practices in 186 societies using the Human Relations Area Files, note:[2]

> information of any sort on sexual habits and beliefs is hard to come by. . . . when data do exist concerning sexual attitudes and practices, they are often sketchy and vague; what is more, such information is usually suspect in terms of its reliability, either because of distortions on the part of the subjects or because of biases introduced by the ethnographer.

Cross-cultural data on homosexual behavior is further complicated by the prejudice of many observers who consider the behavior unnatural, dysfunctional, or associated with mental illness, and by the fact that in many of the societies studied the behavior is stigmatized and thus not usually carried out openly. Under these circumstances, the behavior is not easily talked about. At the turn of the twentieth century such adjectives as disgusting, vile, and detestable were still being used to describe homosexual behavior; and even in the mid-1930s some anthropologists continued to view the behavior as unnatural. In discussing sodomy with some of his New Guinea informants, Williams (1936), for example, asked them if they "had ever been subjected to an unnatural

2. The Human Relations Area Files (HRAF) contain information on the habits, practices, customs, and behavior of populations in hundreds of societies around the world. These files utilize accounts given not only by anthropologists but also by travelers, writers, missionaries, and explorers. Most cross-cultural surveys of sexual behavior, like those of Ford and Beach and Broude and Greene, have been based on HRAF information. A major criticism of the HRAF information on sexual behavior relates to the difficulty of assessing the reliability of the data collected in different time periods by different people with varying amounts of scientific training as observers.

practice." With the acceptance of the view in the mid-1930s that homosexual behavior should be classified as a mental illness (or at best dysfunctional), many anthropologists replaced "unnatural" with the medical model. This model still finds adherents among researchers at present, especially those in the branch of anthropology referred to as psychological anthropology.

Because of the prejudice with which many researchers and observers approached the subject, statements about the reported absence of homosexual behavior, or the limited extent of the behavior where reported, should be viewed with some skepticism. Mead (1961) suggests that statements of this kind "can only be accepted with the greatest caution and with very careful analysis of the personality and training of the investigator." She further notes that: "Denials of a practice cannot be regarded as meaningful if that practice is verbally recognized among a given people, even though a strong taboo exists against it."

This chapter will mainly utilize the published research findings of empirical studies which have considered homosexual behavior in some detail. It will examine homosexual behavior in preliterate, peasant, and complex modern societies in all the major geographical regions of the world.[3] Where necessary, these findings will be supplemented with information found in accounts given by travelers, missionaries, and novelists.

Sociocultural Factors

A number of sociocultural factors help explain variations of homosexual behavior between societies. Two of the most important are: cultural attitudes and proscriptions related to cross-gender behavior, and availability of sexual partners.[4] The latter is in turn related to such variables as segregation of sexes prior to marriage, expectations with respect to virginity, age at marriage, and available economic resources and/or distribution of income.

3. "Preliterate" refers to essentially tribal societies that do not have a written language; "peasant" refers to essentially agrarian literate societies; and "complex modern" refers to highly industrialized societies.

4. In one of the first scholarly surveys of homosexual behavior done by an anthropologist, Westermarck (1908) concluded that: "A very important cause of homosexual practices is absence of the other sex."

CROSS-GENDER AND HOMOSEXUAL BEHAVIOR

Different expectations for male persons as opposed to female persons are culturally elaborated from birth onward in every known society. Although behavioral boundaries between the sexes may vary culturally, male persons are clearly differentiated from female persons; and progeny is assured by normative societal rules which correlate male and female gender roles with sexual behavior, marriage, and the family. There is a general expectation in every society that a majority of adult men and women will cohabit and produce the next generation. Social pressure is thus applied in the direction of marriage. The general rule is that one should not remain single.

The cross-cultural data on human sexual behavior suggest that a significant relationship exists between much of the homosexual behavior reported cross culturally and the continuing need of societies to deal with cross-gender behavior. Feminine male behavior, and the set of anxieties associated with its occurrence in the male part of the population, appears to have brought about more elaborate cultural responses temporally and spatially than has masculine female behavior. There are no doubt many reasons why this is so, but it appears to be related in general to the higher status accorded men than women in most societies; and, in particular, to the defense role that men have historically played in protecting women and children from outsiders.

Societies in which homosexual behavior can be linked to cultural responses to cross-gender behavior may be categorized according to the type of response made. Three major cultural types have been identified: those societies which make a basic accommodation to cross-gender behavior, those societies which outlaw the behavior as scandalous and/or criminal, and those societies which neither make an accommodation to such behavior nor outlaw it but instead have a cultural formulation which tries to ensure that cross-gender behavior does not occur.

ACCOMMODATING SOCIETIES

Societies making an accommodation to cross-gender behavior in one form or another have been reported in many different parts of the world. Munroe et al. (1969), for example, put together a list of societies having what they call "institutionalized male transvestism . . . the permanent adoption by males of aspects of female dress and/or behavior, in accordance with customary expectations within a given society." Their list includes Indian societies in North and South America, island societies in Polynesia and Southeast Asia, and preliterate and peasant societies in mainland Asia and Africa. Although reported for both sexes, male cross-gender behavior appears in the literature more often than female.

A folk belief exists in some of these societies that in every generation a certain number of individuals will play the gender role of the opposite sex, usually beginning at or prior to puberty and often identified at a very early age. The Mohave Indians of the American Southwest, for example, used to hold the following belief—typical of many Indian societies in North America—about cross-gender behavior of both sexes:

> Ever since the world began at the magic mountain . . . it was said that there would be transvestites. In the beginning, if they were to become transvestites, the process started during their intrauterine life. When they grew up they were given toys according to their sex. They did not like these toys however. (Devereux, 1937)

In southern Mexico one group of Zapotec Indians believes that "effeminate males" are born not made: "Typical comments include: But what can we do; he was born that way; he is like God made him. A related belief also exists that . . . it is a thing of the blood" (Royce, 1973). In Tahiti, the belief exists that there is at least one cross-gender behaving male, called a *māhū*, in all villages: "When one dies then another substitutes . . . God arranges it like this. It isn't allowed (that there should be) two *māhū* in one place" (Levy, 1973).

Cross-gender behavior is accepted in other societies because it is believed that some supernatural event makes people that way prior to birth, or that the behavior is acquired through some mystical force or dream after birth. In India, for example, the following belief exists about the *Hijadā,* cross-gender behaving males thought to be impotent at birth who later have their genitals removed:

> When we ask a Hijadā or an ordinary man in Gujarat "Why does a man become a Hijadā?" the usual reply is "One does not become a Hijadā by one's own will; it is only by the command of the mātā that one becomes a Hijadā." The same idea is found in a myth about the origin of the Hijadās. It is said that one receives the mātā's command either in dreams or when one sits in meditation before her image. (Shah, 1961)

Among the Chukchee of northeastern Asia, a role reversal was accepted because of an unusual dream or vision:

> Transformation takes place by the command of the *ka'let* (spirits) usually at the critical age of early youth when shamanistic inspiration first manifests itself. (Bogores, 1904)

Among the Lango in Africa:

> A number of Lango men dress as women, simulate menstruation, and become one of the wives of other males. They are believed to be impotent and to have been afflicted by some supernatural agency. (Ford and Beach, 1951)

Although not necessarily accepted gladly, the various folk beliefs make the behavior acceptable, and a certain number of cross-gender behaving individuals are to be expected in every generation. Expectations about the extent to which the opposite gender role is to be played, however, appear to have changed over time with acculturation. Affected individuals in the past often were required to make a public ritualized change of gender and cross-dress and behave in accordance with their new identity. Among the Mohave, for example, there was an initiation ceremony and it was important for the initiate "to duplicate the behavior pattern of his adopted sex and make 'normal' individuals of his anatomic sex feel toward him as though he truly belonged to his adopted sex" (Devereux, 1937). The *māhū* in Tahiti were described in the latter part of the eighteenth century as follows:

> These men are in some respects like the Eunichs [*sic*] in India but are not castrated. They never cohabit with women but live as they do. They pick their beard out and dress as women, dance and sing with them and are as effeminate in their voice. (Morrison, 1935)

Affected individuals in most societies at present are allowed a choice as to the extent they want to play the role; e.g., how far they want to identify with the opposite sex, whether they want to cross-dress or not, etc. Levy (1973) notes, for example, that in Tahiti: "Being a *māhū* does not now usually entail actually dressing as a woman." The North American Indian societies who used to have initiation ceremonies discontinued them long ago; and, although expectations about cross-gender behaving individuals persist, only remnants of the original belief system are remembered currently. They continue, however, to be tolerant and "there apparently is no body of role behavior aimed at humiliating boys who are feminine or men who prefer men sexually" (Stoller, 1976).

The link between cross-gender behavior and homosexual behavior is the belief that there should be concordance between gender role and sexual object choice. When a male behaves like a female, he should be expected therefore to want a male sexual partner and to play the female sex role—that is, to play the insertee role in anal intercourse or fellatio. The same concordance should be expected when a female behaves like a male. As a result of beliefs about concordance, it is important to note that a society may not conceptualize the sexual behavior or its participants as "homosexual."

There is some evidence in support of this linking of gender role and homosexual behavior in societies making an accommodation and providing a social role for cross-gender behaving individuals. Kroeber (1940), for example, concluded from his investigations that: "In most of primitive northern Asia and North America, men of homosexual trends adopted women's dress, work, and status, and were accepted as non-physiological but institutionalized women." Devereux's Mohave informants said that the males who changed their gender role to female had male husbands and that both anal intercourse and fellatio were practiced, with the participants playing the appropriate gender sex role.

The informants noted the same concordance for females who behaved like males.

Unfortunately, the anthropological data do not always make clear whether cultural expectations in a given society were for concordance between gender role and erotic object; or, in terms of actual behavior, how many cross-gender behaving individuals chose same sex, opposite sex, or both sexes as erotic objects. In the paper I just quoted, Kroeber also concluded: "How far invert erotic practices accompanied the status is not always clear from the data, and it probably varied. At any rate, the North American attitude toward the berdache stresses not his erotic life but his social status; born a male, he became accepted as a woman socially."

Many anthropologists and other observers confounded their findings by assuming an equivalence between "transvestite" and "homosexual".[5] Thus, when an informant described cross-gender behavior, they may have concluded without foundation that a same-sex erotic object choice was part of the behavior being described, and that they were eliciting information on "homosexuals." Angelino and Shedd (1955) provide supporting evidence. They reviewed the literature on an often used anthropological concept, berdache, and concluded that the "term has been used in an exceedingly ambiguous way, being used as a synonym for homosexualism, hermaphroditism, transvestism, and effeminism." They also note that the meaning of berdache changed over time; going from kept boy/male prostitute, to individuals who played a passive role in sodomy, to males who played a passive sex role and cross-dressed.

In spite of the confusion between "transvestite" and "homosexual," the available data suggest that in many of the societies providing a social role for cross-gender behavior, the selection of sexual partners was based on the adopted gender role; and, though they might be subjected to ridicule, neither partner in the sexual relationship was penalized for the role played.

The *māhū* role in Tahiti provides a contemporary look at how one Polynesian society continues to provide a social role for cross-gender behavior. According to Levy (1973), villagers in his area of study do not agree on the sexual behavior of the *māhū*—some "believe that *māhū* do not generally engage in homosexual intercourse." Information from both *māhū* and *non-māhū* informants, however, leads to the conclusion that probably a majority of the *mahus* prefer adolescent males with

5. The confounding of transvestism with homosexuality still occurs. For example, Minturn, Grosse, and Haider (1969) coded male homosexuality with transvestism in a recent study of the patterning of sexual beliefs and behavior, "because it is often difficult to distinguish between the two practices, and because they are assumed to be manifestations of the same psychological processes and to have similar causes."

whom they perform "ote moa" (literally, "penis sucking"). The following are some aspects of the role and the community response to it:

> It is said to be exclusive. Its essential defining characteristic is "doing woman's work," that is, a role reversal which is *publicly demonstrated*—either through clothes or through other public aspects of women's role playing. Most villagers approve of, and are pleased by, the role reversal. But homosexual behavior is a covert part of the role, and it is disapproved by many villagers. Men who have sexual relations with the *māhū* . . . do not consider themselves abnormal. Villagers who know of such activities may disapprove, but they do not label the partners as unmanly. The *māhū* is considered as a substitute woman for the partner. A new word, *raerae*, which reportedly originated in Papeete, is used by some to designate nontraditional types of homosexual behavior. (Levy, 1973)

It should also be noted that in Levy's village of study *māhūs* were the only adult men reported to be engaging in homosexual intercourse.

Another contemporary example of a social role for cross-gender behavior is the *Hijadā* role provided cross-gender behaving males in northwestern India. Given slightly different names by different observers *(Hijarās, Hinjrās,* and *Hijirās),* these males appear to be playing the same role. There is general agreement on the fact that they cross-dress, beg alms, and collect dues at special ceremonies where they dance and sing as women. There is a considerable difference of opinion, however, as to whether they engage in homosexual intercourse or in any sexual activity for that matter. From the available data, it appears that they live mostly in towns in communes, with each commune having a definite jurisdiction of villages and towns "where its members can beg alms and collect dues" (Shah, 1961). They are also reported to live separately by themselves. From the findings of Carstairs (1956) and Shah (1961), one can at least conclude that the *Hijadās* living alone are sexually active:

> Carstairs is wrong in considering all the Hijadās as homosexual, but there seems to be some truth in his information about the homosexuality of the Deoli Hijadā. (Note: Deoli is the village of Carstairs study.) Faridi and Mehta also note that some Hijadās practice "sodomy." This, however, is not institutionalized homosexuality. (Shah, 1961)

The finding by Opler (1960) that "they cannot carry on sexual activities and do not marry" may apply to the majority of *Hijadās* living in communes. The question of what kind of sexual behavior the *Hijadās* practice, if any, cannot be answered definitively with the data available. That they are still a viable group in India is confirmed by a recent Associated Press release:

> About 2,000 eunuchs dressed in brightly colored saris and other female garb were converging on this northern town from all over India this weekend for a private convention of song, dance and prayer.

Local reaction to the gathering was mixed. "They're perverts," commented a local peanut vendor. "We should have nothing to do with them. They should be run out of town."

A New Delhi social worker . . . said they sometime supplement their income as paid lovers of homosexuals. (Excerpts from AP, 6 February/1979)

DISAPPROVING SOCIETIES

Societies in which cross-gender behavior produces strong emotional negative reactions in large segments of the population tend to have the following commonalities: (1) negative reactions produced by the behavior are essentially limited to the male part of the population and relate mainly to effeminate males; (2) cross-gender behavior is controlled by laws which prohibit cross-dressing, and by laws and public opinion which consider other attributes associated with the behavior as scandalous; (3) gender roles are sharply dichotomized; and (4) a general belief exists that anyone demonstrating cross-gender behavior is homosexual.

A number of complex modern and peasant societies in the Middle East, North Africa, southern Europe, and Central and South America have the commonalities listed. The author's research in Mexico (Carrier, 1976 and 1977) illustrates how homosexual behavior in these societies appears to be linked to social responses to cross-gender behavior. The comments that follow are limited to male homosexual behavior. Female homosexuality is known to exist in these societies, but too little is known about the behavior to be included in the discussion.

Mexican Homosexual Behavior. The Mexican mestizo culture places a high value on manliness. One of the salient features of the society is thus a sharp delimitation between the roles played by males and females. Role expectations in general are for the male to be dominant and independent and for the female to be submissive and dependent. The continued sharp boundary between male and female roles in Mexico appears to be due in part to a culturally defined hypermasculine ideal model of manliness, referred to under the label *machismo.* The ideal female role is generally believed to be the reciprocal of the macho (male) role.[6]

As a consequence of the high status given manliness, Mexican males from birth onward are expected to behave in as manly a way as possible. Peñalosa (1968) sums it up as follows: "Any signs of feminization are severely repressed in the boy." McGinn (1966) concludes: "The young Mexican boy may be severely scolded for engaging in feminine activities, such as playing with dolls or jacks. Parents verbally and physically punish 'feminine' traits in their male chil-

6. The roles described represent the normative cultural ideals of the mestizoized national culture. Mestizos are Mexican nationals of mixed Indian and Spanish ancestry. They make up a large majority of the population, and their culture is the dominant one.

dren." The importance of manly behavior continues throughout the life span of Mexican males.

One result of the sharp dichotomization of male and female gender roles is the widely held belief that effeminate males basically prefer to play the female role rather than the male. The link between male effeminacy and homosexuality is the additional belief that as a result of this role preference effeminate males are sexually interested only in masculine males with whom they play the passive sex role. Although the motivations of males participating in homosexual encounters are without question diverse and complex, the fact remains that in Mexico cultural pressure is brought to bear on effeminate males to play the passive insertee role in sexual intercourse, and a kind of de facto cultural approval is given (that is, no particular stigma is attached to) masculine males who want to play the active insertor role in homosexual intercourse.

The beliefs linking effeminate males with homosexuality are culturally transmitted by a vocabulary which provides the appropriate labels, by homosexually oriented jokes and word games *(albures)*, and by the mass media. The links are established at a very early age. From early childhood on, Mexican males are made aware of the labels used to denote male homosexuals and the connection is always clearly made that these homosexual males are guilty of unmanly effeminate behavior.

The author's data also support the notion that prior to puberty effeminate males in Mexico are targeted as sexual objects for adolescent and adult males, and are expected to play the passive insertee sex role in anal intercourse. Following the onset of puberty, they continue to be sexual targets for other males because of their effeminacy. The consensus of my effeminate respondents in Mexico is that regardless of whether they are at school, in a movie theater, on the downtown streets, in a park, or in their own neighborhood, they are sought out and expected to play the anal passive sex role by more masculine males. As one fourteen-year-old respondent put it, in response to the question of where he had looked for sexual contacts during the year prior to the interview: "I didn't have to search for them . . . they looked for me."

The other side of the coin is represented by masculine male participants in homosexual encounters. Given the fact that effeminate males in Mexico are assumed homosexual and thus considered available as sexual outlets, how do the cultural factors contribute to the willingness of masculine males to play the active insertor sex role? The available data suggest that, insofar as the social variables are concerned, their willingness to participate in homosexual encounters is due to the relatively high level of sexual awareness that exists among males in the society, to the lack of stigmatization of the insertor sex role, and to the restraints that may be placed on alternative sexual outlets by available income and/or by marital status. The only cultural proscriptions are that "masculine" males should not play the passive sex role and should not be exclusively involved with homosexual intercourse.

The passive sex role is by inference—through the cultural equivalence of effeminacy with homosexuality—prescribed for "effeminate" males. It becomes a self-fulfilling prophecy of the society that effeminate males (a majority?) are eventually, if not from the beginning, pushed toward exclusively homosexual behavior. Some do engage in heterosexual intercourse, and some marry and set up households; but these probably are a minority of the identifiably effeminate males among the mestizos of the Mexican population.

Brazilian Homosexual Behavior   Both Young (1973) and Fry (1974) note the relationship between cross-gender behavior and homosexuality in Brazil:

> Brazilians are still pretty hung-up about sexual roles. Many Brazilians believe in the *bicha/bofe* (femme/butch) dichotomy and try to live by it. In Brazil, the average person doesn't even recognize the existence of the masculine homosexual. For example, among working-class men, it is considered all right to fuck a *bicha,* an accomplishment of sorts, just like fucking a woman. (Young, 1973)

> In the simplest of terms, a male is a man until he is assumed or proved to have "given" in which case he becomes a *bicha.* With very few exceptions, males who "eat" *bichas* are not classified as anything other than "real men." Under this classificatory scheme they differ in no way from males who restrict themselves to "eating" females. (Note: the male who gives is an insertee, the one who eats is an insertor.) (Fry, 1974)

Southern European Homosexual Behavior.   Contemporary patterns of male homosexual behavior in Greece appear similar to those observed by the author in Mexico. An American anthropologist who collected data on homosexual behavior in Greece while working there on an archeological project (Bialor, 1975) found, for example, that preferences for playing one sex role or the other (anal insertor or anal insertee) appear to be highly developed among Greek males. Little or no stigma is attached to the masculine male who plays the active insertor role. The social setting in modern Greece also appears to be strikingly similar to that in modern Mexico. Karlen (1971) describes it as follows:

> The father spends his spare time with other men in cafes; society is a male club, and there all true companionship lies. Women live separate, sequestered lives. Girls' virginity is carefully protected, and the majority of homicides are committed over the "honor" of daughters and sisters. In some Greek villages a woman does not leave her home unaccompanied by a relative between puberty and old age. Women walk the street, even in

Athens, with their eyes down; a woman who looks up when a man spe
to her is, quite simply, a whore. The young male goes to prostitutes and n
carry on homosexual connections; it is not unusual for him to marry at thi
having had no sexual experience save with prostitutes and male friends.
(P. 16)

In an evaluation of the strategy of Turkish boys' verbal dueling
rhymes, Dundes, Leach, and Ozkok (1972) make the following observations about homosexual behavior in Turkey:

It is extremely important to note that the insult refers to *passive* homosexuality, not to homosexuality in general. In this context there is nothing insulting
about being the active homosexual. In a homosexual relationship, the active
phallic aggressor gains status; the passive victim of such aggression loses
status. It is important to play the active role in a homosexual relationship; it
is shameful and demeaning to be forced to take the passive role.

Moroccan Homosexual Behavior. The author does not know of
any formal studies of homosexual behavior in Morocco. The available information suggests, however, that contemporary patterns of
homosexual behavior in Morocco are similar to those in Mexico; that
is, as long as Moroccan males play the active, insertor sex role in the
relationship, there is never any question of their being considered
homosexual. Based on his field work in Morocco shortly after the
turn of the century, Westermarck (1908) believed that "a very large
proportion of the men" in some parts of the country were involved
in homosexual activity. He also noted that: "In Morocco active pederasty is regarded with almost complete indifference, whilst the passive sodomite, if a grown-up individual, is spoken of with scorn. Dr.
Polak says the same of the Persians." Contemporary patterns of
homosexual behavior in the Islamic Arab countries of North Africa
are probably similar to those in Morocco.

The following dialogue abridged from a recent novel illustrates
Moroccan male attitudes toward homosexual contacts:

o What do you need money for?
- What for? I'm a person just like everyone else. I like to have some money
   for clothes, and for wine and whores.
o You need a lot of whores?
- I can niki twenty whores in one night. And if a pretty little boy passes
   in the street after that—twenty one.
o Little boys, too?
- I niki everyone.
o Even old men.
- Old men? Sure, they pay you money.
o To niki you?
- No, for me to niki them.
o And *they* pay you for that?
- Sure.
o You're the same as a whore.
- Why?

o You are.
- But why? I niki *them*.
o But I still don't see how you could: old men.
- A zook is a zook. What's the difference? I niki it.

(Tavel, 1968 Pp. 52–53)

(Note: niki = fuck; zook = ass)

SOCIETIES WITH RITUALIZED MASCULINITY

Cross-gender behavior, as noted previously, is something usually feared among the adult male part of populations. It is not surprising, then, that many societies around the world utilize an elaborate set of rituals to ensure that at or near puberty male members of the society will successfully make the transition from boyhood to masculine adulthood.

Highland societies in New Guinea are particularly noted for their rigid separation of gender roles, male dominance, and varying amounts of tension or hostility between men and women. Most of the nonacculturated highland societies maintain an elaborate set of male rituals related to masculinity. Achieving manhood in these societies "is never regarded as the certain result of a natural process, nor is it established by sexual maturity alone, for its supreme expression is cultural, the result of a demonstrated ability in those activities which are designated male" (Read, 1954).

Some of these highland New Guinea societies have incorporated homosexual acts in male rituals and initiation rites. Semen is transfered from an adult male to a young boy either anally or orally to ensure masculinity and proper growth, and to maintain a source of semen for future generations.[7] Females are both envied and feared in these societies. They are envied for the fast growth which is observed at puberty and correlated with menstruation; and feared because of what are considered the polluting effects of menstrual blood. Although not explicitly stated in any of the available research findings, one has the feeling that a genuine gender role reversal would be unthinkable in these particular societies.

Examples of two highland New Guinea societies that incorporate homosexual acts in their male rituals, the Kaluli (Schieffelin, 1976) and the Etoro (Kelly, 1976), are presented in order to show the complexity of relationships between males and females; and to provide some details on the male belief system that correlates semen with masculinity and growth. Although the transfer of semen is utilized in male rituals in these two societies and in other societies in New Guinea and other parts of Melanesia, it is important to note that it is

7. It is interesting to note that these societies apparently specialize in the way semen is planted; that is, they use one method, anal or oral, exclusively.

not utilized in other societies that have similar social characteristics and male rituals.

Schieffelin concludes from his research that by New Guinea standards the relations between Kaluli men and women are unusual "for their lack of hostility and, indeed, for their affection. Nevertheless, male and female represent two poles in a fundamental cultural-metaphysical opposition that keeps relations between them awkward and problematic." He notes the baleful influence of females is believed to be concentrated in their genitalia and menstrual discharge. Women are seen as clumsier, slower, weaker, and less knowledgeable than men; and this is related to the debilitating state that women present during menstruation. Thus it is that:

> The man who spends too much time in the women's section of the [longhouse], who touches his wife too often, or who eats food a woman has stepped over is likely to become emaciated, develop a cough, or lose his endurance on the trail. (1976, P. 123)

Kaluli men, on the other hand, see themselves as wiry, alert, strong, energetic; and as having considerable endurance. According to Schieffelin: "This male influence is concentrated in semen. Semen has a kind of magical quality that promotes physical growth and mental understanding." He also notes that Kaluli men believe:

> Semen is . . . necessary for young boys to attain full growth to manhood. Kaluli men maintain that women attain maturity by themselves (first menses?) but that boys do not. They need a boost as it were. When a boy is eleven or twelve years old, he is engaged for several months in homosexual intercourse with a healthy older man chosen by his father. (This is always an in-law or unrelated person, since the same notions of incestuous relations apply to little boys as to marriageable women.) Men point to the rapid growth of adolescent youths, the appearance of peachfuzz beards, and so on, as the favorable results of this child-rearing practice. (P. 124)

It is interesting to note that despite the beliefs about the benefits of homosexual contacts, Kaluli men look on them "as a vulnerable point in the male image of strength and consequently a subject of considerable embarrassment in relation to the women. Men try unsuccessfully to maintain it as a secret that women do not know."

Kaluli maleness had its highest expression, according to Schieffelin, in a ceremonial hunting lodge "in which the virgin youths and young unmarried men from a number of longhouses lived for periods of up to fifteen months." Not quite an initiation program, participation in the ceremonial lodge was not required for attainment of full manhood. Nevertheless, homosexual intercourse—which is anal among Kaluli males—"was practiced between the older bachelors and the younger boys to make them grow, some boys and men developing specific liaisons for the time." It is important to note that though the transfer of semen is necessary for the attainment of manhood, it is only through coupling with a female and marriage "that a man can develop the connections and influence that render him fully effective in his life."

Relations between Etoro men and women differ from those of the Kaluli. Kelley (1976) concludes from his research that, although under certain specific conditions women have a weakening influence upon men, "they are not a source of pollution and therefore do not pose a continuous threat to male well-being." He further notes that: "While intercourse is depleting, the female persona is not contaminating, and men therefore need not avoid contact with women *per se.*" Men, however, do not have to worry about undue depletion because heterosexual intercourse is prohibited for various reasons for an estimated 205 to 260 days a year; and Kelley found indirect evidence of general adherence to the prohibitions.

Etoro beliefs about two discrete spiritual aspects of human beings directly affect sexual behavior. The two aspects are the *"ausulubo,* an immaterial spirit double, and *hame,* a life-force or animating principle."* Of particular importance about the *hame* is that it is a reservoir of life-force which can be augmented or diminished. Adult Etoro males believe they possess a limited quantity of life-force which resides in the body as a whole, but is especially concentrated in the semen. Every act of sexual intercourse, therefore, depletes a man's *hame.* Through the process of conception, the man's life-force expended in sexual intercourse is transferred to the children he begets—or in the absence of conception, is lost. A man can also transfer his *hame* and provide semen to a prepubescent boy through fellatio. Kelly summarizes Etoro beliefs as follows:

> Boys differ most importantly from men in that they completely lack the most critical and essential attribute of manhood, i.e., semen. The Etoro believe, moreover, that semen does not occur naturally in boys and must be "planted" in them . . . Moreover, all aspects of manliness are seen as consequences of this acquisition. A youth is continually inseminated from about age ten until he reaches his early to mid-twenties. This period is also marked by rapid growth in stature, increased physical strength and endurance, the sprouting of facial and body hair, and the development of masculine skills and characteristics such as hunting ability and courageousness in war. These empirically observable changes are uniformly regarded as the direct results of insemination. (This is accomplished orally. The boy manipulates the man to the point of ejaculation and consumes the semen. The above effects are only realized through ingestion, and therefore are not applicable to heterosexual relations; women do not acquire strength, etc., in this way.) (P. 45)

The initiation of Etoro youths into manhood takes place in their late teens or early twenties when they go into seclusion from women at a lodge on the edge of primary forest. Most men participate in the activities to some extent. A lot of the initiates' time is spent hunting and trapping and "everyone residing at the lodge goes about nude and, it is said, with their penises erect. This is part of a general celebration of masculinity (and especially that recently attained by the initiates)." Kelly also points out that there is a generalized insemination of the initiates by older men. This takes place because of fears of witchcraft. If a young man should be later deemed a witch, his principal inseminator (secured earlier by his father) is then not necessarily implicated.

It is important to note that legitimate homosexual acts occur only within the context of the ritual which established them. Among Etoro males inappropriate sexual liasions are further controlled by beliefs about witchcraft. Homosexual contacts between young men would carry the psychological burden that one of them would have to become a witch; that is, one would be enhancing his growth and vitality at the expense of the other. This same belief system would also restrain sexual relations between males and females:

> A woman who encourages, entices, or demands her husband to engage in needless copulation—from which he alone will suffer—thereby approaches the purely negative role of witch. She sates her sexual appetite selfishly, knowingly causing harm, and perhaps with malicious intent. (This conotation applies with double force to a woman who consorts with an immature youth whose growth and development will be permanently arrested by loss of semen.) (Kelly, 1976)

These data on the use of homosexual acts in male rituals and initiation rites in the preliterate highlander societies of New Guinea call into question observations about male sexual behavior in lowlander New Guinea societies like Van Baal's (1966) on a Marind-Amin cult: "The men . . . are homosexuals who practice institutionalized sodomy on an uncommonly large scale."

It does seem reasonable to conclude, however, that homosexual acts initiated ritually, and lasting over extended periods of time, may lead to homosexual relationships that are not sanctioned by the society. Restraints placed on Etoro males by their belief system would seem to limit their homosexual behavior outside its approved form. But this may not be the case in other societies. Herdt (1979) found in the New Guinea society of his study, for example, that there is an erotic component in the male initiation rites where semen is transferred to small boys through fellatio in order to bring about growth and masculinity. The following was observed during a first stage initiation for novices who were from six to eight years old; the bachelors described are third-stage initiates from fourteen to sixteen years old:

> The bachelors . . . now come alive. It is nightfall and what should now commence are the first erotic encounters of fellatio between themselves and the novices. The bachelors momentarily engage in outlandish erotic exhibitionism, as is customary . . . The bachelors lift up their arse covers exposing their naked buttocks to the lads.

What soon follows, mostly at the behest of individual boys, is erotic horse-play inside the house and, private homosexual intercourse outside on the darkened dance-ground area. Not all boys join in this but most of them took part. And before the conclusion of the initiation, five days later, all but a handful of novices had served as fellators not once, but twice and more. (Herdt 1979, Pp. 41–42)

AVAILABILITY OF SEXUAL PARTNERS

Irrespective of individual preferences, when suitable heterosexual partners are unavailable to certain segments of a society for whatever reason, some individuals will turn to members of their own sex for sexual satisfaction. Part of the variance of homosexual behavior observed cross-culturally may therefore be related to the availability of sexual partners.

A number of sociocultural factors, operating separately or in varying combinations, may curtail or completely shut off the supply of hetero-sexual partners. Some of the important ones are expectations with respect to virginity, segregation of sexes prior to marriage, age at marriage, polygamy, sex ratio, segregation of sexes as a result of incarceration, and available economic resources and/or distribution of income.

Taboos on sexual behavior between opposite sex partners, for given time periods like adolescence, for example, may facilitate homosexual behavior. Many preliterate, peasant, and complex modern societies place a high value on the virginity of females prior to marriage. Heterosexual intercourse is thus forbidden or restricted between puberty and marriage—a time period of high sexual need for both sexes. Sexual experimentation between members of the same sex appears to be the major outcome of the forbidden or restricted behavior and is often encouraged further by the segregation of sexes in schools. Societies that place a high value on virginity, like those in Latin America, southern Europe, and North Africa, tend to segregate the sexes in schools and to use chaperons for females during courtship. Additionally, the majority of males in these societies have limited economic resources and thus cannot afford to pay female prostitutes on a regular basis; and they are not stigmatized as homosexual as long as they play the active sex role.

Segregation of males in some African societies also results in homosexual behavior. Wilson (1957) reports, for example, that in the boys' villages where Ngonde males were confined from the age of ten on until marriage, sexual activity was permissible between boys so long as mutually acceptable. Polygamy also encouraged homosexual behavior by limiting the supply of females available for marriage. Homosexual activity was not reported among Ngonde girls, who married young, but was reported among the older wives of polygamists.

Separation of adult males from their wives, while the males are away working to support their families, may similarly result in homosexual activity. Such activity has been reported, for example, among men from many different tribal societies around the world when they have been concentrated to work in plantations, port cities, or mines. Junod (1927) provides an early example of this pattern of behavior in his study of an African society, the Thonga. Confined to all-male camps while working in South African mines, Thonga males screened newcomers for those who might be willing to play the female sex role. Those who were willing to play the role were given special privileges such as not having to work underground in the mines. Some marriages were reported between male inhabitants of the camp. Junod, a missionary, did not know much about homosexual behavior among the Thonga in their tribal setting. Those working at the mine, however, did not consider the behavior "sinful."

Segregation of the sexes in jail or prison may also lead to homosexual behavior. A certain percentage of inmates, deprived of heterosexual outlets, turn to what is available. Thus, some inmates may have their first homosexual contact; while others, conditioned by their outside culture, may be continuing a sexual outlet utilized before incarceration. Giallombardo (1966), for example, notes that in the United States

> the male and female inmate cultures *are* a response to the deprivations of prison life, but the nature of the response in both prison communities is influenced by the differential participation of males and females in the external culture.

With respect to homosexuality, she found that females structure their relationships in a totally different way than males. Female inmates set up a complex series of social relationships formed on the basis of marriage and kinship. The prison homosexual marriage alliances play a central role along with the larger informal family groupings. Because of their cultural orientation, male inmates, on the other hand, cannot consider this a feasible alternative since

> the serious adoption of a female role is contrary to the definition of the male role as masculine. It is noteworthy that in the male prison the fags and punks are both held in derision by the vast majority of male inmates, as it is felt that they have sacrificed their manhood, but the homosexuality of wolves is looked upon as a temporary adjustment to sexual tensions generated by the prison setting. (Giallombardo, 1966, p. 186)

It should be noted that a large percentage of prison inmates in the United States come from the lower-class strata of the society.

Widespread polygyny in a society may likewise result in increased homosexual behavior. It may lead to a serious shortage of female heterosexual partners for single males, and may limit the heterosexual activity of the women wedded to one man. Thus both male and female homosexuality may occur in response to polygynous marriages. Graer (1929) reports both as occurring in the Azande society in Africa. Nadel (1942) reported only female homosexual behavior among the Nupe in Nigeria. Widespread homosexual activity has also been reported in harems of Muslim societies around the world. (Edwardes, 1959)

Discussion

Heterosexual intercourse, marriage, and the creation of a family are culturally established as primary objectives for adults living in all of the societies discussed above. Ford and Beach (1951) concluded from their cross-cultural survey that "all known cultures are strongly biased in favor of copulation between males and females as contrasted with alternative avenues of sexual expression." They further note that this viewpoint is biologically adaptive in that it favors perpetuation of the species and social group, and that societies favoring other nonreproductive forms of sexual expression for adults would not be likely to survive for many generations.

Homosexual intercourse appears to be the most important alternative form of sexual expression utilized by people living around the world. All cultures have established rules and regulations that govern the selection of a sexual partner or partners. With respect to homosexual behavior, however, there appear to be greater variations of the rules and regulations. And male homosexual behavior generally appears to be more regulated by cultures than female homosexual behavior. This difference may be the result of females being less likely than males to engage in homosexual activity; but it may also just be the result of a lack of data on female as compared with male homosexual behavior cross-culturally.

Exclusive homosexuality, however, because of the cultural dictums concerning marriage and the family, appears to be generally excluded as a sexual option even in those societies where homosexual behavior is generally approved. For example, the two societies where all male individuals are free to participate in homosexual activity if they choose, Siwan and East Bay, do not sanction exclusive homosexuality.[8] Although nearly all male members of these two societies are reported to engage in extensive homosexual activities, they are not permitted to do so exclusively over their adult life span. Davenport (1965) reports "that

8. Both societies are small, each totaling less than one thousand inhabitants. The Siwans live in an oasis in the Libyan desert. The people of East Bay (a pseudonym) live in a number of small coastal village in an island in Melanesia.

East Bay is a society which permits men to be either heterosexual or bisexual in their behavior, but denies the possibility of the exclusively homosexual man." He notes that "they have no concept and therefore no word for the exclusive homosexual." There are not much data available on the Siwans, but it has been reported that whether single or married Siwan males "are expected to have both homosexual and heterosexual affairs" (Ford and Beach, 1951).

In East Bay there are two categories of homosexual relationships. One category appears similar to that found in a number of Melanesian societies; an older man plays the active (insertor) sex role in anal intercourse with younger boys "from seven to perhaps eleven years of age." Davenport notes:

> The man always plays the active role, and it is considered obligatory for him to give the boy presents in return for accommodating him. A man would not engage his own son in such a relationship, but fathers do not object when friends use their young sons in this way, provided the adult is kind and generous. (P. 200)

The other category is between young single men of the same age group who play both sex roles in anal intercourse. The young men, however, "are not regarded as homosexual lovers. They are simply friends or relatives, who, understanding each other's needs and desires, accommodate one another thus fulfilling some of the obligations of kinship and friendship." This category may be related to several social factors which limit heterosexual contacts of young single men. First, the population is highly masculine with a male/-female ratio of 120:100 in the fifteen- to twenty-five-year-old age group. Second, females have historically been brought in as wives for those who could afford the bride price. Third, sexual relations between unmarried individuals and adultery are forbidden. Both relationships are classed as larcenies and "only murder carries a more severe punishment." At first marriage a bride is expected to be a virgin. Chastity is highly valued in that it indicates adultery is less likely to occur after marriage. And fourth, there is "an extensive system for separating the sexes by what amounts to a general social avoidance between men and women in all but a few situations." From early adolescence on, unmarried men and boys sleep and eat in the men's house; and married men spend much of their time there during the day. Davenport notes that both masturbation and anal copulation are socially approved and regarded as substitutes for heterosexual intercourse by members of the society. Female homosexual activity is not reported in East Bay.

Among Siwan males the accepted homosexual relationship is "between a man and a boy but not between adult men or between two young boys" (Bullough, 1976). They are reported to practice anal intercourse with the adult man always playing the active (insertor) sex role. In this society, boys are more valued than girls. Allah (1917) reports that

> bringing up of a boy costs very little whereas the girl needs ornaments, clothing, and stains. Moreover the boy is a very fruitful source of profit for the father, not for the work he does, but because he is hired by his father to another man to be used as a catamite. Sometime two men exchange their sons. If they are asked about this, they are not ashamed to mention it.

Homosexual activity is not reported for Siwan females.

The way in which cross-gender behavior is linked to homosexual behavior, and the meaning ascribed to the "homosexual" behavior by participants and significant others, differ between the three categories of societies identified in this study. What is considered homosexuality in one culture may be considered appropriate behavior within pre-scribed gender roles in another, a homosexual act only on the part of one participant in another, or a ritual act involving growth and mascu-linity in still another. Care must therefore be taken when judging sexual behavior cross-culturally with such culture-bound labels as "homosex-ual" and "homosexuality."

From a cultural point of view, deviations from sexual mores in a given society appear most likely to occur as a result of the lack of appropriate sexual partners and/or a result of conditioning in approved sexual behavior which is limited by age or ritual (for example, where homosexual intercourse is only appropriate for a certain age group and/or ritual time period and inappropriate thereafter). Homosexual activity initiated by sociocultural variables may over time through in-teraction with personality variables, produce an outcome not in accord-ance with the sexual mores of the society.

The findings presented in this chapter illustrate the profound influ-ence of culture on the structuring of individual patterns of sexual be-havior. Whether from biological or psychological causation, cross-gen-der behaving individuals in many societies must cope with a cultural formulation which equates their behavior with homosexual activity and thus makes it a self-fulfilling prophecy that they become homosexually involved. There are also individuals in many societies who might *prefer* to be exclusively homosexual but are prevented from doing so by cul-tural edicts. From whatever causes that homosexual impulses originate, whether they be biological or psychological, culture provides an addi-tional dimension that cannot be ignored.

REFERENCES

Allah, M. 1917. Siwan customs. *Harvard African Studies.* 1:7.

Angelino, A., and Shedd, C. 1955. A note on berdache. *American Anthropologist* 57:121–25.

Associated Press. 1979. Eunuchs gather for convention in India. Panipat, 6 February 1979.

Bialor, P. 1975. Personal communication.

Bogores, W. 1904. The Chukchee. *Memoirs of American Museum of Natural History* II:449–51.

Broude, G., and Greene, S. 1976. Cross-cultural codes on twenty sexual attitudes and practices. *Ethnology* 15(4):410–11.

Bullough, V. 1976. *Sexual variance in society and history.* New York: John Wiley. Pp. 22–49.

Carrier, J. 1976. Cultural factors affecting urban Mexican male homosexual behavior. *Archives of Sexual Behavior* 5(2):103–24.

———. 1977. Sex-role preference as an explanatory variable in homosexual behavior. *Archives of Sexual Behavior* 6(1):53–65.

Carstairs, G. 1956. Hinjra and Jiryan: two derivatives of Hindu attitudes to sexuality. *British Journal of Medical Psychology* 2:129–32.

Davenport, W. 1965. Sexual patterns and their regulation in a society of the southwest Pacific. In *Sex and behavior* (New York: John Wiley), pp. 164–207.

Devereux, G. 1937. Institutionalized homosexuality of the Mohave Indians. In *The problem of homosexuality in modern society.* (New York: E. P. Dutton), pp. 183–226.

Dundes, A.; Leach, J.; and Ozkok, B. 1972. The strategy of Turkish boys' verbal dueling. In *Directions in sociolinguistics: The ethnography of communication* (New York: Holt).

Edwardes, A. 1959. *The jewel in the lotus.* New York: Julian Press Pp. 254–56.

Ford, C. S., and Beach, F. A. 1951. *Patterns of sexual behavior,* New York: Harper & Bros.

Fry, P. 1974. Male homosexuality and Afro-Brazilian possession cults. Unpublished paper presented to Symposium on Homosexuality in Cross-cultural Perspective, 73rd Annual Meeting of the American Anthropological Association, Mexico City.

Giallombardo, R. 1966. *Society of women: A study of a women's prison.* New York: John Wiley.

Graer, A. 1929. *L'art de guérir chez les Azande.* Brussels: Goemaere. P. 362.

Herdt, G. 1979. Fetish and fantasy in Sambia initiation. In G. Herdt, and M. Meggitt, eds. *Male initiation in New Guinea* (Berkeley: University of California Press).

Hooker, E. 1965. An empirical study of some relations between sexual patterns and gender identity in male homosexuals. In *Sex Research: New Developments* (New York: Holt), pp. 24–25.

Junod, H. 1927. *The life of a South African tribe.* London: Macmillan. P. 493.

Karlen, A. 1971. *Sexuality and homosexuality: a new view.* New York: W. W. Norton.

Kelly, R. 1976. Witchcraft and sexual relations: an exploration in the social and semantic implications of the structure of belief. In *Man and Woman in the New Guinea Highlands* (Washington, D.C.: American Anthropological Association).

Kroeber, A. 1940. Psychosis or social sanction. *Character and Personality* 8:204–15. Reprinted in *The nature of culture* (Chicago: University of Chicago Press, 1952) p. 313.

Levy, R. 1973. *Tahitians.* Chicago: University of Chicago Press.

Marshall, D., and Suggs, R. 1971. *Human sexual behavior.* New York: Basic Books Pp. 220–21.

McGinn, N. 1966. Marriage and family in middle-class Mexico. *Journal of Marriage and Family Counseling* 28:305–13.

Mead, M. 1961. Cultural determinants of sexual behavior. In *Sex and Internal Secretions* (Baltimore: Williams & Wilkins), Pp. 1433–79.

Minturn, L.; Grosse, M.; and Haider, S. 1969. Cultural patterning of sexual beliefs and behavior. *Ethnology* 8(3):3.

Morrison, J. 1935. *The journal of James Morrison.* London: Golden Cockerel Press.

Munroe, R.; Whiting, J.; and Hally, D. 1969. Institutionalized male transvestism and sex distinctions. *American Anthropologist* 71:87–91.

Nadel, S. 1942. *A black Byzantium: The kingdom of nupe in Nigeria.* London: Oxford University Press.

Opler, M. 1960. The Hijarā (hermaphrodites) of India and Indian national character: a rejoinder. *American Anthropologist* 62(3):505–11.

Peñalosa, F. 1968. Mexican family roles. *Journal of Marriage and Family Counseling.* 30:680–89.

Read, K. 1954. Cultures of the central highlands of New Guinea. *Southwestern Journal of Anthropology* 10(1):27.

Royce, A. 1973. Personal communication.

Schieffelin, E. 1976. *The Sorrow of the lonely and the burning of the dancers.* Queensland, Australia: St. Martins Press. Pp. 100–101, 123–28.

Shah, A. 1961. *A note on the Hijadās of Gujarat. American Anthropologist* 63(6):-1325–30.

Stoller, R. 1976. Two feminized male American Indians. *Archives of Sexual Behavior* 5(6):536.

Tavel, R. 1968. *Street of Stairs.* New York: Olympia Press.

Van Baal, J. 1966. *Dema.* The Hague: Martinius Nijoff.

Westermarck, E. 1908. *The Origin and Development of the Moral Ideas,* London: Macmillan. Chapter "On Homosexual Love."

Williams, F. 1936. *Papuans of the trans-fly.* London: Oxford University Press.

Wilson, M. 1957. *Good company: A study of Nyakyusa age-villages,* London: Oxford University Press. Appendix.

Young, A. 1973. Gay gringo in Brazil. In L. Richmond, and G. Noguera, eds. *The gay liberation book* (San Francisco: Ramparts Press), Pp. 60–67.

6 / Homosexuality and Stigma

CAROL WARREN

This chapter is concerned with the social roots of homosexuality in a society that stigmatizes homosexuals. The argument made here is that stigmatization affects the adoption of a homosexual or lesbian identity and the formation of gay communities.[1] The model presented here is not intended as an explanation of homosexuality, but as one element in the many physiological, psychological, and social roots of homosexuality.

Stigma: The Social Context of Homosexuality

Goffman (1963) uses the concept of stigma to describe the process by which some people are treated as morally unworthy. The concept has been applied to the area of homosexuality and bixexuality by Blumstein and Schwartz (1976, 1977), Humphreys (1972, 1975), Lyman and Scott (1970), Ponse (1977, 1978), Warren (1974, 1976), and others. Goffman states that when a stranger

> is present before us, evidence can arise of his possessing an attribute that
> makes him different from others . . . in the extreme, a person who is quite

1. The impact of stigma on females and males has, presumably, both differences and similarities. This chapter will focus on commonalities.

This revised version has benefited considerable by the input of the following people, to whom I am most grateful: Peter Berger, Barry Dank, Judd Marmor, Mildred Pagelow, Barbara Ponse, and Joe Styles.

thoroughly bad, or dangerous, or weak. He is thus reduced in our minds from a whole or usual person to a tainted, discounted one. Such an attribute is a stigma. (1963, p. 3)

Goffman distinguishes three types of attributes which are stigmatized in our society:

First, there are abominations of the body—the various physical deformities. Next, there are blemishes of individual character perceived as weak will, domineering or unnatural passions. . . . these being inferred from a known record of, for example, mental disorder, imprisonment, addiction, alcoholism, homosexuality. . . . Finally there are the tribal stigma of race, nation and religion. (1963, p. 5)

The moral stigma of homosexuality has both differences from and similarities to the stigma of physical condition or racial group. Like physical handicap or racial group, moral failings are seen as "tainting" the entire individual. Blacks or the physically handicapped are viewed as different by virtue of a bodily condition. Logically, homosexuality refers to a type of behavior rather than to a condition. However, homosexuals are viewed generally not just as people who do a certain type of thing, but, rather, as people who are a certain type of being. This definition of homosexuality as a condition is reflected in the fact that the English language has no verb "to homosexual" as it does for many other behaviors such as "to swim" or "to write" (see also Ponse, 1978; Sagarin, 1974; Warren, 1974).

Homosexuality also differs from the physical and racial types of stigma in its degree of visibility. Goffman (1963) refers to the visibly stigmatized as "discredited"—most of those with a physical handicap, or belonging to a minority racial group cannot hide their stigma. But those with a moral failing, whom Goffman calls "discreditable," are only potentially stigmatized—they *can* hide their stigma, and may pose as "normal" among other normals. Many homosexuals are, in fact, invisible (Humphreys, 1975; Ponse, 1978; Warren, 1974), with the consequence that "they are incapable of projecting any definition of themselves to the straight communities" (Barry Dank, personal communication).

The Extent of Antihomosexual Stigma

Stigma depends upon the social context. A homosexual may be stigmatized by heterosexuals, but not by fellow homosexuals. Some non-Western societies tolerate or even encourage homosexual behavior under certain conditions (Carrier, chapter 5, this volume; Tripp, 1975). Even in the United States, heterosexuals' views of homosexuals are mixed rather than uniformly condemnatory. In a 1977 California poll, 5 percent of the polled group said that homosexuals should be punished and kept away from "normal" people, while 17 percent said they should be approved by society and allowed to live their own homosexual lifestyle.[2] Most respondents took intermediate positions; 43 percent said that homosexuals should be tolerated, but only if they do not publicly show their way of life, while 31 percent said they should be accepted by society and protected by law from unfair discrimination against them because of their homosexual life-style (*Los Angeles Times,* part 2, p. 4, June 6 1977).[3]

But homosexuals as a group remain stigmatized in the United States and in most other nations. They are forbidden to serve in the armed forces (Williams and Weinberg, 1971), experience employment and housing discrimination (Pagelow, n.d.), and suffer rejection by friends and family (Miller, 1971; Ponse, 1978). The knowledge of the fact that they *might* be rejected and shunned, even if they never experience stigmatization directly, keeps many homosexuals in a state of diffuse anxiety about their relationships with the heterosexual world (Weinberg and Williams, 1974).

THE HOMOSEXUAL: PREDISPOSITION, BEHAVIOR AND IDENTITY

The causes of homosexual behavior are significant subjects in the current debate over homosexual rights; this debate over cause is directly related to the question of stigma. People with racial or physical stigma may be shunned or rejected, but they will not be blamed for their condition; they are not regarded as having deliberately chosen to be dark-skinned or quadraplegic. Homosexuality, however, is seen as symptomatic of an underlying moral failing and as involving deliberate choice (Goffman, 1963). If homosexuality is indeed an arbitrary choice, then, moralists argue, homosexuals can be brought to account for their behavior.

But current psychoanalytic theory holds, on the contrary, that homosexual predispositions are not a matter of choice—as one would choose between asparagus and peas for dinner—but are established in very

2. California is often seen to be at the forefront of liberal tendencies, therefore these figures may be more "liberal" than similar attitudes in other states.

3. The problem with this type of poll is that sociologists do not find out what the term "homosexual" means to respondents—in their answers, are they thinking of the abstract category, a stranger they have encountered, or a friend or relative? In addition, the proportion of homosexuals in the sample of respondents is unknown; ideally, a measure of heterosexuals' attitudes towards homosexuals should exclude responses from persons who, unknown to the pollsters, are actually homosexual. But this cannot be done. Therefore, the "positive" dimension of the homosexual attitude is inflated by responses from "hidden" homosexuals—and to an unknown degree.

early childhood as a result of familial factors (Marmor, "Overview", this volume) or hormonal ones (Tourney chapter 2; Money, chapter 3, this volume). The incidence of persons with constitutional homosexual predispositions is unknown, but it is probably very small (Marmor, this volume).

But homosexual predispositions, like heterosexual ones, must be translated into behavior. Because of stigma, homosexual predispositions are translated into behavior at a later age than heterosexual ones (Dank, 1971, 1974)—at a considerable personal and social cost. Case studies and autobiographies of homosexual women and men attest to the difficulty of repressing their desires for love and contact. For many homosexuals, repression prevents their fullest development as human beings:

> It is curious to speculate how much more might have been accomplished had the time spent on needless guilt and evasiveness been put to the service of self-fulfillment. The waste is one which is felt not only by myself and my lover, but by nearly every other homosexual—male or female—I have ever known. (Quoted in Miller, 1971, p. 48)

For some, repression leads to much more severe consequences, such as suicide or schizophrenia. Both the milder and the severer consequences of stigma and repression for the individual also have social repercussions. Personal talent is lost to the society through a constant preoccupation on the part of some homosexuals with guilt, fear, and anxiety. Our already overburdened social services must deal with the additional unnecessary burden of those whose physical and mental handicaps are caused quite directly by the strain of stigma and repression.

People are labeled by others and also by themselves. As Goffman (1963) notes, a social identity is someone else's conception of the type of person you are; a personal identity is your own conception of the type of person you are. Many lay persons and even social scientists assign the identity "homosexual" to others on the basis of behavior. But the individuals who engage in the behavior may see themselves as homosexual, heterosexual, or bisexual. Behavior and personal identity are not identical, either among males (Blumstein and Schwartz, 1977; Humphreys, 1975; Warren, 1974) or females (Blumstein and Schwartz, 1976; Ponse, 1977, 1978).

The lack of fit between behavior and identity has been interpreted as a matter of existential identity choice (Sagarin, 1974; Warren, 1974; Ponse, 1978). But it can also be seen as a consequence of stigma. Since the homosexual stigma is invisible, people *can* deny the label. In addition, since homosexuals are seen as morally evil types of persons, individuals who do *not* see themselves as morally evil perceive themselves as not fitting the category: "As far as I knew homosexuality was a horrible thing and I knew sex with Gerald was fantastic, so I knew I couldn't be homosexual" (Warren, 1974, p. 155). Those who both accept themselves as homosexuals and believe the negative imagery experience considerable pain and self-doubt:

> It was so difficult for me . . . to get over feeling that I was what everybody says I was: scum of the earth, perverted, sick—you know all the labels. I didn't feel that way about myself—that's what really drove me over the edge —the terrific conflict of knowing that I really was OK, and I was right . . . and yet I wanted other people to like me. (Quoted in Ponse, 1978, p. 283)

> Even after I came out, there was a time when I couldn't hear the word "homosexual" or say it to myself, without trembling. (Neuhring and Fein, 1976, p. 9)

Adaptation to Stigma

People who engage in homosexual behavior in the face of stigma may avoid pain by denying that they are homosexuals, just as people who repress their desires and refrain from homosexual behavior often suffer serious psychic consequences. For example, the lower-class males studied by Reiss (1964) allowed homosexuals to fellate them, but denied that they were homosexual, and asserted that they engaged in these sex acts only for the monetary gain.

Stigma denial is one of the many adaptations to stigma elaborated by Goffman(1963); it is easier for the invisibly stigmatized than for the visibly stigmatized. The many ways in which homosexuals pass as heterosexuals have been studied by Lyman and Scott (1970), Ponse (1977, 1978) and Warren (1974, 1976), among others; these authors suggest that passing may be the most common adaptation of homosexuals to stigma.

Passing involves acceptance of the homosexual identity for oneself but concealing it from the potentially hostile straight world. Homosexuals may be secretive with family, friends, work colleagues, or with everyone. This secretiveness has both positive and negative consequences for the individual. The most important positive consequence is the experience of a close knit and highly significant gay community (Warren, 1974). Another consequence is the avoidance of discrimination in work and in other areas of social life. Among the negative consequences are a limited social life in the gay world, with time spent in the straight world perceived as unreal (Warren, 1974), a paranoid style of living in the straight world (Lyman and Scott, 1970; Warren, 1974),[4]

---

4. Psychological and sociological explanations of human behavior are often potentially well-fitting, since they take place at different levels of analysis (for example, the model of stigma presented here could conceivably be fitted in to almost any psychological or

anxiety about the discovery of their gayness by straights (Neuhring and Fein, 1976; Weinberg and Williams, 1974) and a sense of betrayal of other gays (Warren, 1974; Ponse, 1978). These themes of the safety and anxiety of secrecy are expressed by one of Ponse's lesbian respondents:

> Most of the people with whom I'm associated in business are *very* conservative in every respect—I know specifically that my boss in particular has a big thing against gay women, because he's been very overt about it, never dreaming that he's stepping on my toes. I've been very uncomfortable. I never give in to the urge to say anything and I don't like that. (Ponse, 1977, p. 62)

Another common form of adaptation to self-identified homosexuality is covering (Goffman, 1963, pp. 102–4). The person who covers makes "an effort to restrict the display of those failings most centrally identified with the stigma." The covering homosexual does not attempt to pass as heterosexual by displaying signs of heterosexuality such as opposite-sex dating (Warren, 1976), but restricts those secondary symbols of the stigma, such as effeminacy or promiscuity, which might offend the straight world.

Tripp (1975, pp. 142–44) regards covering as the most socially integrative form of adaptation to stigma, avoiding the confrontive tensions inherent in disclosure and the anxiety inherent in passing. He asserts that persons who cover may be relatively safe from attack by straights:

> But what about the person who . . . lives and works in a conventional social setting that brings him into daily contact with many people who might quickly join any moral clamor against him? This is a situation which is almost

---

physiological theory of the etiology of homosexual motivation). Sometimes, however, the different disciplines present competing explanations. For example, both psychiatrists and sociologists have characterized homosexuals as "paranoid." But their explanations for the manifestations of paranoia are quite different:

Freud said that paranoid projection also plays a big role in homosexuality; in fact he eventually decided that homosexuality is a defense against paranoia etc. . . . In classic paranoid fashion, (the homosexual) projects onto someone else the urge he cannot tolerate in himself. (Karlen, 1971, pp. 265–66)

Homosexuals, who have sometimes been treated as clinically paranoid, can be seen as persons embedded in a permanently problematic environment so long as they inhabit heterosexually-oriented societies. Their alleged paranoid behavior—indicated by a heightened suspiciousness, conspiratorial interpretation of events, and strategies of deviance disavowal or concealment—can be seen as behavior oriented to their particular problematic status. (Lyman and Scott, 1970, p. 87)

Clearly, the conceptions of paranoia used by Freud on the one hand and by Lyman and Scott on the gay community on the other are quite different. For Freud, paranoia is a *cause* of homosexuality; (in) the medical model . . . homosexuality is a disease or sickness affecting the entire personality. The members' conception, however, is that paranoia is an interactional *effect* of homosexuality—more specifically, secret homosexuality which the actor attempts to conceal from stigmatizing straight audiences. In situations of concealment, gays can easily exhibit a paranoid style. (Warren, 1974, p. 138)

universally imagined to be frightening to the homosexual and perilous to his position. But often it is neither.

A professor in a small-town college may be homosexual and even fairly actively so with little danger *provided* he is discreet in certain ways . . . By the time he has been at his post several years, many of his colleagues and quite a few students may have at least a tacit understanding that he is a homosexual. Yet as long as there is no scandal, and gossip is held within reasonable limits, he is surprisingly safe. (Tripp, 1975, p. 143)

Some homosexuals do not cover or hide their homosexuality; they disclose it either to everyone (that is, by wearing a "gay power" button), or to particular work colleagues, friends, or family members. Some gays see disclosure as a matter of collective political action, which will be discussed later. For the individual, disclosure—like secrecy—brings both rewards and penalties. Overt homosexuals may find difficulty in obtaining adequate employment and housing (Pagelow) and may become alienated from family and friends (Neuhring and Fein, 1976; Ponse, 1977, 1978). But they may also experience a sense of relief from the strain of passing, and a lessened sense of guilt or shame at being gay (Neuhring and Fein, 1976). Disclosure, like secrecy, can bring a sense of ambiguity and uncertainty about the rightness of the decision:

Among the more than two thousand letters I've received . . . have been a great many saying that having written it, I must surely feel relieved, feel freer somehow; it was all out in the open at last.

But that's like asking whether I regret having written it. I'm not sure whether I feel more free. I may simply feel more naked than before, somehow more exposed, more vulnerable. And—it will be some time before I know for sure, if I ever know for sure. (Miller, 1971, pp. 55–56)

Finally, some homosexuals live their lives in a state of self-hatred and despair, unable to repress their homosexuality, and unable to come to terms with it. Some of Humphreys' (1975) "tearoom" respondents, who engaged in impersonal restroom sex, expressed extreme dislike for homosexuals, perhaps reflecting their own self-hating dilemma. It is a truism—but probably quite psychologically true—that many of those with an excessive preoccupation with and dislike of homosexuals are the victims either of this type of self-hatred or of repression of their own desires.

Some of those who cannot come to terms with their own homosexuality attempt what Goffman (1963) calls stigma repair—they try to change themselves into heterosexuals. Like many other moral conditions such as alcoholism or drug use, homosexual stigma repair has both a psychiatric and a self-help dimension. Some homosexuals, like Merle Miller, seek psychiatric help in their endeavor to change their orientation. Still others attempt change through behavior modification, which can involve either painful aversion therapy, or the manipulation of rewards, or both (DeLora and Warren, 1977, pp. 483–488). A few, at least in Los Angeles, join the self-help fundamentalist Christian organization EXIT, which functions, as its promotional literature asserts, to turn gays into exgays through Jesus Christ.

There are many ways in which the homosexual can struggle to reconcile her or his desires or behavior with the stigma against homosexuality. All these ways involve a considerable investment of emotional energy, and most take a considerable psychic toll. At least until very recently—and probably at least into the late 1970s—the most common way of dealing with the stigma was to remain secret and pass as heterosexual: to become part of the homosexual invisible minority.

Homosexual Role-Models and Reference Groups

Not surprisingly, the current controversy over homosexual rights has centered on the relative visibility of homosexuals and their unwilling-ness to remain "in the closet." In the mid-1970s, Dade County, Florida, became the arena for an important debate over the civil rights of gays: whether *acknowledged* homosexuals should be protected against dis-crimination in jobs and housing. The key word here is "acknowledged" —many homosexuals, of course, live in housing and work at jobs. But most of these homosexuals are invisible; therefore they do not provide role-models for young children and adolescents. In the Dade County controversy, the leader of the antigay movement, Anita Bryant, focused on the role-model issue:

> This ordinance brings it out in the open, and I'm concerned about how it might influence the children . . . I mean people who are role models being able to stand up and say "I'm homosexual and I'm proud of it"—implying to our children that they have another legitimate choice open to them. (Quoted by Raspberry, 1977, p. 7)

The antigays see homosexuality as a matter of the deliberate *choice* of homosexuality, in adolescence or adulthood, as one might choose asparagus rather than peas for dinner. If homosexuality were indeed such a choice, the existence of homosexual role-models in the environ-ment might make some difference. But, as indicated, the overwhelming psychiatric evidence is that homosexual predispositions, like heterosex-ual predispositions, are set in early childhood. And, since nearly all children are raised in heterosexual households, the development of homosexuality seems uninfluenced by role-models.

Many gays, like the majority of psychiatrists, view homosexuality as more deep-rooted than a simple preference for peas or asparagus. The desire of gay activists to act as role-models is a desire to act as role-models *for homosexuals*—to show young gays that they need not experience the suffering that attended the lives of so many homosexual adults:

> Mike Scott, a homosexual [says] . . . "All I want to be is a role model . . . *only so I can put a youngster at ease after he discovers he's gay.*" (*Los Angeles Times,* 1977, part I, p. 7; italics added)

There is almost no literature on childhood acquaintance with the concept of homosexuality. Children know little of the details of adult heterosexual behavior; they know less of homosexual behavior. Instead, they have a shadowy image of homosexuals as "perverts." Joseph Epstein (1970, p. 30) comments on what may be a common childhood introduction to homosexuality:

> In the beginning, I felt confusion, revulsion and fear. I must have been nine or ten years old when my father . . . who carefully instructed me never to say the word "nigger"—one night sat me down in our living room to explain that there were "perverts" in the world. These were men with strange appetites, men whose minds were twisted, and I must be on the lookout for them. . . . There were not many such men in the world, but there were some, and they might wish to "play" with my brother and me in ways that were unnatural. (Epstein, 1970, p. 37)

Insofar as homosexuals are role-models in childhood, they are role-models only as filtered through the "pervert" imagery of heterosexual adults. Since children do not connect "perverts" with any specific behaviors, they may engage in homosexual experimentation; thus, the social stigma against homosexuality does not serve to inhibit sexual play in childhood. But once the adolescent learns to combine the pervert imagery with knowledge of the sexual behaviors involved, she or he may repress homosexual desires, or engage in them only with guilt and fear. Dank summarizes:

> Interviewees who had homosexual feelings during childhood were asked how they would have honestly responded to the question "Are you a homosexual?" at the time just prior to their graduation from high school. One typical response follows:
> "Truthfully I wouldn't have know what a homosexual was etc. . . . There was this kid who I was attracted to and I made a pass at him, and he was a good enough friend of mine to say 'What's wrong, are you a homo?' and I didn't even know what he was talking about. I heard the kids at school use the expression 'homo' and I didn't know what it meant." (Dank, 1974, p. 6)

While role-models provide individual identification for the growing child, reference groups provide group identification. Role-models of homosexuals are absent in early childhood, and hazy and negative later; homosexual reference groups tend to be completely absent. The child lives in a world where heterosexuality is taken for granted. In adolescence, there may be some exposure to positive gay role-models through gay liberation activities or writings; still, the adolescent has no picture of what the life-style of *groups* of gays might be. In contrast, those with a visible stigma inevitably provide role-models and reference groups for others like themselves. Blacks who become Muslims, black middle-class communities, black church groups, and black gangs provide reference groups. But the majority of those who share the invisible stigma of homosexuality are still "in the closet," invisible as reference groups, and visible as role-models, generally, only as filtered through straight adults who portray them as "dangerous perverts."

The adolescent with homosexual desires, who perhaps has experienced childhood sexual experimentation, typically engages in a search for some type of positive social definition of homosexuality, which can lead, eventually to a homosexual self-identification. This search often leads to the library. Dank (1971) found that 15 percent of his respondents "came out" into a homosexual identity by reading about homosexuality; in this electronic age, reading may be supplemented by some positive imagery from the visual media. As Goffman notes:

> It is important to stress that, in America at least, no matter how small and how badly off a particular stigmatized category is, the viewpoint of its members is likely to be given public presentation of some kind. It can thus be said that Americans who are stigmatized live in a literarily-defined world, however uncultured they might be. If they don't read books on the situation of persons like themselves, they at least read magazines and see movies; and where they don't do these, then they listen to local, vocal associates. An intellectually worked-up version of their point of view is thus available to most stigmatized persons. (1963, p. 25)

Gay Communities and the Gay World

As Berger and Luckmann (1967) point out, individuals in contemporary society inhabit a number of conceptual and interactional "worlds" of meaning which have more or less contact with one another: the world of biochemists, the world of radical rightists, the gay world. Within these worlds are actual communities: the Midwestern Biochemical Society, the American Nazi Party of Minnesota, or the secret gay community in Brooklyn.

The sociological and anthropological literature on gay communities in the United States and beyond reveals a varied membership: middle-class males (Hooker, 1967; Leznoff and Westley, 1967; Warren, 1974), female impersonators, middle-class females (Ponse, 1977, 1978; Simon and Gagnon, 1967; Warren, 1976), feminists (Ponse, 1977, 1978), tearoom habituees (Humphreys, 1975), gay activists (Humphreys, 1972), lower-class Mexican males (Carrier, 1977), and married men. One of the effects of stigma on the gay world is that many of these communities, since they are secret, are very hard to find by people who want homosexual companionship and sexual contact. Indeed, one of the effects of secrecy and the lack of homosexual reference groups may be that the "choice" of gay communities on the part of newly identified homosexuals may be partly a matter of chance: whether the "leather," middle-class, secret, gay liberation or other group is contacted first through initial gay contacts.

Whatever the choice of gay community, however, adaptation to life as a homosexual is shaped by that community. The most important function of the gay world for the individual's adaptation is its provision of positive role-models and reference groups which can act as counters to the negativity of the larger society. Ironically, conversion to a gay identity can be facilitated by this very negativity. Socialized into the belief that homosexuals are nasty perverts, persons experience a "phenomenological shock" of realization that homosexuals appear as "normal" as themselves:

> When shock is added to previous homosexual interests and activities, the possibility of conversion becomes a very real one, once again highlighting the irony that stigmatization can ... promote affiliation with the stigmatized group. The shock of normalcy would not be possible if the learning of bizarreness had not preceded it. (Warren, 1974, p. 157)

There are several additional ways in which stigmatization serves to promote gay identification. The gay world is isolated from the straight world, in the main, and gays are subject to persecution by members of the straight world. Both these factors tend to enhance the significance of the community for its members (Simmel, 1950). Further, the fact that the homosexual stigma teaches that homosexuals are types of persons, not simply persons engaging in certain behaviors, further convinces the gay that she or he is a committed homosexual, today and in the past and future.

Today individuals have an overt as well as a secret gay community with which to identify. The overt gay world sees disclosure not only as a personal choice but as a political weapon in the fight against stigma; reluctant gays may be encouraged to "come out of the closet" despite any potentially harmful consequences for the individual (Humphreys, 1972; Neuhring and Fein, 1976; Ponse, 1977, 1978). Nevertheless, many gays within the activist communities remain reluctant to disclose their homosexuality to family, friends or perhaps work colleagues (Ponse, 1978), while some gays within the secret communities have disclosed their homosexuality to others (Warren, 1974). Thus, secrecy and overtness characterize individual relationships as well as types of community.

Not surprisingly, the overt gay communities show similarities to the activist communities of the visibly stigmatized. Like blacks and other minorities, gays have a range of political organizations from the conservative Mattachine society (compare the NAACP) to the relatively radical Gay Butterfly (compare the Black Panthers). Like blacks, women, the aged, and other minorities, gays have sought to encourage general use of their own identity labels (gay instead of homosexual, black instead of Negro, woman instead of girl). In the overt communities, some groups identify themselves with terms such as "faggot" or "dyke"; joking usage removes the sting from even the most hurtful antigay words.

Humor is one way in which gays learn to cope with stigma. Another way is what Berger and Luckmann (1967) call "nihilation" (see also Ponse, 1978; Warren, 1974), a process which is similar to therapy but with an opposite intent. Therapy attempts to bring "deviants" back into the fold of "normalcy" while nihilation reduces "normalcy" to a subcategory of "deviance":

> Therapy uses a conceptual machinery to keep everyone within the universe (world) in question. Nihilation uses a similar machinery to liquidate conceptually everything *outside* the same universe. The threat of heterosexual life can be conceptually liquidated by looking upon it as inferior, no fun, sexually inhibited. Second, nihilation involves the more ambitious attempt to account for all deviant definitions of reality in terms of concepts belonging to one's own universe. For example . . . homosexual theoreticians may argue that all men are by nature homosexual—or at the very least, bisexual. Otherwise why are there such stringent laws against homosexuality? Antihomosexual prejudice can thus be transformed into secret desires—an affirmation of the homosexual universe which is ostensibly negated. (Berger and Luckmann, 1967, pp. 116–19)

Both the secret and the overt communities make use of nihilation and humor to lessen the hurt of stigma and rejection. Both types of community are significant to their members, both as reference groups and sources of identity and as refuges from the hostile straight world. Beyond this commonality there is some sparse indication of different implications, for gay experience, of secrecy and overtness. Secrecy tends to intensify the split between the gay and straight worlds, giving secret gays the sense of living in an unreal world when they are among straights, and a parallel sense of experiencing reality and the "true self" only when they are in their own community (Warren, 1974). Bisexuals tend to be excluded from the secret gay world, because their presence is a threat to secrecy, and because it dilutes the significance of a committed gay identity.

The overt communities may either attempt integration with portions of the straight world, or remain aloof. For example, some gay political groups attempt affiliation with left-wing radical movements, women, or ethnic minorities, although they may find themselves rejected by these groups (Humphreys, 1972; Warren and DeLora, forthcoming). In some politicized gay groups there is less commitment to gay identity and more tolerance of bisexuality than in secret groups. Ponse (1978) found that a bisexual identity was seen as a viable option, and even sometimes a preferable one, by activist lesbians. Neuhring and Fein (1976) indicate that about half of the female and male activist respondents at a "gay-in" where they distributed sixty-eight questionnaires identified themselves as bisexual. In contrast (although there was unfortunately no parallel questionnaire), Warren's (1974) secretive male respondents expressed dislike of bisexual "fence sitters":

> [M]en who define themselves as bisexual are generally excluded from the secret gay community, although they may be welcome as bed partners. Bisexuality as a self-definition is regarded both as an instance of bad faith and as an exhibition of a lack of commitment to the gay community. (Warren, 1974, p. 135)

The existence of both secret and overt communities within the gay world leads to some alienation and even hostility between them. Each group regards the other as an inadequate representation, to the straight world, of what gays are "really like" (Humphreys, 1972; Ponse, 1978; Warren, 1974). Secret gays may also fear stigmatization through affiliation with overt gays: "Since secret homosexuals usually interact cautiously, if at all, with more open gays, extremely few secret homosexuals appeared in the (open) community and did so only for special occasions" (Neuhring and Fein, 1976, p. 16).

There is additional conflict between the gay world and those groups with whom gays do not wish to be classified by straights—for example, pedophiles, transvestites, and transsexuals (Warren, 1974). Gays are aware that the straight world sees them as child-molesters, as effeminate, or as promiscuous; some gay groups may go out of their way to disidentify with "chicken hawks," transsexuals, or transvestites:

> You get into a transvestite type thing—a person very definitely has a problem all of their own. . . . When you get into people physically wanting to change, it's a mental fixation, it's a type of feeling, I suppose where there's a feeling of inadequacy as far as being a man is concerned, or logically, um, a domineering mother, you know, a very weak father . . . I don't think many gay kids really enjoy transvestites' type thing. (Male respondent, quoted in Warren, 1974, p. 136)

In their attempt to mitigate society's stigma, in turn, transsexuals and transvestites attempt to disidentify themselves in the public mind from homosexuals.

GAYS IN A STRAIGHT WORLD

Individual gays attempt to evade, confront, or repair their stigma: gay groups remain apart from, or attempt to integrate with, the straight world. The future of gay-straight relations in this country depends upon the actions of gay individuals and groups in the face of stigma and upon the reactions of straight individuals and groups to either an overt, activist stance or a secretive, closeted stance on the part of gays.

At first glance the situation appears simple: the overt gays—like blacks and women before them—will fight and vanquish stigma by coming out of the closet and asserting their rights. However, there may be an alternative consequence: an exacerbation of the homosexual stigma by "coming out of the closet." The future development of gay-straight relationships is dependent upon (1) the depth of the homosexual stigma and (2) the way in which the general public perceives the causes of homosexuality.

In taking the position that antihomosexuality—aptly labeled "homophobia" by members of gay liberation—is an extremely deep and strong sentiment, I realize that I am going out on what may be an unsupportive and unsupported limb.[5] Some scholars regard the stigma as less strong, especially among educated groups (Marmor, personal communication). But I would agree with Klaitch (1974) with regard to both male and female homosexuality that

> stigma surrounds lesbianism in our society. In the late sixties, a Gallop poll showed the 76% of respondents felt that homosexuality was a sickness; and a Louis Harris survey showed that 63% of respondents believed that homosexuals were harmful to American life. In addition, a 1969–1973 study conducted by the Institute for Sex Research [Indiana] showed that the attitudes of 3000 respondents were largely negative; 86% objected to homosexual relations without love, 70% objected to homosexual relations *with* love. (1974, p. 11)

Homophobia, I believe is not only widespread but deep-rooted. Tripp concurs and notes that

> murder, graft, and a host of violent crimes, though strongly taboo, fail to stir the intensely personalized emotions that can still be aroused by the homosexual. . . . To the great mass of the population, taut with the rigors of conventionality and heavily invested in the symbols if not the letter of moral law, any suggestion of a fully acceptable homosexuality is worse than abhorrent. It is as if the very foundations of their beliefs are being threatened. . . . The result is a fiercely dangerous set of emotions that has proved itself capable of corrupting every channel of enlightenment. (1975, p. 241)

---

5. There is a possibility that persons are threatened most by homosexual strangers, but far less by homosexuals discovered among their own circles of intimates and family of origin.

Tripp analyzes the psychic forces behind homophobia, and reasons that "homosexuality can touch people, can involve them vicariously, in ways that serious offenses do not," because the sexual behaviors involved are common to everyday experience in ways in which graft and murder are not. Thus, it is not surprising that the fear of homosexuality intensifies in adolescence and adulthood, when sex behaviors of all kinds become better understood and more taboo. Fear of sexuality combines, in homophobia, with fear of those who violate established sex-role conventions in appearance and activity. As Tripp points out, "for most people, one of the most disturbing images of homosexuality is that of two men kissing, for it is easily imagined and sharply at odds with what is expected" (1975, p. 241).

The homosexual is threatening; the overt homosexual is more threatening; the closer the homosexual stranger is in the experience of the homophobe, the more she or he is threatening. Warren and DeLora (forthcoming) found that in attempts by a university gay student union to attain recognition from other students and faculty, more success attended the use of "disembodied access"—the writing and sending of written documents—than "embodied access," where the gays demonstrated in person in an attempt to gain support. It is not surprising, therefore, that the Dade County debate centered on the issue of allowing homosexuals to "come out of the closet." Out of the closets, they would not only be "perverted" role-models and reference groups for growing children, they would also be an immediate reminder of the threat of homosexuality for adults.

A second theme in the Dade County controversy, besides the theme of role-modeling, was a debate concerning the causes of homosexuality. The etiology of homosexuality is not only of interest to social and behavioral scientists; it has ramifications for nonscientists' treatment of homosexuals.[6] William Raspberry, a journalist and self-styled liberal "nonbigot," wrote an editorial in favor of Anita Bryant's position on homosexuals both because of the role-modeling issue and because of the underlying theory of causation upon which the issue hinges:

6. The two theories of the etiology of homosexuality are that homosexuality is an acquired taste (therefore "catching" and also morally blameworthy) or that it is an inborn or determinately acquired condition (therefore not "catching" and not morally blameworthy). Antigays tend to favor the acquired taste explanation, for reasons indicated in the text. Gays tend to favor the inborn preference theory, as Warren (1974) and Hooker (1967) note.

The majority of those whom I have interviewed believe that they were born as homosexuals, or that familial factors operating very early in their lives determined the outcome. In any case, it is a fate over which they have no control, and in which they have no choice. It follows as a consequence that the possibility of changing to a heterosexual pattern is thought to be extremely limited. To fight against homosexuality is to fight against the inevitable, since they are fighting against their own "nature" in essential form, as they experience it. (Hooker, 1967, p. 183).

"Look, as long as a homosexual is doing a good job and not flaunting his homosexuality, there's no problem," one member of the (Dade County Save Our Children) group said. "But if he is allowed to walk up and down and say he's a homosexual, that could affect the morals of our children, particularly in the case of teachers, Scout leaders, recreation leaders, and so on. That's the real fear."

It is a fear widely shared, in large measure because no one seems quite sure how people come to be homosexual. If it is an inborn predisposition, as some believe, then "straight" children would not be subject to major influence.

But if homosexuality is an acquired taste, as Miss Bryant insists, not many parents would want their children placed in circumstances in which they might acquire it. (Raspberry, 1977, p. 7)

As indicated earlier, current psychiatric theory locates the development of homosexual predisposition in early childhood, not during later socialization in a process of conscious choice. But Anita Bryant and people like her believe that homosexuality is just such an arbitrary choice, and that children who are exposed to homosexual teachers will eagerly embrace them as role-models. As Goffman (1963) saw, homosexuality is seen in our society as a moral choice and therefore a moral failing, not as an innate—or early-acquired—predisposition.

The evidence is that the Anita Bryants are in fact wrong; homosexuality is not chosen during the years of sexual development, nor is the development of homosexual predispositions dependent upon the availability of role-models. However, it is quite possible for an adolescent to make a conscious choice of homosexual behavior, but only *because* homosexuality is stigmatized, and therefore can be used as a weapon against parents by hostile teenagers. The removal of the homosexual stigma would prevent this type of conscious choice.

It is probably those whose self-image is "liberal non-bigot" who are concerned with the underlying etiological issue rather than the "badness" of homosexuals per se; the pure homophobic position is adequate, as Tripp (1975, p. 279) suggests, for the majority of conservatives. There is also a minority of heterosexuals who are relatively unprejudiced against homosexuals. It is the size of this group that is an interesting topic for debate, or preferably for some type of empirical investigation. If it is fairly sizable and influential, then the overt response to the homosexual stigma might be the most successful political style. If it is miniscule, as I would fear, then an overt response can only precipitate backlash against homosexuals:

Conservatism will (never) lose its almost single-handed control of the mores. Even when religious and social dogmas undergo radical change, there are other motives for conservatism which tend to keep it at the helm, and that promise never to let it disappear. . . . Human psychology . . . induces an urge for a degree of closeness and like-mindedness that far exceeds what can be attained by mere proximity and cooperation. A sharable similarity is needed. Thus all societies tend to resist diversity and to seek a relatively narrow uniformity, especially in the emotion-laden matter of sex. (Tripp, 1975, p. 280)

Summary

As Mileski and Black (1974, p. 520) note, "At present there are no theories of homosexual behavior in social science; there are only theories of homosexual motivation." They ask, as sociologists, "What besides psychological homosexuals must be present before homosexual behavior can take place? Simply put, what social mechanisms make homosexual behavior possible?" (p. 512). I would argue that society creates its own homosexuality—that the forms homosexuality takes in our society, whether in behavior, identity, or community, are profoundly influenced by stigma.

The homosexual stigma defines homosexuality as a condition rather than a behavior, and—psychiatric evidence to the contrary—as a moral failing. Stigma inhibits homosexual identification in adolescence and adulthood, but fails to inhibit childhood homosexual experimentation. As heterosexual adolescents and adults learn to link the childhood imagery of "perverts" with specific sex practices, they become increasingly fearful of the "perverts" who practice them.

The repression of homosexual desires because of stigma can cause psychological and related social problems. Homosexuals sometimes suffer from direct job and relationship discrimination, but more often suffer from the fear of discovery and the potential loss of jobs, housing, family and friends. Some homosexuals learn to hate themselves because they have learned that homosexuals, as a group, are sick and evil. As Marmor (1975, p. 1517) summarizes:

> The social and legal consequences of stereotypically labeling an entire group of human beings as mentally ill—or suffering from psychopathology, a euphemistic alternative—are quite serious. . . . Psychiatric labeling of homosexuality as ipso facto a form of mental disorder lends authoritative weight to the basis on which homosexuals are often subjected to discrimination in employment, discharged from military service without honor, deprived of various legal rights, and sometimes confined voluntarily in mental institutions.

Individuals and groups of homosexuals may be secretive or overt. Ironically, stigmatization of homosexuals and other groups serves to reinforce commitment to gay identities and life-styles once the homosexual has "come out." Both secrecy and disclosure reinforce commitment to the gay world and the gay self in a situation of persecution by the straight world. Secrecy and disclosure, as individual choices, involve psychological costs and benefits. As collective choices, secrecy and overtness have consequences for the future relationship of straights and gays in the context of a society in which the homosexual stigma is both broad and deep.

REFERENCES

Berger, P. L., and Luckmann, T. 1967. *The social construction of reality.* Garden City, New York: Doubleday.

Blumstein, P. W., and Schwartz, P. 1977. Bisexuality in men. In C. A. B. Warren ed., *Sexuality: Encounters, identities and relationships* (Beverly Hills, Calif.: Sage Publications).

———. 1976. Bisexuality in women. in *Archives of Sexual Behavior* 5: 171–81.

Carrier, J. M. 1977 Family attitudes and Mexican male homosexuality. In C. A. B. Warren ed., *Sexuality: Encounters, identities and relationships,* (Beverly Hills, Calif.: Sage Publications), pp. 99–115.

Cory, D. W. 1951. *The homosexual in America.* New York: Greenberg.

Dank, B. 1971. Coming out in the gay world. *Psychiatry.* 34: 180–97.

———. 1974. *Symbolic interactionism and the homosexual identity.* Paper presented at a joint session of the American Sociological Association and Society for the Study of Social Problems Annual Meetings, Montreal.

DeLora, J. S., and Warren, C. A. B. 1977. *Understanding sexual interaction.* Boston: Houghton Mifflin.

Epstein, J. 1970. Homo/Hetero: The struggle for sexual identity. *Harper's Magazine.* 241:37–51.

Goffman, E. 1963. *Stigma: notes on the management of spoiled identity.* Englewood Cliffs, N.J.: Prentice-Hall.

Hooker, E. 1967. The homosexual community. In J. H. Gagnon and W. Simon, eds., *Sexual Deviance* (New York: Harper & Row), pp. 167–84.

Humphreys, L. 1972. *Out of the closets: The sociology of homosexual liberation.* Englewood Cliffs, N.J.: Prentice-Hall.

———. 1975. *Tearoom trade: Impersonal sex in public places,* 2nd ed. Chicago: Aldine Publishing.

Karlen, A. 1971. *Sexuality and homosexuality: A new view,* New York: W. W. Norton.

Klaitch, D. 1974. *Woman + woman: Attitudes toward lesbianism,* New York: William Morrow.

Leznoff, M., and Westley, W. 1967. The middle class homosexual community. In J. H. Gagnon and W. Simon, eds., *Sexual Deviance* (New York: Harper & Row), pp. 184–96.

Los Angeles Times. Pt. 1, June 6, 1977, p. 7.

Lyman, S., and Scott M. 1970. *A sociology of the absurd.* New York: Appleton-Century-Crofts.

Marmor, J. 1975. Homosexuality and sexual orientation disturbances. In A. M. Freedman, H. I. Kaplan, and B. J. Sadock, eds., *Comprehensive Textbook of Psychiatry,* vol. 2 (Baltimore: Williams & Wilkins), pp. 1510–20.

Mileski, M., and Black D. J. 1974. The social organization of homosexuality. In A. Skolnick and J. Skolnick eds., *Intimacy, Family and Society* (Boston: Little, Brown).

Miller, M. 1971. *On being different: What it means to be a homosexual.* New York: Random House.

Neuhring, E., and Fein S. B. 1976. Deviant identity and disclosure as tacit decisions. Paper presented at the Society for the Study of Social Problems Annual Meetings, New York.

Neuhring, E., and Tyler, M. 1974. The gay college student: Perspectives for mental health professionals. *Counseling Psychologist* 4: 64–72.

Newton, E. *Mother camp:*

Pagelow, M. Lesbian Mothers. An unpublished paper.

Ponse, B. 1978. *Identities in the lesbian world: The social construction of self.* Westport, Conn.: Greenwood Press.

———. 1977. Secrecy in the lesbian world. In C. A. B. Warren, ed., *Sexuality: Encounters, Identities and Relationships* (Beverly Hills, Calif.: Sage Publications), pp. 53–78.

Raspberry, W. 1977. Could gay rights be wrong after all? *Los Angeles Times,* 3 May, part 2, p. 7.

Reiss, A. J. Jr. 1964. The social integration of queers and peers In H. S. Becker ed., *The Other Side* (New York: Free Press).

Sagarin, E. 1974. Homosexuality and the homosexual: An overview of the former and a denial of the reality of the latter. Paper presented at the American Sociological Association and Society for the Study of Social Problems Annual Meetings, Montreal.

Simmel, G. 1950. *The sociology of Georg Simmel.* New York: Free Press.

Simon, W., and Gagnon, J. H. 1967. Femininity in the lesbian community. *Social Problems* 15:212–21.

Tripp, C. A. 1975. *The homosexual matrix.* New York: McGraw-Hill.

Warren, C. A. B., and DeLora J. S. (1978) Student protest in the 1970s: the gay student union and the military. *Urban Life.* pp. 67–90.

Warren, C. A. B. 1974 *Identity and community in the gay world.* New York: John Wiley.

———. 1976. Women among men: Females in the male homosexual community. *Archives of Sexual Behavior* 4:157–69.

Weinberg, M. S., and Williams, C. J. 1974. *Male homosexuals: Their problems and adaptations.* New York: Oxford University Press.

Williams, C. J., and Weinberg, M. S. 1971. *Homosexuals and the military: A study of less than honorable discharge.* New York: Harper & Row.

7 / Identities in the Emerging Gay Culture

LAUD HUMPHREYS
BRIAN MILLER

> The patterns of adult homosexuality are conse-
> quent upon the social structures and values that
> surround the homosexual after he becomes, or
> conceives of himself as, homosexual rather than
> upon original and ultimate causes.
>
> Simon and Gagnon, 1967

This chapter is concerned with cultural factors and their impact upon the formation of personal identities. We deal first with the salient features of identity theory. Second, we present a typology of cultural units, defining and exemplifying three cultural subcategories. Third, we note the emergence of a gay culture during the 1970s. Finally, we illustrate the interaction between individuals and their cultural environment with a discussion of findings from the authors' research on homosexual husbands whose personal histories recapitulate the phylogeny of gay culture. (For discussions of lesbian identity and culture, see: Berzon and Leighton, 1979; Jay and Young, 1979; Lewis, 1979; Martin and Lyon, 1972; Vida, 1978; Wolf, 1979.)

CULTURE AND IDENTITY FORMATION

In discussing identity formation, Erikson sees it as residing *"in the core of the individual* and yet also *in the core of his communal culture"* (1968, p. 22, italics his). Stone (1962), Klapp (1969), and Rainwater (1970) reach nearly identical definitions of this interactional process. Rainwater's summary of the process is as follows:

A valid identity is one in which the individual finds congruence between who he feels he is, who he announces himself to be, and where he feels his society places him. . . . As individuals seek to build identities valid in terms of their own needs, they use the resources—the values, norms, and social techniques—which their culture makes available to them. Each individual tries on identities that emerge from the cultural material available to him and tests them by making appropriate announcements. (1970, p. 375)

Although the person's physiological and psychological resources constitute the raw material from which an identity is constructed, the patterns that govern the task are supplied by the cultural milieu.

The cultural womb supplies both patterns and equipment for identity formation, and its relative amplitude tends to determine the range of meaning which persons may find within it. If individual identities are shaped through interaction with the cultural environment, it follows that the more diverse and complete the cultural unit's normative and institutional characteristics.

By contrast, a relatively impoverished cultural entity provides its members with limited models for building personal identities. When the culture is severely restricted, its participants may see themselves as worthless people (Rainwater, 1970, p. 374). Their sense of self may be characterized as negative or incapable of inspiring pride, or it might produce self-hatred. Observers have described the tendency of oppressed persons to succumb to shame or to be incapacitated by appropriating the social contempt that others have for them (Humphreys, 1979a; Liebow, 1967, p. 71).

Identity formation is a life-long task for everyone, but it has been exacerbated for those groups which have lacked a supportive cultural milieu. Consequently, the history of ethnic minorities, women, and gays has been one of securing a cultural context in which to assuage problems of self worth and identity. In order to explore the developmental paths taken by such groups, the next section establishes a means of classifying the various cultural entities that nourish and shape identity formation.

A Typology of Cultural Units

Given the profound impact of cultural environments on identity formation, it is essential to establish a means of classifying the various cultural entities that nourish, restrict, and otherwise shape personalities. As used by social scientists, "culture" is both too broad in meaning and too ill defined to serve for analytical purposes. Any group that manifests distinctive values and mores may be described as cultural; and these social units are seen as extending over a range that includes the regular patrons of a neighborhood bar, members of a juvenile gang, ethnic minorities, the citizens of a nation, as well as all those who inherit the Judeo-Christian tradition. Our typology, on the other hand, makes clarifying distinctions between cultural units.

We view cultural entities in terms of units that may overlap, but the smaller groups are generally included within or about the boundaries of a larger cultural group. The smallest cultural entities, narrowly confined to a particular place and quite circumscribed in duration, we choose to call "scenes," a term that is often employed by those who participate in them. Our use of this noun to designate the small, normative group is much narrower than that employed by Irwin (1977), who applies the term to any "alternative design for living" in a wide range from popular psychology enthusiasts to surfers, hippies, and drug addicts.

Scenes, by our definition, are cultural groups that have distinctive, if partial, sets of values, a high degree of differential association, and an argot that helps members identify each other. Members support and train novices in special skills that are largely avocational in nature. It is on this point, as we shall see, that they depart from a pattern common to subcultures. Whereas the skills communicated in subcultural groups provide valuable assistance in earning a living, those learned in scenes usually contribute only to recreational development.

Scenes require face-to-face interaction on the part of participants and involve groups which, if not actually small in numbers (a disco scene, for example, might involve over a thousand people in a single evening), are tightly localized. Not only are scenes normally organized around recreational activities, but they manifest a territoriality that is easily mapped. Regular participants in scenes often rely on published directories (as with gay bars, ski resorts, or nudist camps) or leads to be gained from the "personals" columns of newspapers (for singles parties or sadomasochistic contacts), in addition to word-of-mouth referrals. Scenes, then, are distinguished from other cultural units by both their localized and recreational nature. Although scenes frequently evidence a profound impact on the day-to-day behavior of participants, identities formed around such recreational activities tend to be only partial and transient.

GAY SCENES

Many homosexual scenes, like heterosexual ones, are organized around the need for making erotic contacts. Nearly all American towns have at least one homosexual scene. It may be no more than a bus terminal or a freeway rest stop (Troiden, 1974), where men establish contacts for sexual recreation. In other communities, it may be a stylish resort or athletic club.

The scenes of casual sex have often been viewed as typifying the "world" of homosexuality. It is in this connection that Simon and Gagnon write of the homosexual subculture as "an impoverished cultural unit" with only limited content. "This derives from the fact that the community members often have only their sexual commitment in common" (1967, p. 183). There are several reasons for such stereotyping of the homosexual community in terms of its scenes for impersonal, instant sex. In the first place, because they are settings for effecting interpersonal contact—what Hooker (1965, pp. 95–96) appropriately calls "markets"—they are situated in public places. Outsiders may chance upon them, and they are accessible to observation by disinterested parties, the police, and social scientists. Social control personnel, such as those charged with "peacekeeping," are apt to encounter homosexuals only in these scenes; therefore, virtually all homosexual arrests occur in such settings. Finally, due to the dramatic, often erotic, nature of encounters that occur in these scenes, they are apt to be the subject of both fictional and documentary accounts (Rechy, 1977).

Cruising scenes, however, constitute only one of several general categories of scenes that we have been able to identify as connected to the homosexual community. In addition to the social groupings that form around impersonal sex, there are several types of social scenes, recreational or sports scenes, consciousness-raising groups, and religious or political organizations.

Although social scenes in the gay world function, in part, to facilitate sexual liaisons, their purpose extends far beyond that limited role. For example, there are gay student unions, which often serve political, therapeutic, and consciousness-raising goals, as well as social ones. Gay discos and bars, like those in the non-gay world, serve as settings for display and performance of affective behavior. Names of "cowboy," "leather," and "piano" bars, such as Saddles, The Strap, and Napoleon's, emphasize this expressive function.

Other scenes in the homosexual community are organized around recreational pursuits and sports. Baseball teams, motorcycle and yachting clubs, canoeing excursions, and ski trips have been organized in several metropolitan centers. Gay marching bands perform in cities such as San Francisco and Los Angeles. In such settings, one may easily observe the communication of recreational skills that typifies all scenes.

Rap groups constitute a rapidly developing phenomenon in the gay world. Others, spawned by the emphasis on consciousness-raising that followed the emergence of gay liberation in 1969, now involve a wide variety of therapeutic and group-encounter forms.

Finally, there are political and religious organizations that tend to fall between the categories of scenes and subcultures, depending upon the degree of organization and the power achieved by joint action. These would include not only the many congregations of the Metropolitan Community Church but gay Jewish congregations, Dignity for the Roman Catholics, Integrity for the Episcopalians, and other denominational groups. Political organizations have proliferated since the Dade County elections of 1977, but there are several of long standing, such as the Alice B. Toklas, the Stonewall, and the Walt Whitman, Democratic clubs. As congregations are able to support a full-time ministry and political groups manage to enter openly gay candidates in electoral contests, these scenes tend to become subcultural, providing their members with occupational skills.

SUBCULTURES

The concept of subculture was first defined by Gordon (1947) as a regional, ethnic, or class "sub-division of a national culture." Following the lead of Sutherland (1939), who discussed such groups under the heading of "behavior systems," Cohen (1955), Yinger (1960), and Wolfgang and Ferracuti (1967) developed the theory of subculture in order to explain juvenile gangs, to analyze delinquent "contracultures," or to provide an integrated theory for differential rates of violence. Although there is little consensus among these writers as to the precise characteristics of subcultures, they do agree on the general definition of a subculture as "a normative system of some group or groups smaller than the whole society" (Wolfgang and Ferracuti, 1967, p. 139).

In order to operationalize the concept so that it allows systematic classification and meets the principle of mutual exclusiveness (Chafetz, 1978, pp. 66–67), we narrow the definition of subculture and specify its core characteristics:

1. Subcultural groups must manifest differential association in two ways: first, members must be able to engage in face-to-face interaction; second, participants must be able to specify a major portion of their time, both at work and in play, as being spent with others in the subculture.
2. There must be a discernible and distinctive value system evident in the subculture. These norms are distinguished from those of the dominant culture as *refractions* of the general normative system (Gordon, 1947). If the norms are in almost total opposition to those of the overall culture, it is a "counterculture" rather than a subculture (Yinger, 1960). In other words, the distinctive values of the subculture are derivative in terms of the relative emphasis given to particular norms, some being disproportionately magnified and others suppressed or de-emphasized.
3. Subcultures inevitably evidence a distinctive argot that includes not only a specific vocabulary but a manner of expression. This is often found in conjunction with other differences in style, dress, and folkways that distinguish those in the subculture from others in the general culture.
4. Subcultures foster special skills in their members which are consequen-

tial in terms of occupational choice and career development (Humphreys, 1972, p. 72). Participation in the subculture generally involves a period of apprenticeship.

Because subcultural theory owes its development chiefly to American criminologists who were concerned with gangs of youths and others engaged in criminalized or stigmatized behavior, subcultures are often viewed as being "deviant" and culturally impoverished when compared to the parent culture. This characterization does not hold, however, for many social groups that fit our definition. Because subcultures tend to form around certain occupations or to encourage differential participation in work that requires the communicated skills, there are many subcultures with distinctive normative refractions whose members are neither stigmatized or nonconforming. Psychoanalysts in the city of Chicago constitute a subculture, as do the firemen of any particular department, airline crews, television cameramen, policemen, and workers on the high steel. Most occupations that require a great deal of interdependence in dealing with high risks of either a physical or career nature give rise to subcultures.

EXAMPLES FROM GAY SUBCULTURES

With the growth of gay liberation, subcultures have proliferated in the gay community. One type consists of groups of gay merchants, bar owners, and others whose living depends on a clientele that is largely homosexual. San Francisco has a strong Tavern Guild and an Association of Castro Street Merchants; New York and Key West have formed similar groups.

Some cities have gay subcultures that have been in existence for a longer period of time, such as those involved in the business of style: designers, antique and art dealers, decorators, and architects. An even older occupational subculture is that which forms around street hustlers (Hoffman, 1979). Similar to their heterosexual counterparts, these men affiliate to exchange information and provide mutual protection.

Where there are enough gay couples massed in a community, several such pairs may form a subculture. One such group we have observed in a Midwestern city fosters a network of mutually profitable business interests. The six pairs of lovers who make up this subculture invest in the businesses of other participants, refer clients to one another, and make joint purchases of commercial properties.

The same is true of gay teachers groups and the Gay Academic Union. Here, too, professional contacts are made, professors provide direction and encouragement to those engaged in dissertation research, and informal apprenticeships are formed. Freed from a sense of isolation, members of this subculture often shift their scholarly efforts to topics of concern to the homosexual community. Already this group has produced books of readings, a scholarship program for gay graduate students, and a number of national and regional conferences.

Various professional associations have gay caucuses that tend to develop subcultural characteristics. Large and powerful subcultures have emerged in connection with the American Psychological and Psychiatric Associations, the American Library Association, the Modern Language Association, and the American Sociological Association. Through such alliances, members are made aware of publication outlets for papers and are provided with advice for gaining specialized research funding. Physicians for human rights organizations on both coasts have become important reference groups for their hundreds of lesbian and gay members. Other subcultures center around the concerns of their gay lawyer or engineer constituencies, and smaller groups emerge each year in connection with a variety of professional organizations.

There are gay subcultures that center around occupational interests such as recording, writing, filmmaking, and newspaper production: for example, Olivia Records, the Diana Press, the Mariposa Film Group, and Boston's *Gay Community News*. These gay collectives, united by their exclusion from mainstream business and their desire to overcome prejudice, have impacted the values of the emerging gay satellite culture.

SATELLITE CULTURES

Eliot (1949) recommends the use of "satellite culture" to designate a cultural entity that has become so extensive and diverse that it spawns subcultures of its own. In this way, such aggregates may be differentiated from national, society-wide cultures, on the one hand, and from subcultures with differential (exclusionary) membership and specific foci, on the other. Large, geographically dispersed social classes or ethnic groups are more accurately described as satellite cultures than as subcultures.

Participants in satellite cultures may enjoy direct interaction with relatively few of the unit's total membership, which may number in the millions and be distributed over a wide area. Their *interactional* identification may be with a close-knit religious subculture (e.g., Hasidic Jews, a gay congregation, a Black Muslim sect) or a secular one (e.g., an academic or professional group) but their *historical* identification is with larger satellite cultures.

If subcultural participants are isolated for long periods of time from members of their gang, occupation, or religious sect, subcultural participants tend to stray from the group's normative structure and patterns of behavior. Their satellite cultural identity as Jew or Mormon, black or gay, on the other hand, may persevere through years of social isolation from others of their kind. The *heritage* of a satellite culture provides in depth and breadth what subcultures offer only in relatively brief bursts of intensity.

Satellite cultures develop channels of communication that extend far beyond the house organs and word-of-mouth means that characterize subcultural units. They offer published histories and collections of literature, periodicals that include news events of common interest as well as feature articles, along with autobiographical accounts that emphasize participation in the group and its vicissitudes. To a large extent, these forms of communication replace and compensate for the personal interaction that typifies subcultures.

Due largely to this literary manifestation of their values and cultural heritage, the normative systems of satellite cultures are more fully developed and extensive than those evidenced by subcultural groups. Satellite cultures continue to train members in special skills and to maintain distinctive styles of expression, folkways, and jargon; they therefore provide a greater variety of expression for their members than do the fragmented and limited value-sets characteristic of subcultures.

EMERGENCE OF THE GAY SATELLITE CULTURE

The contemporary gay world can no longer be conceptualized as a "deviant subculture," but more appropriately as a satellite culture. It has become increasingly diverse, generating subcultures of its own. Acknowledged gays may now choose from a wide range of career possibilities, benefit from upfront role models, and build pride around a common heritage. Censorship, distortion, and bowdlerization have long excluded homosexual events and persons from history texts. Several major works have now moved the discussion of gay history to the forefront of academic concerns. Leading contributions to gay history have been made by Bullough (1979), D'Emilio (1978), Dover (1978), Hyde (1970), Katz (1976), Martin and Lyon (1972), and Weeks (1978).

We have not yet mentioned the institutional structures that now buttress the homosexual communities of America (Murray, 1978). Newspapers and monthly magazines provide a distinctly gay source of communication and literature, through which the heritage and the history of homosexuality are transmitted to hundreds of thousands of readers. Gay church groups hold regular services in every major urban center of the nation and in some state penal institutions. Social service centers, operated by gays, provide trained counseling staffs, employment services, free medical clinics, and a variety of social events. (Humphreys, 1979b)

It is no longer necessary to seek other homosexuals in bars or clandestine cruising areas. Friends or prospective partners may be found in rap groups, social clubs, political meetings, or at church. The dozen largest urban areas of North America now have readily identifiable gay neighborhoods with heavy populations of same-sex couples. Each of these districts features, not only openly gay bars and restaurants, but clothiers, bookstores, laundromats, a variety of shops, doctors, psychotherapists, lawyers, dentists, and realtors that cater to a gay clientele. The gay ambience of these communities is so pervasive that conventionally-identified persons visiting them may experience culture disorientation.

It should be noted, however, that this catalogue of institutions, scenes, and subcultures applies only to the larger urban areas. The variety of settings for interaction with other homosexuals decreases sharply as one moves from New York, San Francisco, or Los Angeles into smaller cities and towns (Levine, 1979). It is still appropriate to speak of "the homosexual subculture" of Omaha, Albuquerque, or Albany. Residents of these cities, nevertheless, are generally aware of, and attracted to, the cultural richness available in gay meccas either through vacation travel or by reading movement publications.

In addition, the gay satellite culture exerts influence on the dominant culture. For example, it is impossible to discuss American culture without referring to the gay perspectives of Emily Dickinson, Walt Whitman, Herman Melville, Tennessee Williams, Bessie Smith, Edward Albee, Cole Porter, James Baldwin, Christopher Isherwood, Willa Cather, and W. H. Auden. Likewise, it is impossible to discuss French culture without citing the gay perspectives of Proust, Stein, Gide, Cocteau, and Genet. Overcoming resistance and even open hostility, the gay satellite culture enriches the dominant culture and gives it a clearer understanding of iteself.*

Changing Identities of Homosexual Husbands

> Individual perceptions and actions change . . .
> with increasing integration into the community.
> . . . Personal development, in many instances,
> recapitulates group development, as the individ-
> ual moves from isolation to association.
>
> *Adam*, 1978

In our studies of homosexual men who are heterosexually married, the authors discern a clear picture of the nature of the various gay cultural

---

*Although ours is a generally positive description of gay cultural emergence, gay leftists see in it at least two negative aspects: First, the satellite culture provides "an improved environment for 'gay capitalism,'" which exploits the homosexual population. "The second trend has been the emboldening of the upper middle class and cooptation of the movement. . . . adopting the symbols of conformity."(Adam, 1979: 296–297)

Rightwingers also view the development of the gay satellite culture with some dismay but from a very different perspective. Their diatribes are characterized by homophobia and sexism. Our approach is that of participant observers in the culture; whereas, they approach the phenomena as moral entrepreneurs who glimpse it only through the eyes of religious absolutists, psychiatric patients, and literary sensationalists.

entities and their impact on identity construction. Through experiences of married participants in the impersonal sex of public restrooms (Humphreys, 1970) and of gay fathers (Miller, 1978), we are able to trace the moral careers of these marginal actors as their identities are shaped through interaction with the various cultural units.

Miller finds that these men enter into marital unions thinking they can repress or overcome their homoerotic desires. Nearly all report that they married because they perceived that as the only viable means of achieving a stable home life, loyal companionship, and the pleasures of fatherhood. On the other hand, they perceived the gay world as "transitory," "impersonal," "shallow," and "ridden with violence."

Once married, the homosexual husbands are restricted from full participation in the gay culture by family responsibilities and the fear of marital dissolution as a result of disclosure. Many are further limited by a lack of social and occupational resources. Their jobs would be threatened by exposure of their homosexual activities; they lack geographical access to gay institutions; or they are precluded from involvement by poor health or religious considerations. Under these circumstances, participation in gay life is peripheral and furtive.

Having only sexual needs in common with unmarried and more fully acculturated gay men, homosexual husbands meet them usually in clandestine sexual markets: tearooms, parks, highway rest stops, and the streets where hustlers and hitchhikers may provide sexual outlets. Their involvement, therefore, is limited to gay scenes. In these recreational settings, value systems are weak and cultural content is fragmented and circumscribed: "gay" has only a sexual meaning and sex, limited to genital activity, is furtive and highly impersonal. The identities of these marginals, therefore, tend to ambivalence. They see themselves as being like other men, but with a need for supplementary sexual relief; or they define themselves as bisexual. If they admit to being homosexual, they tend to hate that "condition" of their character and to avoid a gay label by emphasizing their marital status and minimizing their homoerotic fantasies (Warren, 1974, p. 158).

Lower-class husbands, frequently of a Roman Catholic or Protestant fundamentalist background, tend to view themselves as "trapped in a miserable marriage." Unable to expand their repertoire of sexual markets or to achieve subcultural involvement, they face the danger of arrest from involvement with teenage boys or as a by-product of frequent tearoom encounters. One such respondent in the gay fathers study has endured ten arrests for "lewd and lascivious conduct" in public restrooms and was beaten up in an automobile outside his daughter's wedding party as a result of propositioning the best man. His wife, who knows of his homosexual activity, feels she cannot leave him because of a combination of religious and financial reasons.

Over the years of marriage, it becomes increasingly difficult for the homosexual husband to reconcile his discordant roles:

> He cannot see himself simultaneously as a worthwhile person and as a homosexual. He cannot reconcile the cognitive dissonance created between his masculine self-image and the popular image of gays as hatefully effeminate. The most he can acknowledge is that he often gets together with other men to ejaculate and that he fantasizes about men during coitus. (Miller, 1978, p. 223)

All these men report high levels of anxiety, generated by having to maintain their compartmentalized lives. They seek therapy, with generally unsatisfactory results, and endure frightening experiences in the course of their furtive cruising activities. Gradually, compartmentalization begins to disintegrate, and the marginal men seek closure.

If the family's financial resources are great enough, the husband may expand his homosexual contacts by hiring call boys and taking business trips or vacations alone, during which excursions he immerses himself in the gay world of a distant city. At this compromise stage, the homosexual husband expands both his repertoire of impersonal sex scenes and also gay social scenes. He may build up an address book of possible sexual contacts and have limited involvement with small social networks of gay friends. If he and his wife are involved in the arts or drama, this adjustment is facilitated by mutual participation in relatively tolerant groups that view homosexuality as an "eccentricity" and provide friendships with other "bisexual" husbands.

Over time, these marginal men tend to "rub the wife's nose in it," becoming increasingly flagrant in their methods of achieving homosexual contacts. Whether in response to a legal prosecution or to their husbands' promptings, wives of homosexual husbands tend to take action to terminate the marriage. When the gay spouse is locked out of his house or served with divorce papers, he experiences relief from at least part of the responsibility for failure of his marriage. Once he no longer lives with his wife and children, the gay husband begins to expand his contacts with the homosexual world, and his marginality decreases rapidly. He may now subscribe to gay publications and join a gay religious congregation or social club. He reports a rapid expansion of gay consciousness and skills, refers to himself as gay, and takes steps to form friendships with others of his sexual orientation.

In most of these cases, the immediate cause for dissolution of the marriage bonds is the establishment of a love relationship with another gay man. As such relationships intensify, homosexual husbands begin to reconstruct the social reality of the gay world as a favorable one. It is now seen as providing viable life-styles which allow for the achievement of companionship and social stability. Simultaneously, heterosexual marriage is increasingly regarded as unfulfilling.

REORGANIZING THE SYMBOLIC WORLD

Openly gay fathers, proud of their newfound identity, tend to organize their symbolic world, to a large extent, around gay culture. With the move out of the nuptial closet, all of these men report a stabilization of self-concept and a greater sense of psychological well-being. Their attitudes toward homoerotic behavior become more casual and better integrated into the fabric of everyday life. Most evidence a change in body-image, exemplified by improved physical fitness and increased pride in their appearance. Several report that, following the dissolution of their marriages, they began to use their seat belts when driving, claiming they now had more reasons to live.

These changes of identity are concomitant not only with changes in individual status but with a reassessment of the gay community. For example, married homosexuals see the gay world as not so much a community as a part-time refugee camp. It seems to be simply a cluster of furtive, impersonal sex scenes that cater to immediate sexual survival. Adding scenes to their repertoire does not free them, but merely builds a larger closet. Gay husbands eliminate the closet and achieve a positive outlook on the gay world only by expanding their connections into the more diverse satellite culture. Migration through these cultural entities is a cleansing process by which these men shed defensive aspects of their personalities and achieve a valid gay identity. For marginal, heterosexually married men, the movement from scenes through subcultures to full participation in the satellite culture is paralleled by a psychological movement from basic need fulfillment to rich self-actualization.

The exodus of one respondent typifies this process. A successful Manhattan attorney, he had long patronized the tearooms of the better hotels. As his marriage worsened, he sought psychiatric counseling in conjunction with his wife. Finding no help in that process, he contemplated suicide. Ejected from his home, he began to patronize gay bars, then participated in the Fire Island scene. Through a lover he became involved in a subculture of gay artists and a gay fathers' group, after which he began to reveal his homosexual identity to selected law partners and clients. Later he was seen to be participating in a gay pride parade up Fifth Avenue. Throughout this process he became less ego-defensive, expressed a growing pride in his appearance, shed chronic psychosomatic ailments, stabilized his self-concept, and increased his self-esteem.

In considering the case of homosexual husbands, we are able to trace parallel processes of social movement and individual development. The respondent whose biography was just summarized speaks for many of those in the gay father study when he says:

Without the gay movement, these great things that have happened in my life would have been impossible. . . . I mean, when the gay world was only tearooms, bars, and baths it offered me nothing but sexual release and shame. How could an ambitious lawyer identify with that? Now, The Movement has created lots for me and other gays to be proud of.

Summary: Cultural Elaboration and Identity Enrichment

This paper traces two parallel and inter-related processes: (1) the exodus of the gay world from a cluster of genitally-focused scenes through subcultures to the emergence of an institutionally diverse gay culture, and (2) the movement of covert individuals from peripheral involvement in gay recreational scenes to the building of enriched identities in a highly developed gay cultural context.

Writing of the homosexual man in 1968, Hoffman (1968, p. 63) states: "He looks to the public places for sex and must look elsewhere for the remaining meaning around which he can center his life." This fragmentation, he continues, "is not conducive to personal happiness or good social adjustment." Today, public places remain as scenes that constitute a portion of the gay experience, but now they can be viewed in a more insitiutionally complete gay cultural milieu where one's meaning systems may be better integrated.

In the recent past, both the cultural content of homosexuality and countless gay men have moved out of closets that precluded any but the most limited development of identity. The gay husbands' biographies illustrate how they construct valid identities from the rich store of tools and patterns provided by the emerging gay culture. Evidence indicates that personal happiness and social adjustment increase in a social context of which one may be proud.

REFERENCES

Adam, B. D. 1978. *The survival of domination: Inferiorization and everyday life.* New York: Elsevier.

———. 1979. A social history of gay politics. In M. Levine (ed.) *Gay Men: The sociology of male homosexuality.* New York: Harper and Row, Pp. 285–300.

Berzon, B. and R. Leighton (eds.) 1979. *Positively Gay.* Millbrae, California: Celestial Arts.

Bryant, A. 1977. *The Anita Bryant story: the survival of our nation's families and the threat of militant homosexuality.* Old Tappan, NJ: Fleming Revell.

Bullough, V. L. 1979. *Homosexuality: a history.* New York: New American Library.

Chafetz, J. S. 1978. *A primer on the construction and testing of theories in sociology.* Itasca, Ill.: F. E. Peacock Publishers.

Cohen, A. K. 1955. *Deliquent boys: The culture of the gang.* New York: Free Press.

D'Emilio, J. 1978. Dreams deferred. *The Body politic* 48–50 (Nov. 1978–Feb. 1979).

Dover, K. J. 1978. *Greek homosexuality.* Cambridge, Massachusettes: Harvard University Press.

Eliot, T. S. 1949. *Notes toward the definition of culture.* New York: Harcourt, Brace.

Erikson, E. H. 1968. *Identity youth and crisis.* New York: W. W. Norton.

Furnald, R. 1978. An exploratory study of male hustlers in Hollywood. Unpublished M.S.W. thesis. Los Angeles: University of Southern California.

Gagnon, J. H. 1977. *Human sexualities.* Glenview, IL.: Scott, Foresman.

Gordon, M. M. 1947. The concept of the sub-culture and its application. *Social Forces.* 26:40–42.

Hodges, A. 1977. Divided we stand. *Body Politic* 30:22–23.

Hoffman, M. 1968. *The gay world: Male homosexuality and the social creation of evil.* New York: Basic Books.

———. 1979. The male prostitute. In M. Levine (ed.) *Gay men: the sociology of male homosexuality.* New York: Harper and Row, pp. 275–284.

Hooker, E. 1965. Male homosexuals and their "worlds." In J. Marmor, ed., *Sexual inversion: The multiple roots of homosexuality* (New York: Basic Books), pp. 83–107.

Humphreys, L. 1970. *Tearoom trade: impersonal sex in public places.* Chicago: Aldine Publishing.

———. 1975. *Tearoom trade: impersonal sex in public places* (enlarged ed.). Hawthorn, NY: Aldine.

———. 1979a. Being odd against all odds. In R. Federico (ed.), *Sociology* (2nd ed.). (Reading, Massachusettes: Addison-Wesley), pp. 238–242.

———. 1979b. Exodus and identity: the emerging gay culture. In M. Levine (ed.) *Gay men: the sociology of male homosexuality.* New York: Harper and Row, pp. 134–147.

Hyde, H. M. 1970. *The love that dared not speak its name.* Boston: Little, Brown.

Irwin, J. 1977. *Scenes.* Beverly Hills, Calif.: Sage Publications.

Jay, K. and A. Young 1979. *The Gay report.* New York: Summit.

Karlen, A. 1978. Homosexuality: The scene and its students. pp. 223–248 in J. Henslin and E. Sagarin (eds.), *The sociology of sex* (revised ed.), New York: Schocken.

Katz, J. 1976. *Gay American history: lesbians and gay men in the U.S.A.* New York: Crowell.

Klapp, O. E. 1969. *Collective search for identity.* New York: Holt, Rinehart & Winston.

Lee, J. A. 1978. *Getting sex.* Don Mills, Ontario: Musson.

Levine, M. 1979. Gay Ghetto. In M. Levine, ed., *Gay men: The sociology of male homosexuality* (New York: Harper & Row).

Lewis, S. G. 1979. *Sunday's women: a report on lesbian life today.* Boston: Beacon.

Liebow, E. 1967. *Tally's corner: A study of Negro streetcorner men.* Boston: Little, Brown.

Martin, D. and P. Lyon 1972. *Lesbian/Woman.* New York: Bantam.

Miller, B. 1978. Adult sexual resocialization: Adjustments toward a stigmatized identity. *Alternative Lifestyles* 1(May):207–33.

———. 1979a. Unpromised paternity: lifestyles of gay fathers. In M. Levine (ed.), *Gay men: The sociology of male homosexuality.* New York: Harper and Row, pp. 239–252.

———. 1979b. Gay fathers and their children. *The Family Coordinator* 28 (October): 544–552.

———. 1980. "Gay men's relationships with women." in D. David and R. Brannon (eds.), The 49% Majority: The Male Gender Role (2nd ed.). Reading, MA: Addison-Wesley.

Miller, B. and Humphreys, L. 1980. Marginality and violence: sexual lifestyle as a variable in victimization. *Qualitative Sociology* 3 (May).

Murray, S. O. 1978. Ethnic communities of limited liability and the meaningfulness of "gay community." Paper read at Canadian Sociology and Anthropology meetings, June 1978, London, Ontario.

Newton, E. 1972. *Mother camp: Female impersonators in America.* Englewood Cliffs, N.J.: Prentice-Hall.

Rainwater, L. 1970. *Behind ghetto walls: Black families in a federal slum.* Chicago: Aldine Publishing.

Rechy, J. 1977. *The sexual outlaw: A documentary.* New York: Grove Press.

Reiss, A. J., Jr. 1961. The social integration of queers and peers. *Social Problems* 9:-102–20.

Simon, W., and Gagnon, J. H. 1967. Homosexuality: The formulation of a sociological perspective. *Journal of Health and Social Behavior* 8:177–85.

Stone, G. P. 1962. Appearance and the self. In A. M. Rose, ed., *Human behavior and social processes* (Boston: Houghton Mifflin), pp. 86–118.

Sutherland, E. H. 1939. *Principles of criminology,* 3rd ed. Philadelphia: J. B. Lippincott.

Troiden, R. R. 1974. Homosexual encounters in a highway rest stop. In E. Goode, and R. R. Troiden, eds., *Sexual deviance and sexual deviants.* (New York: William Morrow), pp. 211–28.

Vida, V. (ed.) 1978. *Our right to love: a lesbian resource book.* Englewood Cliffs, New Jersey: Prentice-Hall

Warren, C. A. B. 1974. *Identity and community in the gay world.* New York: John Wiley.

Weeks, J. 1978. *Coming out.* New York: Quartet.

Wolf, D. G. 1979. *The lesbian community.* Berkeley, California: University of California Press.

Wolfgang, M. E., and Ferracuti, F. 1967. *The subculture of violence.* London: Tavistock Publications.

Yinger, J. M. 1960. Contraculture and subculture. *American Sociological Review* 25:-625–35.

8 / Lesbians and Their Worlds

BARBARA PONSE

The analysis that follows is based on three years of observation and interaction in secretive and activist lesbian worlds, informal talks with many women who relate sexually and emotionally with women, and seventy-five in-depth interviews. In the course of these observations, it became clear that lesbians, or women-related women live in many different worlds. My purpose here is to indicate the configuration of two of these worlds—a world formed by secrecy and a world formed by politics—and the impact of these worlds on the formation of identity among women-related women.

First, it is necessary to define what is meant by "world." A world indicates shared experiences and perceptions by its members. It connotes shared perspectives, shared meanings and definitions, and shared ways of ordering its members, objects, and events. A world has spatial dimensions at any time its members are together, yet, unlike a community, it is not tied to any particular space. A world also implies rules, which may be more or less formalized with respect to differentiating those inside the world from those outside it. So, too, a world has rules of access and rules for establishing membership.

Worlds may be more or less elaborated. They may develop a distinctive language in addition to special meanings for terms shared with other worlds. Worlds may exist self-consciously as subsets of other worlds. That is, they may touch only a facet of human experience and accept the categories, definitions, rationales, and cosmologies of the larger world or society. On the other hand, a world may develop rationales and cosmologies that are distinct from and in conflict with those in other worlds. Worlds may be more or less rationalized, more or less specialized; we might think, for example, of the world of sports or the night world of street people. Again, a world may encompass and define the lives of its members or it may be a part-time world into and out of which members move freely. The significance of being in a particular world, such as the worlds I will discuss here, may have impact on all the other worlds in which the individual lives. Membership in a world such as the lesbian world, if known by outsiders, may block access to other worlds. Lesbians who are mothers may find, for example, that if their membership in the lesbian world is known, it may constitute grounds for circumscribing participation, if not membership, in other worlds.

A world has both experiential and cognitive dimensions. Though a world implies the presence of others, it may be invoked and experienced by an individual in interaction with herself and in the absence of others. Thus an individual may ostensibly be involved in one world but may be experiencing another world intensely. Worlds may overlap, many times unwittingly. In the case of the secretive lesbian world, great care may be taken to obscure its existence.

Simmel (1950, pp. 361–62), the theorist of secrecy in social relations, notes that secret societies emerge in conditions of public unfreedom, an observation clearly pertinent to the situation of lesbians in the larger society. The central external cause of the existence of a secretive lesbian world is the stigma that attends lesbians and lesbianism in the larger society. Lesbian activity is forbidden by law. It is negatively sanctioned by social custom and prejudice. Current legal action (Washington State Supreme Court decision regarding Gaylord in 1977) and legislative initiatives in some states, such as the Briggs initiative in California, would have lesbian *identity* and even a sympathetic or tolerant stance with respect to lesbianism and male homosexuality be grounds for loss of employment. Whether such attempts at social control come to pass, they bespeak the fear and hatred that lesbianism and male homosexuality arouse in significant quarters of American society. Lesbians, thus, are potentially or actually stigmatized in many nongay settings.

Secrecy is the device that protects the existence of the lesbian world and that keeps its members hidden from disapprobation and condemnation. However, secrecy once employed tends to extend far beyond the reasons for employing it in the first place, and begins to encompass, texture, and determine the relations that come within its sway (Simmel, 1950, p. 345). Secrecy affects the lives of the secret-keepers and those from whom the secret is kept. It is the overriding condition of relations between the lesbian world and the straight or heterosexual world, and it also affects the character of life within the lesbian world.

In general terms, relations between the gay and straight world can be characterized by pointing to two effects of secrecy: the counterfeiting of amicable relations, and the escalation of perceived differences between the two worlds, leading to the mystification of both.

Counterfeit Relations

Secrecy facilitates the appearance of amicable relations between secret keepers and those excluded from the secret. However, the relations that secrecy ostensibly permits are necessarily strained. Given the perception, accurate in many instances, that disclosure of lesbianism would disrupt relations with some heterosexuals, relationships between the concealers and those from whom something is concealed are nevertheless weakened by secrecy because it raises a barrier against true intimacy. The gay self must remain masked, and this masking of the self, in turn, colors relations between the two worlds with a sense of inauthenticity.

Social relations between secret keepers and those outside the secret, no matter how intimate they are supposed to be in terms of conventional social roles—such as relationships between mother and daughter, sister and brother, and relationships between intimate friends—become limited in their intimacy. Simmel (1950, pp. 334–35) notes that the strain that secrecy imposes on relations is escalated in the case of intimate relations. The desire to disclose the facts to intimates is always just under the surface of concealment. Lesbians who maintain secrecy with intimate others affirm that they feel cut off from being themselves. Secrecy and the fear of disapproval that its rupture would bring make relations with the heterosexual world "thinner" than they appear.

The perceived need to maintain secrecy tends to promote commitment to the gay world as a place where the gay self can be validated and accepted. At the same time, the care that must be taken in interaction with heterosexual others to obscure the gay self, renders the individual particularly alive to the gay self and the gay world. The gay self becomes salient precisely because it must be hidden. It is reiterated and reinforced in inner consciousness. The gay world is invoked within the walls of the self as a support and sanctuary.

Secrecy promotes cohesion in the secret society and tends to intensify perceived differences between the gay world and the straight world. That is, what constitutes "gayness" and "straightness" is understood as comprising qualities that characterize and structure the entire person.

The secretive lesbian world is organized for the purpose of sociability around socioemotional needs and needs for concealment and security. It is organized around needs for a milieu amenable to the development and maintenance of same-sex relations, needs for acceptance of the gay self, and needs for affiliation at times and places that will not be visible to heterosexual others.

The secretive lesbian world is located in private and semipublic places. It becomes manifest in social gatherings, in homes, in clubs and organizations, and in bars. Because its purpose is sociability, meeting places and times are informally organized. The clubs and organizations in the secretive lesbian world exist to serve a particular class or kind of lesbian, such as gay professional women, or they arise in response to a particular interest held in common by the members such as music, the visual arts, or sports. Some secretive groups of lesbians are formed in order to contribute to educational efforts in the heterosexual world about lesbianism and male homosexuality. Organizations such as the Whitman-Radcliffe Foundation may be known in the heterosexual world, but their members are not known. The Daughters of Bilitis is an organization that predates the politicization of the lesbian world. It was formed in part as a self-help organization—a source of education, information, and support for lesbians. Again, though the organization was known outside the lesbian world, its membership remains secret. What I will be focusing on here, however, is the secretive world of sociability.

The secretive lesbian world is a world of leisure. In the main, it is a world of adults. It designates times and places where lesbians can acknowledge their lesbianism in a validating, supportive environment. The secretive lesbian world is an arena for the gay selves of its members, selves which are obscured in interaction with the heterosexual world. It is places and spaces where the secret can be externalized and acknowledged.

Several features serve to delineate the lesbian world from the larger world: the form and content of relationships and interaction, gay referencing, rules of access, rules of membership and identity rules. I shall discuss each of these in turn, save identity rules. These rules obtain in both the secretive and activist lesbian worlds. I shall reserve the discussion of them until after the description of the politicized lesbian world.

Interaction in the Lesbian World

In the main, the secretive lesbian world is a world of women. However, to an extent far greater than is true among political lesbians, the secretive world intersects with the male gay world. Thus lesbians might go to "boy's" bars and to restaurants that cater to both gay men and women. In the secretive lesbian world one would encounter gay men and women with about equal frequency at private dinner parties and other social gatherings. At these mixed gay gatherings there was typically no systematic distinction about who took the lead in initiating conversation or interaction, though individual differences of course did exist. There being no gender basis for a division of labor in this regard, it seems to be negotiated on the basis of personality differences rather than from any imposed sense of roles.

"Role-playing"—that is, the approximation of male/female role-patterning—was little in evidence among the lesbians who were the subjects of this study. This lack of division—or, to put it more positively, this egalitarian form—seemed to be the mode both in groups of gay men and women as well as in those of women alone. In marginally public places such as gay bars and restaurants, one would observe separate clusterings of men and women. In private spaces with mixed groups of gay men and women, however, these clusterings did not occur. This might well be due to the fact that sexual interest is not salient between gay men and women, so that concerns of sociability predominate without the tension generated by sexual interest.

Simmel (1950, p. 370) comments on the tendency of secret societies to claim their members in a total sense. The secret excludes all persons and groups external to the secret, serving to bind the members of the secret society more closely than ever. Within the lesbian world, the bonding nature of secrecy is evidenced in the rapidity with which friendships, at least on a superficial level, are formed (Simmel, 1950, p. 369). While it is true that the more enduring bonds of friendship are developed over time in the lesbian world (as is true in the larger society as well), the mutuality of gayness makes the more casual forms of friendly interaction readily accessible to the gay actors within the protective, secretive framework of the lesbian world. The mutual identification of the other as gay serves to facilitate the initiation of casual friendship and sociability.

Simmel (1950, p. 369) notes the necessity of staying on good terms with other members of the secret society. In this regard, most lesbians I met perceive the lesbian world as small, one in which it is difficult to extend the boundaries of one's friendship networks. This perception encourages members to maintain the form of friendship, if not the content. Friendship groups in the lesbian subculture are thus strengthened by the lack of alternative ways of meeting other gay women. To a greater degree than is true of the male community, lesbian friendship groups are an important source of romantic and sexual relationships; gay bars serve a much less important function in this regard than is the case for homosexual males.

Friendship groups among lesbians are frequently composed of couples in long-term relationships. Thus the breakup of a long-term relationship can be at least temporarily disruptive to the social life of one or both parties of the relationship in a manner analagous to what may happen in a heterosexual group when a marriage breaks up. There is, however, an important distinction between the two. Because the gay woman does not have alternative sources of gay sociability readily available to her, there is considerably more pressure for her to maintain her ties with her friendship groups.

Gay Referencing

One of the signal features that marks off gay sociability and the gay world from the straight world is what I call gay referencing, that is, in gay places and in conversations among gays, persons, places, events, and situations are designated as gay. If this is not done, the designation is asked for: "Is he/she gay?" "Are your neighbors gay?" "Were there gay people there?" Gay referencing and the gay content of conversation linguistically distinguish the gay world from the straight world. The world of work, of family, and of school are the arenas for the expression of the many issues and concerns that lesbians share with heterosexuals. Gay talk is proscribed in such settings. The gay world is the unique locus where gay concerns, issues, and relationships can be openly shared and gay relationships celebrated. Clearly, "straight" relationships, children, and other "heterosexual topics" are admissible in conversation with personal gay friends. However, in general, where gay people are gathered together for sociable purposes, straight topics are put to the side.

Gay referencing provides a continual renewal of solidarity within the gay world and serves to demarcate that world from the larger society. Not only is the basis of commonality enhanced in conversation, but the relevance of categorizing the world in terms of straight or gay—including indicating gayness to the lesbian herself—is reiterated through gay referencing. The basis for solidarity in a common sexual orientation within the larger context of a stigmatizing society is thus elaborated and extended in social interaction among gay people.

Rules of Access

Access to the lesbian world is restricted by lack of knowledge of its existence and of its members. Generally speaking, access is limited to members or to trusted others that Goffman refers to respectively as the "own" and the "wise" (Goffman, 1963, pp. 20–31). The own designates the in-group; the wise, persons who have a special status. They have pierced the veil of secrecy by virtue of their relationships with members. However, with respect to the secretive lesbian world, another distinction should be made. Not all of one's own have easy access to, or are welcome in, the secretive lesbian world. Some persons who appear to fit the stereotype of lesbian and who are committed to a philosophy of openness about gayness may not be welcome among secretive groups. Such persons may be considered a threat to the secrecy that protects the group.

Secrecy exists in degrees. Members of groups of secretive lesbians and friendship networks are aware of the "secrecy level" in the groups to which they belong and would thus be trusted to make judicious selections in bringing newcomers within the group's borders. The avenue of access to the secretive lesbian world is thus through the establishment of trust with one or more of its members through fortuitous meetings in the straight world.

The secrecy that obscures the lesbian world may also serve as a barrier to potentially gay persons or to persons who are uninitiated with respect to the locations and occurrences of the secretive lesbian world. When some women first begin to define themselves as gay, or possibly gay, they are unable to locate others like themselves. Women who make this tentative identification report feeling unique in the world—different from anyone that they know and ignorant of how to go about meeting others like themselves, if, indeed, such others exist. In such contexts, the finding of community is frequently experienced with great relief, as finally finding where one belongs.

Implicit in all this is the notion that the secrecy of the lesbian world is something that is accomplished and maintained in concert with others. The discussion that follows outlines the primary ways in which secrecy is accomplished among lesbians. It should be noted, however, that an everyday feature of interaction in the heterosexual world functions to facilitate the maintenance of secrecy for lesbians. I call it the *heterosexual assumption.* The heterosexual assumption means that parties to any interaction in the straight world are generally presumed to be heterosexual unless otherwise indicated. The normative rules of social interaction generally preclude inquiry into sexual behaviors and sexual identity.

Fear of stigma, however, engenders both active and passive strategies for maintaining secrecy beyond relying upon the heterosexual
assumption. Lesbians keep their gayness secret from outsiders by passing, restriction, separation, and counterfeit secrecy. Different strategies
are used with different audiences such as persons known in the world
of work, the family of origin, friends and associates, and fellow gays.

Passing refers to accomplishing a social identity of being "just like
everybody else" when in fact some aspect of the person's character or
biography, if known, would set the individual apart from others. For the
secretive lesbian, passing refers to the accomplishment of a "straight
front" among straight persons.

Strategies of Passing

Passing strategies involve impression management, the camouflaging
use of dress and demeanor, and sometimes a conspiracy of others. It
may require the conscious management of oneself, of others, and of
situations, which means that passers must develop a heightened awareness of ordinary events and everyday encounters (Lyman and Scott,
1970, p. 78). A lesbian who wishes to pass must not only obscure the gay
self, but must present a convincing straight front to straight audiences.
Passers must be alive to the subtleties and nuances of communication
and relationships and attentive to the details of speech and other clues
to identity in social interaction.

Conversations that are relatively matter-of-fact for straight people
may occasion elaborate impression management for the secretive gay
woman. One strategy used by gays who wish to pass as straight within
straight settings is to remain neutral in the face of detrimental remarks
about gay people. Some respondents stated that they felt they had to
silently withstand casual slanders about gay people or risk drawing
attention to their gay selves.

Simon and Gagnon (1967, p. 262) note that it is easier for gay women
to pass than it is for gay men as it occasions little suspicion in the straight
community for women to live together. Further, the category of "asexual" single woman is both believable and acceptable in the larger society. Some gay women, however, choose to reinforce their straight
image by referring to "boyfriends" and/or by having a male friend
accompany them on appropriate occasions. The men who serve as a
legitimating "cover" for gay women are frequently gay themselves.

An important aspect of passing is scrupulous conformity in dress and
appearance to the feminine styles prevalent in the straight community.

It is not unusual to hear very feminine-appearing lesbians express concerns about features of dress which they fear might be clues to the gay self. Dress style and appearance can be used as "protective coloration" to conceal or reveal information about the self.

People who pass are alive to the techniques and strategies employed by others who are passing. The failure to say certain things—for example, being secretive about one's personal life, or an expressed lack of interest in males, or never having been married, or the presence of a roommate, or the consistent failure to present a male companion at appropriate times—can start the speculative ball rolling on the part of a gay woman that another woman may indeed be gay.

A standard feature of gay lore is that "it takes one to know one." It seems to me that this is not due to any mystical sixth sense, but rather to a sensitivity—honed by the experience of passing—to the nuances of various cues.

The process of passing requires the concealment of gay identity and the suppression of clues to gayness. In the very process of constructing a straight image, the gay self is reiterated in inner awareness. The constraint reported by lesbians in having to hide their "true" identity works to increase commitment to that very identity.

Counterfeit Secrecy

Lesbians who conceal their gayness usually express the conviction that the attempt at secrecy is effective and that the straight masks they present are unquestionably accepted. In the experience of some of these women, however, relationships with friends and family are more accurately characterized as patterned by the tacit negotiation of mutual pretense in which the gay self is not acknowledged. I call this pretense "counterfeit secrecy." Both straight audience and gay actor cooperate to maintain a particular definition of the situation and both parties tacitly agree not to make what is implicit explicit by direct reference to it.

In relations where counterfeit secrecy prevails, interaction flows smoothly if lesbianism is not explicitly referred to, suggesting a kind of acceptance. However, this seeming knowledge and seeming acceptance cannot be tested for fear of rejection. The whole structure of this ambiguous acceptance is founded upon *not* acknowledging the gay self, and thereby functions to confound the possibility of disclosure. In this way, the etiquette of counterfeit secrecy entails a kind of discretion which becomes more and more difficult to disrupt as time passes.

Restriction

Among the women with whom I spoke, a few prefer to avoid straight people altogether as potential friends. For these women, the world of work provides the single avenue of contact with straight people. In a very special sense, the "real lives" of these secretive lesbians are spent with gay people in gay spaces which demarcate the gay subculture.

The secrecy that surrounds lesbianism and the employment of techniques for maintaining it serve to render being in and of that world special to its members: under the protective cloak of secrecy, new and favorable meanings and understandings of lesbianism are developed. Out of the secret world, too, emerge ideological justifications for lesbianism.

Secretive lesbians, by and large, do not challenge the rightness or legitimacy of the heterosexual order. They favor interpretations of lesbianism which view it as a sexual preference rather than a life-style and their explanations of homosexuality emphasize genetic, hormonal, or "innate" factors. Cosmologies develop which attempt to place lesbianism and homosexuality in the context of the larger heterosexual order of things; for example, lesbianism may be seen as a natural form of birth control to prevent overpopulation.

Such explanations provide interpretations of gayness that are not disruptive to relationships with heterosexuals and commitments in nongay spheres. Secretive groups that support these notions emphasize their similarities with heterosexuals in all spheres except that of sexual activity.

In some secretive groups, then, there is an emphasis on conforming to social norms in nonsexual aspects of life and a consequent minimization of life-style implications of gayness and lesbianism. Indeed, the concern with conforming to the heterosexual normative order may make relationships with "obvious" gay people problematic as mentioned earlier. Humphreys (1970, pp. 131–48) points out that concern with conformity can lead to an extremely conservative stance, which he calls "the breastplate of righteousness." But whether these concerns with conformity and the minimization of gayness lead to conservative positions in other areas, the accommodation to the current status of secretiveness implies the normality and naturalness of the heterosexual order.

Some secret groups, though not speaking directly to the issue of the larger society's treatment of homosexuals, assert the superiority of the lesbian way of life over and against the heterosexual way of life. These groups, while acknowledging the normativeness of heterosexuality, nevertheless emphasize the distinctiveness and preferability of lesbianism. Lesbians, in this view, constitute a special minority; lesbianism is thus aristocratized.

The Aristocratization of Lesbianism

Aristocratization entails the attribution of special qualities and desirable attributes (Simmel, 1950, pp. 364–66) to gay women (aristocratization also characterizes the male gay world [Warren, 1974]) and is accomplished in two ways: first, by asserting the superior character of relationships between women as compared to relationships between men and women; and second, by attributing special qualities to women, particularly qualities of nurturance, sensitivity, empathy, warmth, and understanding. While these qualities evoke characteristics traditionally attributed to women in our culture, another set of qualities is also accorded lesbians. This second set contains qualities demonstrated in relation to the devalued status of women such as forbearance, strength and endurance. Yet other lesbians claim qualities, traditionally defined as male, such as competence, assertiveness, and aggressiveness.

Relationships between women are often presented in ideal terms as being more egalitarian, mutual, and sensitive than those of male-female dyads, as evincing an intuitive understanding between partners, and as having greater intimacy. Sexual relationships are characterized as having a greater degree of intimacy and sharing than is reputedly possible between the sexes. There is, lesbians claim, an intuitive understanding of the sensual possibilities of the other and a high degree of emotional as well as sexual satisfaction in lesbian relationships.

The lesbian world I have described exists with both the strengths and vulnerabilities that secrecy implies. Its strengths lie in the binding power of secret societies, which promote a sense of closeness, specialness, and shared fate among their members. However, secrecy is a double-edged accommodation to and protection from stigma. The other side of secrecy—disclosure and revelation—are ever-present possibilities that can rend the protective veil that secrecy affords (Simmel, 1950, p. 346). The negative understandings of lesbianism and their consequences can be reimposed.

In recent years, in parts of the lesbian world, the stance of secrecy and accommodation to the heterosexual world has been replaced by a new assertiveness among lesbians. Those who move away from secrecy see lesbianism in political terms. The new assertiveness, under the combined thrust of the gay liberation movement and the feminist movement, presents a challenge instead of an accommodation to the existing heterosexual order.

Challenging the Heterosexual Order

The political lesbian world calls into question the whole relationship between straight and gay worlds and explicitly challenges the normativeness of the heterosexual social order. It does not accept the preferability, naturalness, and givenness of the heterosexual order. This activist ideology sees the status of the gay world vis-à-vis the straight world as a function of political and social oppression and believes that the current division of society into masculine and feminine roles is inherently disadvantageous to women. It views this role division as an expression of the political hegemony of males. Activist groups propose that the qualities that are commonly conceived of as attributes of particular sexes are in fact human qualities. The educational efforts of political lesbians are often directed at their own constituency. Gay people are encouraged to see their position in society in political terms, and to see the political implications of personal choices. Jill Johnson (1973, pp. 277–78), for example, proposes the necessity of interpreting the lesbian's position in society in the light of power politics.

The ideology that repudiates the inferior status of homosexuals and lesbians takes a confrontive stance with respect to the heterosexual society. This may be done in the arena of private conviction, or it may take the form of political action such as picketing at public places, lesbian "guerrilla theater" whereby gay people enter straight settings and either act flamboyantly gay or perform elaborate parodies of straight role-relationships, or other open challenges to the normative order.

The political lesbian world exists in a variety of forms, and its members have varying commitments to the politics of gay liberation, feminism, and separatism. Divisions in the political lesbian world emerge around whether persons see their primary fidelity and commitment to gay people—both men and women—or see their interests most closely tied with those of other women, irrespective of sexual orientation. A third group is composed of lesbians who see their interests and fates as tied to those of gay women only. These women eschew relationships and coalitions with both gay males and straight women and espouse an ideal of separatism.

The political lesbian world and the women's movement stress the life-style implications of lesbianism as opposed to seeing lesbianism in terms of sexual-object choice. One of the primary functions of the political lesbian world is to educate and socialize lesbians into these new ways of conceiving of lesbianism and of living it. Gay self-help groups are concrete realizations of the new political ethos and philosophy.

Self-Help Groups

Self-help groups, particularly those formed by political activist groups, may serve as bridges between the straight world and the gay world. Self-help groups explicitly recognize the lack of socialization and positive support for gay or lesbian identities in the larger society. They focus on identity work which is designed to help the potentially gay person to recognize and accept a lesbian identity and which involves the destigmatization of the labels "gay" and "lesbian."

Identity work is implemented by providing role-models of "proud gays," explanatory rationales and positive interpretations of gayness, accounts of other gay people's experiences, and the opportunity for the novice to talk about her own experience of lesbianism in a supportive milieu.

On the assumption that acknowledging gayness is often traumatic in a society that either ignores homosexuality or is actively antihomosexual, counseling is usually a feature of self-help groups. Besides developing a gay identity per se, self-help groups for women typically focus on identity as a woman and on feminist issues. Such groups feature consciousness-raising sessions during which the experiences common to women are emphasized.

In addition to being concerned with issues of identity and destigmatization, self-help groups provide an alternative to the gay bar as a meeting place and offer a variety of social activities such as dances, dinners, parties, and other get-togethers.

Lesbian Life-Styles and Lesbian Culture

Groups form and reform within the political lesbian world, coalescing around various concerns. These groups conceive of lesbianism as an alternative life-style in various ways. The content of these alternatives

emerges from themes nascent in the women's movement—concern, for
example, with the redefinition and restructuring of roles—particularly
women's roles. Principal among these themes is the idea of a lesbian
culture deriving from lesbian experiences in the world. Lesbian poetry
and music, for example, are conceived of as manifestations and repre-
sentations of the lesbian women's culture. These expressions are not
only lesbian in their content but attempt to move in form beyond forms
which are designated "male." One of the ideological concomitants of
the lesbian/feminist political movement emphasizes a perspective that
"genderizes" existing norms, institutions, and cultural manifestations of
every sort of "male." There is, likewise, an emphasis in these politicized
groups on women articulating their own experience and differentiating
it from that of the male culture.

Groups within the lesbian culture develop activities and institutions
such as women's dances, plays, and poetry readings which are designed
specifically for women and sometimes exclusively for women. Some
lesbian poets, singers, or comedians, for example, will not perform if
men are present. Men are also typically excluded from women's dances.
However, irrespective of whether men are permitted as members of
the audience or as participants, many women's concerts and women's
theater events develop as a combined expression of the lesbian
woman's experience as well as that of the heterosexual woman.

Separatism

In certain sectors of the political lesbian world, feminist ideology even-
tuates in a separatist philosophy analogous to separatist elements in the
black movement. Separatism implies the absence of common interest
with gay males. Even though gay males may be seen as oppressed
because of their homosexuality, gay females are seen as doubly oppressed, both as gays and as women. Some women who hold a separatist
philosophy emphasize the distinction between the lesbian subculture
and the male gay subculture; others emphasize separation from the
heterosexual society.

Among some radical lesbians, separatism entails proscribing relations
between lesbians and all men, including gay men. For other separatist
lesbians, sociable relations with women who also have relations with
men, as well as sociable relations with men themselves, are proscribed.
Such radical separatist groups provide strong ideological support for
lesbianism and for lesbian identities, but their support entails many
constraints on individual interpretations of lesbianism. Such groups

construe lesbianism in such a way that the individual's ties to the heterosexual community, if not looked upon as "treason," are strongly suspect. While they provide strong support for lesbian identity, their stance toward other identities tends to limit their appeal and effectiveness both in terms of the secretive gay community and even in parts of the politicized lesbian community. Radical lesbians and separatists nonetheless form the cutting edge of a community which is in the process of redefining itself and of developing new standards for viewing lesbians, lesbianism, and their relation to society.

The secretive lesbian world and the world of the political lesbian differ in many respects: in their style of relating to the larger society, in their ways of handling stigma, and in the stances taken with respect to disclosure and overtness about lesbianism. The concerns of the political lesbian world go beyond sociability, though that is certainly an important focus of that world. The variegated political lesbian world is concerned with changing the position of the lesbian both in relation to herself and to the larger society. The relationship between the two worlds of lesbians is complex. On the one hand, many secretive lesbians, who have experienced secrecy as a most oppressive feature of gay life, see the political lesbian as helping to change their situation for the better. Other secretive lesbians, however, who have made an accommodation to secrecy, see the political lesbian as a threat, fearing that these women who are "out of the closet" may drag others, unwilling, with them.

The political lesbian, for her part, has an ambivalent attitude toward the secret stance of her sisters. Many political lesbians see disclosure and overtness as signaling the end of oppression. However, most political lesbians have themselves emerged from the secret world. This typically entailed a slow process of disclosure to successive audiences, rather than a wholesale announcement of the gay self. Thus most political lesbians are sensitive to the strain and disruption in relationships that disclosure can occasion.

The two worlds, however, share a paradigm for the construction of lesbian identity. The way in which identity is constructed in the lesbian world is a source both of identity support and of pressure toward the adoption of lesbian identity for its members.

Identity Rules in the Lesbian World

Sexual behavior is only *one* criterion for imputing a lesbian identity to the self or others within both the political and secretive lesbian world. In addition to sexual behavior, and ultimately more important than behavior from the perspective of the lesbian world, are feelings of sexual-emotional attraction to the same sex, *whether or not these feelings have been acted upon.* Thus ascribed motivations and feelings may be the basis for the imputation of lesbian or homosexual identity among lesbians, paralleling the notion of latency in the psychiatric community.

The rules for constructing a lesbian identity in the lesbian world assume that lesbian identity is the public acknowledgment of and reflection of the subjective experience of the self. The community describes certain events and/or states as precursors and evidence of lesbian identity. These include: feeling different from heterosexuals because of feelings of sexual-emotional attraction to one's own sex, becoming sexually and emotionally involved in a lesbian relationship, and seeking out the community. When these experiences or states are evidenced, it is expected that the acceptance and acknowledgment of lesbian identity (at least in the company of other lesbians) will follow.

In the lesbian world, unattached females who associate with gays by going to gay meeting places such as bars, clubs, and organizations will probably have gayness ascribed to them. As noted earlier, the exceptions to these ascriptions are persons who are considered "wise" by the community. A status of wise is facilitated by membership in a heterosexual couple. Once established, the status of the wise straight person may not be questioned, but it may be difficult to achieve for some persons. For example, a single or unattached woman who seeks out and seems to prefer the company of gay women is likely to have gayness attributed to her. She may be said to be in a process of discovering her "real" identity. Dank (1971) notes that there is an average lapse of six years in male homosexuals between an initial sense of attraction to persons of the same sex and the assumption of a gay identity. *Identity lag* has been institutionalized in the gay community. In the argot of the community, it is called "coming out."

Coming Out

The initial process of indicating to the self that one is gay is called "coming out." It marks the beginning of a lesbian career. The term also describes the interaction between gays and the rest of the world. In addition to indicating gayness to oneself, coming out refers to disclosing a gay self before an expanding series of audiences. This second use is more characteristic of political groups, for whom disclosure is a political and ideological stance. Both secret lesbians and activists refer to coming out before various audiences, for example, "I came out with my parents," or "She came out with her straight friends at work."

Coming out is conceived of as a process that takes place over time —a series of acknowledgments and instances of self-labeling. The self is the first audience in the coming out process. One is virtually "all the way out" when most others with whom one is in contact are aware of one's gay identity.

Full membership as a lesbian is often extended to participants who have not yet fully come out. Thus the community gives permission for a period of transition in which the individual's identity may not have caught up with her feelings and behavior. But one is not expected to tarry too long in the transitional phase. If a person continues to assert an identity that is perceived as incongruent with feelings and behavior, sanctions ranging from mild disapproval to public denouncement (the latter in highly political circles) may ensue. Explanations for the person's identity lag will move from a sympathetic understanding of the exigencies of the coming out process to accusations of inauthenticity, stigma evasion, or fence-sitting. Thus although the individual's experiences with respect to lesbianism may vary in their temporal order, the identity rules of the lesbian community do include implicit time norms. If over the course of time a woman "talks differently than she walks"—if she is perceived as being "long overdue" with respect to "realizing" her gay identity—she may become unwelcome in gay circles.

The identity rules of the secretive and activist lesbian worlds and the idea of the coming out process provide a common sense rhetoric or explanation for the variations in identity that exist in the gay world. Identity rules in the lesbian worlds also provide a method for locating the "true self," because here, as in the heterosexual world, gayness is considered definitive of the self in an essential way. These rules presume the existence of the true self and presume to know the character of the "true self" of individuals who supply the cues of feelings, sexual attractions, interests, or associations with gay people. Thus, the lesbian world provides both support and pressure for conformity for those who come within its purview.

REFERENCES

Becker, H. S. 1963. *Outsiders, studies in the sociology of deviance.* New York: Free Press.

Berger, P. L., and Luckmann, T. 1967. *The social construction of reality.* Garden City, N.Y.: Doubleday/Anchor.

Blumer, H. 1969. *Symbolic interactionism: Perspective and method.* Englewood Cliffs, N.J.: Prentice-Hall.

Blumstein, P. W., and Schwartz, P. 1974. *"Lesbianism and bisexuality,"* Unpublished manuscript. University of Washington.

Brecher, E. 1975. History of human sexual research and study. In A. M. Freedman, H. I. Kaplan, and B. J. Sadach, eds., *Comprehensive textbook of psychiatry,* vol. 2 (Baltimore: Williams & Wilkins), pp. 1352–57.

Caprio, F. S. 1954. *Female homosexuality, a psychodynamic study of lesbianism.* New York: Citadel Press.

Chesler, P. 1971. Patient and patriarch: Women in the psychotherapeutic relationship. In V. Gornick and B. K. Moran, eds., *Women in a sexist society* (New York: Basic Books), pp. 362–92.

Dank, B. 1971. Coming out in the gay world. *Psychiatry* 34 (May): 180–97.

Douglas, J. D. 1971. *American social order.* New York: Free Press.

Emerson, J. 1970. Nothing unusual is happening. In T. Shibutani, ed., *Human nature and collective behavior* (Englewood Cliffs, N.J.: Prentice-Hall), pp. 208–22.

Freud, S. 1933. The psychology of women. In *New introductory lectures of psychoanalysis,* (New York: W. W. Norton), pp. 153–85.

———. 1959. *Collected Papers,* vol. 2. New York: Basic Books.

———. *Three Essays on the Theory of Sexuality,* James Strachey, trans. New York: Basic Books, 1962.

Gagnon, J. H., and Simon, W. 1967. *Sexual deviance.* New York: Harper & Row.

Glaser, B., and Strauss, A. 1964. Awareness Context and Social Interaction. *American Sociological Review* 29:669–78.

Goffman, E. 1959. *The presentation of self in everyday life.* Garden City, N.Y.: Doubleday.

———. 1963. *Stigma, notes on the management of spoiled identity.* Englewood Cliffs N.J.: Prentice-Hall.

Gordon, C. 1968. "Self conceptions: Configurations of content. In C. Gordon and K. J. Gergen eds., *The self in social interaction classic and contemporary perspectives,* vol. 1 (New York: John Wiley), pp. 115–37.

Hooker, E. 1963. The adjustment of the male overt homosexual. In H. M. Ruitenbeek, ed., *The problem of homosexuality of modern America.* New York: E.P. Dutton, pp. 141–61.

Hopkins, J. H. 1969. The Lesbian Personality. *British Journal of Psychiatry* 115: 1433–36.

Humphreys, L. 1970. *Tearoom trade: Impersonal sex in public places.* Chicago: Aldine Publishing.

———. 1972. *Out of the closets: The sociology of homosexual liberation.* Englewood Cliffs N.J.: Prentice-Hall.

Johnson, J. 1973. *Lesbian nation: The feminist solution.* New York: Simon & Schuster.

Katz, J. 1972. Deviance, charisma, and role-defined behavior. *Social Problems* 20: 187–202.

———. 1975. Essence as moral identities: Verifiability and responsibility, in imputations of deviance and charisma. *American Journal of Sociology* 80: 1369–90.

Klaich, D. 1974. *Woman + woman: Attitudes toward lesbianism.* New York: William Morrow.

Larkin, J. 1976. Coming Out: "My story is not about all lesbians." *Ms.* 9: 72–2, 84, 86.

Lief, H. I. 1975. "Introduction to sexuality," In Freedman, et al., eds., *Comprehensive textbook of psychiatry,* vol. 2 (Baltimore: Williams & Wilkins), pp. 1349–52.

Lemert, E. 1976. *Human deviance, social problems, and social control.* Englewood Cliffs N.J.: Prentice-Hall.

Lofland, J. 1969. *Deviance and identity.* Englewood Cliffs N.J.: Prentice-Hall.

———. 1971. *Analyzing social setting.* Belmont, Calif.: Wadsworth Publishing.

Lyman, S. M., and Scott, M. B. 1970. *A sociology of the absurd.* New York: Appleton-Century-Crofts.

McCall, G., and Simons, J.L. 1966. *Identities and interactions.* New York: Free Press.

McIntosh, M. 1968. The homosexual role. *Social Problems* 16: 182–92.

Marmor, J. 1965. *Sexual inversion: The multiple roots of homosexuality.* New York: Basic Books.

Martin, D., and Lyon, P. 1972. *Lesbian/Woman.* New York: Bantam Books.

Mills, C. W. 1972. Situated Actions and Vocabularies of Motives. In J. G. Morris and B. N. Meltzer, eds. *Symbolic Interaction, A Reader in Social Psychology,* 2nd ed. (Boston: Allyn & Bacon), pp. 393–404.

Money, J., and Ehrhardt, A. A. 1972. *Man and woman, boy and girl: Differentiation and dimorphism of gender identity from conception to maturity.* Baltimore: John Hopkins Press.

Raphael, S. 1974. Coming out, the emergence of the movement lesbian. Ph.D. dissertation, Department of Sociology, Case Western Reserve University, Cleveland, Ohio.

Rosen, D. M. 1974. *Lesbianism, a study of female homosexuals.* Springfield, IL: Charles C Thomas.

Rule, J. 1975. *Lesbian images.* Garden City, N.Y.: Doubleday.

Schutz, A. 1971. *Collected papers, studies in social theory,* vol. 2. Arnid Broderson, ed. The Hague: Martinus Nijhoff.

Shelley, M. 1972. Gay is good. In K. Jay and A. Young, eds., *Out of the closets: voices of gay liberation.* (New York: A Douglas Book), p. 34.

Simmel, G. 1950. *The sociology of Georg Simmel.* Kurt H. Wolff, trans. and ed. New York: Free Press.

Simon, W., and Gagnon, J. H. 1966. Feminity in the lesbian community. *Social Problems* 14: 212–21.

———. 1967. "The lesbians: A preliminary overview. In J. Gagnon and W. Simon, eds., *Sexual deviance* (New York: Harper & Row).

———. 1969. On psychosexual development. In D. A. Grodon, ed., *Handbook of socialization theory and research.* (Chicago: Rand McNally).

Strauss, A. 1959. *Mirrors and masks.* New York: Free Press.

Szasz, T. S. 1961. *The myth of mental illness.* New York: Harper & Row.

Tripps, C. A. 1975. *The homosexual matrix.* New York: McGraw-Hill.

Warren, A. B., and Johnson, J. 1972. A criticism of labeling theory from the phenomenological perspective. In R.A. Scott and J. D. Douglas eds., *Theoretical Perspectives in Deviance* (New York: Basic Books).

Warren, C. A. B. 1974. *Identity and community in the gay world.* New York: John Wiley.

Warren, C. A. B. 1976. Labeling theory: The individual, the category, and the group. Unpublished manuscript. University of Southern California.

9 / Homosexuality and Aging

JAMES KELLY

The Aging Gay[1] Person in Scientific Literature

The existence of only a few fragmentary and frequently inaccurate accounts about aging gays may be explained in part by the "deviant" status of the gay population. As Evelyn Hooker (1967) noted:

> The necessity of escaping the penalties of social or legal recognition impels many homosexuals to lead a highly secret private life. Only when caught by law enforcement agents, or when seeking psychiatric help, are they usually available for study. (p. 169)

Data are scarce additionally because so many aging studies have concentrated on heterosexual populations, or have failed to break down categories of unmarried participants to provide information on gay subpopulations, or have failed to ask questions relevant to gayness to "supposedly" heterosexual groups. The assumptions of some gerontologists that their subjects are uniformly heterosexual is illustrated by the following quotation from Goldfarb:

> The widespread ignorance about sex and the high frequency, in our society, of excessive inhibition with respect to behavior that can lead to gratifying heterosexual relationships and the relief of sexual tensions make sexual problems one of the most common causes of helpless feelings among the aging. (Goldfarb in Berezin, 1969, p. 133)

1. "Gay" is the widely preferred subculture term for those who engage primarily in homosexual relations. Judd Marmor's (1965) interpretation of the term "homosexual" appears to be one of the most definitive: "One who is motivated in adult life, by a definite preferential erotic attraction to members of the same sex and who usually (but not necessarily) engages in overt sexual relations with them."

THE OPINIONS OF SIGNIFICANT OTHERS: THE IMPACT OF STIGMA

Other social scientists have formulated concepts of the essence of homosexuality. Warren sees the gay individual as "a free social actor with choices and possibilities and [one who] is not determined in his future actions and identities by the social labels of any person or group, no matter how powerful" (1974, p. 7).

However, she also describes a gay man she observed who had accepted society's negative connotations of gayness as a stigma and who was tortured, for a time, by his own negative self-feelings (pp. 8–9). Lemert (1951) confirms this dynamic: the stronger the *self*-identification of an individual, the less credence he is likely to give to society's putative definition of him as a deviant (p. 64).

The idea that some gay men, at least for a time, may accept or internalize societally held beliefs about what their aging process is supposed to be like can also be explained by a theory called "the looking glass self":

> This notion suggests that a person's feelings about himself are derived from imagining how others regard him. Thus, a person's evaluation and image of himself, as well as his general psychological state, are affected by how he imagines other people react to him, regardless of whether these imputations are accurate or not. (Weinberg and Williams, 1974, p. 153)

Furthermore, the impact of the reactions of others to the self is accentuated if the "others" doing the reacting are considered significant by the self. This suggests that the attitudes of the general society towards the concept of an "aging gay man" may have an impact on the attitudes some gays hold toward their own aging process. However, if it can be assumed that most gay men will probably have at some point in time significant others (e.g., lovers, close friends) who are also gay, it can then be imagined that the attitudes and opinions of other gay men toward aging and toward what an aging gay man is like may take on an equal if not greater importance than those of society at large. This type of assumption is bolstered in another sense by Warren's participant observations of a gay community:

> The delight of secrecy resides in the amplification of the gay experience, a *further* amplification of an experience which already assumes great significance because of the stigmatization of the rest of society. The overt adaptation to stigmatization makes the gay world more important to its members than other worlds: the secret response, I feel, adds excitement to stigma and makes the gay world doubly important (1974, p. 5).

STIGMA AND AGING INSIDE THE GAY COMMUNITY

With regard to stigma and aging inside the gay community itself, Weinberg points out that the stereotypes[2] concerning adaptation to aging held by many heterosexuals, and perhaps also by some social scientists, are held as well by large segments of the gay community, particularly the young (1970, p. 536). One young author, for example, whose work is reprinted in *Out of the Closets: Voices of Gay Liberation,* renders a richly detailed stereotype of gay men over thirty:

> Fairyland is still alive . . . for most of those half-decloseted gays over 30, and I don't think most of our older brothers will ever escape from it. Those aging princesses will simply linger on unto death as past relics of a bygone era in their fantasy world of poodle dogs and Wedgwood teacups and chandeliers and all the fancy clothes and home furnishings any queen could ever desire. . . . (Hanson, 1972, p. 266)

Similarly, in her study community Warren describes the prevalence of the catch-all idea of a "lower class," composed of types of deviants assumed to have "unacceptable" characteristics (1974, p. 84).[3]

The "faggot's faggot" was the phrase chosen by a columnist in the *Pittsburgh Gay News* recently in an article deploring the Pittsburgh subculture's stigmatization of two such deviant groups, sadists/masochists (S & M's) and older gays. Just as gay people in general form a predominantly "secret" society within the larger society, columnist Kochera describes these groups as doubly stigmatized "unseen victims of ignorance and oppression" about which a hazy folklore seems to exist:

> What I know about this group is only vague. There are two groups of people that I know of which, sadly, qualify as the Faggot's Faggots in Pittsburgh. These are the Sadists/Masochists (S & M) and the gay senior citizens. The first I have rarely seen in the area; I don't know of any "leather" bars in Pittsburgh. The second I am aware of only from cruel talk about "wrinkle rooms" and the inconspicuous presence that age has in our culture.
>   This distresses me deeply, that in this city, my gay brothers and sisters are making "faggots" out of people who are also brothers and sisters but some-

2. Bengtson (1973, p. 27) defines stereotypes as "widely shared expectancies, without specific sanctions, regarding the behavior or characteristics of a particular category of people . . . (which) do not acknowledge individual differences among those who are members of that social category . . . (and which are) often acquired on the basis of limited contact with the group, (and) are usually (but not exclusively) negative, associated with some sort of stigma."

3. In the particular Pacific Coast beach town she studied, Warren did not observe or sense that older gay men were being classified in the "lower class" category: "The lower class is a residual category into which the elite . . . put a variety of troublesome deviants: transvestites, child molesters, male prostitutes, and others" (1974, p. 84). She stresses, throughout her book, that gay communities in smaller towns and gay cliques in large cities may vary widely in demographic composition, behavior, and other characteristics.

how alienated from most of us. It even disturbs me deeper that I myself am just as ignorant, confused and oppressive towards S & M Gays and senior citizen Gays. (Kochera, 1973, p. 5)

Despite the distress that Kochera describes and the "looking glass self" notion implies, Warren suggests on the basis of her field work that effects of stigmatization may not be nearly so debilitating as is commonly assumed. She seems to feel that the gay community itself often serves as a healing influence transforming stigma into "something positive and valuable" (1974, p. 9). In fact, she believes that:

A final seduction of the secret world is that it fosters the sense of an elite, chosen-people status, which Simmel calls the "aristocratizing principle." Often the stigmatization of the surrounding, hostile society is used in a kind of martyrdom of the elite, breeding a heightened sense of both superiority and unjust persecution. The Jews of the Diaspora, the black community and the gay community exemplify the aristocratizing effect of stigma and secrecy. (p. 6)

While Weinberg and Williams (1974, p. 218) found the older gay men in their samples to be adapting well, for the most part, to a situation of social and sexual isolation, Warren observed many to be members of "elite cliques" within her gay "chosen people" elite, who frequently entertain lavishly and who often enjoy the stability of a long-term love relationship with another man (1974, p. 84).

However, in her discussion of "gay vocabulary," Warren reported both negative and positive connotations for terms such as "old auntie" and "mother" which were used to describe older gay members of the group she observed (1974, pp. 110–11). The ambivalence she sees in gay perceptions of older gay men can be linked to what both Altman (1971, p. 51) and Lemert (1951, p. 60) observe to be a subtle combination of acceptance and rejection, tolerance and hostility, often operating in larger societal reactions.

It is documentable that stereotypes, myths, and negative attitudes toward older gay men exist and that they are generated and perpetuated both from outside and inside the gay subculture. However, the currently popular sociological perspective for examining the dynamics of such stigmatization in deviant populations was considered inapplicable by Warren in her participant observation with gays, and while Weinberg and Williams apply the conception, they describe it as "unclean" on many important points and "not specific and detailed enough to avoid ramifications and overgeneralizations" (1974, pp. 268–69). Even if it is recognized that society devalues the aging homosexual, the examination of such stigmatization is complicated by the complex nature of this reaction in which hostility can combine, in little understood ways, with compassion.

The Aging Gay Person in Recent Literature

MICHAEL: It's called, "getting old." Ah, life is
such a grand design—spring, sum-
mer, fall, winter, death. Who*ever*
could have thought it up?
DONALD: No one *we* know, that's for sure.
MICHAEL: [*Turns to study himself in the mirror,
sighs*] Well, one thing you can say for
masturbation . . . you certainly don't
have to look your best. (Crowley,
1968)

The older gay person, lonely and depressed, has been a common theme
in fiction. Four recent films—*Reflections in a Golden Eye, The Sergeant,
Staircase,* and *The Boys in the Band*—all depict sad, twisted existences
for their aging gay characters. In *The Sergeant,* for example: "True to
the Hollywood formula, . . . Steiger was required to blow his brains
out upon discovering his homosexual tendencies. . . . The movie has
been described as being 'basically about loneliness' " (Phillips, 1971, p. 22).

The concept that being gay leads to failure in interpersonal relationships, which leads to loneliness in later life, which leads to suicide, is also
presented in *The Boys in the Band:*

Michael: And the pills!
Harold has been gathering, saving, and storing up Barbiturates for the last
year like a goddamn squirrel. Hundreds of Nembutals, hundreds of Seconals,
all in preparation for and anticipation of the long winter of his death.
[*Silence*]
But I tell you right now, Hallie. When the time comes, you'll never have
the guts. It's not always like it happens in plays, not all faggots bump themselves off at the end of the story.

(Crowley, 1968, pp. 113–14)

Despite this somewhat stereotypical view of the aging gay man,
novelist Christopher Isherwood, writing in 1964, even prior to the appearance of Crowley's play, has been described as creating in his fifty-
eight-year-old hero George (a character much older in chronological
age than that in *The Boys in the Band*) an image of a man who "has
resolved his homosexuality, made it a part of his life, without any of the
great *Sturm and Drang* that pervades most homosexual fiction" (Altman, 1971, p. 39).

Isherwood's George seems to make a positive adaptation to the aging
process and to his age. He reminisces about the many pleasant memories of life with his now deceased lover, Jim: "Breakfast with Jim used
to be one of the best times of their day. It was then, while they were
drinking their second and third cups of coffee, that they had their best
talks . . ." (p. 11).

While George mourns his lover's death, he does not seem to be suicidal or desperate but appears, rather, to find relief in living:

> George is very far, right now, from sneering at any of these fellow-creatures [Christmas shoppers]. They may be crude and mercenary and dull and low, but he is proud, is glad, is almost indecently gleeful to be able to stand up and be counted in their ranks—the ranks of that marvelous minority, The Living. (p. 87)

The aforementioned fictional accounts depict two very different types of aging homosexuals. Gay men and women share many of the same stresses of aging as do individuals in heterosexual society. However, because of the unique subculture to which they belong, these individuals must additionally confront the problems involved in the aging process within that stratum.

The Aging Gay Man

PROBLEMS IN THE STUDY OF STIGMATIZATION

Recent findings (Weinberg and Williams, 1974; Warren, 1974) by social scientists who have included material on older gay men in major studies seem to conflict somewhat in descriptions of the life circumstances of their subjects. Also, none of the authors *focuses* on any aspect of the lives of older gay men: Weinberg and Williams include one short chapter on "Age" (pp. 216–22) in their 289-page study, *Male Homosexuals;* Warren devotes an occasional page or paragraph to older gays in her research, *Identity and Community in the Gay World.*

In fact, a review of English language social science literature uncovers little material devoted directly to the subject of aging homosexual men or women. To what extent do gay people share the widely disseminated stereotypes, beliefs, hypotheses, and attitudes which routinely stigmatize "what it's like to be old and gay"? What *are* the attitudes, beliefs, opinions, and valuations of gay men, across the life span, toward their own aging process and the aging processes of others in the gay community? Are there age differences related to the expression of certain attitudes and opinions?

Until the completion of a recent study[4] by the author (Kelly, 1974),

4. Data were collected through questionnaire, interview, and participant observation techniques over a two-year period (1973–74). As there are no accurate accounts of the racial, age, or socioeconomic parameters of the American gay subgroup, probability sampling techniques were virtually impossible to employ. This study must therefore be considered an exploratory account; its findings are not meant to be generalized to all aging gay men.

these questions constituted virtually unexplored phenomena. Relevant theory, data, and definitions are sparse, ambiguous, and sometimes contradictory. Let us explore the substance of those questions.

SOME STEREOTYPES AND ACTUAL CHARACTERISTICS

Data for this recent comprehensive survey of aging gay men were compiled in several ways. These included participant observation in the Los Angeles gay community to discover alternative sample sources. In order to allow for the widest range of respondent characteristics, it was decided to avoid the sampling of bars, baths, and similar establishments which charge fees and which are generally recognized in the gay community as primarily "sexual hunting grounds." It was thought, on the basis of participant observation, that sampling these places might systematically exclude the very poor, and perhaps also some persons in settled gay liaisons and some older persons.

Continued observations led to the selection of a popular gay beach and the Los Angeles Metropolitan Community Church (the mother church) congregation as major sample sources, along with advertisements in several gay-oriented newspapers, and the use of friendship networks.

One hundred ninety-three questionnaires and forty-eight interviews were analyzed. Thirty of the men stated they were over sixty-five; seven in the older group refused to divulge their age, and six were over seventy-five (all interview material quoted in this chapter comes from conversations with men over sixty-five).

During data collection, trust and confidence were established primarily through viewing the gay men involved as experts with experience in "living in a certain milieu." Study participants were viewed not simply as research "objects" but as valuable informants helping the researcher to become aware of the characteristics and types of attitudes existing in their community. One participant observed:

> It's good that you are interviewing a cross-section of people because I've only read a couple of books and it seems like they get their examples from people who are from the psychiatrist's office or something like that or they go out and interview straight people, they go out and interview the most bizarre people they can find and they really don't take a realistic cross section of people. (Interview)

Cooperation of several gay organizations such as ONE, Inc., SPREE, or Los Angeles Metropolitan Community Church, provided background information and entrée into the Los Angeles gay community.

There is a composite stereotype of the supposed characteristics and activities of the aging gay man. He no longer goes to bars, having lost his physical attractiveness and thereby his sexual appeal to the young men he craves. He is oversexed, but his sex life is very unsatisfactory. He has been unable to form a lasting relationship with a sexual partner, and he is seldom sexually active anymore. When he does have sex, it is usually in a tearoom. He has disengaged himself from the gay world and from his acquaintances in it. He is retreating farther and farther into the "closet"—fearful of disclosure of his "perversion." Most of his associations are increasingly with heterosexuals. In a bizarre and deviant world centered around youth, he is labeled "an old queen" as he has become quite effeminate.

The component parts of this mythical man were compared to the characteristics and activities of some real gay men in a real gay setting.

MYTH AND REALITY IN THE BAR SCENE

As a baseline question for how active the individuals studied were within the social structure of the gay subculture, the respondents were asked if they had visited a gay bar[5] within the preceding six months. Approximately 80 percent of the entire questionnaire sample answered in the affirmative. Agewise, however, bar-going was highest among the thirty-six to forty-five age group, with 87 percent of the people in this age bracket attending. Although the rate of attendance was about twenty percentage points lower for the next age grouping, it was still 64 percent.

In some of the popular dance bars which cater to a "young crowd," the appearance of a man much over thirty-five was indeed considered an intrusion. However, Los Angeles and some other major cities have gay bars which are popular with older men. We see that stereotypes about age cutoffs for bar activity seem largely to be overgeneralizations derived from observations which are valid only in some contexts.

DISENGAGEMENT AND THE OLDER GAY MAN

Regarding the assumption of disengagement[6]—that is, the *lack* of participation of aging gays in the gay community—this survey found little evidence to support the theory (see Table 9.1). Most gay respondents believed their level of participation in the gay world's round of activities was low (30 percent) to moderate (52 percent). Within this framework only 12 percent of those forty-six to fifty-five years of age listed their involvement in gay activities as low, while 50 percent of

5. The choice of a bar was made because the gay bar is one of the few establishments that attracts a uniformly homosexual clientele in large numbers.

6. The disengagement theory of aging presented by Cumming and Henry, (1961) suggests that: "The individual gradually withdraws socially as well as psychologically from his environment as he moves into old age. Most importantly, the process of withdrawal is suggested by theory to be mutually satisfying. For the individual, the withdrawal brings a release from the societal pressures for instrumental performance that tax a weakening body. For the society, this withdrawal allows younger (and, presumably, more energetic and competent) individuals to assume the functional roles which must be fulfilled for the survival of the social system" (Bengtson, 1973, pp. 43–44).

TABLE 9.1

Low Degree of Involvement in Gay Activities (By Age)*

Age	Number of Respondents	Percentage of Involvement in Gay Activities as Low
Under 26	19	35%
26–35	24	31%
36–45	8	27%
46–55	2	12%
56–65	4	50%
65+	0	0%

*Questionnaire sample only.

those fifty-six to sixty-five did so. However *no one* over age sixty-five in either questionnaire or interview samples indicated that they had disengaged from activities in the gay milieu.

SEX AND THE OLDER GAY MAN

Concerning the degree of sexual satisfaction within the gay population, 87 percent of the total questionnaire respondents indicated that they were on the satisfactory side of the continuum. By comparison, among a group of predominantly heterosexual men who responded to the *Psychology Today*[7] questionnaire on sex, only 69 percent rated their sexual satisfaction as adequate.

In terms of the age distribution of sexual satisfaction, percentages of satisfaction were high in all gay age groups. While the highest percentage (91 percent) was in the under-twenty-six group and the lowest in the fifty-six to sixty-six bracket, the low was still a substantial 50 percent rate of satisfaction. Also, 83 percent of the respondents over age sixty-five reported being sexually satisfied.

STEREOTYPES AND LONG-TERM RELATIONSHIPS

Regarding the ability of the aging gay man to be involved in a long-term relationship, the number of persons involved in liaisons seemed to *increase* with age, peaking with 59 percent in the forty-six to fifty-five group and then declining significantly in the older groups (see Table 9.2).

There are a multitude of possible reasons for this decline. An attempt to explain them all would seem naive. One of them, however, mentioned by several older gays, is the death of the loved one.

7. In 1970 *Psychology Today* published a survey on sexual attitudes and behaviors of American men and women. While this survey was not based on probability sampling and was not intended to be descriptive of the American public, findings are, according to the researchers, "descriptive of a well-educated, intelligent group that just might be the wave of the future" (Athanasiou, et al., July 1970, p. 40).

He had a lover and they lived for years and years. This guy must be about, he's getting close to 70. Having always to live with this other guy, it's like living with another woman, you know. All of a sudden the guy dies. Just the natural course of events. So now this guy is now high and dry. He doesn't know how to get another friend. He misses all, all that companionship, all that living together meant, that is when he comes home to find someone there or to be with someone. He doesn't have any means of going out and finding anyone because there's no framework. If he was 35 he can go cruising and find anyone, you know. What does a 70 year old gay man do? He's always in good health, he has always taken good care of himself, so forth, in a sense, but he doesn't have any framework. (Interview)

While this death resulted in the kind of loneliness popularly associated with the older gay who "lacks supports," this type of situation was not reported by other interviewees.

I notified his cousin and aunt back in Milwaukee that he died. They were broken up; and called me the next day to see if I needed anything. They told me that whatever we had, whatever Wally left, they wanted nothing of it and it was all mine. You worked together and lived together all these years, it has to be yours and not ours. Isn't it nice? (Interview)

There also seemed to be some older gays as well as many younger men who rejected the notion of having *one* lover and adopted alternative life-styles more satisfactory for them. An interview with a seventy-one-year-old man went like this:

Interviewer:
    "Are you now partner in a gay marriage or liaison of one year or longer?"

Interviewee:
    "No, I just refer to my Jewish husband and my butcher husband and my salesman husband, like that, camping, but I would like to make a lot of them happy, than to live and be and try to be true to one. And both of us being more or less miserable. (Interview)

TABLE 9.2
Partnership in Gay Liaison (by Age) *

Age	Number of Respondents	Percentage in a Gay Marriage of One Year's Duration or Longer
Under 26	11	20%
26–35	27	35%
36–45	12	40%
46–55	10	59%
56–65	3	38%
65+	0	0%

*Questionnaire sample only.

THE "REAL" OLDER GAY MAN

Thus, the aging men in this study bear little resemblance to the stereotyped composite image circulating in society at large. In contrast to the mythical man, the "composite" older man in the study group does not frequent tearooms but occasionally goes out to bars, particularly those that serve his peer group. The extent of his participation in the gay world is moderate but based largely on his individual desires. He has many gay friends and fewer heterosexual friends. His sex life is quite satisfactory and he desires sexual contact with adult men, especially those near his own age, but he is not currently involved in an exclusive relationship. He does not consider himself effeminate, nor does he like to define himself in terms of gay age-labels, but he remembers the terms that were commonly applied to "old gays" when he was younger.

This older gay man is himself a generalization. However, his life seems somewhat different not only from the general stereotype but also from the adaptational pattern of aging which Weinberg observes in the gays in his study and which Gurin, Venoff, and Feld (1960) have described in older people in general: "But neither are they particularly happy or optimistic about their lives. Their satisfactions seem to be based on limited expectations and a passive acceptance of their status" (Gurin in Weinberg, 1970, p. 536).

Attitudes: Gay Men and the Aging Process

Another major objective of the Los Angeles study was to ascertain the extent to which adult gay men of all ages shared the widely disseminated stereotypes, beliefs, hypotheses, and attitudes that symbolically stigmatize what it is like to be old and gay. The attitudes, beliefs, opinions, and valuations of gay men, across the life span, toward their own aging process and toward the aging process of others in the gay community were analyzed by age groups. Conceptual areas the survey focused on included the salience of aging, success, sexual desirability and age, and the personal and societal politics of aging.

THE SALIENCE OF AGING

In terms of the salience of aging, the thought of aging itself did not seem to be completely foreign to most of the gay men in this study, but it was not very relevant for many, nor was it an overriding concern for most. The majority of questionnaire respondents said that they thought about aging "seldom" to "a moderate amount of the time," and fewer thought "constantly" about aging than "never" thought about it. As a baseline question, the study group was asked where youth and middle age begin and end and where old age begins. The plurality or majority agreed that youth began before age eighteen and ended at about thirty years, at the point where middle age began. The end of middle age was seen as fifty years (twenty years later than many stereotypes would seem to indicate) and this time period also heralded the onset of old age.

THE NATURE OF AGING

When asked about the nature of aging within the gay subculture, the majority expressed either neutral or positive opinions (see Table 9.3). In general, the older the respondent, the more positive was his concept of what happened to old gays.

Attitudes regarding "specific problems" of older gays were also explored (see Table 9.4). The men surveyed appeared most concerned about loneliness, loss of physical attractiveness, and failure to accept the aging process.

SEX AND SUCCESS

When asked about "success" and "sexual desirability," most respondents to the questionnaire survey considered the twenty-to-twenty-nine age bracket and the thirty-to-thirty-nine bracket to be the most sexually attractive. Of note is the fact that more respondent groups found the forty-to-forty-nine ages appealing than considered the under-twenty most desireable. Those preferences support the concept that the over-fifty gay man, in general, is not sexually appealing. However, the uniqueness of individuals may be overlooked in these generalizations. Several interviewees specifically mentioned young gay men who find only older men appealing, and one man described personal participation in a relationship which ignored all society's ethnic, racial, and age "barriers."

TABLE 9.3

Expression of Negative Beliefs about What Happens to Old Gays, (by Age)*

Age	Number of Respondents	Expressed Negative Beliefs
Under 26	20	36%
26–35	19	25%
36–45	7	23%
46–55	5	29%
56–65	1	13%
65+	0	0%

*Questionnaire sample only.

TABLE 9.4

*Specific Problems of Older Gays Reported by Questionnaire Respondents**

Problems	Number of Respondents
Loneliness	37
Increasing isolation from gay social activities	7
Sexual rejection	5
Loss of loved ones	13
Loss of physical attractiveness	27
Failure to accept the aging process	27
Loss of youth which is valued in the gay world	19
Lack of family supports	3
Lack of friendship supports	8
Same problems as other aging people	11
Problems are uniquely individual	4
Other problems	11
No problems	18
Don't know, blank	25

*Respondents may have given more than one response.

The question of "attractiveness" and "youthful appeal" seems related to the more global issue of "success" in the gay world. The majority of questionnaire respondents (46 percent) indicated that a "youthful appearance" was definitely an asset in one's social interactions within the gay community. Among those who believed that a youthful appearance was a plus, the respondents were equally spread throughout the age continuum.

GAY ATTITUDES TOWARD AGING: SITUATIONALLY DETERMINED

These gay men, collectively, knew relatively few men whom they would define, as a group, as "old." According to the cultural rules of categorizing people, these individuals would be expected to apply stereotypes more quickly and more broadly than those with more familiarity with older gay men. However, stereotyping and other reactions may also be uneven and very different depending on the context of questioning. While the study indicated that gay men did not stereotype age, in particular their *own* age, their beliefs about the general nature of aging for gay men remain more stereotypical than any of their other beliefs.

For example, while the findings regarding success, sexual desirability, and age ran somewhat counter to the myth that all gay men pursue "the eighteen-year-old Adonis," it is still evident that gays over age fifty are not considered sexually appealing. Also, many related an attractive, youthful appearance to success in the gay world—with many defining success for themselves in sexual terms.

While a slight majority continued to view success and sexual desirability in terms of age norms, most expressed anger, dismay, or similar emotions when asked about a situation involving discrimination against elderly gay men, with older men being somewhat more likely to express defeat or acceptance in regard to the hypothetical discrimination.

However, in describing their personal policies toward aging, many rejected the salience of age with advice to "forget about it" or to "resist it." While rejecting thoughts about aging and, to some extent, the physical process for themselves, they believed, increasingly with age, that some type of societal reforms must come—either for all the elderly, all gay people, or for older gays specifically. Many felt that such actions must come first or solely from gay society, either because they believed society at large to be hostile or apathetic or because they felt that older gay men are stigmatized most by the gay subculture.

The overall attitudes of these gay men seem to be situationally determined. The picture of the old gay facing discrimination brings indignation and compassion, while when asked about what old gays are "like," responses are stereotypical and, in some instances, where social distance may be great, answers are even cavalier or cruel. While some of these gay men continue to stereotype an image of *the* old gay, they have, for the most part, rejected the internalization of such stereotypes for themselves. This in itself may represent the beginning of the end of stigmatization.

THE POLITICS OF AGING

With regard to social policies as they affect aging, the problem areas most frequently cited included hospital visiting rights, employment discrimination, insurance company policies, housing considerations, and the need for retirement homes. Although society at large was blamed for the stigmatization of older gays, several respondents agreed that gay society itself has been the worst offender.

Older Lesbians

It may appear that the subject of aging gay women has been relegated to a secondary place in this chapter; although there is a paucity of survey data on the sexuality of both older gay men and women, less information is available on older gay women. In *Sexual Behavior in the Human Female* (1953), Kinsey et al. provided data on only one individual in the survey group who was over sixty. The

NOW Task Force on Older Women (1976, p. 1) recently compiled data that demonstrated that the information available on older women was still negligible.

Many factors may be implicated in our failure to produce a substantial amount of sex research about older women. The taboo that most directly prevented this research in the past was the antiquated notion that the purpose of sex for women was solely that of procreation. In addition, women had been viewed culturally as sex-objects for men. Older women's sex lives were therefore of little consequence to researchers. Other disincentives included the concept that aging women were unattractive and sexually unmarketable as well as extensions of the incest taboo against sex with "mother."

THE FUTILITY OF "HAPPINESS MEASUREMENT"

In their chapter, "Deviate Sex Behavior in the Aging," in *Psychopathology and Aging,* Johnson and Kelly (1978) compiled much of the available research on the lives of homosexual women. They cited the advice of Dee Martin and Phyllis Lyon (1972) who recommended, on the basis of many years of experience counseling lesbians, that researchers abandon the practice of attempting to measure the lesbians' "happiness." Due to the stigma of illness and deviance ascribed to gay women, many in the older age groups have had to deal with decades of blackmail, employment penalties, lack of compensation for heavy individual obligations to aging parents, and therefore also with some degree of frustration, masochism, and severe depression.

OLDER GAY MEN AND WOMEN: KEY DIFFERENCES

Unfortunately social scientists have, in the past, researched gay men and women together and have even implied that data gathered from studies of gay men were equally applicable to gay women. It must be clearly understood that there are many key dissimilarities between gay men and women, and that not to be aware of this concept is to do a grave injustice to both groups.

However despite the miniscule amount of research on lesbian women, there certainly exists enough information to disprove the stereotypical image of the older gay woman as heartless, unemotional, merciless, and a child molester.

RECENT RESEARCH

In some of the recent literature concerning homosexuality, there have been occasional references to lesbianism and aging. When Saghir and Robins (1973, pp. 311–12) asked respondents in their study of homosexuality, "How do you feel about aging?" women indicated that aging and the problems associated with it were less a source of concern than they were for male respondents. Far more women in that study also indicated that they wished to grow old within the framework of a long-term gay liaison.

A relatively recent study by Christenson and Johnson (1973), surveyed seventy-one single (never married) women over fifty. The results showed that eight of these or 11 percent were lesbians. All of the lesbians had had sexual experiences with men. Most of the lesbians had experienced relationships with other women in their younger years and had a-dopted heterosexual behavior afterwards (then returning to lesbianism).

In another recent study, the *Redbook* Report on Female Sexuality, Carol Tavris (1977) interviewed several lesbian couples over the age of fifty, as well as many straight women in the same age group. She reported that the gay women's concerns about aging concentrated on feelings of loneliness in old age as well as on a loss of physical attractiveness. These paralleled the problems faced by many straight women interviewed.

THE UNIQUENESS OF THE AGING LESBIAN EXPERIENCE

On the other hand, several other reports document a real difference between lesbians and heterosexual women with reference to aging problems. For example, Galana and Covina (1971) compiled a comprehensive nationwide survey of lesbian women and came to the conclusion that these individuals exhibited an "overwhelming ability to change the negative into the positive." The vast majority had strongly positive self-concepts and identifications and very few described the stereotypical butch/femme-style role-playing within their relationships.

While not a social scientist, lesbian poet Elsa Gidlow (1976), now in her seventies, has portrayed the aging process as one that is a great deal easier for lesbians than for straight women. Her belief stems from her conviction that the gay woman is insulated from what Gidlow describes as a nonfeminine emphasis on remaining youthful and retaining one's physical attractiveness.

NEEDED RESEARCH

Thus, some generalizations may be gleaned from available research on gay women and some stereotypical images may be dismissed. However, it remains quite evident that the definitive studies on lesbian life and, in particular, on the effect of aging within lesbian society, remain to be done.

Conclusion

The aging process and the problems inherent within it are difficult ones with which to come to grips. The gay woman and man share many of the same concerns and attitudes as the heterosexual woman and man. However, there are many differences, as have been documented, in the impact of aging on the gay and the heterosexual individual as well as dissimilarities between the effects of aging on the gay man and the lesbian woman.

When society can unite in support of social policy revisions which declare equal worth for all human beings "in spite of individual uniqueness and cultural (and age and race and sexual) differences ... [entitling them], therefore, to essentially equal social, economic, civil and political rights, liberties and responsibilities" (Gil, 1973, p. 7), then all gay men and women can feel that they are "brothers" and "sisters," and then . . .

> it seems we (all humans) will converge
> until we explode
> sisters and sisters
> brothers and brothers
> together
>
> (Winant, 1972, p. 6)

REFERENCES

Altman, D. 1971. *Homosexual oppression and liberation.* New York: Avon Books.

Athanasiou, R., et al. 1970. Sex. *Psychology Today* July: 39–52.

Bengtson, L. 1973. *The social psychology of aging.* New York: Bobbs-Merrill.

Berezin, A. 1969. Sex and old Age: A review of the literature. *Journal of Geriatric Psychiatry* 2:131–49.

Christenson, V., and Johnson, A. B. 1973. Sexual patterns in a group of older never-married women. *Journal of Geriatric Psychiatry* 6:80–89.

Crowley, H. 1968. *The boys in the band.* New York: Farrar, Straus & Giroux.

Cumming, E., and Henry, W. E. 1961. Growing old: The process of disengagement. New York: Basic Books.

Galana, L., and Covina, G., 1971. *The new lesbians.* Berkeley, Calif.: A Moon Books.

Gidlow, E. 1976. A view from the seventy-seventh year. *Women: A Journal of Liberation* 4:32–35.

Gil, D. 1973. *Unraveling social policy.* Cambridge, Mass.: Schenkman Publishing.

Gurin, G.; Veroff, J.; and Field, S. 1960. *Americans view their mental health.* New York: Basic Books.

Hanson, C. 1972. The fairy princess exposed. In K. Jay and A. Young, eds., *Out of the closets: Voices of gay liberation* (Moonachie, N.J.: Pyramid Publishers, Inc.).

Hite, S. 1976. *The Hite report.* New York: Macmillan Publishing.

Hooker, E. 1967. The homosexual community. In J. H. Gagnon and W. Simon eds., *Sexual deviance* (New York: Harper & Row).

Huyck, M. 1977. Sex and the older woman. In L. E. Troll et al., eds., *Looking ahead: A woman's guide to the problems and joys of growing older* (Englewood Cliffs, N. J.: Prentice-Hall), pp. 43–59.

Isherwood, C. 1964. *A single man.* London: Methuen.

Johnson, M. T., and Kelly, J. J. 1980. Deviate sex behavior in the aging. In O. Kaplan, ed., *Psychopathology and aging* (New York: Academic Press).

Kelly, J. J. 1974. *Brothers and brothers: The gay man's adaptation to aging.* Unpublished doctoral dissertation. Ann Arbor, Mich.: University Microfilms.

Kinsey, A. C., et al. 1965. *Sexual behavior in the human female.* New York: Pocket Books.

Kochera, B. 1973. The faggot's faggot . . . gay senior citizens and gay S & M. *Pittsburgh Gay News* 1 (5; 1 September): 6.

Lemert, E. M. 1951. *Social pathology.* New York: McGraw-Hill.

Marmor, J. 1965. *Sexual inversion: The multiple roots of homosexuality.* New York: Basic Books.

Martin, D., and Lyon, P. 1972. *Lesbian/Woman.* San Francisco: New Glide Publications.

NOW Task Force on Older Women. 1976. *Age is becoming: Annotated bibliography on women and aging.* San Francisco: New Glide Publications.

Phillips, G. D. 1971. Homosexuality. *Sexual behavior* Pp. 18–37.

Saghir, T., and Robins, E. 1973. *Male and female homosexuality.* Baltimore: Williams & Wilkins.

Tavris, C. 1977. The sexual lives of women over 60. *Ms.* (July), pp. 62–65.

Warren, C. A. B. 1974. *Identity and community in the gay world.* New York: John Wiley.

Weinberg, M. S. 1970. The male homosexual: Age-related variations in social and psychological characteristics. *Social Problems* 17:527–37.

Weinberg, M. S., and Williams, C. J. 1974. *Male homosexuals.* New York: Oxford University Press.

Winant, F. 1972. Christopher Street liberation day, June 28, 1970. In K. Jay and A. Young, eds., *Out of the Closets: Voices of Gay Liberation* (Moonachie, N.J.: Pyramid Publishers, Inc.).

10 / Homosexuality and the Law: From Condemnation to Celebration

RALPH SLOVENKO

The law on homosexuality is changing rapidly. It is moving from condemnation to legitimation and next, some say, to sponsorship. By and large, though not without a setback here and there, the law is in the process of turning from foe to friend of the homosexual. The development began in 1961, following a riot in New York's Greenwich Village. Homophiles in large numbers began to mobilize for the first time and soon became a political and economic force. Like women and blacks, they emerged from obscurity to fight for rights, and they have been winning these battles, at least in theory if not in practice. In 1976, for example, Governor Milton Shapp of Pennsylvania along with other political leaders publicly declared a "Gay Pride Week." If such public declarations can serve as an accurate barometer of public sentiment and legal protection, it can now be said that, in the span of less than two decades, homosexuality has moved from condemnation to celebration.

In the larger historical sense it was only yesterday that English society was rocked by the trial of one of its best-known writers. Oscar Wilde was prosecuted and found guilty in 1895 of a homosexual relationship with Lord Alfred Douglas. He was sentenced to two years in prison under the most horrible conditions. His health ruined by the imprisonment, he died a few years later at the age of forty-six. Although this sentence seems disproportionately severe to the contemporary observer, at the time the judge said that he wished he could have sent him to the gallows.

The alternating societal rejection and celebration (by some) of homosexuality is not a new story. The Bible tells of the inhabitants of ancient Sodom who pridefully proclaimed their homosexuality. Later a reaction set in and the prophet Isaiah condemned homosexuality along with bestiality.[1]

Toward the end of the seventeenth century, with the declining influence of religious beliefs and institutions and the corresponding rise in power of the secular state, what was formerly sin became crime. In some cases, though, the religious language was retained. Thus, some statutes continued to describe the crime as "the abominable and detestable crime against nature, not to be named among Christians, with either mankind or beast." The homosexual's crime was not merely against society, nor only against humanity, but "against nature."

In the eighteenth century these sins and crimes took new names; they became illnesses or diseases. Medicalizing replaced theologizing and criminalizing. Reformers urged the grammar of sickness as a replacement for the grammar of sin or crime in order to deal more effectively and less punitively with homosexuality and other types of behavior. It was all part of a general effort to move away from a punitive or moralistic approach to socially unacceptable behavior (Menninger, 1973; see also Berman, 1974).

But the grammar of sickness often backfires. For example, Vladimir Bukovsky, the Russian dissident, points out that during Stalin's time the label "mental illness" saved people from the labor camps, but today the psychiatric label is more harmful than helpful as far as the dissident is concerned, because of the lack of procedural safeguards in psychiatric hospitals, the indefinite period of confinement, and the type of treatment imposed. In the United States, too, the "sickness" label has worked against the homosexual. Government and many private employers justified employment discrimination against the homosexual by referring to the *Diagnostic and Statistical Manual of Mental Disorders (DSM)* of the American Psychiatric Association (APA) listing of homosexuality as a mental disorder. While very few homosexuals have been convicted of any "crime against nature"—the vast majority of homosexuals have as clean a criminal record as heterosexuals—they all fell under this "mentally disorder" label. As a consequence, various gay liberation

1. Isa. 3:9. In ancient Greece, following a period of discrimination, the famed lawmaker of Athens, Solon, gave civil rights to those who practiced homosexuality. This reflected the view of the philosopher Diogenes, that at least among the wise, free choice is the basis of every action and every relationship. This view was also reflected on the island of Lesbos, where the poet Sappho had her school for women, and from which the sexual intimacy of women takes the name lesbianism.

groups, supported by some psychiatrists, began to urge that homosexuality not be considered a form of mental illness. In 1973 the APA Board of Trustees voted unanimously (with two abstentions) to delete the term "homosexuality" from *DSM,* and to substitute in its place the term "sexual orientation disturbance," which would apply only to homosexuals who are either subjectively distressed by or in conflict with that orientation.[2]

What of the criminal law? Writings on homosexuality and the criminal law tend to be unsatisfactory because they ignore the question of how to deal with patently offensive public behavior. While the great majority of homosexuals are unobtrusive and therefore apparently indistinguishable from the rest of the population, there are some who feel so thwarted or exhibitionistic that they continually make passes or otherwise flaunt what many in society consider to be offensive behavior. Open homosexual activity has traditionally offended public decency more than public heterosexual intimacy. Many people agree that, because sex involves the most intimate aspects of a person's life, the state should not invade an individual's privacy in this respect any more than is necessary to protect other individuals and the public. As a corollary, public activity does invite and warrant the state's attention. It is not a matter of sex per se, or a question of homosexuality versus heterosexuality. It is a matter of discretion: the community needs to control, as well as to express its feelings about, gross violations of established social amenities. As I have written elsewhere, however, this can be done without specific sex laws. The use of laws neutral to sex, such as kidnapping, assault and battery, or disturbing the peace, can more fairly and adequately accomplish this goal than any specific sex laws (Slovenko, 1967, p. 265; 1971, p. 142).

For example, the sodomy cases that come before the courts today invariably involve either gross indiscretion or forceful action. Two decisions may illustrate. In one case the accused, two males, were sitting on a bus stop bench in front of a bar, embracing and kissing each other on the lips, while one was masturbating the other.[3] In the other case, the defendant savagely beat a sixteen-year-old and attempted to perform sodomy with him.[4] In both cases, in majority or dissenting opinions, the court discussed the validity or merit of the sodomy laws. This focus, however, seems misdirected as it was the notoriety or the brutality of the behavior that should have concerned the respective courts. Yet

2. In 1974, APA members voted by ballot to ratify the trustees' decision. The vote was 5,854 for the trustees' position, 3,810 against, and 367 abstentions. About half of the membership did not vote. "The professions, particularly those concerning human behavior, are a growing locus of the struggle for homosexual liberation" (Spector, 1977, p. 52).
   3. *State* v. *Mortimer,* 105 Ariz. 472, 467, P.2d 60 (1970).
   4. *State* v. *Trejo,* 83 N.M. 511, 494 P.2d 173 (1972).

these considerations are almost universally absent from sodomy statutes, and from discussion about them.[5]

The criminal law on homosexuality is rarely enforced, and even when it is, the offender is referred to a psychiatric clinic. There, more often than not, he is placed on "psychiatric probation." Although frequently unenforced, these laws have consequences: (1) they make possible the constant threat of criminal prosecution;[6] (2) they support a number of explicit legal sanctions, such as ineligibility for employment, housing, service in the armed forces, and immigration; and (3) they supply the warrant for countless other public and private discriminatory acts that lack express legal sanction. But while the criminal law may be used to justify the discrimination, it is well established that criminal laws punish acts, not status or diagnosis—and the homosexual more often than not has no criminal record of sodomy.

Homosexuality stirs anxiety, and it is this reaction—not the law, which at most buttresses the stigma—that causes the homosexual to suffer discrimination. Such is the intensity of the anxiety that ever since homophiles adopted the term "gay," to brighten their image, the word has dropped out of general usage, rendering the earlier use obsolescent.

So as a result of this anxiety aroused by even casual mention of homosexuality, when laws on sodomy are ostensibly discarded, liberalized, or decriminalized, not much really happens within the popular ethos. Approximately one-third of the states have exempted from legal sanction sex in private between consenting adults, but no change is apparent in either attitude or practice.[7] Sodomy statutes are constitutionally permissible;[8] but as a matter of enforcement, "notoriety" or "brutality" were read into them by the courts as essential elements for an offense long before the advent of the gay liberation movement.

5. See, e.g., Barnett, 1973; Boggan et al., 1975. The facts of cases are often written as an adversarial brief to the court. For example, the citation of cases involving gay people dancing together in public places may fail to note the evidence that the parties were fondling their primary sexual organs on the dance floor. That type of behavior would have been illegal for heterosexuals as well. For this omission, see the discussion of *Becker* v. *New York State Liquor Authority,* 287 N.Y.S. 2d 400, 21 N.Y. 2d 289 (1967), in Boggan et al., 1975, p. 98.

6. Judge Harold Carswell, a prior nominee for the Supreme Court, was indicted for homosexual activity.

7. The following nineteen states have repealed laws on adult consensual sex acts: California, Colorado, Connecticut, Delaware, Hawaii, Illinois, Indiana, Iowa, Maine, Nebraska, New Hampshire, New Mexico, North Dakota, Ohio, Oregon, South Dakota, Washington, West Virginia, and Wyoming. Acts of sodomy are done by heterosexuals as well as homosexuals, and so these statutes technically apply to both groups.

The English Sexual Offences Act of 1967 (which does not apply to Scotland and Northern Ireland) provides that "a homosexual act in private [rather widely interpreted] shall not be an offence provided that the parties consent thereto and have attained the age of twenty-one years." The Japanese Criminal Code is similar. See Art. 174, Penal Code; Art. 1 (20), Minor Offenses Law.

8. The U.S. Supreme Court in 1976 summarily affirmed a lower court decision upholding the constitutionality of Virginia's law barring consensual sodomy.

In general, full sanctions for deviations from standards of conduct are not applied when there is a valid excuse. In common parlance, the formula for excuse is, "I didn't know what I was doing," or "I couldn't help it." One is not blamed for an undesirable involuntary act though one may be blamed for the voluntary act which caused or promoted the involuntary act's occurrence.

An individual may be excused for having become a homosexual, through no fault of his own, but it is the public—not private—manifestation of homosexuality (and, for that matter, heterosexuality) which the ordinary citizen finds unpleasant and annoying. The privacy of one's home is one thing, the view on the street is another. Those who insist that homosexuality may be regarded as a problem even when it is done in private are still split in their opinions as to what sort of problem it must be considered to be. Some worry about it as a health problem (homosexuality is an "illness"), others as a moral or legal problem. But even if one considers homosexuality as a health or psychological problem, the law by providing some external control may contribute to its resolution—at least to the extent of deterring the overt behavior.[9]

Compared to the United States and other Western countries, there are few overt homosexuals in the Soviet Union. Homosexuality is against the law in a number of countries,[10] but among them, only the USSR uniformly enforces the law with a heavy hand. A penalty of five years' imprisonment is imposed for overt homosexual behavior or the strong suspicion of it (up to eight years if committed with a minor or by exploiting the position of a dependent or if accompanied by physical force or threats).[11] Soviet psychiatrists consider homosexuality to be an unquestionable manifestation of emotional illness which should be treated, but they report few cases. There are certainly homosexuals in hiding, and one cannot precisely estimate their number. There is rarely, if ever, to be seen in the USSR a male who walks with a swishy gait or talks like a woman.

Should homosexuality be deterred, and if so, by what means? The answer depends upon answers to other questions: Is homosexuality a handicap to the individual, or to the social fabric? Does homosexuality in and of itself disturb one's well-being or inner serenity, warranting a

9. The English Sexual Offences Act (1967), based on the Wolfenden Report, provides that, subject to exceptions, a homosexual act in private is not an offense. The most important exception relates to participating persons who have not attained the age of twenty-one.

10. In these countries provision is made for the punishment of homosexual behavior per se, but the sanction is practically a dead letter where there is no peculiar element involved (e.g., an element of duress, extortion, assault, etc., which would in any event render the particular behavior punishable in terms of other crimes). This, for instance, is the case in Bulgaria, Ireland, Rumania, Scotland, Yugoslavia, Latin American, and African countries, and in certain states in the United States (Van Niekerk, 1970).

11. From the Revolution until 1933, sodomy between consenting adults was not a crime in Russia.

psychiatric label? Can the homosexual adequately function vocationally and socially? How does homosexuality affect, if at all, nonsexual morals, values, ideals, commitment to goals? Is homosexuality, by chance, an advantage? History, we know, is replete with illustrious homosexuals— was the creativity generated by or in spite of their homosexuality? Are homosexuals more creative or sensitive than others, as is sometimes claimed? The questions go on and on, but most of the answers are inadequate or simply conjecture.

At one time, homosexuals looked upon the law as an enemy; now they look upon it as a potential ally—as a means to bar discrimination in employment, housing, and public accommodations. Fund drives and national committees have been organized, including several that are lobbying for federal legislation and White House support.

The gay community suffered a setback in the 1977 Miami election concerning the rights of homosexuals,[12] but generally the tide is running the other way. The homosexual community has become active politically, and the growing political consciousness, gay activists say, will be a factor to be reckoned with.

Freedom of Speech and Association

At a number of universities, gay student service organizations have sought university recognition in order to have the benefit of facilities enjoyed by other recognized groups. To date, the First, Fourth and Eighth Circuits, United States Courts of Appeals, have ruled that a state-run university may not constitutionally withhold recognition of a student organization, composed largely of homosexuals, whose basic purpose is to provide a forum for a discussion of homosexuality.[13] The Eighth Circuit stated that even if it were to accept the argument that the presence of a gay organization on campus would render homosexual activity more likely, this would still be "insufficient to justify a governmental prior restraint on the right of a group of students to associate for the purposes avowed in their [policy statement]." The

12. With evangelical fervor, Anita Bryant, a religious gospel singer and television purveyor of Florida orange juice, led a fundamentalist "Christian Crusade Against Homosexuality." "If homosexuality were the normal way," asserted Miss Bryant, "God would have made Adam and Bruce." During a debate she would break into a patriotic rendering of "The Battle Hymn of the Republic." Bumper stickers said: "Squeeze a fruit for Anita," and "Kill a queer for Christ."

13. *Gay Students Organization of University of New Hampshire* v. *Bonner,* 509 F.2d 652 (1st Cir. 1974); *Gay Alliance of Students* v. *Matthews,* 544 F.2d 162 (4th Cir. 1976); *Gay Lib* v. *University of Missouri,* 558 F.2d 848 (8th Cir. 1977).

court noted the absence of any finding that the gay organization, at least in the record presented, advocated any unlawful activity or would infringe reasonable campus rules, interrupt classes, or substantially interfere with the opportunity of other students to obtain an education. The court said that to ascribe evil connotations to the group simply because they are homosexuals "smacks of penalizing persons for their status rather than their conduct, which is constitutionally impermissible." Suits are pending against a number of universities in other circuits.

Access to the Press

Freedom of speech is linked to publication. The wider the dissemination, the wider and heavier the impact. To what extent does one's freedom of speech justify shackling another with the burden of publication?

Do the media have the right to be silent on issues about which they do not want the public to know? What is fit to publish, in news or advertisement? Should the society page of a newspaper cover gay activities? Should it give publicity to the union of "lovers"? Under the law of libel and slander it has long been considered defamatory upon its face to (untruthfully) say that a person is a homosexual, because it "obviously tends to affect the esteem in which he is held by his neighbors,"[14] but many avowed gays now actively seek rather than shun publicity.

Any guarantee to those interested in homosexuality of the right freely to associate with one another is linked to access to information relevant to their concerns. In this connection, gay groups seek to place advertisements in publications to notify persons who are homosexuals, who are interested in the subject of homosexuality, or who have problems relating to homosexuality that certain services are available to them at a "gay center." The First Amendment does not protect speech soliciting criminal activity, but is criminal activity involved here? One may not be prosecuted for *being* a homosexual—no statute makes criminal the status of being a homosexual; indeed, no statute could do that and survive constitutional challenge—but one may be prosecuted for the commission of homosexual acts under the traditional law.[15] Hence, in such jurisdictions, arguably no publication may be required to advertise solicitations for homosexual contacts, any more than a paper could be expected to advertise solicitations for contacts with prostitutes.

14. Prosser, W. L. *Law of Torts.* St. Paul, Minn., West, 1971, p. 740.
15. *Robinson* v. *California,* 370 U.S. 660 (1962).

Many newspapers restrict or reject prurient ads that are "offensive to good taste." In a recent case, the Mississippi Gay Alliance sought judicial compulsion to require a student newspaper to publish an advertisement which that paper did not want to print. It was agreed that the advertisement did not directly solicit anything approaching criminal activity. The American Civil Liberties Union contends that such restrictions are "a blow to the concept of free speech, freedom of expression and the rights of people to have information." Ordinarily, a First Amendment case seeks to set aside an order prohibiting publication; this case, on the other hand, sought an order compelling publication. According to prevailing law, in the absence of state action the choice of material to go into a newspaper is within the exercise of editorial control and judgment. In the Mississippi case, it was held that inasmuch as students elected the editor and the university officials did not supervise or control what was to be published or not published, the First Amendment interdicted judicial interference with the editorial decision not to accept the proposed advertisement.[16]

Access to Broadcasting

Access to the press is one thing; to the electronic media, quite another. In the electronic media, outlets are more difficult to obtain, so in seeking a larger piece of the pie, there is less available to others.

The electronic media, unlike the press, are regulated by the Federal Communications Commission. Broadcasters have a responsibility under the law to serve the public interest. The FCC compels a broadcast licensee to ascertain the problems, needs, and interests of the community and to arrange informational programming to meet those needs. "Problems, needs, and interests" must be determined on the basis of a random public survey and a series of interviews with representative leaders of various segments of the community. Not surprisingly, the ascertainment requirement has stirred the opposition of various organized groups.[17]

Gays contend that, considering their number, they constitute a substantial and distinct community group, and are entitled to a significant voice. They claim that their concerns are not presently being given adequate attention, notwithstanding the national publicity they have

16. *Mississippi Gay Alliance* v. *Goudelock,* 536 F.2d 1073 (5th Cir. 1976).

17. E.g., *Office of Communications of United Church of Christ* v. *FCC,* 359 F.2d 994 (D.C. Cir. 1966). See Emerson, 1976.

been receiving. A conservative "guess-timate" is that 1 in 20 people in the United States, approximately 10 million, are homosexual (the figure includes about 2.5 million male homosexuals, 1 million lesbians, and 6 million bisexuals). Many experts in sexuality believe the homosexual population percentage is as high as 10 percent, or more than 20 million people. In any event, whatever the estimate, gays contend that they are not properly represented on the airwaves.[18]

In general, the important question lingers: how closely do First Amendment justifications actually fit the practical operation of the ascertainment requirement and of related doctrines regulating content in the interest of the consumer? Does the requirement of ascertainment of community concerns and correlative programming threaten the First Amendment rights of broadcasters without significantly advancing the First Amendment rights of the audience? Professor W. C. Canby (1976), writing in the *Texas Law Review,* argues that the constitutional interest of the audience should not be labeled a "right to hear" because the desires of all listeners can never be even partially satisfied. There will always be at least one wholly dissatisfied segment of the audience. Rather, he suggests analyzing the consumer interest as a speech interest and advocates a system of limited public access to best accommodate the First Amendment interests of broadcasters and broadcast consumers (Canby, 1976, p. 67).[19]

Housing and Accommodations

The availability of housing and other food and lodging accommodations play an important role in the style of habitation that prevails in a society. "Living in sin" is impeded by limitations on housing, hotel, or automobile. In Eastern Europe, where housing is scarce, preferential

18. A Miami judge refused to order two television stations and a dozen radio broadcasters to air advertisements sponsored by opponents of Dade County's hotly debated homosexual rights ordinance (*UPI news release,* 27 May 1977).

19. Professor Canby adds (in correspondence): "I would visualize a group of gays having the same status as any other organized group in seeking the access to radio or television. And, like other groups, I would apply the same analysis to them; namely, that they have a right to speak but that there is no particular right in the audience either to hear or not to hear their message. The real problem, of course, is that as yet there has been no recognition of a right of access, and whether or not gay groups are given access depends greatly on the discretion of the broadcaster. I would not impose access as part of the listeners right to hear, but I would impose it as part of the right of the group to speak, and let it take its place in line with other organized groups. I suppose that it may all be academic if the FCC never approaches the problem the way I have. I can hope, however" (correspondence of 23 September 1977, to author; quoted with permission).

placement is given to married couples. Singles and the unmarried living-together have no priority. In those countries even heterosexuals often enter into a fictitious marriage in order to get an apartment, then divorce, and quarrel over who gets the place.

In the United States, there is private and public housing. In the case of private housing, the "fundamental right normally associated with the ownership of property is that of an owner to decide who may reside on the property."[20] That right is not absolute, however; it is cut across by zoning laws. Zoning may define living patterns. It may prohibit the use of dwellings by unrelated individuals, whatever may be the wishes of the owner of the property.

Public housing is available for "families of low income." Public housing has been thought of as a means to help traditional families through adverse economic circumstances and, in particular, as a way to protect children from the full force of poverty. In reality, traditional families headed by both mother and father make up only a fraction of those seeking public housing.[21] It may be argued that public funds should not be used to subsidize what many consider to be immoral conduct, but it may also be argued that government is not responsible for changes in life-styles; it is simply responsive to them.

It is within the jurisdiction of the Department of Housing and Urban Development, subject to approval of the local housing authorities, to set up guidelines in this area. It is not to discriminate on "any arbitrary basis." Faced by the pressure of changing life-styles, on 9 May 1977, HUD opened public housing to unmarried couples living together and to homosexual couples if they can show a "stable family relationship." "The expanded concept of the family is 'very brand new' and liberalizes the country's housing policy," said the HUD housing program specialist who wrote the new rules.

In the past couples accepted for public housing have been low-income, married, and heterosexual or have met state tests for a common-law relationship. (About 1.3 million adult men and women lived together as unmarried heterosexual couples in 1976, according to the Census Bureau. The number had doubled since 1970.) Under the HUD regulation issued in 1977, a family consists of "two or more persons, sharing residency whose income and resources are available to meet

20. A lease may limit use of a house or apartment to a tenant and "immediate family." In the case of unmarried heterosexuals living together, some courts have ruled against evictions under the provision. In a recent case in New York, for example, a landlord sought to oust a tenant from the rent-controlled apartment he had been sharing with a woman for over four years. The landlord cited the "immediate family" clause in the lease. The court said that while the woman was not technically a member of the tenant's immediate family, "she certainly is in the eyes of today's world" (Dullea, 1977, p. C–12).

21. A majority are single-parent families headed by women who have been divorced from, deserted by, or never married to the father or fathers of their children. An unknown number are, in fact, living with men other than their legal husbands.

the family's needs and who are related by blood, marriage or operation of law, or have evidenced a stable family relationship." Local HUD officials were left to interpret what constitutes a "stable family relationship"; HUD officials in Washington said they hope local housing authorities will interpret the new rules "generously."

The HUD regulation admittedly was drawn to accommodate homosexuals in programs of rent or mortgage subsidies. Within a month, on 15 June 1977, the House of Representatives, with little debate, voted to nullify the regulation. It may be more than a coincidence that, by a large majority, the voters of Dade County, Florida, had just endorsed Anita Bryant's much-publicized crusade for the repeal of its ordinance outlawing discrimination against homosexuals in housing, employment, and public accommodations.

A word about other accommodations is appropriate here. The keeper of a hotel or restaurant bar may be charged with suffering or permitting his premises to become disorderly and thus subject his liquor license to revocation, so he is advised to eject homosexuals from the premises.[22] Turning to their own places, gays often find them inadequate in many respects. Gay activist leaders protest what they call unequal enforcement of city health and safety laws at homosexual meeting places such as the Everard Baths in New York City where nine people died in a fire. They accused the city of "selective enforcement" of standards; the standards of safety, they said, were not the same for gays as for mainstream society.[23]

Employment

There is current legislation before the Congress striking at discrimination against members of the gay community in the area of employment as well as in housing and public accommodations.

Discrimination of some sort is inherent in the employee selection

22. A number of courts have ruled that a liquor license of a bar or restaurant may not be revoked merely because apparent homosexuals are permitted to congregate there. *One Eleven W. & L., Inc.* v. *Division of Alcoholic Beverage Control,* 50 N.J. 329, 235 A. 2d 12 (1967); *Stoumen* v. *Reilly,* 234 P.2d 969 (Cal. 1951). However, such places may be particularly susceptible to political pressure and accused of being places in which there is solicitation or disorderly conduct.

23. *New York Post,* 27 May 1977, p. 4. The Civil Rights Commission recently announced that, while it does not have legal authority to investigate homosexual rights complaints in general, it will look into specific cases involving alleged unequal administration of justice against homosexuals. The Commission cited as examples the courts and prisons. *AP news release,* 6 September 1977.

process. One surely does not put a mental defective at the helm of a ship. The question is always: What is important, what matters, and what is the rational connection between the alleged defect and the performance of the job? And in all cases of alleged improper discrimination, how can the real reason for the rejection be ascertained? The stated reason is, of course, always a lawful reason. Antidiscrimination legislation would be difficult to enforce, gays admit, but nevertheless they want it for its symbolic value. They want the seal on their style of life to say "good" or, at least, "acceptable."

Private Employment In private employment, the basic common-law principle was that individual citizens are free to make such transactions as they choose to make—advised or ill-advised, wise or foolish, morally right or morally wrong, indeed, prejudiced or unprejudiced. The freedom envisaged is based upon the assumption that free people would, as a body, ultimately choose wisely and righteously. Another assumption is that, in order to be free, an individual must be free to do wrong. For a people to be free to do only that which is right necessarily assumes that there will be some government or other institution to say, with authority, what is right.[24]

Nevertheless, many restraints have been placed upon the employer-employee relationship over the years (e.g., Norris-LaGuardia Act, Labor-Management Act, Fair Labor Standards Act, Age Discrimination in Employment Act, and Title VII of the Civil Rights Act of 1974). There is no longer reserved to the employer completely unfettered discretion to pick and choose as he wishes, wisely or foolishly, from good motive or bad.

A number of federal, state, and local laws now proscribe discrimination in employment on grounds of gender, race, and religion. Title VII guarantees equal job opportunities for males and females. This law, though, says nothing about forbidding discrimination based on "affectional or sexual preference" of an applicant. By its silence, the law gives an employer the option of rejecting an employee because he cannot abide his sexual life-style. It is not considered sex discrimination to refuse to hire a male displaying feminine characteristics.[25]

So far, no state legislatures have passed laws proscribing discrimination based on a person's sexual preference, nor has the Congress, but approximately forty cities have passed ordinances to that effect.[26] In

24. *Smith* v. *Liberty Mutual Insurance Co.*, 395 F. Supp. 1098 (N.D. Ga. 1975).
25. *Smith* v. *Liberty Mutual Insurance Co.*, 395 F. Supp. 1098 (N.D. Ga. 1975); see Siniscalco, 1976, p. 495.
26. Gay rights protections have been adopted in the following municipalities: in 1972—Atlanta, Ga., San Francisco, Calif., New York, N.Y., East Lansing, Mich., Ann Arbor, Mich.; in 1973—Columbus, Ohio, Minneapolis, Minn., Alfred, N.Y., St. Paul, Minn., Palo Alto, Calif., Ithaca, N.Y., Sunnyvale, Calif., San Jose, Calif., Portland, Ore.; in 1975—Mountain View, Calif., Cupertino, Calif., Madison, Wis., Marshall, Minn., Yellow Springs, Ohio, Austin, Texas, Santa Barbara, Calif., Chapel Hill, N. C., Bloomington, Ind., Urbana, Ill.; in 1976—Cleveland Heights, Ohio, Boston, Mass., Pullman, Wash., Amherst, Mass.,

contrast, in the much publicized referendum mentioned earlier, the first of its kind in the United States, Miami area residents voted against an ordinance protecting homosexuals from discrimination in employment, housing, and accommodations. Much concern has been expressed that the fallout of the Miami election may lead to new restrictive legislation in other parts of the United States.

Public Employment   As a rule, the government as employer may not discriminate against employees on the basis of their sexual orientation. The Constitution protects individuals against mistreatment by official bodies. Protection against discrimination by private employers or hotels requires civil rights legislation of the kind Miami voters vetoed for homosexuals.

The constitutional requirement that governmental agencies act fairly to all citizens applies to local, state, and federal agencies, but the principle has developed most fully at the federal level. In 1975 the U.S. Civil Service Commission stated that people may not be found unsuitable for federal employment "solely on the basis of homosexual conduct." Before then, the Civil Service Commission had publicly announced a discriminatory policy on the basis of sexual orientation. Nevertheless, gay groups point to discrimination in a number of governmental agencies, including the State Department, the Federal Bureau of Investigation, and the Central Intelligence Agency. In fact, the new governmental guidelines contain specific prohibitions against hiring homosexuals in the FBI and the CIA.

In the early 1950s, when there was great concern about communist subversion among the employees of the executive branch of the federal government, a special investigating subcommittee was created in the U.S. Senate to make recommendations concerning the employment of homosexuals by the federal government. This subcommittee concluded that "those who engage in acts of homosexuality and other perverted sex acts are unsuitable for employment in the federal government. This conclusion is based on the fact that persons who engage in such degrading activity are committing not only illegal and immoral acts, but they also constitute security risks in positions of public trust." The report of the subcommittee further stated that the "emotional instability and weak moral-fiber" of the homosexual made him untrustworthy.[27]

Los Angeles, Calif.; in 1977—Tucson, Ariz., Iowa City, Iowa, Champaigne, Ill., Wichita, Kan., and Eugene, Ore. Also in 1975, the counties of Santa Cruz, Calif., Howard, Md., and Hennepin, Minn., and in 1976, the State of Pennsylvania (in regard to state employment) adopted gay rights protections.

27. U.S. Senate, Interim Report submitted to the Committee on Expenditures in Executive Depts. by its Sub-Committee of Investigations, "Employment of Homosexuals and Other Sex Perverts in Government," 81st Cong., S. Doc. 241. See *Federal Personnel Manual Supplement* (Washington, D.C. United States Governemnt Printing Office), pp. 731–71; Note, Government Created Employment Disability of the Homo-

In 1969 the Court of Appeals for the District of Columbia imposed limits on this policy, holding that it was overly broad and a denial of due process.[28] Other courts followed the precedent. As a consequence, the application form for public employment now does not ask about homosexuality. The Civil Service regulations, as amended in 1975, deleted "immoral conduct" from the list of specific factors for disqualification from employment. "Criminal, dishonest or notoriously disgraceful conduct" may still be considered as reasons for disqualification from employment, but "immoral conduct" may not.[29]

Investigation may turn up material that affects the applicant's "suitability for the job." Today, confronted by the gay liberation and other civil rights movements, the federal or state employers, like their private counterparts, rarely give homosexuality as a reason for disqualification. Instead, other reasons are stated which may or may not be a rationalization of antigay discrimination. Even the first-year law student quickly learns that the values or motives that lie beneath the reasons given for a particular decision, even by a court, are often unexpressed. Legal doctrines are all too often ways of disguising the real issues.

If homosexual behavior is actually given as the reason for termination of public employment, the courts now require proof of "a rational nexus between the conduct complained of and job performance."[30] The court considers the specific requirements of the position. As one court put it: "Conduct that may not be deleterious to the performance of a specific governmental position—i.e., a Department of Agriculture employee— may be deleterious to the performance of another governmental occupation—i.e., teacher or houseparent in a mental ward."[31] Jeopardization of security due to the potential for blackmail is a well-known proposition. Also, the credibility of a witness at trial is diminished by an allusion that he is a homosexual; it brands him as a liar (see Hiss, 1977).

Homosexuals who are employed by the government may have some protection, but the Civil Service Commission is not obliged to "sponsor" homosexual activity, the U. S. Court of Appeals for the

---

sexual, *Harvard Law Review* 82 (1969):1738.

28. *Norton* v. *Macy*, 417 F.2d 1161 (D.C. Cir. 1969). See Note, Government Employment and the Homosexual, *St. John's Law Review* 45 (1970):303.

29. 40 Fed. Reg. 28047 (1975).

30. The Supreme Court recently declined to accept an appeal by a Washington state school teacher, James Gaylord, who was fired under a school district rule against "immorality" after he disclosed he was a homosexual. State courts had ruled that homosexual teachers may be fired because of their sexual preference. *Gaylord* v. *Tacoma School District No. 10*, 88 Wash.2d 286, 559 P.2d 1340 (1977). The Supreme Court also declined to review a case involving a homosexual teacher in New Jersey who was ordered by the board of education to undergo a psychiatric examination after he became president of the state's Gay Activist Alliance. *Gish* v. *City of Paramus*, 145 N.J. Super. 96, 366 A.2d 1337 (1976), *cert. den.*, 74 N.J. 251, 377 A.2d 658 (1977).

31. *Safransky* v. *State Personnel Board*, 215 N.W. 2d 379 (Wis. 1974). Sexual conduct as ground for dismissal of teacher or denial or revocation of teaching certificate is discussed in 73 ALR3d 19.

Ninth Circuit has said. It held in a 1975 case that the Commission had established a rational connection between the employee's deliberately public homosexual involvement and detriment to the efficiency of the federal service. In this case the employee, a clerk-typist, had on several occasions publicly disclosed his sexual preference while identifying himself as an employee of a federal agency. He had, with full media coverage, applied for a license to marry another male, and he was also active in a gay organization. The Ninth Circuit concluded that the government's interest in promoting the efficiency of the public service outweighed the employee's interest in freedom of expression.[32]

It has been the lower courts (not the appellate courts) in recent years that have demanded that the Civil Service Commission show how the individual's conduct relates to his occupational fitness. It had been unquestioned federal policy to regard homosexual acts as ipso facto basis for dismissal from the Civil Service until very recently. Illuminating the old policy is this 1966 communication by the Chairman of the Civil Service Commission, which is now a matter of public record:

> Suitability determinations also comprehend the total impact of the applicant upon his job. Pertinent considerations here are the revulsion of other employees by homosexual conduct and the consequent disruption of service efficiency, the apprehension caused other employees by homosexual advances, solicitations or assaults, the unavoidable subjection of the sexual deviate to neurotic stimulation through on-the-job use of common toilet, shower, and living facilities, the offense to members of the public who are required to deal with a known or admitted sexual deviate to transact Government business, the hazard that the prestige and authority of a Government position will be used to foster homosexual activity, particularly among the youth, and the use of Government funds and authority to furtherance of conduct offensive both to the mores and the law of our society.[33]

32. *Singer* v. *United States Civil Service Commission*, 530 F.2d 247 (9th Cir. 1976). In a two-sentence order, the Supreme Court remanded the case to the Court of Appeals for reconsideration in light of a memorandum submitted to the Court by the Solicitor General on behalf of the Civil Service Commission. The memorandum suggested that the case be returned to the Civil Service Commission so that Singer can be given a new hearing under the standards embodied in the Commission's new, more favorable policy regarding the employment of homosexuals. Under the new policy, homosexuals can be terminated where there is evidence that their homosexual conduct affects job fitness, but terminations based on unsubstantiated conclusions about possible embarrassment to the federal service are not permitted. In a somewhat unusual move, the Solicitor General, on behalf of the Commission, joined Singer in urging the Supreme Court to grant certiorari. The Solicitor General stated that the Commission, since it has adopted new guidelines concerning the employment of homosexuals, has no interest in judicial resolution of the issue of whether it is permissible to terminate an employee for advocating homosexuality and has determined to give Singer the benefit of a hearing under the new guidelines. 3 Sex. L. Rptr. 1 (1977). See Siniscalco, 1976, p. 494.

33. Appendix D to Brief for Certiorari, *Murray* v. *Macy, Chairman, U.S. Civil Service Commission*, 393 U.S. 1041 (1969).

Increasingly, as employment is viewed more as a constitutionally protected right than as a mere privilege, that view is either being abandoned or going unacknowledged.

Military Policy

The United States bars homosexuals from service in the armed forces on the theory that they hurt recruiting, create disciplinary problems, lower morale, and raise security issues. It is official policy to discharge such persons (including men and women who have won Purple Hearts) with less-than-honorable discharges and no veterans' rights. The Navy and Air Force, however, have recently upgraded dishonorable discharges given homosexuals. In 1977, Navy Secretary W. Graham Claytor upgraded to honorable the discharge of a Naval Academy graduate, Ens. Vernon Berg 3d, who had acknowledged committing homosexual acts while in the service. The Air Force did the same a year earlier in the case of Sgt. Leonard Matlovich, who had been commended for his Vietnam War record but was ordered discharged when he likewise admitted being a practicing homosexual. Notwithstanding the American Psychiatric Association's statement that "homosexuality per se implies no impairment in judgment, stability, reliability or general social or vocational capabilities," the Air Force decided that Sgt. Matlovich's continuance in uniform would be too stressful—for the Air Force. Federal District Judge Gerhard Gesell, though dismissing a suit by Sgt. Matlovich for reinstatement, said that the time had come for the Air Force to reexamine its "knee-jerk reaction to some of these cases."

Judge Gesell also refused to order the Navy to reinstate Ensign Berg. Judge Gesell said that Berg's dismissal "due to his homosexual activity places no restriction to his right to associate with whomever he chooses, and clearly does not contravene the First Amendment." Berg's claim that his right to privacy had been invaded was "more troublesome," Judge Gesell said, but he concluded that "an individual's right to privacy does not extend to homosexual conduct even when it occurs in private between consenting adults." Despite this opinion, Judge Gesell urged the Navy to clarify its policies on homosexuals in the service. "In the final analysis, there is an obligation to accommodate personnel policy to changing scientific knowledge and social standards to the fullest extent so long as conduct which threatens to interfere with defense objectives can be avoided."[34]

34. 3 Sex. L. Rptr. 26 (1977); The *New York Times,* 28 May 1977, p. 35.

The announcement of the upgrading of Berg's and Matlovich's discharge from dishonorable to honorable marked the first indications of a change in military policy toward homosexuals. But Berg himself says: "Stating that *all* future discharges would be fully honorable unless other reasons existed for a dishonorable discharge, the Navy seems to feel that its 'problem' has been solved. It has not. Where no violent crime has been committed, where no act of indiscretion has occurred, where no noticeable effects are transferred to job performance, there should be *no* discharge at all."[35]

The military now says that it does not automatically rule that there is a nexus between homosexuality and qualification. It asks, "Will the presence of this individual in the military be conducive to 'good order'?" In every case, it has found that homosexuality is not in the interest of "good order." The reasoning is new, the conclusion is old.

Immigration and Naturalization

The United States bars homophiles from visiting or becoming citizens. Gay groups and their supporters claim this is a violation of the Helsinki Declaration and the freedom to travel.

The entry of aliens into the United States is governed by the Immigration and Naturalization Act of 1952, as amended.[36] Subsection (4) of section 212(a) of the act excludes aliens "afflicted with psychopathic personality or sexual deviation or a mental defect." Such an alien may be deported if the condition is discovered after entry.[37] The U.S. Supreme Court has stated its conclusion that the Congress used the phrase "psychopathic personality" not in the clinical sense but to effectuate its purpose to exclude from entry "all homosexuals and other sexual perverts."[38] The change in nomenclature of the American Psychiatric Association, removing homosexuality from the list of sexual deviations and mental disorders, has not resulted in a change in immigration and naturalization policy.

With regard to the incidence of cases involving women as com-

35. Berg, V. E., letter to The *New York Times*, 27 May 1977, p. 24.
36. 8 U.S.C. § 1251.
37. Evidence that an alien had given false testimony concerning alleged homosexual proclivities more than five years prior to filing of a petition for naturalization sustains denial of a petition for naturalization. *Kovacs* v. *United States*, 476 F.2d 843 (2d Cir. 1973).
38. *Boutilier* v. *Immigration & Naturalization Service*, 387 U.S. 118 (1967).

pared to men, the Immigration and Naturalization Service at the Port of Detroit advises: "We do not recall ever seeing a case involving female homosexuality. We are either overlooking or unwittingly missing the females. This may be attributed to many causes such as easier outward identification or suspicion of males, and most probably the sheer lack of numbers. In the future we will keep a closer eye on the women."[39]

The Immigration and Naturalization Service not only excludes, it also deports or refuses citizenship to homosexual aliens on the ground that they do not possess the "good moral character" required for citizenship.[40] For naturalization, a person must "prove" he is of good moral character and, as the law now stands, the Service assumes that the homosexual is precluded from such a characterization.[41]

Health, Education and Welfare

Federal grants for research and social services have been severely limited, gays say, as they apply to gay issues and programs. Gay groups urge that such existing programs as services for the aged and volunteer services for community self-help programs be expanded to meet the needs of the gay community.

In the private realm, a developer in California is planning what is announced as the first male homosexual retirement home. Lesbians in

39. Correspondence of 20 April 1977, from the Immigration & Naturalization Service, Detroit, Michigan, to author.

40. 8 U.S.C. § 1427(a).

41. This position was upheld in *Petition of Olga Schmidt*, 289 N.Y. Supp. 2d 89 (1968). In contrast, a federal district court in 1971 held that a petitioner's private homosexual conduct did not prevent his naturalization. In this case the petitioner had led a quiet life as an immigrant, his homosexual relations were purely private with consenting adults. He did not corrupt morals of others, such as minors, or engage in publicly offensive activities, such as solicitation or public display; he was gainfully employed, highly regarded by his employer and associates; and he had submitted to therapy that was unsuccessful. The court held that he was a person of "good moral character." *In re Labaddy*, 326 F. Supp. 924 (S.D. N.Y. 1971). This being an isolated decision, the Service continues to recommend to the courts that homosexuals be denied citizenship on the ground that they do not possess the good moral character required for citizenship. Correspondence of March 22, 1977, from Immigration & Naturalization Service, Detroit, Michigan, to Ralph Slovenko.

On August 2, 1979, the Public Health Service announced that it would no longer conduct examinations on sexual orientation, thus removing from the INS the means to apply the law. Immigration authorities say they do not know, at the moment, what their next step will be. However, they seem disinclined to follow the Public Health Service's lead in administratively changing policy toward homosexuals and they question whether the Health Service's action was legal. *New York Times*, 12 August 1979, p. 20.

New York envision a "lesbian Workman's Circle" for the same purpose (Lichtenstein, 1977, p. 37).

Tax Status

Certain organizations are given tax-exempt and tax-deductible status; a donor to such an organization may deduct his contribution in computing his federal taxable income. These are organizations organized and operated exclusively for one or more of the following purposes: religious, charitable, scientific, testing for public safety, literary, educational, or for prevention of cruelty to children or animals. Such organizations are generally prohibited from "carrying on propaganda, or otherwise attempting, to influence legislation" and from "participating" or "intervening" in political campaigns on behalf of particular candidates.[42]

An organization formed "to promote American ideals," or "to foster the best interests of the people," or "to further the common welfare and well-being of the community" is not given tax exemption status because "such purposes are vague and may be accomplished other than in an exempt manner."[43]

The Internal Revenue Service has denied the applications of gay organizations for tax-exempt status. Gay organizations want to state the view that homosexuality is an acceptable alternate life-style. That has not been considered an acceptable tax-exempt purpose by the Service.

Prisoners' Rights

The "prison-law explosion" of the past two decades is traceable to religious cases. Black Muslim prisoners in the early 1960s sought changes in prison administration and complained about interference with the free exercise of religion. Starting with this litigation, federal courts engaged in a broad review of prison programs and activities. What was before an essentially unregulated administrative matter has now become subjected to a significant measure of judicial control.

42. Internal Revenue Code of 1954, § 170; IRS Regulations, 26 CFR § 1.170.
43. Internal Revenue Service, Publication 557.

Gays have followed the approach of the Black Muslims. Inmates in California requested the ministry and congregated services of the Metropolitan Community Church (MCC), the "gay church." The state authorities banned all activities of the group in prison, contending that the MCC is not a bona fide religion and that the ban on the MCC's congregated services and group activities was justified by concern for the security of the institutions and the welfare and safety of the inmates. A three-judge court, however, found that the MCC has the "cardinal characteristics" of a religion, "in that it teaches and preaches a belief in a Supreme Being, a religious discipline and tenets to guide one's daily existence." As such, the inmates were held to have standing to contest the state's total ban on their group activities. The court held that state authorities would have to show a compelling state interest in orderly prison administration to the extent that, were it not for the ban, a clear and present danger of breach of prison security or inmate safety would be present.[44] Following this decision, California prison authorities, agreeing to a consent order to resolve the complaint, allowed MCC representatives to enter the institutions and conduct services and other ministry to inmates.

In appraising this decision, one should recall that restrictions may be placed on religious activities to the extent that such restrictions can be proven necessary in order to protect the security, health, or orderly running of the institution.[45] The Constitution ordains an absolute guarantee of freedom of religious beliefs, but *actions,* taken upon those beliefs, do not have absolute protection, and may be regulated to the extent necessary to protect the health, welfare, and good order of society.[46] With the Black Muslims, for example, the organization's newspaper and publications may be excluded by prison authorities if they are shown to be inflammatory, posing a threat to the internal order and security of the institution.

In the same sense, federal prisoners have been denied the right to receive gay publications on the ground that such publications will make their recipients subject to sexual abuse from nongay prisoners. Gay rights groups contend that homosexual prisoners have been denied equal educational and recreational opportunities on similar grounds, while at the same time, it is alleged, prison officials have failed to protect gay inmates from abuse and assault and have often been parties to such abuse.

---

44. *Lipp* v. *Procunier,* 395 F. Supp. 871 (N.D. Cal., 1975).
45. Cripe, 1977; Comment, The Religious Rights of the Incarcerated, *University of Pennsylvania Law Review* 125 (1977):812.
46. *Cantwell* v. *Connecticut,* 310 U.S. 296 (1940).

Child Custody and Visitation Rights

The issues of child custody and parental visitation rights are generally determined by the "best interest of the child" rule. Since there appears to be a link between "best interest" and "better" parent, the issue becomes one of comparative fitness of the parents. Today, as a matter of trial practice, the husband generally carries the burden of proving the mother is unfit. How is that to be done? As in other areas, allegations on fitness are made which are likely to bring results. In child custody disputes, one allegation that tends to be very successful is that the mother is a lesbian. While there is no rule of law equating lesbianism with unfitness, the judge, exercising discretion, tends to equate the two.[47] Judges appear to frown on both beer-drinking and lesbianism, as if the two formed the quintessence of an unfit mother.

As a matter of law, lesbianism is not deemed irrelevant to a determination of fitness.[48] A lesbian may provide adequate care and attention, it is argued, but a homophile is not a good role-model. Moreover, it is contended that not only is a homophile an unsuitable role-model, but such a parent may prompt stigmatization and ridicule of the children by their peers. Hence, to an allegation of homosexuality, one may not demur or shrug one's shoulders and say, "So what?"—but must answer with facts rebutting the allegation. Since evidence of homosexuality is deemed legally relevant, the respondent in these cases usually denies the allegation: "It's a lie, I'm not a homosexual."

As a rule, however, the factual basis of the decision in such cases of alleged homosexuality is omitted or truncated; some other reason is usually given for denying custody. Some courts have allowed custody to a lesbian mother provided she not live overtly with her lover. (Armanno, 1973, p. 1; Harris, 1977, p. 75; Riley, 1975, p. 79). Gays also are stymied in adopting children. In other cases, homosexual fathers (including the executive codirector of the National Gay Task Force) have been denied visitation privileges. In no state are avowed homosexuals permitted to adopt children.

No less than in cases of criminal responsibility, psychiatric testimony in cases to decide whether a homosexual parent should be denied custody or visitation rights produces contradictory views. For example, in a case where a lesbian mother and her estranged hus-

---

47. *Nadler v. Superior Court*, 244 Cal. App.2d 523, 63 Cal Rptr. 352 (1967); See Klaich, 1974.

48. See Gibson, 1977. A few and growing number of cases have taken the position that the existence of a lesbian relationship has no significance in determining fitness. *People v. Brown*, 49 Mich. App. 358, 212 N.W. 2d 55 (1973); *M. P. v. S. P.*, 169 N.J. Super. 425, 404 A. 2d 1256 (1979).

band battled for custody of their daughters, one child psychologist advised the court that the children should remain with the mother, provided her lover move out of the house. A psychiatrist, who called homosexuality a "character disorder," recommended the children be placed in the custody of their father. Another psychologist also said the mother's lover should not remain in the house if the children were to stay there.[49]

Is sexual orientation in and of itself indicative of attributes of personality or character, such as integrity, reliability, responsibility or devotion to, and ability to care for children? Is divorce or the parent's current choice of partner the more burdensome event in a child's life? Is the suitability of a parent to have custodial or visitation rights something that needs to be judged independently of that parent's homosexual, bisexual, or heterosexual history? In the worst cases of the battered child syndrome, the injury was inflicted upon the child by a heterosexual mother or father. By contrast, some of the most tender devotion and care of sick and ailing children recorded has been performed by a mother or father with an active homosexual history. Accordingly, it is increasingly being urged that homosexual men and women should be individually evaluated on their total human qualities and not discriminated against stereotypically on the basis of their sexual orientation.[50]

Cohabitation Agreements / Benefits of the Legally Married

Not permitted to marry, homosexuals (like heterosexuals cohabiting without legally marrying) often seek to define the terms of their relationship by contract. (Heterosexual married couples not satisfied with conventional rules may also turn to written contracts to define or vary their responsibilities within the marriage.) The state law's definition of marriage is a union of a man and a woman.[51] and thus it precludes

49. *Detroit Free Press*, 16 June 1977, p. 3.
50. The American Psychological Association recently adopted the following resolution: "The sex, gender identity, or sexual orientation of natural or prospective adoptive or foster parents should not be the sole or *primary variable* considered in child custody or placement cases." Meanwhile, the Conference of Delegates of the California State Bar Association disapproved a resolution which recommended that a parent's marital status or sexual orientation should *never* be considered in child custody litigation.
51. See, e.g., La. Civil Code, Art. 88

marriages between persons of the same sex. The most important test case of the law occurred in Minnesota in 1971, when two men attempting to get a marriage license were turned down by the state's highest court.[52] The U.S. Supreme Court refused to review the case. The two men in the preceding case also failed in their attempt to file a joint income tax return.

Deductions allowed for the care of "dependents" are also precluded.[53] The inability to marry also precludes advantages afforded to the legally married such as special fares, insurance, hospital visitation, housing restricted to one-family occupancy, and other benefits. Among these is "battered spouse" legislation which provides for action only against legally related members of the same household; it does not cover unrelated members living in the same home. In the course of debates in the New York legislature, the legislators refused to go along with any hint of recognizing common-law marriages or homosexual relationships. There was fear that the family court would be called upon to mediate homosexual disputes.

Insurance

The availability of insurance—and its rate—is based on the status of the individual. Insurers attempt to predict risk by category: marrieds and unmarrieds, young and adult, male and female, urban and rural, etc.

Health insurance of a household covers the legally married. Both life insurance under group insurance coverage and workers' compensation provide benefits for a "spouse" (and in an individual policy a friend or "lover" may be named as beneficiary). Heterosexual married couples under twenty-five years of age can buy automobile insurance at discounts of up to 40 percent less than can a single unmarried heterosexual male. The thinking is that marriage is an indication of the stability of the relationship, and that with responsibilities, like family responsibilities, one is a better driver. Ten years ago, this may have been the case, but in view of the divorce trend, it seems to be true no longer. Now it is asked: Should heterosexual cohabitators and partners in gay unions

52. *Baker* v. *Nelson*, 191 N.W. 2d 185 (Minn. 1971), noted in *Drake Law Review* 22:206 (1972).

53. The Internal Revenue Code states: "An individual is not a member of the taxpayer's household if at any time during the taxable year of the taxpayer the relationship between such individual and the taxpayer is in violation of local law." Internal Revenue Code Sec. 152(b). The provision applies to unmarried heterosexuals living together as well as to homosexuals. *Martin* v. *Commissioner*, 32 TCM 565 (1973); *Eichbauer* v. *Commissioner*, 30 TCM 581 (1971).

have the benefit of the married, heterosexual discounts? Is a de facto economic union to be recognized as a de jure one? Recent studies have indicated that male homosexuals are capable of having relationships that last as long as those of heterosexuals. The State of New York recently issued regulations prohibiting discrimination in automobile insurance on the basis of cohabitation versus legal marriage. Gays say that homosexual unions should be treated no differently. They raise the question of whether insurance companies should be allowed to "tell people how to live their life, rather than finding a way to insure them."[54]

In general, "alternate life-style" people, but especially gay people, have difficulty obtaining automobile insurance. When an insurance underwriter views a risk, he asks himself, "How will the applicant hold up on the witness stand in the event of a claim we wish to litigate? What will be his credibility? Can it be shaken?" Whether life-style is admissible as evidence or not, an astute trial attorney will find some way to get it to the attention of the jury.

Conclusion

The love that once "dared not speak its name" is today not only mentioned, but freely discussed, openly expressed, and sometimes even celebrated. Yet the general attitude toward homosexuality is still beset by conflict and anxiety. Public policy concerning homosexuals has changed dramatically in recent years, but the feelings of contempt and hostility continue to run deep and are still reflected in many of the laws of contemporary society.

REFERENCES

Armanno, B. F. 1973. The Lesbian Mother: Her Right to Child Custody, *Golden Gate Law Review* 4:1.

Barnett, W. 1973. *Sexual freedom and the constitution.* Albuquerque, N.M.: University of New Mexico Press.

54. Comment by Lloyd M. Levin, President and Founder of "All Together," in correspondence of 2 May, 1977, to the author. "All Together" is a nonprofit corporation that purports to represent people with untraditional life-styles. *National Observer,* 23 April 1977, p. 9.

Berman, H. J. 1974. *The interaction of law and religion.* Nashville, Tenn.: Abingdon Press.

Boggan, E. C., et al. 1975. *The rights of gay people/The basic ACLU guide to a gay person's rights.* New York: Avon.

Canby, W. C., 1976. Programming in response to the community: The broadcast consumer and the First Amendment. *Texas Law Review* 55:67–98.

Cripe, C. A. 1977. Religious freedom in prisons. *Federal Probation* 41:31–35.

Dullea, G. 1977. A legal guide to cohabitation. The *New York Times,* 8 June, p. C-12.

Emerson, T. I. 1976. Legal foundations of the right to know. *Washington University Law Quarterly* (1976), pp. 1–24.

Gibson, G. G. 1977. *By her own admission/A lesbian mother's fight to keep her son.* Garden City, N.Y.: Doubleday.

Harris, B. S. 1977. Lesbian Mother Child Custody: Legal and Psychiatric Aspects. *Bulletin of the American Academy of Psychiatry and Law* 5:75.

Hiss, T. 1977. *Laughing last.* New York: Houghton Mifflin.

Klaich, D. 1974. *Woman plus woman: Attitudes toward lesbianism.* New York: Simon & Schuster.

Lichtenstein, G. 1977. Homosexuals in New York find new pride. The *New York Times,* 24 October, p. 37.

Menninger, K. A. 1973. *Whatever became of sin?* New York: Hawthorn. Reviewed in R. Slovenko, Review essay, *DePaul Law Review* 23 (1974):1437–1453.

Riley, M. 1975. The Avowed Lesbian Mother and Her Right to Child Custody: A Constitutional Challenge That Can No Longer Be Denied. *San Diego Law Review* 12:799–864.

Siniscalco, G. R. 1976. Homosexual discrimination in employment. *Santa Clara Law Review* 16:494.

Slovenko, R. 1967. Sex mores and the enforcement of the law on sex crimes: A study of the status quo. *University of Kansas Law Review* 15:265–286.

———. 1971. Sex laws: Are they necessary? In D. L. Grummon and A. M. Barclay, eds., *Sexuality—A search for perspective* (New York: Van Nostrand Reinhold). pp. 142–59.

Spector, M. 1977. Legitimizing homosexuality. *Society* 14:52–56.

Van Niekerk, B. 1970. The "third sex" act. *South African Law Journal* 87:87.

11 / Homosexuality and the Churches

SEWARD HILTNER

Until about ten years ago, most churches (denominations) and most of their clergy and theologians said as little as possible about homosexuality. This prudential silence was consistent with the defensive public posture about human sexuality in general that the churches had been unable (or unwilling) to break through, even though the attitudes of many clergy and other church people toward sexuality had become more positive from the 1920s onward.

The first positive statements were about sexuality as a constructive factor in marriage, but they were cautious and euphemistic. Among Protestant churches, with their usually strong ties to the Bible, it was not until 1941 that any competent biblical scholar ventured a statement of what the Bible said about human sexuality as such, separating these views from the many ways in which the Bible deals with sex metaphorically, for example, the church as the bride of Christ, Israel in its worst moments as a harlot, or progeny as a kind of political evangelism (Piper, 1941). Another illustration of this reticence is the length of time that it took for Protestant groups to make clear positive statements about contraception (Hiltner, 1967). Until the 1950s such statements remained euphemistic. Only after contraception was being universally practiced by Protestants (save for small right-wing groups) did the official statements become clear.

When the ground-breaking studies of Alfred C. Kinsey appeared (in 1949 about males, and in 1953 about females), comment by churches, clergy, and theologians was at a minimum (Kinsey et al., 1948). Although I thought Kinsey was far better as an interviewer and scientist than as a philosopher, I regarded his findings as of great importance, published a book appreciative of the findings, and offered suggestions of how a Christian understanding of sexuality could profit from them (Hiltner, 1953). I was astounded that even my best theological friends, so to speak, ignored my discussion because I was consorting with Kinsey. Even Reinhold Niebuhr, then perhaps the greatest American theologian, was negative about my appreciation for Kinsey, although he was prepared, with characteristic openness, to debate the issue, as most theologians of the time were not. Twenty years afterward I reviewed all that history and wrote it up (Hiltner, 1972).

What has amazed and puzzled and frustrated me for at least thirty years about various areas of human sexuality including homosexuality has been the discrepancy between the emerging constructive attitudes and the reluctance to share these openly even with the members of one's own group (where of course the public and the media might find them out). I have thought often of Galileo. The Curia members of his time knew quite well that the claims of Christian faith were not dependent upon a geocentric view of the universe, but they feared that the people, believing the earth not to be the center of the universe, would renounce both Christianity and its communal embodiment in the Church. The psychology of some modern Protestant leaders has been uncomfortably like that of the Curia of Galileo's time.

I

I have seen many documents and have had access to other situations by oral communication in which the attitude toward homosexuals has been anything but punitive or legalistic, extending back as far as the 1930s. For the reasons just discussed, none of these has ever been published. The situations have usually involved persons with a considerable degree of homosexual orientation who have been discovered in some compromising situation. They have often been clergy, but sometimes youth workers, church musicians, or others active in church affairs. Instead of sheer condemnation or ouster, even when adolescents have been involved, there has often been strong concern for the person.

As far back as the 1930s, and more frequently later, the persons caught in such situations, especially clergy, were put on a kind of probation of required psychiatric consultation. For some clergy with only a partial degree of homosexual orientation, especially if their homosexual behavior had been infrequent and sporadic and guilt-ridden, this approach worked. I still receive Christmas cards from a happily married clergyman caught in such a situation twenty-five years ago. But obviously there was no change in orientation for most persons who were found out.

So long as most psychiatrists regarded a homosexual orientation either as sickness or as evidence of a need for psychiatric therapy, the churches could assure themselves that they were exercising pastoral care (through bishops, committees on ministerial relations, or other appropriate officials or groups) by recommending or requiring psychiatric treatment. If no change of attitude or orientation resulted, the person could be seen either as a noncooperative patient or as not working hard enough at the therapy. It is likely that some such persons got help through their therapy quite apart from their sexual orientation. Certainly even coerced psychiatry was in some respects better than automatic rejection or ouster. But the net effect of the efforts of that era was to enable the churches to continue avoiding the homosexual orientation question in the false conviction that psychiatrists could produce a heterosexual orientation if the persons were sufficiently cooperative in their therapeutic work.

During that same period, however, another movement was going on in the churches that would eventually have considerable influence on church attitudes toward homosexuality. It was a reconception of the church's ministry to persons, families, and small groups, promoted since the 1920s mainly through the movement for "clinical pastoral education"; essentially it consisted of an internship or residency training program under close supervision of a qualified pastor or chaplain. After World War II, this kind of education also found its way directly into the programs of theological schools, first Protestant and Jewish, and later Roman Catholic. The primary purpose of the movement has been to enable clergy in local churches to do better direct helping work, no matter what the problem area. There has also been a spin-off movement of specialists in "pastoral counseling."

The greater understanding and skill demonstrated by many clergy with the new training brought to them, among others, more persons who feared they had a homosexual orientation as well as more people who clearly had such an orientation. Sometimes the relatives came instead. Whether the clergy attempted the counseling themselves, or made psychiatric referrals, they soon acknowledged the fixity of a genuine homosexual orientation. Seeing that counseling or therapy would not alter that orientation, they were confronted with the issue of shifting to a kind of "prophetic" stance or remaining silent.

One of the earliest pastoral care leaders who chose a prophetic or interpretative stance was H. Kimball Jones in 1966. In a realistic way, Jones showed that many of the problems of homosexual persons came from misunderstandings, willful or otherwise, of their condition on the part of both church and society. About the same time, Norman Pittenger, an Anglican priest who had taught in the United States as well as in England, published a book with a similar theme (1970). Then followed some symposium publications edited by Ralph W. Weltge (1969) and W. Dwight Oberholtzer (1971). The movement toward a similar position by somewhat more conservative Protestant opinion was shown in the 1974 book by Clinton R. Jones.

As far back as 1963, some English Quakers had shown a similar attitude (Heron, 1963). Consistent with Friends tradition, they had noted both the unnecessary sufferings of the persons and the social deficiency in terms of de facto deprivation of both human and civil rights. It may well have been the Quakers who first turned the thought of many church leaders to the rights issue. The rights question was not absent from any of the works cited above. But most of those authors had come through the new tradition of enlightened pastoral helping with a principal concern for injured persons. The Quakers, mostly without clergy, properly combined the persons and rights concerns, but their social impact was greater on the latter. What is noteworthy is that, toward the end of the 1960s, church concern for personal suffering and church concern for human and civil rights began to converge in the consideration of homosexuality.

Except for D. S. Bailey, an Anglican theologian, there was little scholarly work on homosexuality among church intellectual leaders. In 1955 Bailey published *Homosexuality and the Western Christian Tradition,* dealing with both the Bible and the history of the church, Catholic and Protestant, in the West. Bailey's study attempted two things: a demonstration of how the condemnatory, or "crime against nature," view of homosexuality arose and developed; and suggestions that the whole line of thought needed changing in light of the modern understanding of homosexual orientation. Bailey regarded the biblical references to homosexuality as inapplicable for today because of their ignorance about orientation.

Although in his *The Ethics of Sex* (1964) Helmut Thielicke, a highly regarded Continental theologian, was somewhat more cautious than Bailey, he found himself unable to go along with the "orders of creation" (God made them male and female) approach of his predecessors according to which persons of homosexual orientation were either excluded from the creation scheme or left dangling.

Especially with respect to Protestantism, we may summarize the situation up to 1970 in the following way: Even though the churches said as little as possible about homosexuality, they had acquired an uneasy conscience about the older attitudes on three kinds of grounds. First, a better informed pastoral care had revealed much unnecessary suffering. Second, the issues of human and civil rights could not be ignored. Third, even though scholarly work on the tradition was small in quantity, it pointed in the direction of inadequate scholarly bases for the traditional positions.

In Catholic thought something similar was going on before 1970, although statements criticizing earlier positions came even later than among Protestants. A statement from the Vatican as recently as 1976 reiterated the traditional basis of objection to homosexual acts as "intrinsically disordered" because they "lack an essential and indispensable finality."[1] The basis of the judgment is the theory of natural law combined with the "finality" of procreation. At least indirectly, the statement did acknowledge differences among persons who commit homosexual acts, so that the notion of orientation, while not espoused, was nevertheless not denied either.

The degree to which these changes in attitude among Christian groups are paralleled in Judaism is simply unknown to me. So far as attitudes toward sexuality in general are concerned, the traditional Jewish attitude has been much more positive than the Christian. But it is not clear that Jewish communities have been more understanding toward homosexuals than their Christian counterparts. One Jewish scholar, Robert Gordis, who has spoken on the issue recently regards his as a "center" position, on the one hand rejecting the view of homosexuality as an "abomination," but on the other hand equally rejecting it as simply an "alternate life style" (1978). Certainly Jewish groups do not appear to be as worked up about the question as many Christian groups currently are.

II

As organized homosexual groups became more numerous and more active during the present decade, they recognized the presence of an uneasy conscience of many clergy and other church members. Frequently as a genuine religious question, but sometimes as a strategy, some of them talked of religious rights, especially acceptance into a worshiping community. In the 1960s Troy Perry (1972), a minister, was the principal leader of a group of small churches in metropolitan centers that clearly accepted homosexual persons and that tried hard to avoid becoming ghettos by including other persons as well. But the danger of self-segregation in churches with a homosexual core group seemed great. Especially as more people and groups have come into the open and become active, the right to participation in regular churches

1. Reported in The *New York Times*, 16 January 1976.

is being pressed. Concomitantly, the ecclesiastical sense of guilt is being touched with the result that, insofar as the churches have power over public opinion, they may help to bring about some other changes desired by homosexual groups.

The desired agenda, or "propaganda line," now being brought to the churches by groups and individuals is different from that of just a few years ago. Then it appeared a gain to get homosexual acts among consenting adults off the criminal lists, and especially to eliminate automatic discrimination in jobs or housing solely on the grounds of homosexual orientation. Although those battles are not entirely won, the present agenda goes much further. It seems to include not only acceptance of persons but also agreement with certain theoretical positions, for instance, that a homosexual orientation is a life-style or only a difference and in no way a developmental variance or deviance, that adult sexuality in the absence of coercion is exclusively a private affair, and that nothing of significance is known about the causes of homosexual orientation.

The first national church group to accept officially the agenda of the organized homosexual groups has been the Unitarian Universalist Association, often referred to as Protestantism's left wing. Its statements are clear that homosexuality represents only a difference or an alternate life-style. Curriculum materials that develop this theme consistently have been prepared for the education of people of different ages. Unitarian interest was aroused largely through the issues of civil and human rights and has been carried to a logical conclusion. The simplicity of the Unitarian position seems to make the Unitarians relatively uninterested in the complicated issues with which churchmen in other groups have begun to wrestle.

It has become the practice in most Protestant denominations, in dealing with various social as well as ecclesiastical questions, to issue only brief statements of viewpoint from a representative national assembly, while either before or afterward a committee works to prepare a more thorough background and position paper. The latter is seldom adopted, but is more often accepted for study and action by local churches. The distinction between these two types of statement needs to be kept in mind for the discussion that follows.

One of the early modern official statements came from the Lutheran Church in America in 1970. Its central point was that "the sexual behavior of freely consenting adults in private is not an appropriate subject for legislation or police action," and it declared that homosexual persons are "entitled to understanding and justice in church and community." In the previous year the Council for Christian Social Action of the United Church of Christ had recommended a similar statement, and had deplored exclusion of homosexuals from public service and the military; but this resolution was not an official statement like that of the

Lutherans. In 1977 the United Church of Christ received an extensive report on subjects including homosexuality from a committee, and this is now being studied throughout the church.

The Methodist General Conference of 1972 stated:

> Homosexuals no less than heterosexuals are persons of sacred worth, who need the ministry and guidance of the church in their struggles for human fulfillment, as well as the spiritual and emotional care of a fellowship which enables reconciling relationships with God, with others and with self. Further we insist that all persons are entitled to have their human and civil rights insured, though we do not condone the practice of homosexuality and consider this practice incompatible with Christian teaching.

At the corresponding conference of 1976 an effort was made to make this position more liberal, cutting out the point of the last three lines above, but it was defeated.

It is probable that most mainline Protestant denominations today who are moved to make statements on homosexuality have included or will include the substance of the first two Methodist points: that such persons ought not to be excluded from the ministry of the church, and that their basic human and civil rights should be respected. Beyond those declarations, however, there is difference of conviction.

Denominations differ in the extent to which they are prepared to acknowledge the reality of a homosexual orientation. That acceptance is one of the strongest points in a study document presented in 1977 to the General Assembly of the Presbyterian Church, U. S. (Southern Presbyterian Church), and accepted for study across the constituency. Although it advocated concern for ministry to homosexuals and for their human and civil rights, as do the Methodist and other statements, this document posed the issue of accepting the equality of orientation approach, with the consequence of "living faithful and obedient Christian lives within it," in lieu of previous condemnatory attitudes. On basic theoretical issues, the study document posed alternatives rather than flatly arguing for one position or the other.

My own denomination, the United Presbyterian Church, has had a special study committee at work for nearly two years. Its 1977 preliminary report included a sample of opinion on homosexuality throughout the church. The most liberal views were found among national church executives, with ordained ministers coming next, and with lay members a bit more conservative. The views as a whole were, however, less traditionalist than had been expected.

In June 1978 the study committee recommended to the General Assembly of the United Presbyterian Church that persons of homosexual orientation not be automatically barred from ordination as ministers, even though the district organizations that do the ordaining (presbyteries) may say yes or no as they see fit. The General Assembly voted down the majority report, basically on the issue of ordaining ministers who state their homosexuality publically. On the matter of general acceptance of homosexuals as persons, with implications for civil rights, housing, church participation, and the like, however, the tone of the discussion was understanding and accepting. Future reconsideration of ordination was not ruled out.

The Episcopal Church has been so busy for several years in considering the ordination of women to its priesthood that it has had no time, or perhaps inclination, to reexamine homosexuality. Discussion in that church is rife, however, especially because of the decision of the Bishop of New York to ordain to the priesthood a woman who is an avowed homosexual in orientation. In explaining his decision, the bishop noted that the candidate met all qualifications including a psychiatric examination, and declared that, "in the absence of public scandal," the "personal morality, lifestyle, and behavior" of this candidate, like any other, is "a matter between him or her and a confessor, pastor, or bishop." It has been the general interpretation of the bishop's remarks that the new ordinand is not actively practicing in a sexual way her homosexual orientation.

Some conservative Protestant churches have either maintained silence on the question, or have given reinforcement to positions taken or assumed earlier under which homosexuality is usually declared to be sin. If one takes this to mean that homosexual acts are sin (or give evidence of sin), it leaves unresolved the question of the status of a homosexual orientation. And if such a statement is not followed by noting that all human beings are sinners, it is suspect of special pleading.

There is a large group of conservative Protestants, belonging to various denominations, who usually refer to themselves as "evangelicals," by which they mean to suggest their fidelity to the message of the Christian gospel (good news). Some of them, as well as some other conservatives, were with Anita Bryant in Miami. But a sizable minority among them are not only well informed about homosexuality, but are currently compiling a book from within the evangelical framework that will be a direct attack on the Bryant type of position.

In Roman Catholicism, the big news of the past three years has been John J. McNeill, a Jesuit priest, whose book, *The Church and the Homosexual* (1976), is probably the ablest ecclesiastical interpretation and defense of homosexual persons that has been written. He declares himself to have a homosexual orientation, but not to practice it sexually. He is literate both historically and scientifically; his argument moves carefully and without abrasive overtones; and his influence appears to be growing. Before publishing his book, he secured the necessary approval from superiors. A few months later, however, that approval was withdrawn. It is hard to escape the conclusion that the very success of the book was the occasion for retracting approval. If damage it is, however, the damage has largely been done.

III

What are the prospects for more just and humane attitudes and practices on the part of churches and church leaders toward homosexual persons in the next ten or fifteen years? If the history that has been traced here is at all accurate, and if change continues either quietly underneath (as it has been doing in much of the recent past) or openly, there is a reasonable prospect of greater acceptance of homosexual persons and of action on behalf of their human and civil rights on the part of the churches in the years ahead. As never before, however, such constructive change could be delayed or even arrested by a kind of backlash if organized homosexual groups, no matter how understandable in light of injustices done to them in the past, exercise little restraint in pushing their objectives or show little consideration for the kinds of sensibilities that, right or wrong, are present in even the most liberal of churches. In the comments that follow, I assume that some such restraint and consideration will prevail.

It seems likely that the churches, in their own life and work, will increase their acceptance of participation by persons of homosexual orientation. Worship and other formal events will come first, along with pastoral care. Participation in religious education will be slower because children and adolescents are involved. The greatest problems are likely to arise because churches are social and fellowship groups as well as worshiping and service bodies. Attendance at family night suppers by homosexual couples seems unlikely. Homosexual persons will probably develop local fellowship groups of their own within churches, and their activities might become occasions for backlash. Nevertheless, while it may come slowly, increasing acceptance is probable.

Some churches, as noted already, are now more ready than they have ever been to support the cause of human and civil rights for homosexuals. So far, such support has been rather unspecific or limited to local situations. Taking a stand against job discrimination simply because of a homosexual orientation will probably come first. Discrimination in housing is likely to prove a more stubborn issue, for living across the street or across the hall is closer to the personal center than working across the office or plant. The increased political influence that homosexual groups are likely to gain may be viewed with suspicion. If much of the present discrimination is eliminated by law or in principle, it will remain to be seen whether the churches remain sensitive to de facto discrimination, which is bound to continue.

There are many signs that homosexuality as an orientation will be increasingly acknowledged by the churches. That means understanding the condition, whatever its causes, to be "here to stay" for persons of such orientation, so that they must be considered as they are. Since reluctance on this point has been a major stumbling block to attitude change in both the past and the present, the shift will have large consequences. But the churches—probably along with scientific, therapeutic, and educational groups—are unlikely to interpret the orientation issue as minimizing the need for study of ways of changing the orientation of people who want it changed, and especially of finding ways of preventing the orientation from arising or taking hold in children now being reared.

Further, the churches are unlikely to accept the view that adult sexuality, even when uncoerced, is purely a private affair. Some of the legalisms of the past about the bedroom will be altered. And church ethics are still in process of restatement without such legalistic props of the past. But opposition will remain to the "no harm" or the "anything goes" philosophies of adult sexuality. The kind of sexual libertinism— even athleticism—that is on the rise in our culture, the churches will eventually remember, is quite similar to that which was strong in the Hellenistic world when Christianity arose, and which was rejected by Jews and Christians alike.

There will always be Christian groups which insist on what they regard as literal interpretations of the Bible. As the understanding of homosexuality as an orientation becomes more widely accepted, however, most churches will accept the fact that the ten or eleven biblical references to homosexuality did not address themselves to the phenomenon as we understand it today. What the Bible does have to say that impinges upon attitudes to homosexual persons will be sought, therefore, at points other than the explicit homosexual references: the place of human sexuality in creation, love of one's neighbor, the nature of creation, and similar points. I have already noted that there is today a considerable group of influential "evangelical" Christians who already take this position, despite their general conservatism in biblical interpretation.

The application of modern principles of biblical scholarship to those passages, less than a dozen in number, which translators render as being about homosexuality is well illustrated in the recent United Presbyterian report. It is noted that some of the passages do not deal with homosexual acts among consenting adults (Genesis 18–19, Judges 19, II Peter 2:6–10, Jude 7), that other passages deal with sexual abuses in cultic practice but probably not of a homosexual kind (Deut. 23:17–18, I Kings 14:24, 15:12, 22:46, and II Kings 23:7). Two Old Testament passages (Lev. 18:22 and 20:13) do condemn consenting homosexual acts, which is probably true also of Paul in two references (I Cor. 5–6 and Romans I:18–32 and perhaps I Tim. 1:1–11). It is noted, however, that none of the passages understood homosexuality, to use the modern phrase, as an "orientation." That means that modern interpreters must either acknowledge that the Bible does not speak directly to the issue of behavior by consenting adults of homosexual orientation, or they must interpret at least some of the passages as disapproving the behavior even if it is based on orientation. At present the second alternative still seems stronger than the first.

Closely related to the exegetical question is that of homosexuality as "sin." Traditionally, any kind of homosexual act, regardless of context, was regarded as sin. Supporting the judgment were the biblical references, plus either a theory of natural law or one of the "orders of creation," according to which God's intent in creating the two sexes was procreative, with homosexual activity running counter to that.

Christian theology generally has held, however, that all human beings sin, so that, even if homosexual activity is regarded as sin, the persons who carry it out are not unique in their sinfulness. Much church opinion, however, even today, believes that persons who commit homosexual acts should repent. Repentance may mean simply no further such behavior, even for persons of homosexual orientation. For a smaller number, repentance includes making every effort to alter the orientation itself. More liberal groups, like the majority in the Presbyterian report, do not believe that homosexual behavior as such, in responsible relationships, by persons of fixed homosexual orientation, is to be regarded as sinful.

Part of the problem lies in different theological perceptions of the meaning of sin. If sin is regarded as simply another word for calling acts bad or displeasing to God, then it emerges (as in common speech) as a term of blame. In theology, however, "the news of sin is good news," in that only the person in whom God's grace has already begun a redemptive process can understand the malignity of his sin. Thus, sin and grace are inseparable; and sin, while it is to be set aside or repented of, is never just a word for blame. It is more like a diagnosis.

The real issue is whether persons of homosexual orientation who engage in certain kinds of homosexual relationships are thereby disapproved of by church communities. To some extent, the talk of whether homosexual activity is itself sinful or not distorts that issue. In view of the general theological agreement about the ubiquity of human sinfulness, the questions that have to be faced about homosexual orientation and behavior can be viewed more accurately when they are not singled out for association with a presumably unique kind of sinfulness.

What is likely to happen with regard to ordination to priesthood or ministry of persons with an avowed homosexual orientation? The trouble with this question is that the churches are damned if they do and damned if they don't. If they say no to otherwise qualified candidates, when it is well known that there are many unavowed homosexual persons in the ministry and priesthood, the charge can be made of concealment and hypocrisy. But if they offer a simple yes, they are dangerously close to accepting the philosophy that sex is purely a private affair. Unless the question is seen in a larger context, my opinion is that either answer to it will evade the underlying issues.

Churches have always taken the position that the sexual behavior of their clergy is of peculiar church concern because of their leadership and exemplary functions. Guidance has been exercised all the way from enforced celibacy in the Catholic church to almost compulsory marriage in some Protestant circles. Legalisms have abounded. It is only in the past few years that Protestant ministers, when caught in impossible marriages, have been able to become divorced and retain their ministerial status. Adultery by ministers, when forgiven, is usually regarded as emotional illness.

Many of the specifics of the churches' concern for the sex lives of clergy are changing. Some of those concerns that remain will undoubtedly continue to be regarded with hostility by some priests and ministers. But it is difficult to see how the churches could operate at all if they exercised no concern whatever. Reports that pastor and mistress spent the post-Easter season in Bermuda or that the manse had group sex on Saturday night are not likely to be received with equanimity. Such illustrations may be caricatures, but they suggest why the churches must inevitably have some special concern for the sexual behavior and philosophy of their clergy.

If persons of avowed homosexual orientation are ordained to the ministry, how can the churches exercise a legitimate concern over their sexual behavior without reviewing (and equalizing, so to speak) that concern in relation to persons of heterosexual orientation? There is a sense in which the Catholic church has solved the problem in advance by compelling celibacy for all priests. For Protestants, the story is different. There is extreme reluctance on the part of Protestant churches to review in general such policies.

Unlike Catholics, Protestants cannot easily say to homosexual candidates for the ministry: we accept your orientation, but promise that you will engage in no sexual behavior. If it is tacitly understood that some sexual relationship is permissible, what are the criteria? If they are simply "discretion," then the person, although open about orientation, is still closeted in regard to relationships. Or if a permanent relationship is avowed, how would such a partnership be treated in the actual life of the church? And on what grounds would its rupture, and the creation of another relationship, be tolerated? Until Protestant churches are prepared to review and think through such issues in relation to both heterosexual and homosexual clergy, any decisions they make to ordain or not ordain persons of homosexual orientation contain a strong element of cop-out.

In regard both to clergy and other church members, the question of so-called "homosexual marriages" has already arisen. Sensing that the desire for something of this kind often comes from homosexual persons with a sense of guilt about their orientation and behavior, organized homosexual groups are little concerned with this matter even though they support those who desire or need it. If the churches do become more accepting of homosexuals, more homosexuals may become active in churches and many may want some symbolic indication of their acceptance, not only with their orientation but also with their current way of exercising it. So ceremonies of some sort are likely to become more frequent. A lot of headaches could be averted if the analogy to marriage were not invoked.

REFERENCES

Bailey, D. S. 1955. *Homosexuality and the Western Christian tradition.* New York: Longmans Green.

Gordis, R. 1978. *Love and sex: A modern Jewish perspective.* New York: Farrar, Straus & Giroux.

Heron, A., ed. 1963. *Toward a Quaker view of sex.* London: Friends Home Service Committee.

Hiltner, S. 1953. *Sex ethics and the Kinsey reports.* New York: Association Press.

————. 1967. Religious viewpoints on family planning: Protestant. *Southern Medical Bulletin* 55 (December):54–59.

————. 1972. Kinsey and the church: Then and now. *Journal of Sex Research* 8(August):3. Reprinted in *The Christian Century* XC:22 (30 May 1973).

Jones, C. R. 1974. Homosexuality and counseling. Philadelphia: Fortress Press.

Jones, H. K. 1966. *Toward a Christian understanding of the homosexual.* New York: Association Press.

Kinsey, A. C., et al. 1948. *Sexual behavior in the human male.* Philadelphia: W. B. Saunders.

————. 1953. *Sexual behavior in the human female.* Philadelphia: W. B. Saunders.

McNeill, J. J. 1976. *The church and the homosexual.* Kansas City: Sheed Andrews & McNeel.

Oberholtzer, W. D., ed. 1971. *Is gay good?* Philadelphia: Westminster Press.

Perry, T. 1972. *The Lord is my shepherd, and He knows I'm gay.* Los Angeles: Nash Publishing.

Piper, O. 1941. *The Christian interpretation of sex.* New York: Charles Scribner's.

Pittenger, N. 1970. *Time for consent: A Christian's approach to homosexuality,* 2nd ed. London: SCM Press.

Thielicke, H. 1964. *The ethics of sex.* New York: Harper & Row.

Weltge, R. W., ed. 1969. *The same sex.* Philadelphia: Pilgrim Press.

12 / Society and the Gay Movement

BRUCE VOELLER

In order to understand the nature, history, and directions of the gay movement, it is, I believe, valuable to recognize some distinctive attributes of most lesbians and gay men in our Euro-American culture. These attributes are not widely appreciated. They include: First, that we are extensively present in our society—socioeconomically, geographically, ethnically, racially, and by gender. Second, that gays, for the most part, are as unable to recognize or identify other gay people as nongays are; that is, we are an *invisible* minority, even to one another. Third, that *we* are taught *homophobia* (the irrational fear, hatred, or loathing of homosexuals and homosexuality) by peers, parents, church, state, and sadly, most medical authorities with an intensity that compares with the hatred inculcated in the young between Irish Protestant and Catholic, Arab and Israeli, or communist and capitalist. Fourth, that because of fear, through adolescence and young adulthood we grow relatively unable to share our awareness of the nature of our sexual and affectional feelings with our friends, families, or others. Fifth, that we are oppressed and discriminated against in all the classic ways known to other despised minority groups, overtly and quietly. Sixth, that we are deprived of access to positive gay role-models and information about estimable lesbians and gay men throughout history.

An exploration of these basic facts of life shared by most lesbians and gay men will help in understanding the problems our human rights movement faces as well as in understanding the history of steps taken in our programs to secure changes in law and, more important, in public attitudes and understanding.

Prevalence and Distribution of Homosexuality in Our Culture

The first point, our ubiquitousness and widespread distribution in our society, is still extensively unrecognized even in medically sophisticated circles. Consequently, numerous authorities will state that about 1 to 3 percent of the American population is homosexual. Many do not even know that they are utilizing data from the Kinsey Institute (Kinsey et al., 1949, 1953). If we look at the data more closely, we find that about 37 percent of all white American males, for example, have had at least one adult homosexual experience to the point of orgasm; moreover, approximately 10 percent of all adult American women and men have an extensive homosexual experience, that is to say, some 20 million Americans have had or will have such a history. Other data show that, broadly speaking, gays are about equally abundant in various races, religious backgrounds, professions, occupations, and rural and urban settings.

Although big cities act in some measure as magnets for gays, we are but little ghettoized in comparison with blacks, Hispanics, Jews, and native Americans, and thus have major problems in developing a strong sense of community; we lack communication based on proximity that has facilitated the building of other minority movements. Many gays and nongays think we do have large communities. They point to Greenwich Village in New York, the Melrose area in Houston, West Hollywood in Los Angeles, Newtown in Chicago, and the Castro district in San Francisco. But gay concentrations in these areas number only in the tens of thousands, compared with some 20 million gays throughout the nation. Nevertheless, drawn by the anonymity of big cities, their greater tolerance, more extensive and organized social and sexual opportunities to meet other gays, and the improved self-image and self-confidence and sense of security engendered by being surrounded by gay friends, the "immigrant" gay in the big city shares in the impression that gays are very abundant in such places. A good example of this is the almost universal notion in San Francisco that some 40 percent of the population is gay, that is, four times the national figure. Gays, and others, attribute authority for such a view to statements from a United States governmental agency in San Francisco. The imagined studies have not been made; nor *could* they be done other than through rather elaborate surveys such as Kinsey made, inasmuch as even in San Francisco the overwhelming majority of lesbians and gay men remain deeply secretive about their sexual orientation.

Gay Visibility

Many, if not most, people think they can recognize homosexuals by mannerisms, speech, dress, or behavior. But those within the gay community have long been aware that the popular stereotypic cues are shared by but a tiny portion of lesbians and gay men. There are, however, few concrete data from competent sex researchers on the degree of frequency of stereotypic behavior. According to Kinsey associate Dr. Wardell Pomeroy (in a personal communication), about 15 percent of exclusively gay men are in some degree effeminate, but so are some exclusively *heterosexual* men. When one recalls that a third of American men, for example, have had adult homosexual experience and that 13 percent of men have had extensive homosexual experience, and 25 percent have had more than casual experience, it should be evident that such large numbers of men are not manifestly effeminate.

Indeed, the public, including those in medicine, are only now beginning to learn that *most* lesbians and gay men are extraordinarily successful at "passing," undetected even by their families, friends, and colleagues. The public announcements of their homosexuality by several well-known figures have begun to alert the world to the invalidity of popular stereotypes. Physicians who have publicly indicated their homosexuality have included noted neurosurgeon Dr. Henry Messer and former New York City Health Commissioner Dr. Howard Brown. Major sports figures who have taken this step are Rose Bowl football captain David Kopay, and U.S. Olympic decathlon star, Tom Waddell, M.D. Others are President Carter's International Women's Year Commissioner, Jean O'Leary, state legislators Elaine Noble in Massachusetts and Alan Spear in Minnesota; and Purple Heart war hero, Air Force Sgt. Leonard Matlovich.

Even in the realm of psychiatry, traditional societal views about gay visibility prevail, as a couple of examples will illustrate.

When I was in my third year at Reed College in the mid-1950s, I feared I was a homosexual and sought assistance from the college psychiatrist. After several meetings, he assured me I could not possibly be homosexual: I neither looked nor acted like one, I was an accomplished athlete, an honors student, had a good and warm relationship with both my parents, and had no desire to cross-dress or view myself in reverse gender terms. Therefore, I couldn't possibly be a homosexual!

Second, at a social event during a professional meeting, one of the best known leaders of the opposition to the removal of the "sickness" designation of homosexuality in the American Psychiatric Association's nomenclature expanded on his perceptiveness and boasted of his ability to recognize gays across a crowded room, unaware that the clinic director with whom he was speaking was gay. To add to the tragicomedy, he then introduced three of the senior residents in his training program in psychiatry, and left to talk with other psychiatrists. During the conversation between the residents and the clinic director, two of the three residents acknowledged their own homosexuality and expressed grave fear that their professor might discover their secret.

It is not only the medical world which reinforces myth and fear. The media, especially television and movies, help perpetuate the familiar characterizations much as they do the long reinforced stereotypes of blacks as servants and shuffling people: Aunt Jemima, Stepin Fetchit, Amos and Andy. Even in the face of tens of thousands of lesbians and gay men marching in the annual Christopher Street Liberation Day parades in major cities—ordinary-looking men and women who might just as easily be mistaken for participants in a St. Patrick's Day parade (minus the shamrocks)—the media will focus its cameras on the dozen extravagantly dressed people who give showy visuals for the home viewer's amusement, by-passing the thousands who don't conform to the public's stereotypes.

Interestingly, many lesbians and gay men also believe *they* can recognize other gays even though they think nongays would be unable to do so. There is a partial truth in this, but it is largely erroneous also. Some gays are indeed recognizable by others, through their adopted behavior and dress. As the climate toward gays has become more tolerant, increasing numbers have taken steps away from full hiding, particularly in urban areas and around universities. However, the cues are not at all those imagined by the general public.

Dress cues may range from the traditional lesbian and gay male stereotypic patterns (*rarely*, however, transvestite) to strongly stated, gender-typic clothing. The common mode of dress seen at many of the male gay enclaves for the last few years is characterized by rather macho denim or leather jackets, blue jeans, and flannel or denim shirts. This "Marlboro Country" image is highly popular among gay males (for better or worse) and is strongly reflected in the printed advertising aimed at that male market. Some populations of gays recognize *this* image of denim and leather: "bikers" jacket, boots and jeans, keys hung on the hip; and often a handkerchief (color coded for particular sexual interests) in the hip pocket. Similarly, a subtler but clear "disco image" characterizes thousands of gay men who dance and socialize at the nation's many gay discotheques. Gays who are open enough to engage in the bar/bath/discotheque/gay groups' social scenes are attuned to recognizing these dress codes and others.

Similarly, lesbian dress ranges through all the variety seen at nongay women's gathering places, from a convention of the National Organization for Women to elegant social events at the Hamptons on New York's Long Island. Jean O'Leary, Rita Mae Brown, and Elaine Noble—frequent lesbian speakers at conventions, on national television, and at universities—are proud and attractive women and fit no usual stereotypes. Yet even they provide subtle cues to other women with fine-tuned perceptions, through their strong independent-mindedness, their self-assurance around others, and their lack of deference to men: not arrogance or hostility, "merely" a healthy sense of equality not common among other women.

But these cues do not apply to the great majority of gays. Those whose gay circles extend rather more widely than such gay social and political institutions as bars, discotheques, beaches, and gay organizations recognize that the great majority of lesbian and gay men have very successfully passed and are quite undetectable. Networks of gays in all walks of life have come to know one another but usually not through direct observation. For example, one senior police officer in New York informed me that he knows personally about fifty other policewomen and men who are gay on the New York force. He *recognized* none of them as such, but "gay grapevine" reports led him to them, and to lowering his own protective cover; discrete discussion led to mutual exchange of information and eventual friendship. He has also cautiously "come out" to a small number of his closest nongay colleagues, none of whom at first would believe he was homosexual.

A major consequence of our invisibility to each other is the difficulty in building a movement. Most gays remain afraid to join a movement or to help it because their employers, friends, or family may discover their secret. Because they choose not to identify themselves to the gay movement and are mostly undetectable by us, we cannot easily target our campaigns at a specific audience. Rather, we must direct much of our effort at the *entire* American populace in the hope that a portion of the gays in the general population will come forward and become involved. That this has in fact worked is evidenced by the growth of the Christopher Street parades each June, commemorating the New York gays' resistance to police harassment in 1969, when the gay movement became a widespread, nonviolent activist movement. From a few hundred marchers the first year in New York, it has progressed to parades in cities throughout the country, with from 50,000 to 250,000 participants in New York and San Francisco in 1977.

A deeply important consequence of the widespread distribution of gays and of our relative invisibility even to each other has been the necessity of developing routes for contacting one another, of publicizing our very existence to one another, and of developing a sense of self-esteem and worth. One of the most common experiences that prominent, openly gay women and men have is the receipt of a flood of letters and phone calls from gay youngsters who thought they were the only homosexuals in the world and from older isolated gays who know few others.

To remedy this situation the gay movement has attempted to do such things as:

1. create publishing vehicles for gay people to communicate with one another;
2. utilize nongay media which, though commonly resistant or uninterested, reach millions of Americans throughout the country, including numerous gays;
3. develop media events sufficiently newsworthy that the major media can no longer ignore them—for example, peaceful protests, mass marches, public confrontations with mayors, Presidential candidates; introduce legislation and schedule meetings such as that of the National Gay Task Force at the White House;
4. persuade prominent gays publicly to announce their homosexuality, for example, Merle Miller or Dr. Howard Brown.
5. form social, religious, and political groups that encourage people to meet one another and to evolve programs to serve their collective needs and to effect social change.

The importance of the media, both gay and nongay, is evident. Gay papers and magazines are sometimes private, profit-oriented ventures, but more commonly they are the organs of gay religious, social, or political groups. Their function is to reach out to an audience of dispersed gays, and to inform, educate, and establish contact with those too fearful or geographically remote to have substantial direct connection with other lesbians or gay men.

A considerable number of small local periodicals (none of them dailies) have come into existence, many of them short-lived. The few larger national periodicals have rather small distributions (between 50,000 and 150,000) compared with those of blacks or other groups. Most of these papers and magazines have catered to gay males, rather than lesbians, and usually survive financially by considerable use of sexually oriented advertising and writing of a more or less sexually explicit nature.

This sexual tone attracts a segment of gay male readership but has acted as a limit to wider readership by a large number of males and most lesbians. Because of the present limited readership of the gay press and the embryonic state of gay programming in the electronic media, gay groups with professional expertise aiming to reach large numbers of people have concentrated on capturing the nongay printed and electronic media. One article in *Time* magazine or the *New York Times* reaches millions of readers including about 10 percent who are gay. Thus, gay articles or information in such vehicles reach more gays than are reached by all the principal gay publications combined.

Self-image

Gays have been taught self-hatred much as other minority groups have. Those with religious training have not only been taught the *basic* societal negativity about sex but ideas about homosexuality that can only be considered deep phobias of a very serious nature. The major religions represented in Western society have shared few conceptions as strongly as their aversion to loving or sexual relationships between members of the same gender. The inculcation of these taboos is deeply reinforced by peer pressure, ridicule, and the threat of ridicule. Medical authority has long underscored the sin notion with its own sickness notion, and few Americans lack some combination of these views in their attitudes, whether they are predominantly heterosexual or homosexual. Sadly, much of the medical view of homosexuality seems to have its roots in what Alfred Kinsey liked to refer to as "defending the mores," rather than in real science.

To these deep-rooted attitudes is added the criminalizing effect of popular ideas about "sodomy laws." While such laws have been removed in nearly all Western European and New World nations, they continue to exist in about two-thirds of the states in the United States. Moreover, these laws almost universally apply to heterosexuals as well as to homosexuals. From 70 percent to 90 percent of heterosexuals engage in violations of these laws in the form of cunnilingus, fellatio, and anal sex (Levin and Levin, 1975, p. 52; *Time* 1977). The criminalizing impact of these laws, however, is largely visited upon homosexuals.

But even those homosexuals who are not easy subjects for the sin and sickness notions are often embarrassed or ashamed of their sexual orientation because of other popular myths and stereotypes about gays. Thus, a major effort of our movement has been to collect and distribute accurate data to *both* gays and nongays. For example, very few lesbians or gay men are transvestites, or cross-dressers. Indeed, a majority of those who cross-dress are heterosexually oriented (Feinbloom, 1976; Benjamin, 1966). Similarly, scholarly data reveal that about eleven out of twelve pedophilic arrests involve men with *female* minors—that is, are heterosexual crimes (DeFrancis, 1966)—and that in all likelihood "the adult heterosexual male constitutes a greater risk to the underage child than does the adult homosexual male" (Groth, 1978).

Such data are, sadly, little known even among gays.

Intrafamilial Isolation

Nowhere has the hostility to homosexuality been more frightening to large numbers of gay men and lesbians than in their own families, forcing them to feel like minority group members in their own homes. A black child growing up in a white neighborhood or a Jewish, Catholic, or Mormon child in nonminority areas may have many problems with bigoted neighbors, peers, and teachers. But he or she does not usually face these same bigotries at home. There a refuge of sorts exists, where it is not necessary to fear attacks on the issue of race or faith. There a person need not defend, explain, apologize for, or hide minority status. There one finds others who share the status, and, at least in good families, share the cultural experience of handling internal and external oppression.

But the young gay person is usually sharply separated from this kind of sharing and mutual support. The last place most gays wish their secret to be known is in their own families. The fear by teenagers of being thrown out of their homes if their feelings are discovered is intense, and, as those who counsel in gay groups well know, too often this fear is well founded rather than paranoid. Even if one is not disinherited or ejected, the ostracism, ridicule, rejection, and unpleasantness visited upon a young gay individual by parents and siblings is much feared and is one of the things giving deepest concern to lesbians and gay men (see, for example, Weinberg and Williams, 1974). Unwittingly, parents and siblings intensify this fear every time they talk about "tomboys" or "sissies" or make a "fag or dyke" joke.

Ironically, even otherwise well-adjusted, self-confident women and men in leadership positions in the gay movement often postpone telling their parents about their homosexuality, only to have the parents discover the secret in news media.

The forces which generate this fear—rejection, ridicule, physical abuse—are too obvious to belabor to the thoughtful observer. The consequences may not be.

At the early stages of the movement, in the late 1960s, gay organizations received numerous suicide telephone calls, especially from young lesbians and gay men because of their loneliness and despair. After almost a decade of intensive publicity and activism in the gay movement, young gays are now at least aware they are not the only one in the world. Although they are still lonely, the sense of utter isolation that used to exist is tempered now by the knowledge that there are some two thousand gay groups around the nation. Consequently, homophile organizations, including the National Gay Task Force, now quite rarely receive suicide calls.

Some young gays perfect their abilities for hiding their orientation from family and friends, while recognizing they are gay. But many others, under heavy pressure from family and peers, refuse to see the truth about themselves for many years. Whether to hide and protect themselves, or out of the self-deception encouraged by society ("How can a good, decent person like me be one of those perverts my family's warned me about?"), many people date, marry, and become parents, only to realize too late the error they have made. They then find themselves deeply pained, fearful of losing their children through court suits, of losing spouses they care for but are ill suited to, of depriving their spouses and themselves of more deeply appropriate and meaningful relationships, and of causing their friends and other relatives deep pain.

This pattern has been widespread. Increasingly, however, young gays are refusing to view themselves with the negativity and fear of earlier generations. Six or eight years ago when I spoke at meetings of college and high school gay groups and asked how many of my audience had shared their sexual orientation with their families, only a few hands were raised. Now it is rare to see the hands of less than half the audience go up. A younger generation, with self-esteeming role-models, absent in earlier times, is less willing to lead a double life.

One possible *positive* result of the traditional familial situation of gays may well be the better "centering" suggested in some studies (e.g., Freedman, 1975). That is, some data suggest gays seem to be better adjusted than heterosexuals to fend for themselves and less inclined to accept societal views and goals uncritically. They seem to be less devastated, for example, by the fear of facing old age alone or by the loss of a spouse.

Because, until recently, the media have usually been deeply uncomfortable about featuring news or information concerning homosexuality, few people have been aware that lesbians and gay men face all the familiar forms of discrimination known to blacks, Jews, Catholics, Hispanics, Asians, and native Americans. Awareness of this discrimination has been made even more difficult, compared with these other minorities, because those who have suffered fear to come forward and document what has been done to them. Although some 1,500 to 2,500 women and men are fired from the armed services each year (Weinberg and Williams, 1971), few individuals protest because they fear they will lose their civilian jobs or hurt family and friends.

Air Force Sgt. Leonard Matlovich, with years of service as a model soldier and with a chest covered with medals including a Bronze Star and a Purple Heart, is an exception. He spoke up and immediately was fired. He somewhat bitterly comments, "My country gave me medals for killing men and a less-than-honorable discharge for loving one."

Another exception, Barbara Love, well-known magazine editor and lesbian author, told the New York City Council how she and her lover, who was dying from cancer, were thrown out on the street, along with their furniture, by their landlord on Christmas Eve because a neighbor suspected they were gay.

City councils across the nation have heard innumerable similar tales and have felt compelled to help. As a consequence, about forty North American municipalities have adopted protections for gays.

But most gays, as we have indicated, are not ordinarily detected. Thus, as a group, gays have not suffered *direct* discrimination to the extent that other minorities have. Rather, we have learned to pretend to our families that our lover is just a roommate; to our colleagues and friends at the office water cooler that we spent the weekend with a "him" or "her" who was, in fact, a "her" or "him"; to separate our family, social, and business lives from our personal and intimate ones in a manner known to heterosexuals only if they have affectional or sexual relationships they must hide—relationships with someone of the wrong race, class, religion, or marital status.

The instant we are honest and forthright about ourselves, we face intense *open* discrimination in our jobs, homes, and lives. As long as we are hypocritical, hide, lie, and pretend, the world likes us, but we are *quietly* ostracized through our awareness of what would be done to us if we were otherwise.

Roots and Role-Models

In a vicious cycle resulting from all the above and perpetuating its continuation, we have been systematically deprived of our history and of role-models. My personal experience growing up in Oregon is characteristic. I was assured by those around me that homosexuals were demented and disgusting and that I was not one of them. Dictionaries and encyclopedias underscored that. If any teacher or adult knew, none dared tell me that Dag Hammarskjöld was gay, that Alexander the Great, Sappho, Tchaikovsky, Willa Cather, Howard Brown, Wittgenstein, John Maynard Keynes, da Vinci, and others were homosexuals. No book told me that, nor did *Time* or *Newsweek*.

Gays ask by what logic are young gays less needful of gay role-models than heterosexuals are of heterosexual models? By what perverted notion are young heterosexuals *taught to despise and hate* lesbians and gay men, in part through the absence of teachers and other adults who are decent, concerned, and accomplished human beings who happen to be homosexual? Is this not like the centuries of refusal of southerners to allow blacks to teach in white children's schools? It is too reminiscent

of the Nazi edicts forbidding Jews to be teachers because they were
"degenerate."

These, then, constitute some of the problems and issues with which
the gay movement has had to deal. Our task is to effect changes in the
law, in the attitude of society, and in ourselves and to do so by all
available peaceful and educative means.

The Developing Gay Movement and Its Perception of Its Role: Early Years

Because of societal attitudes towards gays and the difficulty of identifying the gay constituency, effective efforts to organize gays began only
after the Second World War. Earlier efforts in Chicago and elsewhere
did not take solid root or spread. But in the early 1950s several groups
emerged, mostly in California and based on secret membership of
friends linked in a chain of contacts. These early groups comprised both
gay men's organizations (e.g., Mattachine and The Society for Individual Rights) and lesbian ones (Daughters of Bilitis, or DOB). After a
relatively brief period of secrecy, these groups became increasingly
public and other groups using the same names arose elsewhere around
the country—New York Mattachine, New York DOB, Washington Mattachine, for example.

During their early stages, these organizations were usually discussion
groups, providing social contact for participants and opportunities for
exploring the newly emerging studies and reform policies that were
reaching the public. These included the Kinsey studies (Kinsey, Pomeroy, and Martin, 1948; Kinsey, Pomeroy, and Gebhard, 1953), which
revealed for the first time that the extent of homosexual experience was
far wider and deeper than the public (or "scholars") had previously
imagined. The U.S. Model Penal Code recommendations, prepared and
published by the American Law Institute in 1955 and now adopted by
nearly half the fifty states, eliminated legal sanctions against those engaging in consensual adult sexual relations between competent persons
and not involving exchange of money. The concurrent removal of similar restrictions throughout Western Europe was brought to particular
prominence when England's celebrated parliamentary report of the
Wolfenden Committee was published in 1957 (and subsequently
adopted as law), recommending decriminalization of the restrictions on
homosexual acts.

The growing awareness of gays that change was in the air and badly needed was heightened by the governmental witch hunts of the McCarthy era when hundreds of persons were dismissed from the U. S. State Department on allegations of homosexuality, and even the Duke of Windsor was arrested in a gay police raid (Tripp, 1975). At this time, a major news event emerged surrounding an arrest in Boise, Idaho, which netted many wealthy and politically prominent men. These events frightened most gays but angered and polarized others.

All these forces, coupled with the general social changes of the 1960s (blacks' and women's civil rights; antiwar sentiment; the flower children culture) led to a growing militancy among some gays who wished to see a change in law and public understanding. In San Francisco, between 1968 and 1969, the Society for Individual Rights organized open protests and picketing of homophobic businesses. The Mattachine Society of New York conducted a now celebrated "sip-in" at about the same time in protest of the New York State Liquor Authority laws which forbade a licensed establishment to serve a homosexual. At this time several brave souls, led by Dick Leitsch, head of Mattachine, sought arrest, and carried their case through the courts, eventually winning repeal of the odious and absurd law—a law which directly violated the Equal Protection Clause of the Constitution. Also in New York, in February of 1969, the management of a popular gay bathhouse assumed legal defense of a highly publicized and deeply resented police raid.

The growing militancy felt among gays came to a focus in June of 1969 when police raided a Greenwich Village bar, The Stonewall Inn, and arrested the staff and ejected patrons. A major fight arose and the police barricaded themselves inside the bar as a large, angry crowd congregated outside throwing bricks, cans, and stones at the police. A series of riots began and constituted the first violent rejection by gays of their role of hiding and silently accepting police brutality and public violence.

Out of this event and the changing attitudes of gays emerged a series of groups, especially the Gay Liberation Front, determined to change laws and public policy. Splinter groups with differing internal structures and external policies developed relatively quickly, many of them identifying with one or another antiwar, black, or civil rights group—some of politically leftist bent, others more attuned to traditional political process, yet others largely attending to the social, social service, and religious needs of portions of the gay populace. By 1972 some twelve hundred gay groups had been formed within the United States. Many of them were on college and university campuses. The largest and most powerful, however, were not on campuses, but in large cities. Although many of these groups bore common names in different cities, Gay Liberation Front (GLF), Gay Activists Alliance (GAA), Daughters of Bilitis (DOB), or Mattachine Society, the groups had little intercommunication and no formal or legal connections, let alone regional or national structure.

Nevertheless, many of these groups published leaflets and newspapers and recognized the need to communicate with largely invisible and unrecognizable populations of other gays. Although some groups, such as San Francisco's Society for Individual Rights and New York's Mattachine Society had mailing lists of a few thousand people, the active, participatory, or dues-paying membership of even the largest and most visible groups did not exceed a few hundred persons.

The Development of "Zaps" as Nonviolent Confrontation

Despite this, several groups, and especially the GLF splinter group, GAA, became highly visible and sophisticated in confronting public officials, antigay or homophobic businesses and the press. Using nonviolent confrontational tactics adopted from Martin Luther King and Ghandi, GAA evolved the concept of the "zap." A zap was a well-planned, quick hitting publicity event designed to publicly embarrass an individual or organization which refused to negotiate in civil fashion or which conducted policy offensive to and hostile to gays.

The tactic was widely adopted by groups around the country and served several purposes deliberately recognized and sought by gays: overcoming the nearly ubiquitous media blackout on news and discussion of homosexuality in the press and on television (the presence of reporters and TV camera crews at sit-ins and demonstrations also inhibited the otherwise too familiar excesses and brutality of police against gays); notifying the public and other gays that, like Rosa Parks, we would no longer sit at the back of the bus and meekly accept whatever was done to us; showing the public and other gays that lesbians and gay men came in all forms and were as diverse in dress, appearance, and behavior as members of the Democratic and Republican parties, ranging from hippies to pin-stripe suits; notifying isolated gays, whether in Brooklyn, New York, or Boise, Idaho, that they were not alone or the only ones in the world; dramatizing the absurdity and inequity of the legal and social treatment of a large segment of citizens and taxpayers, and, most important, fellow members of humankind. It should be noted that although these goals were all served by zaps, the leadership of GAA was extraordinarily judicious in use of the tactic because of the risk to life and limb of the membership. Although it may have seemed to some that GAA was "zap-happy" because of the frequency of their actions, this was actually a result of the large number of offenders in established society and their intransigence to quietly meet, discuss, and resolve discord. The leaders of GAA authorized such actions only after failure of exhaustive effort to meet with police, press, or politicians through customary and orthodox channels.

This period of the early 1970s saw a major reassessment by gays of their lives and their place in society. Even those who, like some blacks, counseled, "Don't rock the boat; you're moving too fast!" felt an increased sense of self-esteem as some gays refused to experience torment or discrimination, and as slogans such as "Gay pride," "Gay is good," "Gay is beautiful," and "Gay lib" became popular. Labeling theory tells us that part of our self-image comes from the labels put on us. For the first time in modern history gays were hearing some positive names and labels.

The Emergence of Professional Gay Civil Rights Workers and National, Coordinated Efforts

Until about 1973 no ongoing regional or national clearing house existed to unify the burgeoning groups and active populace of gays. Nor did a professional cadre of full-time, paid civil rights workers develop. With few exceptions, those working in the movement were unpaid volunteers who commonly worked a few months only to be forced to go back to earning a regular livelihood outside the movement.

In the autumn of 1973 the National Gay Task Force was created and has grown by leaps and bounds. It now has over nine thousand members from around the country, including individuals from each of the fifty states and over twenty foreign countries. Thus we are the largest gay civil rights organization in United States' history. In comparison with national organizations representing other minority groups, however, we are small. The National Organization for Women and the American Civil Liberties Union, to name but two, are large in comparison. We wanted to find ways to link the country's thirteen hundred gay and lesbian groups through a communications network and through national projects in the media and legislation. Excitement grew as we took stock of the national projects on which we could work. But our chief goal was to try to expand the base of the gay movement—to make it a genuine grass-roots movement which would include people from all sorts of backgrounds and walks of life.

The Sickness Theory of Homosexuality and the APA

One of the first task-oriented goals of the new national organization was to help persuade the American Psychiatric Association to review the growing body of scientific data relevant to the inaccuracy of the "sickness" notion of homosexuality. Members of NGTF met with members of the Nomenclature Committee of the American Psychiatric Association and presented a formal, written critique of research in the area. Over a period of many months, APA committees reviewed the evidence and concluded that a serious error had been made and that homosexuality per se should be removed from the list of emotional disorders categorized in the APA's authoritative *Diagnostic and Statistical Manual of Mental Disorders.* The committees' conclusions and recommendations moved through a hierarchical series of review agencies within the organization and were adopted unanimously by the APA's Board of Trustees at its December 1973 meeting. At the invitation of the APA, the National Gay Task Force participated in the press conference announcing the change.

The Media and the Portrayal of Gays

The media still portrayed gays as sick, as child molesters, and stereotypically. To begin to deal with these problems, NGTF launched a protest effort by gay groups across the nation when the Marcus Welby show was about to portray gays as child-preying people. Again, we triggered a nationwide protest of the lesbiaphobic video episode, "Flowers of Evil," on NBC's *Policewoman* series.

NGTF had been provided a manuscript of a Welby drama in which a male high school biology teacher sexually assaulted one of his male students during a weekend class outing. NGTF protested that the image was an unfair and harmful stereotype of gay men and that, as indicated, heterosexual offenses against minors outnumbered same-sex ones more than ten to one. The ABC network offered to introduce statements that this offense was "the work of a pedophile," not a homosexual, but refused to go further in changing the show. NGTF responded that the "take-home message" the public would retain weeks and months later was of a gay teacher molesting one of his male charges—a familiar, false, ugly stereotype. (Three years later the Anita Bryant campaign to repeal job protections for gays in Florida cited the Welby episode as evidence of the threat from gay teachers.)

Because the network rejected making further changes, NGTF appealed to the nearly two thousand groups around the nation to help obtain refusal of local network affiliates to broadcast the offending episode or provide equal time for the groups to respond on the air, and to write to national advertisers for the series to drop their financial support for that show. A well-coordinated national effort resulted, in which all first and second string advertisers for the show dropped their support, half-a-dozen major affiliates boycotted airing the episode, and local stations throughout the country provided gay groups an opportunity to respond to the show on the air.

Thus, we showed the media we were a serious force and we showed our own community we could work in concert—that with a coordinating center such as NGTF, gay groups in such diverse places as Boston, New Haven, Minneapolis, Atlanta, Los Angeles, and Moscow, Idaho, could share information and pull together on a common project. We could function as a national movement.

Legislative and Legal Efforts

We also wanted to develop a national legislative program for job and home protection, both for the protections themselves and to provide a forum for national public discussion of gay issues and exposure of the public to a wide array of gays who could stretch and eventually destroy the public's stereotype of gay.

Working closely with Congresswoman Bella Abzug's office in the House of Representatives, and with gay groups around the nation, we contacted potential sponsors and lined up twenty-four cosponsors who introduced the Gay Rights Bill into Congress on 25 March 1975. The Bill, HR 5452, would amend the 1964 and 1968 Civil Rights acts to prohibit discrimination based on a person's "affectional or sexual preference" in the areas of employment, housing, public accommodations and facilities, education, and in federally funded programs.

The representation of minority and mainstream politicians from both political parties illustrated the growing belief among legislators that civil rights are not divisible and that no segment of the population can be denied their constitutional rights.

The climate for such legislation was changing rapidly. Gay civil rights laws had already been passed in over thirty-two cities and counties, including Seattle, Minneapolis, Detroit, San Francisco, Washington, D.C., and Austin. Working with gay groups in many of those cities, NGTF supplied copies of legislation from other cities, resolutions of national organizations, and know-how to use in lobbying local legislators. On several occasions, we were asked by local groups to secure special statements on such issues as gay teachers, police officers, etc. We helped by using our national contacts with the ACLU, NOW, and the American Psychiatric Association (APA) to obtain strong statements from the heads of those organizations. A particularly important one was APA. President Dr. John Spiegel's official statement that there is no scientific basis for discrimination against gay teachers, that all negative attitudes about gay teachers are founded on myth and should be ended.

Industry and Employment

In order to begin putting pressure on industry and unions, NGTF conducted a survey of a portion of the corporations in the "Fortune Five Hundred." Responses from several major corporations representing a total employment of more than two million persons were obtained. Each corporation was asked to declare a public policy forbidding discrimination in hiring or advancement based on affectional or sexual orientation.

The corporations responding thus far include American Telephone & Telegraph, the nation's largest corporate employer; the Bank of America, the world's largest bank; International Business Machines, the American, Columbia, and National Broadcasting companies, American Airlines, Eastern Airlines, Avon, Citicorp, Honeywell, Proctor & Gamble, McDonald's, and McGraw-Hill. A typical statement was that from AT&T Board Chairman John de Butts: "An individual's sexual preferences are not criteria either for becoming an employee or remaining an employee of the Bell System. Job retention and promotability are based upon demonstrable job performance and behavior. An individual's sexual tendencies or preferences are strictly personal and information about these matters should not be sought out by company personnel."

Religion

Ultimately, among societal institutions, the church is the primal source of intolerance of homosexuality. The law and medicine have come to buttress religious prejudices and to justify them in the minds of many who consider themselves liberal in most other spheres. This has created particularly severe problems for gays who are religious. In order to further a long-term goal of ending the religious oppositions of the church, NGTF has undertaken wide-ranging projects with the gay churches and within the nongay denominations. For example, NGTF has become part of the National Task Force on Gay People in the Church—the group who prepared the resolution approved in March of 1975 by the National Council of Churches. That resolution requests the support of member denominations for gay civil rights and calls antigay discrimination morally wrong.

Politics and Voting

From early on, members of the movement recognized that the voting booth was one of the safest and most powerful "closets" in the world. If we could begin to affect the outcome of elections by determining the positions of candidates on gay issues, and widely publicize the information to gays, we could gain both publicity and muscle for our movement. Thus, the Gay Activists Alliance and the San Francisco Society for Individual Rights (S.I.R.) initiated surveys and candidates' nights which became highly successful. Focal points in general were a candidate's willingness to sponsor legislation to protect jobs and homes and to repeal restrictions on consensual adult sex.

In many areas gay groups have coupled surveys with voter registration drives and have successfully publicized the registration of thousands of gay voters. Initially, the strongest responses from politicians came from areas known to have large, somewhat ghettoized populations. As gay voter strength has grown, along with publicity about this strength, and the movement has made politicians ever more aware that it has a potential voting block of at least 10 percent of the population (and add parents, friends, and siblings!), politicians have become more accessible and more supportive.

The voting campaign continues as a major effort throughout the gay movement. It received a particular spur when several openly gay women and men were elected delegates to the Democratic National

Presidential Convention. Moreover, several openly gay women and men have been elected to public office in state legislatures. Alan Spear is a state senator in Minnesota and Elaine Noble an assemblywoman in Massachusetts. Gays have been named to human rights commissions in nearly a dozen major cities. Jean O'Leary of NGTF was appointed by President Carter as one of the commissioners of International Women's Year.

In each of these cases, considerable press attention accompanied the election or appointment of gays, furthering our constant campaign to eliminate stereotypes, educate the public, give gays greater self-esteem, and provide role-models for young and old.

Role-Models

Although many of us know well-known people who are gay—U.S. Senators, heads of universities and banks, police, fire fighters, and movie stars—most such people are understandably unwilling to "come out" publicly. Nevertheless, we continue to talk with these people and gently encourage them. A few at a time have done so: David Kopay, football star; Elton John, rock star; Episcopal clergyman Malcolm Boyd; political strategist David Mixner; bisexual singer Joan Baez.

Although the effort to add to the list of prominent openly gay women and men goes on, a new priority is developing to encourage every gay person to "come out" to at least three nongays a year—friends, colleagues, or family members. In part, this effort is based on the belief that one-to-one contact with gays will be one of the most effective means to bring about attitudinal change in the larger society. Most of us have the experience that our friends and associates who learn of our homosexuality change their assumptions about homosexuality, not their attitude toward us. This is strongly underscored by the findings of the survey of the 1977 Oregon State Governor's Task Force on Sexual Preference that twice as many of those who had worked professionally with a homosexual were willing to do so as those who had not. The study concluded that with respect to protecting the jobs of gays, one of the "most important points to be made from this study [is]: contact with co-workers who acknowledge their homosexual orientation produces an increase in positive attitude and a decrease in feelings of discomfort about homosexuals, a reaction contrary to the prediction that knowing that one's colleague or boss is homosexual would have a disturbing effect."

Anita Bryant and Repeal in Dade County

Although only a very superficial analysis can be made here, we have long expected the familiar "backlash" that other civil rights movements have experienced. Anita Bryant and her followers have led such a backlash. But progress is nearly always conducted by three paces forward and one or two back. And a backlash is by definition in *response* to changes. Thus, the present writer believes that we can and will absorb the setbacks involved in referenda. I believe we will lose some referenda, but I do not feel the gay movement is deeply threatened by them. Our movement has made great strides in less than a decade of widespread activism. In another decade we should be able to win referenda. The only real danger is that gays and their supporters will believe a sensation-oriented press that says we are losing. Only if we believe the media's views and become disheartened are we going to be badly set back in our goals.

Ms. Bryant's campaign has done far more to publicize the unfair treatment of gays and far more to further our goals of having the nation see and hear a wide variety of us than we could possibly have done alone.

Conclusions

Through the efforts of the gay movement in conjunction with changing sexual mores, major inroads have been made in disseminating wider public knowledge about lesbians and gay men and in neutralizing myths and stereotypes concerning them; in promoting a stronger sense of self-esteem as well as a decreased sense of isolation and aloneness in gay women and men; and in establishing major challenges to discrimination against gays and to police harassment of them.

Thus, a younger generation of gays has grown up with far greater access to worthy role-models and subject to fewer experiences of hostility and oppression than their predecessors faced. While vast amounts of work remain, the gay movement is well launched.

REFERENCES

Benjamin, H. 1966. *The transsexual phenomenon.* New York: Julian Press.

DeFrancis, V. 1966. *Protecting the child victim of sex crimes committed by adults.* Denver: The American Humane Association.

Feinbloom, D. H. 1976. *Transvestites; Transsexuals: Mixed views.* New York: Delacorte Press.

Freedman, M. 1975. Stimulus/Response: Homosexuals may be healthier than straights. *Psychology Today* 9:28–32.

Groth, A. N. 1978 Adult sexual orientation and attraction to underage persons. *Archives of Sexual Behavior.*

Kinsey, A. C., et al. 1948. *Sexual behavior in the human male.* Philadelphia: W. B. Saunders.

————. 1953. *Sexual behavior in the human female.* Philadelphia: W. B. Saunders.

Levin, R. J., and Levin, A. 1975. Sexual Pleasure: The surprising preferences of 100,000 women. *Redbook* (September), pp. 51–58.

State of Oregon, Department of Human Resources. 1977. Preliminary Report of the Task Force on Sexual Preference to the Oregon State Legislature.

Time Magazine (12 December 1977), p. 106.

Tripp, C. 1975. *The homosexual matrix.* New York: McGraw-Hill.

Weinberg, M., and Williams, C. J. 1971. *Homosexuals and the military.* New York: Harper & Row.

————. 1974. *Male homosexuals.* New York: Oxford University Press.

PART III

The View of the Clinician

13 / Patterns of Sexual Identity in Childhood: Relationship to Subsequent Sexual Partner Preference

RICHARD GREEN

Several variations exist in patterns of sexual identity in male and female children, and many patterns of sexual behavior exist in adult males and females. An intriguing question for clinicians and researchers is the possible relationship between childhood and adult behavioral patterns. The question has theoretical significance for our continuing attempts to unravel the enigma of how heterosexuality, bisexuality, homosexuality and asexuality emerge. From a clinical perspective, the relationship has significance for those who view certain patterns of adult sexuality as generating significant conflict and who may wish to intervene early in life to interdict such an outcome.

During the past decade, a series of retrospective adult clinical reports has indicated a correlation between adult patterns of sexual orientation and childhood sex-typed behaviors. Bieber and his colleagues (1962) published data on approximately 100 homosexual males in psychoanalytically oriented therapy. They reported that approximately one-third of the patients recalled patterns of childhood feminine behavior. This included an avoidance of rough-and-tumble sports play, preference for girls as playmates, and a preference for girls' games and toys. The percentage of adult heterosexuals in therapy with these analysts

who recalled such childhood "feminine" behaviors was significantly
lower. In 1973, Saghir and Robins reported that of about ninety adult
male homosexuals, most of whom were not currently in psychotherapy,
two-thirds recalled a "girl-like syndrome" during boyhood. This included a preference for girls' toys and games, preference for female
playmates, and an avoidance of rough-and-tumble, aggressive boyhood
play. This percentage, too, was significantly higher than that recalled by
the heterosexual contrast group.

Saghir and Robins also studied females. Here, some two-thirds of the
adult female homosexuals recalled "tomboyish" behavior during preteen years, compared to less than 20 percent of the heterosexual contrast group. More than half of the prehomosexual "tomboys" persisted
with "tomboyism" into adolescence versus none of the preheterosexual
"tomboys."

In 1977 Whitam administered questionnaires to 107 male homosexuals and 68 male heterosexuals and asked about childhood interests in
doll play, cross-dressing, preference for the company of girls, and
whether they had been regarded by other boys as a "sissy." For interest
in doll play, 47 percent of the homosexuals reported yes versus none of
the heterosexuals. For cross-dressing, relative to most same-age boys, 44
percent of the homosexuals reported yes versus none of the heterosexuals. As for peer group preference, 42 percent of the homosexuals preferred females versus 1.5 percent of the heterosexuals. As for being
regarded as a "sissy," this was true for 29 percent of the homosexuals
and 1.5 percent of the heterosexuals. Additionally, nearly 80 percent of
the homosexuals preferred childhood "sex play" with other boys, compared to more than 80 percent of the heterosexuals who preferred
childhood "sex play" with girls.

With respect to transsexualism, the correlation between childhood
sex-typed behaviors and those of adulthood is even more striking.
Transsexuals wish to undergo sex-change surgery and to receive cross-
sex hormones in order to appear and live as a member of the other sex.
Their sexual preference is for someone of the same sex as that in which
they were born. Thus, strictly speaking, they are homosexual, although
they deny this, since they feel that they themselves are of the opposite
sex and see their attractions as heterosexual. In 1966, Benjamin reported a series of transsexuals, male and female, in which nearly all
recalled feeling like someone of the other sex, "as far back as I can
remember." As children they recalled preferring the toys, clothes,
dress, and companionship of the other sex and feeling like persons of
the other sex. This nearly universal retrospective recall of childhood
cross-sex identity was confirmed in the text on transsexualixm by Green
and Money in 1969 and by Stoller (1968).

I (Green 1974) further extended this documentation of the adult
recollections of childhood cross-gender behavior with the histories of

adult males and females who wanted to change sex, or who had changed sex through surgical and hormonal means. Additionally, extensive descriptions were published of children, primarily males, who preferred the toys, dress, activities, companionship and role-playing of girls, and frequently stated their wish to be girls. These children were behaving in a manner comparable to that recalled by the adults with atypical sexual patterns.

Finally, many transvestites, heterosexually oriented males who experience sexual arousal when dressing in women's clothing, also report that they commenced cross-dressing prior to adolescence. Of a series of over 500 transvestites, Prince and Bentler (1972) reported that half recalled cross-dressing before puberty and most of the remainder recalled having begun during the early teens.

Thus there is a considerable body of data suggesting that a significantly higher proportion of adults with a same-sex partner preference recall childhood behaviors considered more typical of other-sex children. It must be noted, however, that not all adults with same-sex partner preferences recall such behaviors. Any comprehensive explanation of psychosexual development linking childhood sex-typed behaviors and adult patterns of sexuality must accommodate these discrepant cases.

A prospective study of atypical sex-typed development is underway. In 1976 I reported extensive demographic and behavioral data on a series of sixty boys referred in consequence of extensive feminine behavior and contrast data on fifty demographically matched masculinely behaving boys. The boys ranged in age from four to twelve when initially evaluated. Seventy-eight percent were evaluated before they reached the age of nine. With respect to age at onset of cross-dressing, 94 percent began prior to the sixth birthday and 74 percent prior to the fourth birthday. With respect to friendship preferences, 94 percent of the feminine boys preferred females versus only 2 percent of the masculine boys. Forty percent of the feminine boys were observed by parents cross-dressing more than forty times, with 19 percent having been observed more than one hundred times. This was observed for none of the masculine boys. When playing house, 38 percent of the feminine boys typically role-played as mother, 7 percent as sister, and 13 percent as a male. By contrast, of those masculine boys who did play house, none typically role-played as mother, sister, or another female. With respect to female-type doll play, this was the favorite toy of 17 percent of the feminine boys and the frequently played with toy of 41 percent. By contrast, for the masculine boys, it was not the favorite toy of any and a frequently played with toy of only 2 percent. As for which parent the child would like to resemble when grown, 42 percent of the feminine boys either occasionally or frequently stated they would like to grow up to be like mother, compared to 7 percent of the masculine boys. Sixty-four percent of the feminine boys never stated they wished to grow up to be like their father, compared to 20 percent of the masculine boys. For 73 percent of the feminine boys, mother was the preferred parent, and for 5 percent it was father. Twenty-two percent liked both parents equally. By contrast, of the masculine boys, 25 percent preferred their mother, 17 percent their father and 57 percent liked both equally.

Clearly these are disparate samples of male children. As much as possible, they are being followed longitudinally into adolescence with attempts made to assess personality attributes in general and sexual behaviors in particular.

More recently, we have generated a sample of fifty "tomboys" and are attempting to match this sample with girls whose behavior is not considered "tomboyish." "Tomboyism" has been operationally defined by (1) the parent considering the child to be a "tomboy" (thus having applied the label "tomboy" to the child with all its implications), and (2) the child, at least half the time assuming the role of a male when role-playing, showing little or no interest in female-type doll play, preferring boy-type games and activities, engaging in sports with males more than females, showing no interest in cosmetics and little or no interest in wearing dresses.

The methods of study of the four samples of children (i.e., the "feminine" and "masculine" boys, "feminine" and "masculine" girls) are comparable. Parents are interviewed using the same semistructured interview and they complete the same paper and pencil psychometric instruments. The children are similarly observed in experimental situations and administered a variety of psychometric tests. This method has been documented in *Sexual Identity Conflict in Children and Adults* (Green, 1975). It is hoped eventually to correlate these atypical and typical childhood behavioral patterns with behavioral patterns in later life.

Why should there be an association between gender behavior in childhood and sex-partner preference in adulthood? Or, the question might be asked, why shouldn't there be? If one proceeds from the assumption that a same-sex partner preference in adulthood, i.e., a male choosing a male, is a pattern most commonly sought by most females, then this adult sexual partner preference can be seen as a continuation of an atypical (for the male) developmental pattern. Here one argues for a developmental track beginning in early childhood with the majority of individuals continuing on the track through adolescence and into adulthood. This, of course, does not explain *why* a minority of individuals follow this alternate track, but is merely a facile manner of explaining the continuity.

It has been frequently observed that individuals with a homosocial peer group in preadolescence are typically heterosexual in adolescence and adulthood, and that individuals with a heterosocial peer group in childhood are subsequently homosexual. In plain English, boys whose best friends are girls at age nine are more likely to have male lovers at eighteen, and vice versa. Two explanations have been given for this. One follows the former "track model." It notes that the male child with a female peer group is socialized within the framework of that group. The remainder of the group will evolve a sexual partner preference for males and therefore so will that male child. An alternative view is that males with a female peer group, being socially stigmatized by male peers and typically having an alienated relationship with their fathers, are "male affect starved." The remedy for this in later years is affectional and sexual love from other males. Again, this does not explain those homosexually oriented males who had positive relationships with their fathers and/or preteen male friends.

What do we know about the genesis of atypical sex-typed patterns during childhood? The earliest writings, dating at least from Freud's biographical reconstruction of the life of Leonardo da Vinci, suggest an absent father and a dominant mother for the male child. Difficulties in resolution of the family romance, the triadic rite of passage through which all children must pass for full psychosexual maturation (oedipal phase) has also been given ample coverage. Homosexuals according to this theory are "psychosexually arrested" and did not evolve into the mature pattern of heterosexual object choice.

More recently psychoanalysts have moved to the preoedipal period in which lack of separation and individuation, particularly on the part of the male child from his mother, and fears of engulfment by the mother are seen as predisposing factors to later homosexuality (Socarides, 1968). These theories have received clinical anecdotal support, mostly in the psychoanalytic literature. The more esoteric analytic clinical interpretations found in this literature "confirm" these developmental theories.

Skeptics about the scientific rigor of the psychoanalytic method and doubters of its metapsychological concepts remain unconvinced. A study which attempted to address this issue in a scientific manner (Bieber et al., 1962) found statistically significant differences in recalled childhood relationships between homosexual and heterosexual males. A close-binding, intimate relationship between the prehomosexual male and his mother coupled with an absent or distant father-son relationship was more commonly found than with the preheterosexual male. A methodologic problem here is that these are recollections of questionable validity and are sometimes the interpretations of the treating psychoanalyst. They are data reported by "observers" who may have preconceived notions as to the etiology of homosexuality. Further, there is questionable representativeness of patients in analytic therapy. It is of considerable additional importance that, while there may be a statistical difference between the homosexual and heterosexual samples, there is also considerable overlap.

On the side of confirmation of this triadic early life predisposition toward homosexuality is the questionnaire study of nonpatients by Evans (1969). However, Siegelman in his questionnaire study (1974) of mostly nonpatient samples of homosexual and heterosexual males was not able to confirm this early life pattern. Further, when he excluded the factors of neuroticism and effeminacy in both heterosexual and homosexual males, the pattern crumbled into even finer bits.

What do we see in the parent-child relationships of our feminine boys who may have a higher probability than the masculine boys of being prehomosexual? We see a preference by more of the feminine boys for their mothers compared to their fathers and the wish to be like their mothers. We do not, however, find significant differences in regard to the parents of the feminine and masculine boys feeling closer to or more distant from their sons.

Does the fact that feminine boys more often want to be like their mothers suggest qualities of a pivotal mother-son relationship, qualities of the mother alone, qualities of the mother vis-à-vis the father, qualities of the interaction between the son and father, or qualities of the son alone or the father alone? It can be argued that children who have a male identity early in life (from whatever source) are more likely to want to be like their fathers who are also male. Irrespective of other factors operating in the family, young children who have a feminine identity (from whatever source) are more likely to want to be like their mothers who are female and more feminine than their fathers.

"Role-modeling" of a given parent may emanate from qualities of a parent or from qualities of a child. A child may want to enhance his or her personality which has a masculine or feminine "baseline" and so seek out the available "appropriate" model.

Father-son closeness, mother-son closeness, father-son distance, and mother-son distance are interactional processes. When we clinically interview adults, and they recall child-parent interactions, negative interactions are usually recalled as having been instigated by the parent. However, in research in which we *directly* examine individual families, we find that father-son distance may be son-activated or father-activated, as may be mother-son closeness. There are fathers who attempted to engage their sons in a variety of behaviors which they, the fathers, found enjoyable such as roughhouse play, outdoor recreational pursuits, etc. Moreover, they found their sons' disinterest in such activities nonrewarding to them (the fathers), and so became discouraged. Especially when other children in the family do share the father's interests, the result may be father-feminine boy alienation, father-masculine boy closeness. Other fathers, on the other hand, have little interest or time for a son; the son senses this rejection and turns away from the father toward the other available parent.

Activities and interests of one or another parent may resonate with innate qualities of a child, e.g., domestic chores versus outdoor activities. Temperamental differences in the child may result in that child seeking out one or the other parent and adopting behaviors more like that parent. Thus a socialization pattern evolves which is considered masculine or feminine. This pattern may not be consistent with what is considered socially acceptable for a child of that sex.

All children are not created equal. They differ from birth as any observer of children in nurseries or as parents of more than one child can attest. What accounts for these temperamental differences remains enigmatic, but a few hints are appearing with respect to the prenatal hormonal milieu. Data are appearing which suggest that prenatal levels of androgenic and/or estrogenic hormones appearing at critical developmental periods for the central nervous system may have effects on postnatal behaviors which are culturally sex-typed. The earliest work was by Ehrhardt Epstein, and Money (1968) on females born with the virilizing adrenogenital syndrome. Here, a metabolic defect present *in utero* caused an excessive amount of androgenic adrenal steroid production. While the excessive masculinizing hormone production can be controlled postnatally, the prenatally developing central nervous system was exposed to unusually high levels of androgen. These children have been compared with their sisters not affected with the adrenogenital syndrome. Ehrhardt and Baker (1974) found that girls with the high levels of prenatal androgen were more "tomboyish," had higher general energy expenditure (e.g., roughhouse, physically aggressive play), were less interested in dolls, and less interested in wearing frilly feminine clothes.

More recently there have been studies looking at both male and female children whose mothers received a variety of hormones during pregnancy to control a tendency toward habitual abortion. Results of these studies have not been entirely consistent, in part due to the disparate methods used to study behaviors and the wide ranges of drug dosage, time, and duration of administration. Also, there is the retrospective nature of much of the data collected and the difficulties in obtaining matched samples. Some subjects have received diethylstilbestrol, others have received natural progesterone, others have received synthetic progesterones, and some have received combinations of these. The variations of the dosage have been as much as one hundredfold within a given study, and subjects' mothers may have initially received the drug during any of the three trimesters. Dependent measures have included openended and semistructured interviews, the Cattell Personality tests, the Embedded Figures Test, the Strong Vocational Interest Blank, the Bem Sex-Role Inventory, the Guilford-Zimmerman Temperament Survey, the California Psychological Inventory, observations of teenagers throwing a ball and running, parent ratings, teacher ratings, and so forth.

Rather than attempt a synthesis of these findings, what is important for discussion here is that various personality components with sex-typed connotations and certain behaviors, also with sex-typed connotations, are statistically associated with administration of some of these chemical agents. Some of these behaviors which manifest in childhood, such as preference or aversion for rough-and-tumble aggressive play and preference or aversion for doll play, may influence peer group and parent-child interactions such that different socialization tracks are entered.

Inasmuch as the fetus naturally produces varying levels of sex steroids from the first trimester, it is not illogical that this may be one factor which accounts for "temperamental variability" between young children. This variability may set the stage for varying patterns of psychosexual differentiation.

To synthesize the findings emerging from our current research program, we would tentatively suggest an interaction between innate features of the child (culturally characterized as masculine or feminine), the peer group, and the parents. A necessary, but not sufficient, variable is that parents make no attempt during the first years of life to discourage atypical sex-typed behaviors, even when these behaviors constitute the predominant behaviors. Once on a developmentally atypical track, the ensuing social forces make it difficult to move to the typical track.

A distinction needs be made with respect to the differences between the male and female child with atypical gender-role behavior. The male children we are studying typically *want to be* girls as well as behave like girls. The females are generally *content being females,* but like to behave as boys. Thus, one would expect a more enduring lifelong pattern of atypical development for the male children. Consider too, that in a culture which stigmatizes the "sissy," but not the "tomboy," the inner drive toward femininity must be stronger for the male to persist in the face of social ostracism. By contrast, the female may receive encouragement for her "masculine" behavior so long as it is not of an extreme degree. Those few female children with a male identity who actually wish to be male may be the pretranssexual children. The mystery remains why some of these tomboys evolve into homosexual adults and some do not.

Questions of intervention are a logical concern here. If there is ample evidence that those children manifesting atypical sex-typed behaviors will evolve into sexually atypical adults, is there an ethical responsibility of parents and clinicians to intervene? This question engages value judgments regarding patterns of adult atypical sexuality, psychological and social conflicts experienced by persons during adulthood with varieties of sexual behaviors, social and psychological conflicts experienced by children with atypical sex-typed behaviors, and children's rights.

One problematic issue is the considerable overlap between comparable cross-gender childhood behaviors associated with later diverse patterns of adult sexuality. There is, at present, no clear manner with which to discriminate a "very feminine boy" who is preheterosexual, pretranssexual, pretransvestite, or prehomosexual. This is of significance in that different degrees of social hardship are experienced by adults with these varying patterns of atypical sexuality.

The most profound distress is usually experienced by transsexuals. They relentlessly seek out endocrinologists and surgeons at great personal, social, and financial sacrifice to alter their bodies to "fit their minds." Even after surgery, many continue to experience significant conflict, although most appear better adjusted than prior to surgery when careful preoperative selections are made. However, transsexualism is a rare phenomenon, much rarer than homosexuality. The best estimates are that there are less than ten thousand transsexuals in the United States compared to, perhaps, five million homosexuals (Kinsey et al., 1948, 1953). As for transvestism, the incidence is not known in spite of the fact that in recent years in major cities social organizations have appeared composed of heterosexual, married, cross-dressing males. These individuals generally do not seek psychiatric counseling and there is little in the psychiatric literature describing the social adjustment or inner conflict experienced by them. With respect to homosexuality, patterns of life success or nonsuccess appear to be as varied as for heterosexuals. The great majority of homosexuals do not consult psychiatrists, and more recent, controlled studies comparing heterosexual and homosexual subjects generally do not find significant differences with respect to psychological adjustment. This is not to say that homosexually oriented individuals do not experience unique conflicts in this culture. They do. They are frequently the victims of civil rights discrimination, social prejudice, and, within certain religious groups, stigmatization.

From the perspective of adult conflict one might deduce that if greater precision were available for diagnosing the pretranssexual child, such a child might, through early intervention, learn to experience greater comfort being a member of the sex into which he or she was born. This would preclude considerable subsequent social distress during childhood, adolescence, and adulthood.

Thus, when attempting to evaluate children with atypical sexual identity, clinicians try to disentangle the three components of this identity for a differential diagnosis. The three components are core morphologic identity (the self-concept of being male or female), gender-role behavior (those behaviors culturally defined as masculine or feminine), and sexual partner preference (erotic preference for persons of the same, other, either, or neither sex). It is the first component which may be critical in distinguishing the pretranssexual child. However, this distinction is easier said than made. At the current stage of our knowledge, such distinctions cannot be made with certainty.

Granting that we do not know the outcome of a given child's atypical gender-role behavior, is intervention justified? Differences exist, as noted earlier, for the male and female. The male child experiences social alienation for his "sissy" behavior; the "tomboy" does not. Therefore, unless the tomboy is desperately unhappy being female, there is a little justification for intervention. With respect to the feminine boy, however, both the issues of core morphologic identity and gender-role behavior need be considered. If the male child is desperately unhappy being male, this issue should be addressed. If the child is experiencing considerable social ostracism and peer group stigmatization for his atypical behaviors, this too must be considered. In spite of much that has been read and said during recent years regarding a unigendered or unisexed movement "sweeping the country," at many levels of society hardly a dent is apparent. The atypical male child of today, "the sissy," is often treated in as cruel a manner as his counterpart of a generation or two ago.

In the event a child desperately wants to be of the other sex, the reasons for this can be explored. Oftentimes it is the misassumption that only other-sex children get to do certain things desired by the child. This can be clarified. Examples of individuals who pursue desired occupational, recreational, and dressing patterns and are of the same sex as the child can be highlighted. Also, depending on age and extent of sex education, some children may believe in the magical possibility of changing sex by wishing for it and may not be cognizant of the full range of physiological and anatomical sex differences. Clarification here may be helpful.

With respect to gender-role behavior, modifications can be introduced. A male child whose peer group is exclusively female may be guided into a wider peer group which includes males who are themselves not roughhouse. With a more heterogeneous peer group, the child may be able to develop some masculine social skills, be less set apart from the larger male peer group, and be less subject to teasing. The child needs to know, if he or she doesn't already know, the causes of peer group teasing. In some cases, it is toy selection; in some cases, it is effeminate mannerisms. Children do not like to be teased, and frank discussions with the child about the source of teasing may result in modifications of the behavior. Parents can alert the child to physical gestures, etc., which signal "sissiness" to other children.

Children may ask, "Why can't I do such and such if I want to?" and indeed they can, but they must understand the social price they pay. For those children who do not wish to pay the price, the alternative is modifying their behavior so as to reduce stigmatization. Here one's private ethic may come into conflict with the therapeutic approach.

While the therapist may privately wish that all sexism were immediately eradicated from the culture, along with "sex-typed life-styles," when faced with a suffering individual and troubled parents requesting help, private ethics and clinical responsibilities may collide. I believe our responsibility at the micro level is to the individual patient, while on the macro level it is to attempt to induce changes in the larger culture. These changes would permit a wider latitude of behavior by males and females.

Mention was made earlier of parent-child relationships as an interaction between sex-typed behaviors of the child and parental expectations. In families in which father/son alienation has evolved in association with femininity in the son, the unique nature of the child's interests can be pointed out to the father and attempts can be made to find mutually enjoyable activities. In our experience, Indian Guides (a group father/son, nonathletic, nonroughhouse-oriented activity) has been useful. Here boys develop a greater degree of comfort in relating to a male peer group and the father/son relationship is enhanced. Where parents have been unwittingly or wittingly encouraging feminine behavior by laughing at it in a positive way, by showing it off and giving it social reinforcement, this issue can be addressed. Parents may be unaware of ways in which they have been encouraging behaviors which they now find to be distressing to themselves and to their child. Clearly, no attempt should be made to forge the boy into the "all-American" cultural stereotype or to forge the girl into an ultrafeminine mold. Rather, we are striving for increased psychological and social comfort.

Thus, the question of the relation between sex-typed behaviors during childhood and adult sexuality engages many issues, including the most basic ones of psychological ontogeny, i.e., the development of sexual identity. Research is moving ahead with increased vigor and sophistication at both the physiological and psychosocial levels. Social forces engender and influence patterns of sex-typed expression at all age levels. Prospective studies may provide data on the associations between specific types of early childhood behaviors, specific intrafamily and peer group experiences, and later adolescent and adult patterns of sexuality. These should be of greater heuristic value than previous retrospective reports.

In this quest for knowledge, let us not lose sight of the overriding concern for the rights and welfare of individuals at all ages of both sexes and for the opportunity for maximal growth and expression. As investigators, clinicians, and social scientists, we bear the responsibility to assist those individuals with both typical and atypical patterns of sexuality. Maximum growth potential at the clinical level, responsible research, and social activism can work in concert towards this goal. Any discussion relating gender-role development in children to adult sexuality without such a caveat would be incomplete.

REFERENCES

Benjamin, H. 1966. *The transsexual phenomenon.* New York: Julian Press.

Bieber, I., et al. 1962. *Homosexuality.* New York: Basic Books.

Ehrhardt, A., and Baker, S. 1974. Fetal androgens, human central nervous system differentiation, and behavior sex differences. In R. Friedman, R. Richart, and R. Vande Wiele, eds., *Sex Differences in Behavior* (New York: John Wiley).

Ehrhardt, A.; Epstein, R.; and Money, J. 1968. Fetal androgens and female gender identity in the early-treated adrenogenital syndrome. *Johns Hopkins Medical Journal* 122:160–67.

Evans, R. 1969. Childhood parental relationships of homosexual men. *Journal of Consulting and Clinical Psychology* 33:129–35.

Freud, S. 1910. Leonardo da Vinci and a Memory of His Childhood. In J. Strachey, ed., *The standard edition of complete works of Sigmund Freud, 11th ed.* (London: Hogarth Press, 1957), pp. 59–137.

Green, R. 1975. *Sexual identity conflict in children and adults.* New York: Basic Books; London: Gerald Duckworth; New York: Penguin.

———. 1976. One-hundred ten feminine and masculine boys: Behavioral contrasts and demographic similarities. *Archives of Sexual Behavior* 5:425–46.

Green, R., and Money, J. 1969. *Transsexualism and sex reassignment.* Baltimore: Johns Hopkins University Press.

Kinsey, A. C., et al. 1948. *Sexual behavior in the human male.* Philadelphia: W. B. Saunders.

Kinsey, A. C., et al. 1953. *Sexual behavior in the human female.* Philadelphia: W. B. Saunders.

Prince, V., and Bentler, P. 1972. Survey of 504 cases of transvestism. *Psychological Reports* 31:903–17.

Saghir, M., and Robins, E. 1973. *Male and female homosexuality.* Baltimore: Williams & Wilkins.

Siegelman, M. 1972. Adjustment of male homosexuals and heterosexuals. *Archives of Sexual Behavior* 2:9–26.

———. 1974. Parental background of male homosexuals and heterosexuals. *Archives of Sexual Behavior* 3:3–18.

Socarides, C. 1968. *The overt homosexual.* New York: Grune & Stratton.

Stoller, R. 1968. *Sex and gender.* New York: Science House.

Whitam, F. 1977. Childhood indicators of male homosexuality. *Archives of Sexual Behavior* 6:89–96.

14 / Clinical Aspects of Male Homosexuality

JUDD MARMOR

The assumption that homosexuals are all alike is a stereotype born of cultural prejudice, the absurdity of which becomes obvious if the analogous assumption were made that heterosexuals are all alike. There is as wide a personality variation among homosexuals as among heterosexuals: from extreme passivity to extreme aggressiveness, from quiet introversion to loud and raucous extroversion, from hysteria to compulsiveness, from sexual inhibition and timidity to sexual promiscuity and self-flaunting, from irresponsible sociopathic behavior to highly responsible and law-abiding life-patterns. Their psychiatric diagnoses apart from their homosexual reactivity run the entire gamut of modern nosology.

The physical makeup of male homosexuals is equally diverse. In contrast to the popular myth that all homosexuals are effeminate in appearance and given to effeminate mannerisms, e.g., swishing gait, lisping speech, and "limp wrists," the appearance of homosexual men covers a broad spectrum from extreme "femininity" of physique and manner to extreme "masculinity." Thus the widespread assumption that homosexuals are always recognizable by their appearance or manner is without foundation. The vast majority of homosexuals who conceal their homosexuality from the general public (that is, are "in the closet") are neither recognized nor recognizable as such. Indeed, homosexuals do not always recognize each other except for the deliberate cues that they may choose to present to one another on occasion (see Voeller, chapter 12, this volume).

Another reflection of the stereotyping of homosexuals is the almost universal belief that they are not to be trusted with young people of the same sex. The assumption that they are somehow less in control of their impulses than are heterosexuals is the same kind of misconception that underlies white prejudice against blacks or native born prejudice against foreigners. In all of these instances, the prejudice is a reflection of fear based on a lack of intimate knowledge of the people involved. A homosexual individual is neither more nor less trustworthy, necessarily, with young people of the same sex than a heterosexual person is with young people of the opposite sex. The "dependability" of a homosexual in such a position rests on whether or not he or she is a responsible human being with an adequate "superego," and that is the only factor to be evaluated; otherwise his or her homosexuality is neither more nor less relevant than is the heterosexuality of a male counselor in a girls' camp or of a female counselor in a boys' camp. What I am saying is simply that individual homosexuals ought to be evaluated on their own merits and not on the basis of a stereotyped preconception.

The erotic practices of male homosexuals do not differ markedly from those that characterize heterosexual relations except for the anatomical limitations imposed by the fact that the participants are of the same sex. Kissing, petting, mutual masturbation, and oral-genital relations are essentially similar and analogous to those activities as practiced by heterosexuals. Anal intercourse, however, is considerably more common among male homosexuals than it is between heterosexuals, as is anal stimulation in general, but the assumption that anal intercourse is an inevitable and necessary part of male homosexual practices is simply not true. A substantial number of male homosexuals find this practice distasteful and indulge in it rarely or not at all.

Contrary to popular assumption, most homosexuals, in Western Europe and America, do not show clear-cut active or passive preferences in their relationships with one another. Even though they may have role preferences, in actual practice the majority vary their techniques, assuming the active and passive roles interchangeably or participating in different roles with different partners. As Carrier (1977) has shown, however, role preferences may differ in various cultures as well as in different socioeconomic classes. He points out that in countries like Mexico, Brazil, Greece, and Turkey, and in the lower-class culture of the United States (both Anglo and Mexican-American), where "macho" concepts dominate, there tends to be a much sharper differentiation of sex-roles between men indulging in homosexual practices. Anal inserters are regarded as more masculine than anal insertees and their external behavior and mannerisms are also quite different. The inserters are more masculine in appearance and behavior and also more likely than the more effeminate insertees to have had heterosexual contacts. They also tend to view themselves as superior to the more effeminate types. Carrier's research suggests also that those Mexican homosexual males who do play both sex-roles generally do not do so with the same partner. Instead, he found, they tend to rank prospective partners as to whether they are more masculine or more effeminate than themselves. Once they have made this judgment, then they tend to play the appropriate opposite role, that is, they are active sexually with the more effeminate types and passive sexually with the more masculine types. Similar dichotomization of homosexual sex-roles has been noted in Brazil by Young (1973), in Turkey by Dundes, Leach, and Özkok (1972), and in Greece by Bialor (1975). Farrell and Marrione (1974) have described similar role differentiations among lower-class American youths and Carrier (1976) among Chicano males in Southern California.

A recent Kinsey Institute study by Bell and Weinberg (1978) involving 686 homosexual males and 293 homosexual females has strikingly demonstrated the diversities that exist in male and female homosexual behavioral patterns. The subjects were all recruited from the Bay area around San Francisco. Bell and Weinberg found that public cruising was much more frequent among the male homosexuals in their sample than among female homosexuals, but that most of the sexual activity was conducted in the privacy of homes. Their data did not support the popular notion that male homosexuals do nothing else but search for sexual partners. Almost 40 percent of their male respondents either did no cruising at all or did it no more than once a month. Most of the homosexual males sought their sexual partners in gay bars or baths with relatively few doing their cruising in public areas where they might be arrested.

Bell and Weinberg's study confirms the general view that male homosexuals tend to be relatively promiscuous in their sexual behavior, but it is also interesting to note that a majority of them also sought and had more extended relationships. Although a majority of the extended relationships lasted only one to three years, many of them were long-time "marriages."

Thus, despite the fact that homosexual contacts can be made with relative ease, it is clear that not all homosexuals pursue patterns of promiscuity or impersonal sex. Most of them, indeed, are searching for a meaningful human relationship. The more emotionally mature the person, the more apt he is to seek a more stable liaison with a genuinely loved partner. The fact that so many of these relationships do not last more than a year or two or three is not entirely surprising. It is quite possible that many more heterosexual relationships would end in divorce much sooner if there were no legal restraints or children involved.

The promiscuity of some male homosexuals may rest in some of their common underlying psychodynamic patterns. For example, in many of them there are fears of interpersonal commitment, intimacy, or responsibility that may play a part not only in their avoidance of heterosexual involvement but may also operate with regard to homosexual relationships. For such homosexuals part of the safety of brief homosexual liaisons rests precisely on the fact that such liaisons do not entail expectations of commitment, intimacy, or responsibility.

On the other hand, it may well be that a substantial factor in homosexual promiscuity rests on sociological rather than psychodynamic factors. Is there any reason to doubt that if heterosexual exchanges were as easily available as most homosexual ones, that heterosexual men would be just as promiscuous? Indeed, the advent of the pill and the lessened fear of venereal disease that has accompanied scientific advances in the past two decades has, in fact, led to an enormous increase in heterosexual promiscuity.

Nevertheless, it is worth noting that, as Bell and Weinberg point out, "A relatively steady relationship with a loved partner is a very meaningful event in the life of a homosexual man." Such relationships, when they occur, involve the same kind of significant emotional exchange and commitment that heterosexuals experience in their love relationships.

By contrast, homosexuals who cruise in public parks, streets, and public restrooms are often individuals who are seeking relatively impersonal sex and who have strong neurotic components to their homosexual behavior. The drive for impersonal sex sometimes has an enormously compulsive quality. Some of these individuals may be involved in a dozen or more sexual transactions in the course of a single day or evening. Most homosexuals who seek passing relationships but are less neurotically driven look for them in homosexual baths and gay bars where there is a higher degree of safety. Bell found that cruising in public restrooms and in movie theaters was the least frequent type of cruising among both black and white male homosexuals in their sample. Bars were by far the most popular cruising locale.

Interestingly, the popular conception that all men who pursue impersonal sex in public restrooms are obligatory homosexuals bears little relationship to the actual facts. Humphreys (1970) in a study of participants in the impersonal sex of the public restrooms (sometimes called "tearooms") found that 54 percent of them were married and living in middle-class homes and neighborhoods with their wives and children. For all intents and purposes they were "just average guys next door." They tended for the most part to be on the politically conservative side and many were regular churchgoers. About 40 percent were Roman Catholic and only about 16 percent professed no religious affiliation. Approximately 10 percent were black. Only 38 percent of these "tearoom" frequenters fell into the type 5 and type 6 Kinsey groups. Twenty-four percent could be categorized as being type 3 or type 4 on the Kinsey scale. The more "heterosexual" group usually functioned as fellatees rather than fellators. These men viewed their experiences not as homosexual encounters but rather as quick, inexpensive, and impersonal ways of achieving an orgasm. As might be expected, for the most part these were emotionally withdrawn men whose marriages were deteriorating and whose sex lives with their wives had become unsatisfactory.

Although most male homosexuals appear to be drawn to partners whose attributes reflect a high degree of masculinity, i.e., well-developed physiques and particularly, large penises, there are wide variations of preference. Some are attracted by qualities of intellect or by cultural achievement, and some reach out for partners with obvious feminine characteristics. The widespread assumption that male homosexuals constitute a threat to young children is a totally unfounded notion. In actuality the seeking out of children as sexual objects is much less common among homosexuals than among heterosexuals (Gebhard et al., 1965).

In general, one encounters conflict about homosexuality more frequently in males than in females, although Bell and Weinberg found that the vast majority of their male respondents accepted their homosexuality. Nevertheless, the fact that our society is much more condemnatory of homosexuality in males than in females accounts for part of the difference as well as the fact that homosexuality in males is more likely to be seen as an indication of masculine inadequacy. Obviously, the homosexuals whom most psychiatrists see are the ones who are unhappy and conflicted about their homosexual status.

Bell and Weinberg divide the homosexuals in their sample into five major groupings:

1. *Close-coupled.* These were men who were living in a "marital" relationship with a male partner. These individuals had fewer sexual problems, fewer partners, and did less cruising than most of the others. They constituted 10 percent of the sample.
2. *Open-coupled.* This group, constituting 18 percent of the sample, consisted of men who were involved in a quasimarriage with a male partner but still tended to cruise and seek out other partners. Men in the open-coupled group tended to be more exclusively homosexual, to do more worrying about cruising, to be more active sexually, to have engaged in a wider variety of sexual techniques, and to have more regret about their homosexuality.
3. *Functional.* The functional group constituted 15 percent of the sample. These individuals were "single"—that is, they were not coupled. Their scores were high with regard to sexual promiscuity and the level of sexual activity. These individuals did not regret their homosexuality, for the most part, and had relatively fewer problems of sexual dysfunction. They did more cruising but worried less about being exposed as homosexuals. They tended to be more overt in their homosexuality and to have less guilt about it. As a group they tended to be younger. The black respondents were overrepresented in this group.
4. *Dysfunctional.* This group constituted 12 percent of the total sample. None of these were coupled, but, in contrast to the functional group, although they were high in sexual activity, they were also high in terms

of the number of sexual problems that they presented and in their regret about being homosexual. They were more likely to have concerns about sexual inadequacy, about finding a suitable sex partner, and about difficulties in reaching orgasm. As a group they tended to be somewhat higher educationally than the average male respondent in this sample.

5. *Asexual.* This group consisted of 16 percent of the sample. None of them were coupled but they all scored low in the level of sexual activity, the number of partners, and the amount of cruising that they did. In addition, they had low levels of sexual interest, more difficulties in finding partners, less extensive sexual repertoires, and more regret over their homosexuality. As a group they tended to be less exclusively homosexual and more covert than the other respondents. They tended to feel that they were less sexually appealing to other men and tended to be older than the other respondents in the sample. Blacks were underrepresented in this group.

The Bell and Weinberg study illustrates other diverse aspects of the homosexual life-style, aspects that contradict many of the stereotyped preconceptions about homosexuals. Thus, the men in their sample reported work histories that were fully as stable as those of their heterosexual controls and were quite satisfied with their working situations and salaries. For most of them, being homosexual had not significantly affected their careers, although a number did feel that their homosexuality had restricted their job opportunities. As a group they were less religious than the heterosexual controls, but the spectrum of religiosity in the group extended from conventional religious affiliations to none at all. As a group the homosexual men in the Bell and Weinberg sample tended to be slightly more liberal than the members of the heterosexual sample, but again the spectrum of their affiliations went from quite conservative to quite radical. It must be borne in mind that their sample, having been drawn from the Bay area, tended to represent a more liberal sector of political thought than might be found in other parts of the country. Another interesting finding in the Bell and Weinberg study was that the homosexual men in their sample tended to have more close friends than the heterosexuals did. Also, they were more likely to number both homosexuals and heterosexuals among their friends, while relatively few of the heterosexuals had homosexual friends that they knew of.

Bell (1975) has succinctly summarized the clinical diversity that exists among homosexuals:

Homosexuals differ with respect to the degree to which they are exclusively homosexual in their sexual arousal and behavior. These differences are reflected in the nature of their past and present sexual fantasies and dreams ... and in the emotional contexts in which such arousal is most likely to occur. ... Other ways in which homosexuals differ "sexually" include (1) the number of their partners, (2) the physical characteristics they seek in their partners, (3) the degree of intimacy obtained in a given relationship, (4) the emotional meaning of their sexual partnerships, (5) the locales in which prospective partners are sought and in which sexual contacts take place, (6) the frequency with which sexual contacts are pursued and found, (7) the extensiveness of their sexual repertoires as well as their preferred sexual techniques, (8) the degree to which their sexual impulses are ego-alien, (9) the extent and nature of their sexual problems, (10) the level of their sexual interest and arousal, and (11) the degree to which they are overt or covert. (pp. 423–424)

It should be quite apparent that almost all of these variables apply to heterosexuals no less than to homosexuals.

Aging and Homosexuality

A common assumption, particularly with regard to male homosexuals, is that their older years are inevitably a period of loneliness, sadness, and sexual frustration. As Kelly (chapter 9, this volume) demonstrates, this is yet another popular myth that fails to stand up under objective study. In his study, aging gay men are shown to continue to be involved both sexually and socially, and many are in long-term relationships which are often terminated only by the deaths of their partners.

It is true, nevertheless, that aging does have an almost phobic meaning for some homosexual men. Such homosexuals cling to a youthful appearance with passionate intensity, dress accordingly, and devote themselves with dedicated fervor to the preservation of their youthful figures. To the extent that such concerns constitute a dominant theme in their lives, they reflect a narcissistic preoccupation suggestive of deep underlying feelings of insecurity and fears of rejection. In all fairness it must be stated, however, that although such concerns with youthfulness are perhaps more frequent among homosexual men, they are by no means confined to them. The "cult of youth" is widespread in our culture and can be observed with increasing frequency also among heterosexual middle-aged and older men—witness their increasing preoccupation with physical fitness as well as the tendency among them to visit hair stylists, use cosmetics, wear jewelry, and attire themselves in clothes that once were considered either overly youthful or "effeminate." Yet such is the power of prejudice that many such men still feel free to sneer at gay men for doing exactly the same thing!

By the same token there are many aging homosexuals who accept the aging process with a dignity and objectivity that is in no way different from that observed in mature heterosexuals. Thus in the area of aging, no less than in other areas, one is impressed as much by the similarities between homosexuals and heterosexuals as by the differences.

The Prevention of Homosexual Development

Is it legitimate for a psychotherapist to try to prevent the development of a homosexual life-style if it appears that a child is moving in that direction? Spokespersons for the gay liberation movement argue that to do so is merely another way of expressing the societal prejudice against homosexuality and that children should be left free to develop as they will. This argument is not without merit, yet it seems to me to be pragmatically untenable. The fact is that questionnaires addressed to homosexual parents themselves, asking whether they would want their children to be gay also, indicate that most of them reply in the negative, on the grounds of the difficulties that a homosexual way of life entails in our culture. Obviously, heterosexual parents uniformly feel this way. Until, therefore, our societal mores develop to a point at which homosexual behavior is no longer regarded with prejudice, the issue of preventing its development, where possible, is a legitimate one.

The problem of prevention is far from a simple one, however. It is not by any means always possible to predict that a homosexual pattern is in the process of developing. A significant proportion of both male and female homosexuals present no clear-cut outward indications in childhood or early adolescence of their variant development, so that there is no basis for instituting preventive measures in such instances. One possible indication, however, is where there is a significant failure to develop sex-appropriate gender-role patterns and/or satisfactory peer relationships in childhood. Green (chapter 13, this volume) has demonstrated that effeminate boys show a high propensity for developing homosexual behavior later in life (although a small proportion may become transsexuals, and some go on to become "normally" heterosexual). Such children, therefore, should be considered as potentially susceptible to homosexual development, and preventive treatment should be instituted as soon as possible. Treatment of these children is indicated for another reason also that is no less valid. Effeminacy in boys (much more than tomboyism in girls) usually subjects them to merciless teasing and hazing from their peers; the result is often a seriously impaired self-image and distressing feelings of isolation and alienation.

It must be pointed out, however, that in such cases, it is not the child that should be regarded as the problem, but the family system. Emphasis in treatment should be placed on those aspects of the family relationships that are hindering the development of a satisfactory identification with the same-sex parent, an affectionate and unambivalent relationship with the parent of the opposite sex, and healthy peer associations. This usually involves an exploration not only of the parents' relationships to the child and vice versa, but also of their relationship to one another, to their own gender identities, and their attitudes toward sexuality. With appropriate family therapy and guidance, many of these children can be helped to achieve more appropriate gender-role patterns, and presumably, in some of them at least, a homosexual life-pattern may be forestalled.

Once, however, a homosexual predilection has clearly emerged, the issue is no longer one of prevention but of trying to alter an already existent preference. This is quite a different issue, and in this writer's opinion, such efforts should not be undertaken without the genuine cooperation of the individual involved. It is not at all uncommon for a psychiatrist to be importuned by distraught parents to treat a teenage son or daughter whose homosexual propensities have come to light, but in my experience, unless the adolescent is strongly motivated to change, not much will be accomplished so far as changing his or her erotic preference. In such instances it is more constructive to help the parents to develop a better understanding of the issue of homosexuality and above all not to withdraw their love and support from their child. At the same time, it is equally important to help the adolescents in such instances to accept themselves without guilt or shame, and to cope with some of the problems that their variant sexual preference may entail.

Treatment of Homosexuals

Under no circumstances is there ever any justification for forcing psychiatric treatment on an unwilling or uncooperative homosexual. Homosexual behavior that violates standards of decent behavior in public, or that involves the seduction of minors, should be handled by legal sanctions just as analogous behavior by heterosexuals should be; however, homosexual relationships between consenting adults in private should be neither the law's business nor psychiatry's.

There is a widespread assumption that whenever homosexuals present themselves for psychiatric treatment it is always to get rid of their homosexual orientation. Nothing could be further from the truth, as Sanders (chapter 19, this volume) clearly indicates. They usually come with problems quite analogous to those presented by heterosexuals— loneliness, dissatisfaction with their partners, breakups of meaningful love relationships, problems in self-realization, or a wide variety of neurotic or depressive reactions. The majority of them have no wish to change their sexual orientation, and should be treated no differently than heterosexuals with similar presenting problems.

Not infrequently, a psychiatrist may be confronted by an individual who comes in because he has gotten into difficulty with the law—for cruising or homosexual acts in public places. Most of these patients are not seeking to alter their homosexuality, but they do need help with their impulse-ridden behavior, which like all such behavior is rooted in a neurotic character structure. Treatment of such individuals needs to be directed toward an understanding of the unconscious significance of their need for impersonal sex and their (usual) inability to establish a meaningful dyadic relationship. These patients often can be helped also by behavioral techniques (see Birk, chapter 21, this volume). In recent years some individuals with these problems have established self-help groups in a number of urban centers.

Some homosexuals, however, *are* unhappy with their sexual orientation for a variety of reasons. They may have a wish to have children and a family life, or they may feel excluded from the societal mainstream and want, if possible, to become part of the majority culture. Gay activists argue, not without some justification, that the second reason, at least, is simply a reflection of their reaction to cultural prejudice and discrimination, and that such patients should be encouraged not to change their orientation but rather to accept themselves more fully, indeed, with a sense of "gay pride." I would agree that it is reasonable to ascertain whether individuals seeking to change their sexual orientation are genuinely motivated and not responding to some passing mood. But if their motivation to change is sincere and strong, I believe they deserve an opportunity to try to accomplish their goal, with all the help that psychotherapy can give them. The fact is that a homosexual way of life in most contemporary Western societies does impose special stresses on those who pursue it, and it is not unreasonable to help such individuals, when they request it, to achieve a more homeostatic relationship with their environment.

Not that this is always possible. Even the most optimistic psychotherapists rarely report more than 50 percent success in changing a homosexual orientation to a heterosexual one.[1] On the other hand, the general view in the gay community that treatment is *never* successful is without foundation. The fact that most homosexual preferences are probably learned and not inborn means that, in the presence of strong motivation to change, they are open to modification, and clinical experience confirms this. The kernel of truth in the gay point of view, however, is that once a major pathway to sexual gratification has been established and reinforced by repeated experiences, the tracks of that pathway can never be totally obliterated. Thus although it is possible for successfully treated homosexuals to change their overt behavior

1. Birk (chapter 21, this volume) reports a remarkable 100 percent success with behavioral group therapy in fourteen highly motivated group 6 homosexuals who remained in therapy for two and a half years or longer, but such results are exceptional. Birk's method, in which he uses male-female cotherapists, deserves to be tested more widely.

from homosexual to heterosexual, the tendency toward erotic arousal by the same sex is probably never totally lost.

In reality, this is part of the reason that the reversal of homosexual orientation constitutes a difficult task. This is true of any behavioral syndrome in which the main "symptom" is a prime source of basic gratification. The resistance to giving up a behavioral pattern that is a major, if not the main, source of a person's erotic satisfaction is understandably enormous, and the fact that somewhere between 25 and 50 percent of homosexuals who seek to change their main sexual orientation are able to do so is more of a tribute to the strength of their motivation than it is to the specific therapeutic approach involved.

For the fact is that as of now no specific form of psychotherapy has clearly proven itself to be superior to all others. Psychotherapeutic results are difficult to evaluate at best, but it is particularly difficult to compare reported results of various therapeutic approaches to homosexuality because the precise nature of the patient sample and of the outcome are often not clearly indicated. For example, it is not always clear whether the patients treated are exclusively homosexual or whether they may be 3, 4, or 5 on the Kinsey scale. Similarly, to say that a patient benefited from therapy may not necessarily mean that a total abandonment of homosexual object-choice has been achieved. A group 5 or group 6 homosexual may be enabled to shift to a group 3 or group 4 pattern, or may be helped toward a more stable and satisfying life adjustment in general—certainly positive therapeutic results—yet they should not be put in the same category as a total shift in object-preference.

Thus although percentage results in toto are difficult to evaluate, there is little doubt, from my own clinical experience and that of other therapists, both behavioral and psychodynamic, that a genuine shift from a state in which heterosexual relations are avoided or feared to one in which they are sought and enjoyed can be achieved in a fraction (somewhere between 20 and 50 percent) of highly motivated male and female homosexuals.

Apart from powerful motivations to change—the importance of which is paramount—other factors that tend to contribute to more favorable outcomes are: (1) youth: patients under thirty-five tend to do better than older ones; (2) previous heterosexual experience, or at least, responsiveness: patients who give a history of having been heterosexually responsive in adolescence and/or have had previous heterosexual intercourse have a better prognosis; (3) recency of onset of homosexual activity: the longer the homosexual pattern has been in existence, the more difficult it is to change it; obligatory homosexuals who trace their homoerotic arousal patterns to early childhood are poor therapeutic prospects; and (4) "masculine" looking and acting men tend to have a better prognosis than "effeminate" ones, especially when the effeminate behavior dates back to early childhood. Although I know of no definite data to point to a similar pattern in lesbians, I strongly suspect that it holds true also for them, i.e., "feminine" lesbians probably offer a more favorable prospect for change of their sexual orientation than do strongly "masculine" ones. Sanders (chapter 19, this volume) lists other relevant variables.

Therapeutic techniques that have been employed toward the goal of sex-orientation change have run the gamut of most of the standard approaches. They have ranged from more or less classical psychoanalysis, four to five times weekly (Bieber et al., 1962), to psychoanalytically oriented psychotherapy, one to three times weekly (Lief and Mayerson, 1965; Hatterer, 1970), to group therapies—some exclusively homosexual in makeup, others with mixed groups (Haddon, 1966; Birk and Miller, 1970)—to conditioning techniques using aversive and reinforcing stimuli (Feldman and MacCulloch, 1965). Despite their technical diversity, all these therapies have certain features in common. All of them tend to discourage homosexual reactions and encourage heterosexual behavior, but the therapist is accepting and noncritical of the homosexual patient personally. In addition, either implicitly or explicitly, they all endeavor to increase the patient's self-esteem and self-assertiveness, and to overcome any heterosexual phobic reactions that may be present.

In the final analysis, however, it must be recognized that the percentage of homosexuals, male or female, who seek to change their sexual orientation is very low in proportion to the total. A humane and democratic society must learn to accept homosexuals as they are and give them the same right to respect and human dignity that, in principle at least, we try to extend to all other human beings. When that day comes, all men and women, heterosexual as well as homosexual, will be the better for it.

REFERENCES

Bell, A. P. 1975. Research in homosexuality: Back to the drawing board. *Archives of Sexual Behavior* 4:421–32.

Bell, A. P., and Weinberg, M. S. 1978. *Homosexualities.* New York: Simon & Schuster.

Bialor, P. 1977 (1975). Quoted by Carrier, J. in *Archives of Sexual Behavior* 6:59, 1977.

Bieber, I., et al. 1962. *Homosexuality: A psychoanalytic study.* New York: Basic Books.

Birk, L., and Miller, E. 1970. Group psychotherapy for homosexual men by male-female cotherapists. *Acta Psychiatrica Scandinavica* 218 (suppl.): 7.

Carrier, J. M. 1976. Cultural factors affecting urban Mexican male homosexual behavior. *Archives of Sexual Behavior* 5:103–24.

———. 1977. "Sex-role preference" as an explanatory variable in homosexual behavior. *Archives of Sexual Behavior* 6:53–66.

Dundes, A.; Leach, J.; and Özkok, B. 1972. The strategy of Turkish boys' verbal dueling. In J. Gumperz and D. Hymes, eds. *Directions in sociolinguistics: The ethnography of communication*. New York: Holt.

Farrell, R., and Marrione, T. 1974. Social interaction and stereotypic responses to homosexuals. *Archives of Sexual Behavior* 3:425–42.

Feldman, M. P., and MacCulloch, M. I. 1965. The application of anticipatory avoidance learning to the treatment of homosexuality. *Behavior Research and Therapy* 2:165–83.

Gebhard, P. H., et al. 1965. *Sex offenders*. New York: Harper & Row.

Haddon, S. B. 1966. Treatment of male homosexuals in groups. *International Journal of Group Psychotherapy* 16:13.

Hatterer, L. 1970. *Changing homosexuality in the male*. New York: McGraw-Hill.

Humphreys, L. 1970. *Tearoom trade: Impersonal sex in public places*. Chicago: Aldine.

Lief, H., and Mayerson, P. 1965. Psychotherapy of homosexuals. In J. Marmor, ed., *Sexual inversion: The multiple roots of homosexuality*. New York: Basic Books.

Masters, W. H. and Johnson, V. E.. 1979. *Homosexuality in Perspective*. Boston: Little Brown.[2]

Young, A. 1973. Gay gringo in Brazil. In L. Richmond, and G. Noguera, eds. *The gay liberation book*. San Francisco: Ramparts Press, pp. 60–67.

2. As this volume approaches completion, a study by Masters and Johnson, *Homosexuality in Perspective* (Boston: Little Brown, 1979), has appeared demonstrating what has been increasingly recognized clinically, namely, that homosexuals suffer from the same sexual dysfunctions as do heterosexuals and respond to the same treatment techniques. Less convincing is the claim by Masters and Johnson that they can "revert" or "convert" 65 percent of highly motivated male and femal homosexuals to heterosexuality with their usual fourteen-day treatment program. This claim is misleading not only because their follow-up studies were inadequate, but also because the majority of their sixty-seven subjects were bisexuals, not obligatory homosexuals. Moreover, there is no evidence that the underlying homosexual eroticism or fantasy life in these patients was altered. Finally, there is a fundamental error in the implication that homosexual inclinations are attributable to anxiety about heterosexual performance.

15 / Clinical Aspects of Female Homosexuality

MARCEL T. SAGHIR

ELI ROBINS

Studies on homosexuality have traditionally involved the male homosexual. Systematic investigations of groups of female homosexuals have been few. The first comprehensive study of female homosexuality was conducted by Saghir and Robins (1973). A group of fifty-seven female homosexuals was systematically interviewed through the use of a semi-structured interview. Comprehensive data were obtained on early childhood characteristics, adolescent psychologic responses, psychopathology, sexual behavior as it evolved from childhood to adulthood, and a variety of other variables and parameters of childhood, adolescence, and adult life. The homosexual sample was obtained through an organization for homosexual women and the majority of these individuals were members of the organization. All of them were volunteers. About two-thirds of the subjects were obtained through the organization, while about one-third were obtained through referral by friends and advertisements in homophile newsletters. These individuals were active and functioning members of the community with no history of psychiatric hospitalization or significant antisocial behavior and incarceration. The interview lasted an average of about three and a half hours. Upon completion of the homosexual interview, it was felt that in order to assess reliably the behavioral and psychiatric correlates of being a homosexual, it was essential to estimate the prevalence of these correlates in nonhomosexual women. Therefore, a control group of

This study was supported in part by National Institute of Mental Health Grants MH13002 and MH14677.

forty-three heterosexual women were interviewed, a group which met similar criteria to those met by the homosexual women. We considered age, marital status, religious, and socioeconomic backgrounds to be important variables to be controlled. The heterosexual group of women were obtained from a large apartment complex. These individuals were generally not highly motivated to participate in the study in contrast to the homosexual women who were highly motivated to do so. A small remuneration was given to each heterosexual woman who agreed to be interviewed. The age range of the homosexual women was from twenty-two to fifty-four years, with a mean age of thirty-one. The age range of the controls was comparable, with a mean age of twenty-nine. Over three-fourths of the homosexual and heterosexual women had never been married, while the rest had been married but were presently separated or divorced. Both the homosexual and the heterosexual women tended to have a relatively high socioeconomic status.

The conclusions that are presented in the ensuing pages are based on the findings in our sample, but the fact that these findings have been replicated by other studies lends some credence to their generalizability (Baum et al., 1977; Gundlack, 1967; Kenyon, 1968b and 1968c).

Definition

Owing to our research, we consider homosexuality to be an early childhood phenomenon characterized by psychologic responses that include emotional attachments and fantasies directed primarily at members of the same sex. These attachments and fantasies develop in childhood and adolescence and persist, more overtly and intensely, into adult life. Sexual behavior is only the expression of the basic psychological propensity and, therefore, secondary to it. In our definition of homosexuality, it is recognized that homosexuals, both men and women, may possess a certain degree of psychologic responsiveness towards members of the opposite sex and may at varying periods throughout their lives become involved in heterosexual behavior. However, the predominant component is one of psychologic preference for members of the same sex. Therefore, homosexuality includes a longitudinal development of psychologic responsiveness involving members of the same sex as well as eventual overt sexual expression. Individuals who became involved at times in homosexual behavior or who develop homosexual preferences and life-style as adults are seen as a separate group from the early-onset psychologic responses. Individuals who become involved homosexuality later in life usually fall into the Kinsey 1, 2, or 3 classification. Consequently, we see them as separate groups of individuals that have not been adequately studied. Crucial, therefore, to our definition is the primary nature of psychologic responsiveness in its longitudinal development through time.

EARLY CHILDHOOD CHARACTERISTICS

"Tomboyishness" or the "boylike" syndrome in girls is a phenomenon involving manifestations of boylike behavior. Two components are included in this syndrome. First, persistent aversion to girls' activities and to girls as playmates and, second, a definite preference for the company of boys and for boys' activities. The true prevalence of tomboyishness in a general population of girls is unknown. However, tomboyishness is generally considered to be a common but innocuous behavior, in contrast to "sissiness" in boys that tends to be seen as rather pathologic and deviant. Tomboyishness tends to be a highly common phenomenon in female homosexuals. Over two-thirds of our sample reported childhood and adolescent behaviors that were consistent with the tomboyish syndrome in contrast to only 16 percent of our heterosexual controls. This was a highly significant factor that tended to differentiate clearly the childhoods of homosexual and heterosexual women. Tomboyish behavior tended to persist among female homosexuals into adolescence and often into adult life. Most tomboyishness among heterosexuals usually disappeared or was under control by the onset of the adolescent years. As part of the tomboy syndrome, a majority of female homosexuals tended to report cross-gender wishes with a desire and fantasy to become a boy or a man. These were not true expressions of a need for sex change, but a rejection of the sex-appropriate sociocultural and occupational roles. Only a small minority of heterosexual women reported similar fantasies and desires during childhood.

SEXUAL PSYCHOLOGIC RESPONSES

The development of homosexual psychologic responses in homosexual women parallels the development of heterosexual psychologic responses in heterosexual women. The vast majority of homosexual women experience emotional attachments in preadolescence or before the age of thirteen. These usually involve feelings of closeness that are romanticized but not sexualized to specific persons, often girl friends or adult women in the individual's immediate environment. Homosexual emotional attachments and fantasies, while universal in individuals who are destined to become adult homosexuals, are relatively rare in the young girls who are destined to become heterosexuals. Only a small minority of heterosexual women ever experienced recurring homosexual attachments or fantasies. Despite the universality of homosexual attachments and fantasies in preadolescence and later on in adult life, a significant number of homosexual women tend to experience heterosexual attachments as well. About one-half of homosexual women report such attachments at some point in their early life, usually during the early adolescent years. Heterosexual fantasies occur in a minority, however, and they are reported by about one-third of homosexual women. Most heterosexual attachments, as well as fantasies, tend to be transient and disappear largely towards the end of the adolescent years. Thus, homosexual women experience predominately homosexual psychologic responses that persist in time while a significant number of them experience heterosexual psychologic responses that are usually transient and limited to the adolescent years.

Sexual Practices

SELF-MASTURBATION

Self-masturbation is the earliest sexual behavior in both homosexual and heterosexual women. There is a statistically significant difference in the reported prevalence of self-masturbation between homosexual and heterosexual women. Over three-fourths of homosexual women admit to self-masturbation in contrast to somewhat less than one-half of the heterosexual women. The age of onset of this behavior was comparable in the two groups with over one-half of those who masturbated beginning their activities between the ages of ten and nineteen. It was of interest to note that women, both homosexual and heterosexual, tended to begin masturbation at an earlier age than men. Thus, over 40 percent of homosexual and heterosexual women had reported masturbation before the age of ten in contrast to only a small minority of both heterosexual and homosexual men. The difference was highly significant statistically. In contrast, more men, both homosexual and heterosexual, tended to masturbate compared to heterosexual and homosexual women. Masturbation was almost universal among both homosexual and heterosexual men. Self-masturbatory behavior persists among homosexual women and does not show significant decrease or change with age. However, among heterosexual women, masturbation tended to diminish significantly after the age of thirty. Most homosexual and heterosexual women who masturbate do so at a frequency of less than once a week. Thus, in their self-masturbatory behavior, homosexual and heterosexual women tend to be alike, and they differ from both homosexual and heterosexual men. Still, compared to heterosexual women, more homosexual women tend to masturbate later in life, and more of them masturbate with greater frequency.

HOMOSEXUAL PRACTICES

Manual-genital stimulation is the most common sexual practice among homosexual women, a majority of whom prefer it in order to achieve climax. Homosexual activity in homosexual women tends to begin usually after the age of fourteen. Only a small minority, less than 10 percent of homosexual women, begin homosexual behavior prior to the age of fourteen, in contrast to over one-half of homosexual men. Homosexual women in general tend to begin their homosexual activity at a later time in life—usually in mid to late adolescence (Schafer, 1977).

The second most common homosexual behavior among homosexual women is oral-genital activity, which the vast majority of homosexual women begin practicing after the age of nineteen. This is in contrast to homosexual men, where the majority experience fellation before the age of nineteen. In their oral-genital activity as well as manual-genital stimulation, there is usually no male or female role played in any consistent manner. There is most often an interchange of roles sexually. In addition, a significant proportion of homosexual women tend to use inanimate objects vaginally during sexual relationships with other women. These are used for "kicks" and to increase stimulation. There is also an element of role-playing between inserter and insertee, with the inserter using the inanimate object as a penis representative.

ROMANTIC RELATIONSHIPS

Homosexual women tend to strive towards stable relationships with other women. One-night stands or casual encounters occur but are rather infrequent. Most casual relationships between homosexual women usually last between one and three months while the usual pattern among homosexual men is the one-night stand. Homosexual women in general tend to behave like heterosexual women in this respect. They establish fairly stable and prolonged relationships and become involved in dating and establishing affectionate bonds prior to sexual involvements. Almost all of the homosexual women that were studied had established at one point or another in their lives long-lasting relationships of more than one year's duration with other women (Schafer, 1977). Prolonged affectionate and sexual relationships most commonly occur between the ages of twenty and thirty-nine. In addition, prolonged relationships between homosexual women tend to be characterized by fidelity and an emphasis on faithfulness. Sexual activity among homosexual women occurs on the average of twice a week, with the frequency diminishing markedly with the duration of the relationship. Similarly, the total number of sexual partners of homosexual women was few compared with homosexual men. Both homosexual and heterosexual women are similar in their overall sexual activities including frequency, number of partners, and age of onset of sexual behavior. Both homosexual women and heterosexual women tend to be distinctly different from both homosexual and heterosexual men. Thus, it appears that in general the age of onset of sexual activity as well as its frequency and variety seem to be related more to the gender of the individual rather than to his or her sexual preference.

SEXUAL ROLE-PLAYING

Close to three-fourths of homosexual women usually interchange their sex-roles within a given relationship or between relationships. They assume both an inserter and insertee position with no distinct preference for male or female role-play. However, about one-fourth of the homosexual women do have a consistent preference for the active or passive role. At around middle age or later on, more homosexual women tend to settle into a specific role sexually than did so prior to middle age. Role behavior among homosexual women appears to be most often related to group and individual preference rather than to any basic psychologic imperatives of masculinity or feminiinity. That is, these roles appear to be related to group reinforcers, age, and partner preference.

CRUISING

Cruising is defined as a purposeful activity primarily aimed at finding partners. It involves seeking such partners in bars as well as public places and facilities. In this context, the cruising behavior of homosexual men usually involves a variety of public areas. Among homosexual women, on the other hand, cruising in this context is practically nonexistent except in homosexual bars. Homosexual women most often seek and find their potential partners in the context of social gatherings, parties, friends, school, and the homosexual bar. The homosexual woman usually begins to establish her relationship rather slowly with an introductory period of knowing the other person, dating, and establishing affection and friendship. In this process, homosexual women often become involved with basically heterosexual women who are experiencing difficulties in their heterosexual life-style or their marriages or who are seeking a different form of sexual expression. A significant number of homosexual women become involved at any one point in time in casual or longlasting relationships with basically heterosexual partners. Heterosexual men are less likely to become involved in prolonged homosexual liaisons or to accept as readily homosexual involvements. In addition, homosexual females rarely become involved in financial transactions in their sexual relationships. Homosexual prostitution among female homosexuals does not appear to be common, and paying or receiving money is rare, probably occurring with less than 5 percent of the homosexual women. In addition, there is very little group sexual behavior among homosexual women. Sadomasochistic practices and other deviant sexual behaviors are practically nonexistent. A substantial number of homosexual men, on the other hand, close to one-fourth of them, become involved at some time in group sexual practices and sadomasochistic encounters.

HETEROSEXUAL PRACTICES

Due to social and parental expectations, a homosexual woman often becomes involved in heterosexual behavior similar to her heterosexual counterpart. This occurs primarily during the adolescent and early adult years. There is an almost universal pattern of heterosexual dating among homosexual women between the ages of sixteen and nineteen. By the age of twenty, however, almost one-half of homosexual women drop out completely from heterosexual dating, and by the age of twenty-eight, only a very small minority, less than 10 percent, continues heterosexual dating. In contrast, heterosexual women tend to maintain a steady frequency of dating throughout their adolescence and young adult life and until their marriage. During the peak periods of dating, there does not seem to be a significant difference in the frequency of dates between both homosexual and heterosexual women. However, the vast majority of homosexual women date for fewer than ten years, while two-thirds of heterosexual women date for ten or more years. Heterosexually, "necking" and kissing is also universal among homosexual as well as heterosexual women during the adolescent and early adult years. This again appears to have been part of social expectations, group pressure, and a general uncertainty concerning the direction of sexual responsiveness. Partly in conforming to heterosexual expectations and partly due to internal and external pressures, homosexual women do become involved sexually with men. More than three-fourths of them experiment with sexual intercourse. This behavior usually lasts for a short period of time. About 40 percent of the homosexual women experiment with intercourse over a period of less than one year and the rest over a somewhat extended time. Most homosexual women who become involved with intercourse tend to be nonorgasmic and often express a negative psychologic response to the overall heterosexual involvement. Generally homosexual females report emotional and sexual indifference to their heterosexual experience. They experience it as a limited behavior with some pleasurable results but with highly dissatisfying consequences. Despite this, however, homosexual women do not seem to experience a greater degree of fear, guilt, inadequacy, or pain in their heterosexual relationships than heterosexual women. Their ultimate avoidance and refusal to continue heterosexual relationships is related to lack of psychologic and physical responsiveness and satisfaction rather than to any significant manifest inner fears. During the peak of their heterosexual experimentation, a small number, perhaps a fourth, of homosexual women marry, but ultimately the vast majority obtain a divorce. Marriage, like heterosexual liaison, appears to be an attempt at "warding off" the homosexual tendencies and at establishing "normal" sexual and social life-styles with the hope that this in itself would control the homosexual propensity. Of those homosexual women who marry, about one-third marry a homosexual man whom they knew to be homosexual or suspect of homosexuality. This is done primarily for reasons of convenience. Of the women that marry heterosexual men, two-thirds of those men appear to be passive and disinterested in sex, while one-third are appropriately aggressive and interested.

Psychopathology:

MASCULINITY-FEMININITY

In assessing the degree of psychopathology among homosexual women, it is important to take into consideration the degree of manifest and measurable psychopathology as measured by well-defined criteria and diagnostic categories. For measuring psychopathology, specific criteria for psychiatric disorders were utilized, and an attempt was made at defining areas of disability. The aim was not to assess the degree of conflict, relative contentment, and pathology. Traditionally, homosexual women were considered to be masculine in appearance and temperament with aggressiveness, competitiveness, and peculiarities of physical build. There is a good deal of agreement among homosexual and heterosexual women on outside appearance and dress as measures of masculinity or femininity. Among homosexual women, a majority considered themselves to be nonfeminine and either masculine or "neuter." Still, over one-third of homosexual women see themselves to be appropriately feminine and appear to be so based on their mannerisms and manner of dress. Among heterosexual females, almost all of them consider themselves to be appropriately feminine.

LEVELS OF PSYCHIATRIC CARE

A significant proportion of homosexual and heterosexual women become involved in one form of psychiatric care or another, usually psychotherapy and counseling. Close to one-third of homosexual women and one-fourth of the heterosexual control sample were involved in psychotherapy at some point in their lives. Psychiatrists are most often seen by homosexual men and women, while nonmedically qualified individuals are most often the therapists seen by heterosexuals. Of the homosexual women in therapy, many are referred by family members or school, with homosexuality being the immediate reason. This usually occurs following the discovery of homosexual involvements. Furthermore, a significant portion of homosexual women who seek psychotherapy, possibly about one-third of them, do so during a period of clinical depression, while a small minority, about 15 percent of those who seek psychotherapy, do so with the hope of obtaining a change of sexual orientation. Among heterosexual women, evidence of depression leads to psychotherapy in about one-fourth of them while about three-fourths of those who go into therapy do so to promote insight and emotional growth.

PSYCHIATRIC DISORDERS

When compared with matched heterosexual women, homosexual women do not seem to suffer from a greater degree of neurotic illness, psychophysiologic reactions, affective disorders, psychosis, or other definable psychiatric problems in the form of hysteria, obsessional neurosis, anxiety or phobic symptoms, or paranoid reactions. On the other hand, homosexual women suffer significantly more from excessive alcohol use and abuse than heterosexual women. Close to one-fourth of homosexual women report patterns of alcohol use that are compatible with problem drinking. The lifetime prevalence of neurotic, character, and psychophysiologic disorders as well as affective disorders in homosexual women is no higher than in heterosexual women. On a cross-sectional assessment of psychiatric morbidity, the only differentiating factor is again a pattern of excessive alcohol use among a significant number of homosexual women. Depression, as a well-defined syndrome, is a rather common disorder among both homosexual and heterosexual women. These depressive episodes are often related to traumatic life occurrences particularly following the breakup of affairs and love relationships. There is a somewhat increased pattern of suicidal attempts among homosexual women, with the rate being twice that of heterosexuals. Most of the attempts tend to be during periods of peak conflict in late adolescence and early adult life and often accompany the breakup of a relationship. There is no difference in premenstrual symptoms, depressive or otherwise, between homosexual and heterosexual women. In addition to a pattern of excessive alcohol use in homosexual women, a significantly greater number of homosexual women use nonprescription drugs, often on an experimental basis and as part of the group behavior. Those who drink excessively tend also to use illicit drugs.

In assessing the psychiatric morbidity among homosexual and heterosexual women, overall adjustment to the homosexual orientation was also assessed. Homosexual men and women develop a significant degree of conflict over their homosexuality, particularly during adolescent and early adult life. During these years, close to one-half of homosexual women and two-thirds of homosexual men consider and desire a change of sexual orientation (Saghir and Robins, 1973). After a period of heterosexual experimentation and with greater physical and emotional maturity, however, these individuals ultimately accept their homosexual orientation and develop a working adaptation to their particular life-style. Still, a significant proportion of homosexual women, possibly about one-fourth of them, continue to experience deep conflict, uncertainty, and failure to reconcile themselves adequately to their homosexuality. Still, despite the conflict, it is almost universal for adult female homosexuals to reject attempts at a change of sexual orientation as they come to accept their homosexuality as fixed and unchangeable and as an integral part of their personality structure. On an occupational level, homosexual women as well as men that we have interviewed tend to be high achievers. However, homosexual women have a tendency in general to show greater job instability than heterosexual women. More of them are often fired from jobs and fewer spend three or more years in one job. However, the tendency to be fired somewhat more often than heterosexual women does not necessarily correlate with poor functioning or poor performance and productivity. The annual income of homosexual women compares very favorably with their heterosexual counterparts and with national norms.

Parental and Family Relationships

There is a definite phenomenon of parental loss among homosexual women. Our data showed that 39 percent of homosexual women but only 5 percent of heterosexual controls experienced parental loss by death or divorce prior to the age of ten, with the most common parental loss resulting from divorce. Of the total homosexual sample, about one-fourth (23 percent) lost both parents, while 12 percent lost a father and 4 percent lost a mother. Thus, 27 percent of the homosexual sample, but only 2 percent of the heterosexual controls, had lost a mother prior to the age of ten. The most frequent causes of loss were divorce, death, and illegitimacy (with placement in a foster home), in this order. Two-thirds of homosexual women are either only children or have one sibling, in contrast to one-third of heterosexual women. Female homosexuals also appear to have a generally low sister-to-brother ratio. The same finding is present among male homosexuals. Thus, in both homosexual men and women, there seems to be a relative deficiency of sisters in their sibships, and the most profound deficiency of sisters in the sibships appears in the families of those female homosexuals who were child-hood and adolescent tomboys. A history of emotional breakdown in the relationship between the homosexual women and their mothers was also present; these relationships were often characterized by distance and noninvolvement, whereas closer and more involved relationships generally existed with the fathers.

Some Sociological Considerations

Being a female homosexual is like being a female in general, both sexually and socially. There is a tendency to greater conformity, stabil-ity of relationships, and an absence of indiscriminate sexual involve-ments. There is also a general emphasis on relationships, romantic in-volvements, and faithfulness in relationships. The average male homosexual tends to experience a great deal of instability and even promiscuity in his relationships, as well as the threat of violence in-volved in indiscriminate cruising behavior. The homosexual woman, however, tends to be reserved, selective in her involvements, and gen-erally uninterested in multiple sex partners or varieties of sexual prac-tice. The similarities between male and female homosexuals are limited to their dominant sexual preferences for members of the same sex. Otherwise, the female homosexuals are more like female heterosexuals while male homosexuals are more like male heterosexuals. This is prob-ably related to cultural as well as biological variables. Because of her predictable and limited cruising behavior, the female homosexual rarely encounters violence as part of her sexual behavior. In our own research, close to one-third of male homosexuals experience violence at one point or another in their lives in the form of assault, robbery, or threats against them as the result of their cruising behavior. Such vio-lence appears to be rare or practically nonexistent among female homo-sexuals. Their cruising behavior is limited to predictable situations.

These findings are compatible with similar findings from other stud-ies. Schafer (1977) reported on a group of West German homosexual women and men and found that homosexual men had fifteen times as many sex partners as lesbians and that eleven times as many homosex-ual men as women had had fifty or more partners in the course of their lives. In addition, homosexual men discover their homosexuality earlier than homosexual women. Homosexual women become involved in heterosexual relationships, namely, petting, kissing, and coitus, at an earlier age than homosexual men, who tend to experience during ado-lescence homosexual rather than heterosexual involvement. This appears to give some support to the idea that homosexual women behave like women in general, in terms of their sexual behavior; this is true particularly during the adolescent and young adult years, with a tendency to earlier heterosexual involvements and a continued willingness to become involved heterosexually throughout young adult life. In contrast, homosexual men discover their homosexuality first and then experiment with heterosexuality in an attempt to ward off the homosexual impulses, but towards the end of adolescence they relinquish most of their heterosexual involvements and limit themselves to homosexual relationships.

Despite the many signs that the homosexual woman presents to her family, both during childhood, adolescence, and afterwards, most parents of homosexual women do not usually become aware of the homosexuality of their daughters until later—and usually from outside sources. Only one-half of the homosexual women interviewed felt that their parents definitely knew about their homosexuality, and most of those felt that the parents' knowledge came first from outside sources, including schoolteachers and family friends. Most of the parents that became aware of the homosexuality of their daughters reacted with surprising understanding and eventual acceptance. Initial feelings of pain, disbelief, and rejection were quickly replaced by a genuine attempt to come to terms with the situation.

Being an adult female homosexual involves a relatively low visibility. There are stereotypes of the masculine-looking female with the severely tailored clothes, the short hair, and the masculine mannerisms. However, this stereotype is true of only a small proportion of female homosexuals, while the vast majority are not easily recognized. Because of her low visibility, a homosexual woman tends to be much less socially and economically affected by her sexual orientation than her male counterpart. Accordingly, only a minority of homosexual women feel that being lesbians affects their social and economic life adversely, in contrast to about one-half of the homosexual men, who feel that their homosexuality is a detriment to their overall relationships, job functioning, and stability. Furthermore, few homosexual women feel that being lesbians limits their ambitions or their ability to achieve, while a significantly greater proportion of men feel that being homosexual limits their ability to develop ambitious goals. This is believed to be the result of restrictions placed on homosexuals in much of industry, business, and government.

In addition to the differing patterns of sexual and social perceptions in homosexual women and men, there are also differences in feelings about growing older and losing one's attractiveness to members of the same sex. Homosexual women are less preoccupied with youth and less concerned about their attractiveness or age than homosexual men. Therefore, growing old is not as much of a source of anxiety to homosexual women as it is to homosexual men. Homosexual men and women tend to be a generally active group in terms of their interests and hobbies and possibly more so than their heterosexual counterparts, who are often more involved with family-related endeavors. Most homosexual women develop hobbies and leisure activities, with a significant proportion of them showing interests in sports activities and in artistic endeavors.

Thus, sociologically, as well as sexually and temperamentally, homosexual women tend to be very different from homosexual men and more similar to heterosexual women. Still, there are definite differences between homosexual and heterosexual women with the latter showing fewer tomboyish behaviors in childhood and a greater degree of interest in socially acceptable feminine parameters, including dress, makeup and the emphasis on looks and sexual attractiveness. In addition, there is some evidence to indicate that homosexual women display a greater degree of assertiveness and aggressiveness in their jobs and social lives than heterosexual women. Being a homosexual woman does not correlate in later adult life with a greater degree of subjective unhappiness, however, or with conflict with the immediate environment.

Some Final Remarks

Studies on female homosexuality have been rather limited in the past. Over the past ten years, however, a number of authors have conducted studies with limited groups of homosexual women usually obtained from homosexual organizations, bars, or personal contacts. These have tended to be enlightening and have provided a significant contribution to the literature. Studies of representative samples of homosexual women and men are difficult to develop due to the social and legal status of homosexuality. It is even more difficult to set up such studies among homosexual women because of their relative lack of visibility. Consequently, there are no epidemiological studies of the prevalence of homosexual women or men, although estimates vary around the possibility that 4 percent of adult women are predominantly homosexual in their orientation. What is known so far about female homosexuality suggests that it is a lifelong condition beginning early in childhood and characterized by a constellation of behavioral variables which culminates in late adolescence with recognition of one's homosexuality and involvement in overt homosexual behavior. In homosexual women the earlier sexual involvement is heterosexual in nature, with dating and sexual noncoital behavior with intercourse occurring at similar age periods and with similar frequency to that of heterosexual women. With the "coming out" process homosexual behavior becomes predominant.

Being a homosexual woman carries with it less conflict and internal turmoil than being a homosexual man. But while sexually homosexual women tend to behave more like women in general, their psychiatric and possibly some of their psychological characteristics are more similar to the heterosexual and homosexual male. Among homosexual women there is a high tendency to alcohol abuse that is comparable only to the high prevalence among men in general. There is also a high emphasis on sports, as both participant and spectator. In childhood a homosexual woman displays behavioral characteristics that are more like the young boy next door with predominant tomboyish behavior that usually persists throughout childhood and into adolescent and often adult life.

While a good deal is known about the clinical course and natural history of homosexuality both in the male and in the female, little is known about the etiologic factors. There is evidence to indicate that the home environment sometimes shows stress in the form of parental divorce and a lack of an affectionate and close relationship between the mother and the tomboy. However, there is an absence of prospective studies to validate any of the usually retrospectively elicited data on parental relationships, home environment, and their significance in terms of eventual homosexuality. Therefore, future research in the area of homosexuality, both in the male and in the female, should concentrate on studies of groups of children and adolescents who display cross-gender behavior and whose family relationships are problematic. Such prospective studies should be adequately controlled and followed up after periods of five, ten, and fifteen years to develop adequate data. In addition to prospective and follow-up studies of adolescents, prospective family studies assessing the dynamics of the family environment would be essential.

Although being a homosexual is not necessarily pathologic, manifest homosexuality is a painful and a conflict-ridden life-style, particularly during the adolescent and early adult years. While treatment of a homosexual individual is not indicated just because of the different sexual orientation, psychotherapy to relieve guilt and to encourage adjustment is often desirable and indicated. A large proportion of both homosexual men and women seek psychotherapy for conflict and emotional instability, and many of them appear to benefit from sympathetic short-term psychotherapy. Depression, alcohol abuse, and conflict tend to be detrimental to both homosexual men and women during the earlier years of their lives. There is also a tendency to suffer from an increased college dropout rate. Thus, between age sixteen and twenty-five, the homosexual female is in need of a good deal of support and counseling with an attempt to set reasonable and attainable goals.

There are no reports in the literature of sexual-orientation reversal among female homosexuals. There are a number of studies involving male homosexuality and reports of successful sex-orientation reversal. These reports, however, suffer from methodological difficulties with poorly defined samples, poorly defined methods of treatment, and inadequate follow-up. "Successful cure" of homosexuals must involve not only a suppression of behavior but also a reversal of the primary psychological orientation and of the predominant preference for members of the same sex. Suppression of behavior alone is insufficient, since this reflects most likely a transient and willful control.

Among female homosexuals, there is a tendency to form relationships with nonhomosexual women. This occurs in a fairly significant proportion of homosexual relationships and often involves a heterosexual woman with a discordant life-style, poor heterosexual adjustment, poor marital relationship, or a pathological emotional state. This prior involvement tends to destabilize the homosexual relationship because of the lack of commitment that the heterosexual woman often has for such a relationship. Still, there appears to be presently an increasing tendency for some women who have had a heterosexual life-style for most of their lives to abandon that life-style and to commit themselves to homosexual relationships. The figures for the prevalence of such a shift are not available. However, it appears that this has been a growing tendency that may partially reflect the increased emphasis on independence and assertiveness of women in society. Still, such a group of heterosexual women cannot be considered to be homosexual even though a choice of homosexual behavior was made. The most crucial aspect that defines homosexuality is the lifelong psychological tendencies to homosexual preferences, rather than the behavior itself. A group of heterosexual women who adopted homosexuality later in life needs to be adequately studied and evaluated. They form a separate group of women associated with homosexuality but not truly homosexual.

In summary, being a homosexual woman is an outgrowth of childhood and adolescent variables and involves consistent types of psychological and behavioral responsiveness. Much is known presently from a natural history and clinical point of view, but little is known etiologically. Prospective research with children, adolescents, and adults is essential to provide us with reliable data on early development, course, and etiology.

REFERENCES

Baum et al. 1977. A comparison of professionally employed lesbians and heterosexual women on the MMPI. *Archives of Sexual Behavior* 6:193–201.

Gundlack, R. 1967. Research project report. *The Ladder* 11:2–9.

Kenyon, F. E. 1968a. Studies in female homosexuality, psychological test results. *Journal of Consulting and Clinical Psychology* 32:510.

———. 1968b. Studies in female homosexuality. VI. The exclusively homosexual group. *Acta Psychiatrica Scandinavica* 44:224–37.

———. 1968c. Studies in female homosexuality. IV. Social and psychiatric aspects. *British Journal of Psychiatry.* 14:224–37.

Saghir, M. T. and Robins, E. 1973. *Male and female homosexuality: A comprehensive investigation.* Baltimore: Williams & Wilkins.

Schafer, S. 1977. Sociosexual behavior in male and female homosexuals: A study in sex difference. *Archives of Sexual Behavior*, vol. 6: 355–64.

16 / Psychological Tests in Homosexuality

In the field of sexual behavior, the issue of the status of homosexuality has aroused more heat than light. From the mid-nineteenth century to today, the choice of like-sexed love partners has been seen as either frankly pathological or as symptomatic of deeper illness. Even Freud's famous letter (1951) declassifying homosexuality as an illness still describes it as an "arrest of sexual development."

The a priori positioning of homosexuality as a theoretically defined abnormality has influenced the objective study of the personality of the actors in the partnership. In addition to the theoretical bias, testing for and/or about homosexuality has been contaminated by social attitudes toward sex differences—what holds for the female must be seen as the mirror image of the male role orientation. Therefore, before detailing the studies in which psychological tests have been used, it is necessary to point to the philosophical and methodological difficulties implicit in all of the research on homosexuality.

Why, in general, do persons in the mental health field give or use psychological tests? For the purpose of this chapter, we shall define a test as a standardized or widely used instrument. Thereby we are eliminating questionnaire studies where the items on the paper have not lent themselves to prior study, standardization, and utilization.

When Is Testing Done?

There are at least five major discriminable situations in which testing is done. First, it is used to quantify the amount or degree of an observable type of behavior. The usual intelligence test has this objective. One emerges from the test labeled as having so much of the trait called intelligence. The second use is diagnostic. Here the purpose is to identify, label, or establish the existence of a specific syndrome or condition. A third area is the use of the test to get at the etiology of the observed or reported condition. Hypothesis testing is a fourth use of psychological measurement. Finally, tests are used to assess the outcome of treatment procedures or interventions. The first three uses are aimed at the person who exhibits a specific kind of behavior or at the syndrome which is under scrutiny. The fourth and fifth assume a position about the syndrome and deal with its vicissitudes in treatment or intervention.

The place of psychological testing in the area of homosexuality cannot be assessed or even properly discussed without consideration of the social and theoretical frame within which the testing is done. Until quite recently, despite the earlier work of Kinsey (1948), Ford and Beach (1951), and others, the assumption has been that heterosexuality is superior to and/or more "natural" than homosexuality. Furthermore, it has been assumed that sexuality is more appropriately studied in the male than in the female. Women were seen as passive-receptive persons and hence not as primary movers of sexual behavior.

Although, as Morin (1977) points out, the homosexual rights movement dates back as early as 1869, it was not until Hooker's projective test study in 1957 that a serious challenge was raised about the theoretical bias inherent in the idea that homosexuality was against nature and against the dominant personality theory and hence pathological.

The issue is clear then: if theory says that like-sexed partnership-choice is pathology, the first uses of testing (i.e., to quantify the behavior) are irrelevant, because testing can only reinforce the original premises. The question is, if homosexuality is not a syndrome, how can one test for it? Furthermore there is a prior question of whether there is such a unitary phenomenon as homosexuality. Kinsey questioned this from his data and concluded that there was a continuum from exclusive heterosexuality to exclusive homosexuality. More recently, Stoller, in his book on perversion, defines a syndrome as follows:

> A diagnosis is supposed to be a highly compact explanation. To make a proper diagnosis in any branch of medicine there should be: (1) a syndrome —a constellation of signs and symptoms shared by a group of people, visible to an observer; (2) underlying dynamics (pathogenesis)—pathophysiology in the rest of medicine, neuropathology or psychodynamics in psychiatry; (3)

etiology—those factors from which the dynamics originate. When these exist, we can save time by using shorthand, knowing that a word or two— a label, a diagnosis—communicates to others about what we know. . . . If one uses the three criteria above for considering a condition a diagnosis, homosexuality is not a diagnosis: (1) there is only a sexual preference (so noticeable because it frightens many in our society), not a uniform constellation of signs and symptoms; (2) different people with this sexual preference have different psychodynamics underlying their sexual behavior; and (3) quite different life experiences can cause these dynamics and this behavior. (1975, pp. 197–98)

Methodologically, then, the first issue is whether there is a unitary phenomenon to be diagnosed. Even purely behavioral establishment of a condition of homosexuality has been questioned by Kinsey. How many homosexual experiences determine the finding that the person is a homosexual? Each researcher has an idiosyncratic definition of the population and its behavior. Bieber et al. (1962) used patients, all male, who had many "problems" other than homosexuality. Gundlach and Riess (1968) defined the behavior of their population as an adult relationship with another same-sexed person of at least six months' duration. Saghir and Robins (1971) used self-identification as the basis of their study. Each subject avowed that homosexuality was the preferred kind of relationship. Further complicating the evaluation of research which uses test materials is the elaboration of population selection methods. Test results from patients may be different than those from persons not in treatment. Information drawn from male homosexuals is likely to differ from that of a female population. Data on homosexuals in prison may be at variance with data from an unincarcerated population. Age is another confounding variable, since social and public attitudes towards homosexuality have changed in the last ten years. A sixty-year-old male homosexual has had a different set of sexual experiences than a twenty-year-old if both were tested in the 1970s. Selection of subjects from bars and homosexual gathering places may produce a different sample from one gathered from a college campus.

The Question of "Illness"

There are at least two major ways to develop answers to the question of whether homosexuals are more "disturbed," "sick," or "deviant" than a comparison group of heterosexuals. The first is the clinical procedure in which a skilled interviewer, usually a therapist, engages in an "in-depth" interview of heterosexual and homosexual persons. The second method tries to correct the "subjective" bias possibly inherent in the clinician's interviews by using so-called objective measuring instruments.

Considering the possible sources of error in the clinical interviews, there must be control or responsibility for the comparability of the homosexual and heterosexual population. Among the factors that have to be dealt with are age, sex, patient or nonpatient status, self-identification or self-concept as a sexual person, and a consistent definition of both homosexuality and heterosexuality. For instance, does a casual, two- or three-time homosexual experience during adolescence identify the person as one or the other? It is also mandatory to have some theoretical grounds or research base on which to establish the inference of pathology. Does length of relationship and orgasmic satisfaction define good mental health? Do anger and hostility toward men inevitably signify emotional illness? Does the occupational choice of a so-called feminine vocation indicate lack of masculine self-identification? These potential sources of error should, of course, be avoided in the "objective" tests, but they are more difficult to counter in the clinical interview area.

One generalization seems possible on the basis of all the interview studies thus far published. If the populations to be compared are both groups of patients who come for help, then the homosexuals seem to be different from the heterosexuals, although both groups are, by virtue of the selection process, abnormal, disturbed, or sick. Relative "sickness" is hard to establish quantitatively, and the bias of the interviewer determines the inferences about illness.

When the population of homosexuals and heterosexuals is derived from a nonpatient pool, some differences have been established between the two groups, but the researchers have been unable to find more "pathology" in the homosexual group than in the heterosexual group. Bieber et al. (1962) present the research on patient populations, whereas Saghir and Robins et al. (1970, 1971) and Gundlach and Riess (1968) are examples of studies of nonpatients. It would appear then that nonpatient homosexuals and heterosexuals are more like each other than either group is similar to corresponding patient populations.

In addition to the two methodological issues just cited—that is, theoretical bias and subject selection—the testing instrument plays a part in the confusion. Morin (1977), who has surveyed the literature for the years 1967 to 1974, finds that there are twenty-seven studies in which the researcher tried to assess the homosexual. Of these, ten used projective tests, ten paper-and-pencil instruments, and seven used behavior measures. For the present chapter, a computer search of the literature from 1967 to 1977 uncovered twenty-three studies in which projective instruments were used and thirty-five studies based on some form of paper-and-pencil test or questionnaire. There is little question that the type of measure used involves some methodological considerations. For instance, one of the frequent criticisms of the usual Rorschach research is that the test predisposes the investigator to seek pathology: the scoring and identification of data are weighted in the direction of uncovering maladaptive factors. The questionnaires are also implicitly contaminated. For example, assertive or aggressive answers on paper-and-pencil tests of masculinity or femininity are scored as masculine, and passive responses are scored as feminine. So an aggressive reaction by a woman tends to be interpreted as showing masculine patterning and hence as pathognomonic of homosexuality.

Another difficulty in the use of testing arises from the absence of cross-validational studies. The so-called Rorschach signs of homosexuality were obtained from the Rorschach testing of a group of male homosexuals. The same signs were then used to study female homosexuals. If the original group had been female homosexuals, the selection of identifying responses might have been different. Similarly, no one has studied the incidence of these signs in a wider male heterosexual population.

The whole area of research on homosexuality has been permeated with the preceding sources of error. Morin (1977) states:

> Two basic assumptions are made in the following analysis of recent research in this area. First, research reflects the value systems of its investigators and the social climate within which it takes place. Most research is conducted within the institutional framework of funding, prestige, and scientific respectability. Investigators are most likely to do research that is acceptable to others and that, above all, is publishable.
>
> Second, an analysis of the research questions being asked in a given time period may be used as an indicator of the zeitgeist of that period and/or the values of individual investigators. In particular, the questions being asked in the 8 year period prior to the APA resolution reflect the social climate regarding lesbianism and male homosexuality. (p. 663)

Before discussing the taxonomy of research questions, a brief discussion of research samples is in order. First, the finding that there are approximately four times as many studies of homosexual males as of lesbians supports both the contention that homosexuality is seen as a more serious "problem" in males for a variety of reasons and the contention that lesbians, and to a large extent women in general, have been ignored in research. Findings from research that has employed both lesbians and homosexual males tend to emphasize the uniqueness of the experiences of the two groups. Findings from one group cannot reasonably be applied to the other.

Second, the psychological literature on lesbianism and male homosexuality has been confused by a failure on the part of researchers to agree on sample definitions. Three distinct definitions of homosexuality are found in the published research: (1) the presence of homosexual behavior, where the degree of homosexuality is assessed on the basis of sexual histories (e.g., Kinsey et al., 1948); (2) the erotic preference for same-sex "objects," a definition used in attempts to assess degree of homosexuality by measuring such things as penile volume response to moving pictures of male and female nudes (e.g., McConaghy, 1967); and (3) the self-reported identity of respondents, used in those studies where all the subjects identify themselves as "homosexual" (e.g., Evans, 1969). Results gathered from these three different scores are not comparable with one another.

Testing Instruments

Before describing the results of the use of tests, a brief introduction to the instruments will help in evaluating the research.

Generally, the researchers have used one or more of what have been called projective measures. These are stimulus situations into which the respondents project their interpretations of ambiguous or semistructured material. The most commonly used projective measure is the well-known Rorschach test. The final interpretation consists of inferences based on a vast literature of rules and conclusions.

A second commonly used projective measure is called the Thematic Apperception Test or TAT This is essentially a story-telling exercise for which a picture provides the stimulus. Again, the interpretation of the personality that emerges from the responses is based on specific inferences.

The third most popular projective is the Draw-a-Person (DAP) material. This is a motor task in which the subject is asked to draw a person, then a second person, opposite in sex to that drawn first, and then to tell a story about each drawing. Here again, the drawings are scored objectively, but the personality attributes ascribed to different features of the drawings are inferential.

A second class of measuring instrument is the paper-and-pencil personality inventory. This is basically a collection of items which have to be answered as to whether they apply to the respondent, do not apply, or are irrelevant. The most widely used such measure is the Minnesota Multiphasic Personality Inventory, the MMPI. The usual report from scoring services yields data on ten or more personality factors such as masculinity-femininity, hysterical orientation, depression, etc. The test has been extensively researched and widely used.

Less frequently used materials are adjective tests, the Szondi test and Cattell's 16 PF test. On adjective tests, subjects are asked to check adjectives which describe them. These choices are then scored against

norms derived from testing groups of identified patients, i.e., schizophrenics, neurotics, etc.

The Szondi is a series of photographs of psychiatric patients of varying diagnostic categories. The subjects have to choose the two most and
least liked pictures in each of six series. Scoring is complicated, but,
again, inferentially interpreted.

Cattell's 16 PF test is an inventory type of questionnaire that explores
sixteen personality factors. These were developed from involved statistical analyses of patients' and subjects' responses.

Review Articles

There have been few presentations of the overall coverage of testing
in and for homosexuality in the recent past. Van den Aardweg (1967,
1969) has summarized the use of tests and projective materials on male
homosexuals. The instruments he discusses were the Rorschach, the
TAT, the DAP, the MMPI, the Szondi, and the Zamansky (this last test
consists of pairs of plates like TAT cards, each plate having male and
female persons as part of the contents). His conclusions were:

> (1) The Rorschach is useless for the individual diagnosis of homosexuality. At
> best one may come across clear "give aways" pointing to homosexuality.
> There is no specific "homosexual Rorschach"; the lists of signs (Wheeler
> [1949], Fein [1950]) are of no use in individual cases. . . . (2) The following
> factors for homosexuality have come out with more or less certainty in the
> Rorschach: feminine qualities . . . sexual preoccupation . . . anality . . .
> aversion to female sex. (1969, pp. 8–10)

As to the TAT, van den Aardweg writes:

> (1) The TAT is probably useful for the individual diagnosis of homosexuality
>   as a so-called "broad band test": sometimes one may come up with
>   something—perhaps more often not. The Tejessy-lists* [supplemented
>   by Davids, Joelson, and McArthur, 1956] may have value by way of an
>   orientation, although we have to keep in mind that so-called "homosex-
>   ual" signs occur in the protocols of heterosexuals, where this may not be
>   interpreted as an indication of homosexuality. This pertains especially
>   to those signs that cannot be called specifically homosexual, such as
>   "feminine identification."
> (2) There are no indications that a TAT-protocol specific for homosexuality

---

*These are descriptions of indices on the TAT, which, according to Tejessy (1952), show
differentiated sexual orientations. Among the signs are negative identifications of males
with father and mother figures, the use of females as central characters in TAT stories,
mixed sexual identification on card X, etc.

can be found, except where the story tells of an overtly homosexual relationship.

(3) The testing situation probably exerts some influence: the more relaxed the atmosphere, the more likely it is that repressed homosexual stories will eventually come out.

The Draw-a-Person Test has been the most widely used projective measure in studies of homosexuality. Van den Aardweg (1969) concludes that:

> For the individual diagnosis of homosexuality with the DAP few certainties exist. The sign that a subject draws the first figure as female seems to call for its interpretation as a mark of femininity; hence this sign may sometimes indirectly measure homosexuality. However, in half the cases this sign definitely does not have this meaning. Sign 2 of the extensive DAP according to Whitaker (1961) may be the best predictor of homosexuality yet.*
>
> Feminine traits in the drawings of males appear mostly in the passive type homosexual. (1969, p. 10)

Questionnaires likewise are found to be unimpressive, particularly the MMPI.

It must be noted that all of the summarization cited above is limited to the testing of groups of male homosexuals and male heterosexuals. The only survey of testing with lesbians has been that of Riess, Safer, and Yotive (1974). These authors point to some of the methodological problems when comparing men and women. All of the tests used and the so-called homosexual signs were developed on a male population and then used with female homosexuals. This introduces or reintroduces the old bias that what is true or may be true of males is, in reverse, to be expected of females. Up to this point no one has looked at the test data of women to develop a "sign" system like that produced for men. The prevailing lack of concern for possible male-female differences extends even to the amount of research generated by the problem. The number of studies on lesbians is significantly smaller than that for males. Riess, Safer, and Yotive conclude:

> Notwithstanding all the contradictory evidence with each approach, why are there such differences in the results of projective and nonprojective studies? A partial explanation may be in the inherent differences between projective and nonprojective techniques. Rorschachs, TAT's, and Draw-A-Person Tests diagnose psychopathology; the variety of nonprojective tests used are highly structured, self-report instruments that do not "pull for" evidence of unconscious conflicts. The difference this makes becomes apparent when Hopkins' (1970) results with both kinds of instruments used on the same lesbian sample are compared.
>
> The theoretical orientation and bias of the researcher are subtle determi-

---

*Sign 2 refers to the sex of the first figure. Usually the sex chosen is that opposite to the sex of the subject. Similarity of choice is interpreted as pointing toward homosexuality.

nants both of research methodology and interpretation of data. The psychoanalyst simply approaches the lesbian differently than does the behaviorist.

Sampling is of critical importance in this body of research. Many of the studies cited attempted to match heterosexual and homosexual subjects on what the authors considered relevant variables, but the selection and sources of lesbian subjects have been largely overlooked. In virtually every study mentioned, the homosexual subjects were either psychiatric patients or members of homophile organizations. How representative of the lesbian population as a whole are such women? (p. 82)

At least we do know that there is no evidence of anything like a coherent psychological "syndrome" of female homosexuality. Clinical populations of lesbians cannot readily be distinguished from neurotic nonlesbians. There are indications of inhibited emotionality from some sources, which are contradicted by reports of greater maturity and mental health among homosexuals from other sources. Choice of instruments and methodology may determine the nature of findings. A wide diversity of instruments, designs, and analytic techniques have been used by individual researchers, none of whom has made a systematic attempt to replicate earlier work. Perhaps what is required is the development of a standard battery of projective and nonprojective measures to be administered to both clinical and nonclinical samples of lesbians and controls from a range of socioeconomic classes, and to be analyzed both statistically and clinically.

What, then, despite the methodological insufficiencies, has been the picture that develops about homosexuality as seen by test-using researchers? We summarize here the findings of the period from 1960 to 1977.

Projective Tests

First, as to the Rorschach during the period under review, there were sixteen studies which used it. The size of the population tested ranged, for homosexuals, from 11 to 120 persons. Of these sixteen studies, only four were based on female subjects. The male homosexuals were from hospitals (Anderson and Seitz, 1969; Exner 1969; Seitz et al., 1974), prisons (Raychandhuri and Mukerji, 1970), colleges (Hendlin, 1976; Golding and Rorer, 1972), out-patient services (Stone and Schneider, 1975), and from self-referral (Anderson and Seitz, 1969). The women were hospital patients (Barker, 1970), college students (Hopkins, 1970), and self-identified lesbians (Hopkins, 1970). Control or comparison populations were avowed heterosexuals, college students, unselected, church groups, prisoners, and nonhomosexual hospital patients. The results tended to establish Wheeler's signs, thereby giving some support to differential diagnosis. Again, however, cross-validational studies and double-blind analyses are missing. Furthermore there are no cross-sex studies. The list of references to Rorschach studies includes: Anderson and Seitz, 1969; Anderson, 1975; Auerbach and Edinger, 1976; Barker, 1970; Chapman and Chapman, 1969; Exner, 1969; Goldfried, Stricker, and Weiner, 1971; Golding and Rorer, 1972; Hopkins, 1970; Raychandhuri, and Mukerji 1970; Seitz, Anderson, and Braucht, 1974; Stone and Schneider, 1975.

In summary then of the findings with the Rorschach, it appears that van den Aardweg's (1967) conclusions are supported. The Rorschach clearly does not help to identify homosexuality, whether of the male or female variety. It does not help to differentiate male from female homosexuality. Finally, the analysis of Rorschach protocols throws little if any light on factors that may be involved in like-sexed love partnership choices.

Studies Using the Draw-A-Person Instrument

There have been, in the period under scrutiny, some six or seven reports on comparisons using human figure drawings as a measure of homosexuality. These are as follows: Fraas, 1970; Hassell and Smith, 1975; Janzen and Coe, 1976; Merinfeld-Goldbeter, 1973; Riess, Safer, and Yotive, 1974; and Roback, Langevin, and Zajac, 1974. It has often been assumed that this measure should, a priori, show differential treatment of like and unlike sexed partners because of its human immediacy. The overall results do not substantiate any clear-cut differentiation when the DAP was scored for sexual identity. The populations under study ranged from 256 male and 270 female students (Merinfeld-Goldbeter, 1973) to 9 homosexual "criminals" (Fraas). The characteristics of the drawings that were used to measure sex-role choice and sex behavior included the sex of the first drawn figure. The hypothesis here has historically been that for the homosexual woman, the sex of the first drawing would be female. Roback, Langevin, and Zajac (1974), comparing twenty-one male and twenty-one female homosexuals with like numbers of heterosexuals, found no significant differences. Gundlach and Riess (1968) similarly found no first drawing differences between 101 lesbians and 100 heterosexual women. Janzen and Coe (1976) and Hassell and Smith (1975) make the point that the embellishment of the figure consistent with the sex of the artist and the sexualization of the drawing *did* separate homosexual

from heterosexual women. However, their populations were self-identified as to sexual preference before the test was given, and the units of
embellishment were symbolically interpreted.

It appears then that, despite its surface attractiveness, the DAP has
not given any statistical substantiation to the idea of disparate percep-
tual organization in homosexuals or heterosexuals. The finding of Riess,
Safer, and Yotive (1974) that field independence is more characteristic
of female homosexuals than of heterosexual controls seems to be a
function of the selection of subjects from the Daughters of Bilitis, a
homophile organization of self-identified lesbians.

Again, methodologically, one is struck by the absence of systematic
research. The presence of such factors as field independence in lesbians
needs to be checked against the increase in that trait among women in
age cohorts. It may well be that, as employment and financial independence become more common among women, the incidence of field
dependency will decrease.

It is significant that there were no reports of Thematic Apperception
Test (TAT) studies in the period under review. Obviously, where the
TAT produces an overtly homosexual story, it is relevant to the "diagnosis" but this happens rarely. The older hypothesis of the hostility supposedly found in homosexual women has been so thoroughly discounted both by newer theories of female psychology and by the lack
of experimental findings that the TAT is not used by researchers.

For the whole field of projective testing, the conclusions are clear.
None of the projective instruments can definitively differentiate homosexuality from heterosexuality or male from female homosexuality, nor
can they delineate a significantly different etiology for any of the behaviorally distinct groups. Two possibilities emerge. First, the projective
instruments are insensitive to the differences between homosexual and
heterosexual subjects. The alternative is that the tests are accurate and
that there are few, if any, personality factors which distinguish people
with like-sexed partnership choices from people with opposite-sexed
partnership choices. This alternative seems to concur with larger and
more in-depth studies of homosexuals. Saghir and Robins et al. (1970,
1971) and Gundlach and Riess (1968) have amply demonstrated that homosexual behavior is not more pathological than heterosexual behavior.

Paper-and-Pencil Personality Tests

In view of the difficulty in obtaining a good sample of either hetero- or
homosexual persons for individual examination, it is easy to understand

the greater frequency of usage of so-called objective, standardized, paper-and-pencil tests. Of eleven different instruments used during the period of this scrutiny, the Minnesota Multiphasic Personality Inventory (MMPI) was the test of choice in twenty-four instances. In these studies, most of the basic subscales of the MMPI were examined. As could have been predicted, the masculinity-femininity scale (M/F) was found to be the most predictive of sex-role preference with H sex (homosexual sex) next in line. Despite the loading of the M/F questions with older, stereotypical views of male and female psychology, only six of the twenty-four studies yielded data which suggests predictive value for the M/F scoring.

Dean and Richardson, in an unpublished paper in 1976, state that "such attempts [i.e., to identify differentiating MMPI items] have been limited either by restriction of item analyses to specific scales or by lack of cross-validation of items identified." These authors then proceed to do an analysis of *all* the MMPI items from samples of homosexual and heterosexual adult males. Three groups of data were used: (1) those from an earlier study by the same authors on forty homosexuals and forty heterosexuals; (2) those from forty-nine homo- and forty heterosexual males from the Manosevitz study (1970b); and (3) those from 113 homosexuals tested by Dean in 1967. The responses of the 113 homosexual males were compared with those of 17,079 men seen at the Mayo Clinic. One hundred ninety items were found to be of value in discriminating between homosexuals and heterosexuals. These were cross-validated against the Manosevitz and the Dean and Richardson samples. All in all, in the final validation, thirty-two items were found to discriminate in all comparisons, and 39 percent of these responses were on the M/F scale. Factor analysis of the data produced an element identified as "personal and emotional oversensitivity."

Thus, it appears that even the M/F scale should be applied cautiously and with the knowledge that less than half of its constituent items are of discriminative value.

Loney (1971) reports, in contrast to the other MMPI researchers, that the twenty-nine self-labeled homosexuals in his population scored significantly higher on the F scale indicating an elevated level of nonvalidity for the MMPI responses. Ohlson and Wilson (1974) report that female homosexuals give responses indicating greater self-confidence, less anxiety, and more security than heterosexuals. For those who wish to survey the MMPI literature, the following references in the bibliography deal with this test: Carroll and Fuller, 1971; Cubitt and Gendreau, 1972; Dean and Richardson, 1966, 1976; Fraas, 1970; Fromhart, 1971; Horstman, 1972, 1976; Kenyon, 1968a, 1968b; Loney, 1971; Manosevitz, 1970b, 1971; Ohlson and Wilson, 1974; Pierce, 1972, 1973; Ross, 1975; Singer, 1970; Zucker and Manosevitz, 1966.

Other than the MMPI, the next two most frequently used tests are the Adjective Check List and the Cattell 16 PF Questionnaire. The former was studied by three researchers: Evans (1971), Hassell and Smith (1975), and Thompson, McCandless, and Strickland (1971). The population ranged from 24 lesbians to 127 homosexual men and comparison groups of 111 to 123 heterosexuals. In the latter two studies, the comparisons involved lesbians. Evans studied only males. No hospital or criminal inmates were used. All the investigators found that the checklists, except for the M/F scale, did not differentiate among the groups and that there was no clear-cut evidence for greater neuroticism among homosexuals, whether male or female.

Evans (1970), Hopkins (1970), and Visser (1971) all used the Cattell 16 PF Questionnaire. Again there was agreement that traditional labels of neurosis did not apply to the homosexuals studied.

The remaining studies using a wide variety of inventories or questionnaires found no test-substantiating evidence of pathology among homosexuals nor any evidence of greater deviations in personality when comparisons were made between homosexuals and heterosexuals: Stringer and Grygier (1976), Wilson and Greene (1971), Loney (1973), Ohlson (1974), Andress, Franzini, and Linton (1974), Siegelman (1972), and Clark (1973).

We arrive then at the end of our survey with the firm conclusion that there are no psychological test techniques which successfully separate homosexual men and women from heterosexual comparisons.

More important by far is the conclusion that the commonly used psychological assessment tools do not show any evidence of greater pathology among homosexual women or men than among heterosexuals. That large numbers of mental health professionals still, a priori, identify homosexuality as pathology leads one to conclude that professional practice may blind one to the reality of experimentally established fact.

REFERENCES

Anderson, D. O., and Seitz, C. 1969. Rorschach diagnosis of homosexuality: Schafer's content analysis. *Journal of Projective Technique and Personality Assessment* 33(5): 406–8.

Anderson, E. A. 1975. The elusive homosexual: A reply to Stone and Schneider. *Journal of Personality Assessment* 39(6):580–82.

Andress, V. R.; Franzini, L. R.; and Linton, M. 1974. A comparison of homosexual and heterosexual responses to the Menninger word association test. *Journal of Clinical Psychology* 30(2):205–7.

Auerbach, S. M., and Edinger, J. D. 1976. Factor structure of Rorschach prognostic rating scale and its relation to therapeutic outcome. *Journal of Consulting and Clinical Psychology* 44(4):682.

Barker, G. B. 1970. The female homosexual in hospitals. *Journal of Projective Psychology and Pers. Study* 134(2):2–6.

Bieber, I., et al. 1962. Homosexuality. New York: Basic Books.

Carroll, J. L., and Fuller, G. B. 1971. An MMPI comparison of three groups of criminals. *Journal of Clinical Psychology* 27(2):240–42.

Chapman, L. J., and Chapman, J. P. 1969. Illusory correlations as an obstacle to the use of valid psychodiagnostic signs. *Journal of Abnormal Psychology* 74(3):271–80.

Clark, T. R. 1973. Homosexuality as a criterion predictor of psychopathology in nonpatient males. *Proceedings of the 81st Annual Convention of the American Psychological Association.* 8:407–8.

Cubitt, G. H., and Gendreau, P. 1972. Assessing the diagnostic utility of MMPI and 16 pf indexes of homosexuality in a prison sample. *Journal of Consulting and Clinical Psychology* 39(2):342.

Davids, A.; Joelson, M.; and McArthur, C. 1956. Rorschach and TAT indices of homosexuality in overt homosexual, neurotic, and normal males. *Journal of Abnormal Psychology* 53:161–172.

DeLuca, J. 1967. Performance of overt male homosexuals and controls on the Blackey test. *Journal of Clinical Psychology* 23(4):497.

Dean, R. B., and Richardson, H. 1966. On MMPI high point codes of homosexual versus heterosexual mates. *Journal of Consulting Psychology* 30(6):558–60.

———1976. Identification and cross-validation of MMPI items differentiating homosexual from heterosexual men. Paper presented at Western Psychology Association Convention.

Domino, G. 1973. Homosexuality and creativity. *Proceedings of the 81st Annual Convention of the APA.* 8:409–10.

Evans, R. B. 1969. Childhood parental relationships of homosexual men. *Journal of Consulting and Clinical Psychology* 33(2):129–35.

———. 1970. Sixteen personality factor questionnaire scores of homosexual men. *Journal of Consulting and Clinical Psychology* 34(2):212–15.

———. 1971. Adjective check list scores of homosexual men. *Journal of Personality Assessment* 35(4):244–49.

Exner, J. E. 1969. Rorschach responses as an index of narcissism. *Journal of Projective Technique and Personality Assessment* 33(4):324–30.

Fein, L. G. 1950. Rorschach signs of homosexuality in male college students. *Journal of Clinical Psychology* 6:248–54.

Ford, C. S., and Beach, F. A. 1951. *Patterns of sexual behavior.* New York: Harper & Bros.

Fraas, L. A. 1970. Sex of figure drawing in identifying practicing male homosexuals. *Psychological Reports,* 27 (1): 172–74.

Freud, S. 1961. A letter from Freud (9 April 1935). *American Journal of Psychiatry* 197:786–87.

Freund, K., et al. 1974. Measuring feminine gender identity in homosexual males. *Archives of Sexual Behavior* 3(3):249–60.

Fromhart, M. V. 1971. Characteristics of male homosexual college students. *American College Health Association Journal* 19(4):247–52.

Goldfried, M. R.; Stricker, G.; and Weiner, I. B. 1971. *Rorschach handbook of Clinical and Research Applications.* Englewood Cliffs, N.J.: Prentice-Hall.

Golding, S. L., and Rorer, L. B. 1972. Illusory correlation and subjective judgment. *Journal of Abnormal Psychology* 80(3):249–60.

Greenberg, J. S. 1973. A study of male homosexuals (predominantly college students). *American College Health Association Journal* 22(1):56–60.

Gundlach, R. H., and Riess, B. F. 1968. Self and sexual identity in the female: A study of female homosexuals. In B. F. Riess, ed., *New Directions in Mental Health* (New York: Grune & Stratton).

Hassell, J., and Smith, E. W. 1975. Female homosexual concepts of self, men and women. *Journal of Personality Assessment* 39(2):154–59.

Hendlin, J. C. 1976. Homosexuality in the Rorschach: A new look at the old signs. *Journal of Homosexuality* 1(3):303–12.

Hooker, E. 1967. The adjustment of the male overt homosexual. *Journal of Projective Techniques.* 21:18–31.

Hopkins, J. H. 1970. Lesbian signs on the Rorschach. *British Journal of Projective Psychology and Personality Study.* 15(2):7–14.

Horstman, W. R. 1972. Homosexuality and psychopathology: a study of the MMPI responses of homosexual and heterosexual male college students. *Dissertation Abstracts International* 33(5–13):2347.

———1976. MMPI responses of homosexual and heterosexual male college students. *Homosexual Counseling Journal* 2(2):68–76.

Janzen, W. B., and Coe, W. C. 1976. Clinical and sign prediction: The draw-a-person and female homosexuality. *Journal of Clinical Psychology* 31(4):757–65.

Kendrick, D. C., and Clarke, R. G. 1967. Attitudinal differences between heterosexually and homosexually oriented males. *British Journal of Psychiatry* 113:95–99.

Kenyon, F. E. 1968a. Studies in female homosexuality. VI. The exclusively homosexual group. *Acta Psychiatrica Scandinavica* 44(3):224–37.

———. 1968b. Studies in female homosexuality: Psychological test results. *Journal of Consulting and Clinical Psychology* 32(5, pt. 1):510–13.

Kinsey, A. C., et al. 1948. *Sexual behavior in the human male.* Philadelphia: W. B. Saunders.

———. 1953. *Sexual behavior in the human female.* Philadelphia: W. B. Saunders.

Kromer, M. W., and Ritkin, A. H. 1969. The early development of homosexual: A study of adolescent lesbians. *American Journal of Psychiatry* 126(1):91–96.

Loney, J. 1971. A MMPI measure of maladjustment in a sample of "normal" homosexual men. *Journal of Clinical Psychology* 27(4):486–88.

———. 1973. Family dynamics in homosexual women. *Archives of Sexual Behavior* 2(4):343–50.

McConaghy, N. 1967. Penile volume changes to moving pictures of male and female nudes in heterosexual and homosexual males. *Behavior Research and Therapy* 5:43–48.

Manosevitz, M. 1970a. Early sexual behavior in adult homosexual and heterosexual males. *Journal of Abnormal Psychology* 76(3):396–402.

———. 1970b. Item analysis of the MMPI MF scale using homosexual and heterosexual males. *Journal of Consulting and Clinical Psychology* 35(3):395–99.

———. 1971. Education and MMPI MF scores in homosexual and heterosexual males. *Journal of Consulting and Clinical Psychology* 36(3):395–99.

Merinfeld-Goldbeter, E. 1973. Direction of psychosexual interests and the drawing of the human figure. *Psychologica Belgica.* 13(1):37–54.

Moran, P. A., and Abe, K. 1969. Parental loss in homosexuals. *British Journal of Psychiatry* 115:319–20.

Morin, S. F. 1977. Heterosexual bias in psychological research on lesbianism and male homosexuality. *American Psychologist* 32(6):629–37.

Myrick, F. L. 1974. Attitudinal differences between heterosexuality and homosexually oriented males and between covert and overt male homosexuals. *Journal of Abnormal Psychology* 83(1):81–86.

Ohlson, E. L. A preliminary investigation into the self-disclosing ability of male homosexuals. *Psychology* 11(2):21–25.

Ohlson, E. L., and Wilson, M. 1974. Differentiating female homosexuals from female heterosexuals by use of the MMPI. *Journal of Sex Research* 10(4):308–15.

Pierce, D. M. 1972. MMPI Hs × scale differences between active and situational homosexuality. *Journal of Forensic Psychology.* 4(1):31–37.

———. 1973. Test and nontest correlates of active and situational homosexual. *Psychology* 10(4):23–26.

Raychandhuri, M., and Mukerji, K. 1970. Rorschach differentials of homosexuality in male convicts: An examination of Wheeler and Schafer signs. *Journal of Personality Assessment* 35(1):22–26.

Riess, B. F.; Safer, J.; and Yotive, W. 1974. Psychological test data on female homosexuality: A review of the literature. *Journal of Homosexuality* 1(1):71–85.

Roback, H. B.; Langevin, R.; and Zajac, Y. 1974. Sex of five choice figure drawings by homosexual and heterosexual subjects. *Journal of Personality Assessment* 38(2):154–55.

Robertson, G. 1972. Parent-child relationships and homosexuality. *British Journal of Psychiatry* 121:525–28.

Ross, M. W. 1975. Relationship between sex role and sex orientation in homosexual men. *New Zealand Psychologist* 4(1):25–29.

Saghir, M., and Robins, E. 1971. Male and female homosexuality: Natural history. *Comprehensive Psychiatry* 12(6):503–10.

Saghir, M., et al. 1970a. Homosexuality. III. Psychiatric disorders and disability in the male homosexual. *American Journal of Psychiatry* 126(8):63–70.

———. 1970b. Homosexuality. IV. Psychiatric disorders and disability in the female homosexual. *American Journal of Psychiatry* 127(2):147–54.

Seitz, F. C.; Anderson, D. O.; and Braucht, G. N. 1974. A comparative analysis of Rorschach signs of homosexuality. *Psychological Reports* 35(3):1163–69.

Siegelman, M. 1972. Adjustment of homosexual and heterosexual women. *British Journal of Psychiatry* 120(588):477–81.

———. 1974a. Parental backgrounds of male homosexuals and heterosexuals. *Archives of Sexual Behavior* 3(1):3–18.

———. 1974b. Parental background of homosexual and heterosexual woman. *British Journal of Psychiatry* 124:14–21.

Singer, M. I. 1970. Comparison of indicators of homosexuality on the MMPI. *Journal of Consulting and Clinical Psychology* 34(1):15–18.

Stephan, W. G. 1973. Parental relationships and early social experiences of activist male homosexuals and male heterosexuals. *Journal of Abnormal Psychology* 82(3):506–13.

Stoller, R. J. 1975. *Perversion, the erotic form of hatred.* New York: Basic Books.

Stone, N. M., and Schneider, R. E. 1975. Concurrent validity of the Wheeler signs of homosexuality in the Rorschach. *Journal of Personality Assessment* 39(6):573–79.

Stringer, P., and Grygier, T. 1976. Male homosexuality, psychiatric patient status, and psychological masculinity and femininity. *Archives of Sexual Behavior* 5(1):15–27.

Swanson, D. W., et al. 1972. Clinical features of the female homosexual patient: A comparison with the heterosexual patient. *Journal of Nervous and Mental Disease* 155(2):-119–24.

Tejessy, C. 1952. The thematic apperception test. Unpublished honors thesis. Harvard University.

Thompson, N. L.; McCandless, B. R.; and Strickland, B. R. 1971. Personal adjustment of male and female homosexuals and heterosexuals. *Journal of Abnormal Psychology* 78(2):273–40.

Thompson, N. L., et al. 1973. Parent-child relationships and sexual identity in male and female homosexuals and heterosexuals. *Journal of Consulting and Clinical Psychology* 41(1):120–27.

Van den Aardweg, G. J. M. 1969. Male homosexuality and psychological tests. *International Mental Health Research Newsletter,* 11(4):7–12.

———. 1967. *Homofilie, neurose en dwangzelfbeklag.* Amsterdam: Polak and van Gennep.

Visser, R. S. 1971. The 16 PF scores of a group of homosexual students. *Nederlands Tijdschrift voor de Haarhologie en Haar Grensgebrieden* 26(3):159–68.

Wheeler, W. M. 1949. An analysis of Rorschach indices of male homosexuality. *Journal of Projective Techniques* 13:97–100.

Whitaker, L. 1961. The use of extended Draw-a-Person Test to identify homosexual and effeminate men. *Journal of Consulting Psychology* 25:482–86.

Wilson, M. L. 1974. A new female homosexuality scale. *Dissertation Abstracts International* 34(8–B):4065.

Wilson, M. L., and Greene, R. L. 1971. Personality characteristics of female homosexuals. *Psychological Reports* 28:407–12.

Woodward, R., et al. 1973. A comparison of two scoring systems for the sexual orientation method. *British Journal of Social and Clinical Psychology* 12:411–14.

Zamansky, H. S. 1955. A technique for assessing homosexual tendencies. *Journal of Personality* 24:431–48.

Zucker, R. A., and Manosevitz, M. 1966. MMPI patterns of overt male homosexuals: Reinterpretation and comment on Dean and Richardson's study. *Journal of Consulting Psychology* 30(6):555–57.

17 / Latent Homosexuality

LEON SALZMAN

There is an old children's rhyme that says: "Sticks and stones will break my bones, but names will never hurt me!" Unfortunately in the adult world names frequently do more damage than sticks and stones. In this connection it is worth exploring certain psychoanalytic terms that not only have pejorative connotations but are of doubtful validity either as description or as explanation. The term "latent homosexuality," which has come into prominence since the contributions of Sigmund Freud, belongs in this category. It stems from the bisexual theory of sexual development, a theory that was prevalent during the late nineteenth and early twentieth centuries, when our clinical and laboratory knowledge was more limited than it is today.

In recent years biologists and sexologists have emphatically denied that this theory has any validity. In the face of this denial and the growing confusion about the definition of what constitutes overt homosexuality, it is essential that the concepts of bisexuality and latent homosexuality be examined in a fresh light, free from preconceptions and prejudices. The need for such a reexamination has been underscored by recent proscriptive and primitive measures applied to homosexuals. Such labels can have a major economic as well as psychological impact. To label someone "schizophrenic," "psychopathic," or "homosexual" may permanently alter that person's existence in a devastating way.

The difficulties in defining homosexuality make it even more imperative that the term "latent homosexuality" be clarified. Above all, it is necessary to reexamine the prevalent assumption that everyone is latently homosexual, in the sense that homosexual inclinations are present in all of us to a greater or lesser degree. Freud's authority, which grew out of his pioneering explorations in previously unexplored areas of human behavior, especially in the area of sexuality, gave a sanctified and irrefutable aura to his views. For a long time his views were accepted in toto as ultimate truths, even though some concepts like the libido theory and his theory of instincts have been under attack since the beginnings of psychoanalysis. The tendency to move from an instinctual framework to a more culturally oriented perspective in personality theory has been reflected in a number of alternative theories with regard to infantile sexuality, homosexuality, female sexuality, and sexual deviations. These approaches take into account the scientific developments in psychology, anthropology, sociology, and ethology over the past fifty years. Instinct theory is largely outmoded as a biological model for the understanding of personality development, and the view of sex simply as an instinct limits the understanding of its role in human behavior. In recent years there has been considerable research in human sexual behavior by biologists, sexologists, physiologists, and psychologists, and many cherished dogmas about male and female sexual behavior have undergone marked revisions (Ford and Beach, 1951; Kinsey, 1948, 1953; Marmor, 1954; Masters, 1960; Masters and Johnson, 1960; Salzman, 1954). Revisions have also taken place in the areas of homosexuality and other sexual deviations.

The concept of latent homosexuality especially needs reevaluation even though this concept may have played a useful role in the early development of personality theory. As Einstein said: "Concepts that have proved useful in the constitution of an order of things readily win such authority over us that we forfeit their earthly origins and take them to be changeless data" (Schlipp, 1955). It is not idle play or semantic juggling to review these concepts in order to determine the grounds upon which they have been erected and whether or not they are still valid.

First, it is useful to determine the meaning of "latency." Latency implies either *dormancy,* that is, the presence of a fully developed and matured function in an inactive state (the hibernating bear and portions of memory apparatus are examples of this latent state), or *potentiality,* that is, the possibility that some state of being or process may develop if adequate stimuli and auspicious circumstances are provided. The acorn which becomes an oak tree is a clear example of latency as potentiality. The second use of the term is more consistent with both modern biology and psychology, neither of which views human development as a process in which all is preordained and merely awaits illumination. Modern psychological theory tends to be evolutionary. This goes well beyond the concept of genetic unfoldings of the DNA chain. Thus, recent theories about schizophrenia suggest a genetic potential which must be activated or brought to fruition by environmental factors. This is also true of processes in human maturation such as speech, personality traits, and psychological and emotional maturity which are dependent upon environmental circumstances that impinge on given genetic potentials.

The potentialities inherent in human beings are thus influenced by environmental phenomena, and development is dependent upon the phenomena and stimuli that confront the developing organism. The only preordained state is the potentiality for development. This concept of latency, however, is taken for granted, and the term is therefore never used in ordinary discourse. We do not speak of the latent adult or the latent syphilitic or the latent heterosexual. These possibilities are all intrinsic in the developmental process, and an individual will become syphilitic, adult, or heterosexual if adequate and necessary stimuli are present. In this sense all human beings are also potentially homosexual and may develop in that direction if certain conditions prevail and other necessary influences are absent.

The term "latent homosexuality" was not originally used in this sense, however, nor is it currently applied in this way. It is invariably used to define those qualities in the adolescent or preadolescent male that relate to gender attributes commonly ascribed to being feminine. Used in this way it is a direct application of Freud's concept, derived from the bisexual theory of human sexual development, and therefore it is being used strictly in the sense of dormancy. As a dormancy concept, the term implies that the individual has hidden inside himself a fully grown and developed capacity to be homosexual that covertly influences his attitudes, needs, desires, and behavior. It is presumed to be an aspect of everyone's personality structure, although it may be more apparent in some people than in others.

Such a notion of dormancy is, however, highly questionable when applied to the living, growing organism. Evidence for it is rare, except in some inactive states in lower organisms like spores, or in states of hibernation in some more highly developed species. In hibernation the entire organism is immobilized. Latent homosexuality as a dormancy concept, however, implies that homosexual needs and drives exist in fully developed but concealed form within the individual.

What is the origin of this interesting idea which has influenced psychoanalytic theory so profoundly? On what clinical findings is it based? Does its existence tend to categorize many aspects of behavior as latent homosexual trends that could be equally well understood under different rubrics? Does a tacit and unquestioned acceptance of its validity allow the collection of a whole variety of dissimilar phenomena into a "wastebasket" category that serves to impede the search for more definitive causes of such behavior? Does it tend to limit research into normal sexual development as well as into deviant sexual behavior? It is useful to examine these questions historically as well as clinically.

The concept of latent homosexuality grew out of Freud's acceptance of a biological hypothesis prevalent during the period in which he worked: the bisexual theory of sexual development. This theory was derived from mythological sources, comparative biological studies, and observation of certain histological remnants of the sexual anlagen of both sexes in every individual. This conception of inborn bisexuality was inherited from Freud's predecessors, particularly from his friend Fliess, who found it useful in explaining many aspects of human sexual behavior. It implied that in the course of development, the sexual potentialities for both sexes are present. In this respect the theory is substantiated by embryological studies, and it accounts for the remnants of the opposite sex in each individual (Ferenczi, 1938; Freud, 1933; Freud, 1962). The theory goes further, however, and insists that even after physical sex has been determined and development of the sexual apparatus is proceeding toward maturation, there are present in each person not only physiological remnants but also psychological remnants of the other sex in a complete but dormant form (Rado, 1940).

Refutations of these notions have come from a variety of sources: biological, biochemical, histological, and embryological. In a recent summary of data relating to the psychology of the female, Sherfey (1966) has documented the path of gender development with biochemical and anatomical data which totally nullify the bisexual theory of sexual development. She clearly demonstrates that it is inaccurate to speak of a bisexual phase of embryonic development. Genetic sex is established at fertilization, but all embryos are morphologically female until the effect of the male sex genes is felt during the growth of the fetal gonads. In this way androgens induce the male growth pattern. If the genetic sex is female, germ cells stimulate the production of follicles and estrogen. However, if the fetal gonads are artificially removed before the seventh week, a female anatomy will develop in both males and females. Therefore, female differentiation is the result of the innate, genetically determined morphology of all mammalian embryos unless they are acted on by androgens at a critical period in embryonic development.

The complex problem of gender role in relationship to genital morphology in sex behavior has been illuminated by a large number of physiological, biochemical, and chromosomal studies in recent years. There are a large number of variables which enter into the total sexual pattern: (1) sex-chromatin pattern, (2) gonadal sex as indicated by morphology, (3) hormonal sex which is correlated to secondary sex characteristics, (4) external genital morphology, (5) internal accessory reproductive structure, (6) sex assignment and rearing, and (7) psychological sex or gender role (chap. 3, this volume).

Psychological maleness or femaleness (gender role) is not attributable to any single one of the variables and does not appear to have an innate preformed instinctive basis. On the contrary, it has been found that sex assignment and rearing usually play the major factors in gender role. Thus, gender role in human beings appears to depend on learned experience as well as on somatic variables. Hampson and Hampson (1961) conclude that psychologic sex or gender role appears to be learned, and "becomes differentiated during the course of many experiences of growing up . . . In place of a theory of innate constitutional psychologic bisexuality. . . . we must substitute a concept of psychologic sexual neutrality in humans at birth" (p. 1406).

The attitudes, characterological traits, and behavioral characteristics of the female are not due exclusively to her biological sex but also to the demands, expectations, and restraints which a particular culture may place on her. Biological and physiological differences, nevertheless, are significant. The marked differences in the size and bulk of the voluntary muscles obviously produce some divergent attitudes regarding the male and female when a culture requires strength and endurance. Although this was a paramount need in primitive cultures, the advent of a technology capable of replacing muscular power in recent years has obviated this advantage. Nevertheless, the major differences which revolve around the roles of the male and female in the procreative and child-rearing processes may produce distinctive characterological elements in each sex. In spite of recent changes in women's cultural status, child-rearing functions still influence a significant portion of a woman's personality structure. As child-rearing practices change either through the uses of crèches, early boarding schools, or day-care centers, major changes in this aspect of women's maternal role may occur; however, since there is no likelihood in the foreseeable future that the actual childbearing role of women will be supplanted by artificial techniques, it is fair to assume that this will remain a significant factor in feminine psychology. Nevertheless, the concept of the biologically weak, helpless, and submissive female will ultimately have to be abandoned, even though many women as well as men have come to accept this notion.

The bisexual theory of sexual development postulates that there is a normal phase of homoerotic development which is followed by a heteroerotic phase. The homoerotic tendencies are forever present but dormant, and they may be aroused by both instinctual and experiential factors. Failures of repression or sublimation may allow the emergence of these homosexual impulses which may manifest themselves in a variety of ways. Such symptoms are supposedly revealed in a host of data about passive-submissive attitudes in the male and active-aggressive attitudes in the female. Other manifestations are thought to be evident in expressed fears of homosexuality, in the hidden content of dreams or other unconscious or conscious fantasies of homosexuality, in homosexual panics, in difficulties in adequate heterosexual functioning, and in an endless list of activities or intimacies of a nonsexual nature between individuals of the same sex (Ovesey, 1954). It has long been believed that alcohol and other drugs that weaken repression may bring such latent tendencies into the open, revealing the hidden homosexual inclinations.

Although this concept had its origin in biological theory, modern biological theorists deny its validity. One eminent biologist (Lillie, 1939), in summing up these objections, wrote: "Sex of the gametes and sex in bodily structure are two radically different things." Sandor Rado, in a review of the concept (1940), wrote: "Using the term, bisexuality, in the only sense in which it is biologically legitimate, there is no such thing as bisexuality either in man or in any other of the higher vertebrates." Biological sex activity cannot be partial: the deposit of sperm by a penile organ characterizes the male and the presence of genital and related glandular apparatus to receive and nurture the ovum characterizes the female. The joint embryological origin of the genital system does not speak for a physiological—let alone a psychological—duality of the biological function of sex and reproduction.

According to the bisexual theory, every individual with the supposed heritage of so-called masculine and feminine traits reveals latent homosexual trends if any of his or her attitudes or behavioral characteristics does not conform to the accepted qualities of maleness or femaleness. Where do these so-called qualities come from? The assumption of male aggressiveness and female passivity is metaphorically derived from the need for the male to penetrate and aggressively overwhelm the female for the sex act to occur. The normal female is expected to be the passive receiver, waiting to be invaded to receive the sperm. Her total psychology is presumed to be organized around the curious joke of nature that provides an inner warm and protected area for the development of the ovum. This picture, although superficially descriptive, does not portray with accuracy the sexual behavior of either animals or humans. The male is certainly not always the aggressive member of all animal species —the human species included—even though the penis must be inserted. Without active cooperation and participation, or unless the female were rendered incapable of resistance, sexual activity could not occur. The aggressiveness of the male varies from culture to culture in the nonsexual areas of behavior, but we might speculate that sexually the female is generally a willing participant in the drama and that force has rarely been necessary.

This is not meant to be a historical refutation of the aggressiveness of the male, but rather a brief review of the extraordinary complications that result from calling certain characteristics innately and implicitly masculine because of the sex-role dictated by the sexual organs. While it is clear that the role of each sex in the culture is partly determined by the biological apparatus, psychological characteristics may be determined by many other aspects of life's experiences and cultural pressures. Studies of the actual behavior of each sex during courtship and intercourse throw serious doubt on the biological inevitability of male activity and female passivity (Ford and Beach, 1951; Kinsey et al., 1953; Masters and Johnson, 1960).

In his *New Introductory Lectures* (1933), Freud stated:

> By masculine you mean as a rule "active"; and when you say feminine you mean "passive." Now it is quite true that there is such a correlation. The male sexual cell is active and mobile; it seeks out the female one while the latter, the ovum, is stationary and more or less a model of the behavior of the individual of each sex in sexual intercourse. (p. 1356).

Nevertheless, to attribute passivity to the female because the male genital has to act actively to penetrate the vaginal canal is to base a theory on only one element in a much more elaborate sexual perform-ance. The female genital apparatus is extremely active in the sexual act and is not merely a passive receptor of sperm. The notion of female passivity which has produced untold mischief in the theories of female psychology as well as in the notions of latent homosexuality has, in recent years, been completely negated by the striking research of Mas-ters (1960), who clearly demonstrated that the contractions of the vagina and uterus act as a pump to produce and facilitate the passage of sperm to the uterus. In addition, the participation of the female in intercourse is required for vaginal lubrication, which actively promotes adequate insertion.

Childbearing and the endocrine cycle between pregnancies demand great physiological flexibility and adaptability. The physiological changes that accompany menstruation and conception necessitate, at times, a more sedentary, less active existence, although woman has traditionally carried out practically every function of which man is capable. Yet at certain times her procreative role requires some restric-tion of her motions. The care of the young further limits her mobility. To this extent she is different from the male. Childbearing and breast-feeding are biological roles restricted to the female, and the special demands of these roles determine the differences in the sexes, not the presence or absence of particular genital organs or conventional ideas of sexual activity. Freud's views on sex, female sexuality, and bisexuality were hampered by inadequate data.

In Freudian theory when an individual displays characteristics oppo-site to or deviant from the inherent characteristics of his biological sexuality, he is presumed to be displaying latent homosexual trends. The female thus betrays latent homosexual trends if she acts aggres-sively, i.e., if she becomes interested in such traditionally or convention-ally male pursuits as physical labor, engineering, architecture, etc. (It should be noted that in the last fifty years there has been a marked shift in occupations previously reserved for males; many are now heavily populated by females.) So far as the male is concerned, interest dis-played in homemaking, beauty culture, and other areas traditionally associated with the female is regarded as evidence of latent homosexuality. If the female, on the other hand, evidences so-called masculine interests, it is called "penis envy" or "masculine protest."

The female has so successfully invaded the occupational domain of the male in the past two decades that such superficial categorizations have become meaningless. In spite of continued prejudice and discrimination in hiring, salary, and promotion, the notion of a woman being "in a man's job" is practically disappearing.

The concept of latent homosexuality has come to be reserved largely for the male. Evidence of latent homosexuality was once thought to include the expressed fear of homosexuality or the presence of homosexual fantasies, dreams, or ideas. If one reacted to these ideas or to homosexual advances with excessive fear, disgust, rage, or horror, these reactions would also be evidence of latent homosexual trends. It should be noted that the term is not applied to the overt homosexual but only to the heterosexual individual in whom there lie dormant homosexual tendencies and drives that might influence his behavior and psychology. Latent homosexuality does not refer to repressed or dissociated homosexual drives, and it is believed to be present in all individuals who are not overt homosexuals.

The term "latent homosexuality" is usually applied to those tendencies, attitudes, and behaviors that involve some difficulty with mature sexuality and partake of some of the psychological characteristics of the opposite sex. In therapy the term is applied to those elements in the patient's character structure that involve personality traits not conventionally attributed to his sex. It does not mean that he is actively engaged in homosexual activity. It is not applied to the homosexual who has suppressed his homosexuality and tries to live a heterosexual existence; his homosexuality is not latent. In the course of developing, we must all achieve satisfactory relationships with individuals of the same sex and make our first real efforts at being social creatures. During adolescence this effort becomes the main burden of our development. Some manage it successfully and have few problems with the opposite sex. Such people may never experience even fleeting notions of homosexuality. Others never manage it and become overt, active homosexuals. Still others have only fleeting homosexual contacts or may, in varying degrees, exhibit behavioral traits commonly attributed to the opposite sex. These are the ones to whom the label "latent homosexual" is applied, though it is presumed to be present in all people.

There is thus a tendency to characterize every withdrawal from or difficulty with the opposite sex as either homosexual or arising out of latent homosexual drives. Every evidence in the male of weakness, lack of aggressiveness, timidity, sensitivity, inclination toward nonmasculine pursuits, or interest in the arts becomes evidence of homosexuality or latent homosexuality. The homosexual in our culture is symbolized as a weak, passive male who is incompetent and incapable. Any traits or attitudes that resemble these unmasculine tendencies are also considered evidence of latent homosexuality—whether or not they have any relevance to sexual behavior or interest. The term is also applied to those females who incline toward such conventional male characteristics as aggressiveness, interest in outdoor activities or skills, and general pursuit of the so-called "masculine" concerns.

In therapy so-called latent homosexual attitudes are often described as appearing in the course of psychoanalytic work. At these times abortive attempts to relate to people of the same sex or to a therapist of the same sex are viewed as evidence of latent homosexuality. The activity may actually be indicative of growing capacities and desires for participation in more tender and intimate relationships of a nonsexual nature. They may only indicate a need for expression of interest and affection from the therapist. The need to label this "latent homosexuality" does not arise out of the nature of the phenomenon. Often the therapist's own difficulty in dealing with closeness or intimacy from a patient of the same sex can be acceptably rationalized by labeling the patient's behavior in this way. The tendency to take homosexual fantasies or dreams (manifest content) at face value while searching for the latent content in other dreams often betrays this preconception. Too often the interpretation of behavior in terms of latent homosexuality loses sight of a patient's other problems with competitiveness, fear of aggression, or identification with female figures who may play strong roles in the patient's current life.

The widespread prevalence of doubt about potency, especially in the male, raises in the mind of the intellectually informed the possibility of homosexuality. The recent burgeoning of sex therapy and sex clinics has revealed the widespread extent of sexual problems in men and women. Premature ejaculation is a very common complaint in the male, as is lack of orgasm in the female. It is interesting to note that while the professional does not ordinarily view these problems as evidence of latent homosexuality, the individuals involved, influenced by popular mythology, often see their difficulties as possibly due to "latent" homosexual trends. It is the failure of the experts to clarify this concept that accounts for its continued presence in the layman's mind.

The presence of obsessive ruminations about potency often serves as confirmation to some psychoanalysts of the existence of latent homosexuality. Yet these ruminations represent only one aspect of an individual's doubts and uncertainties about all aspects of his life. The strength of the Freudian impact on our culture is manifest in the way an individual turns these doubts into concerns over potency which then means possible latent homosexuality. It is notable that in lower economic groups, as described in the Kinsey reports, this sequence does not occur nearly so frequently as in middle and upper economic groups. In cultures in which Freudian psychoanalysis has not taken hold as it has in the West (particularly the United States and Great Britain), the tendency to translate inadequacy into homosexuality is far less common (Weinstein, 1962).

At best the term "latent homosexuality" can have meaning only if the definition of homosexuality is precise. Even this word, however, is markedly unspecific and its use is often reciprocally rooted in the concept of latent homosexuality. The definition of one sexual deviation often rests on the imprecise and uncertain status of another deviation, and each draws support from the other, which weakens both structures (Bowman and Engle, 1956).

The term "homosexual" may be applied to anyone who has had contact with the same sex, no matter how fleeting or how long ago, or it may refer only to those individuals whose sexual relations are limited to the same sex. Some psychiatrists label any closeness or intimacy with members of the same sex as homosexual, whether it involves explicit sex activity or participation in poker games or attendance at beer joints. Others label homosexual any sex activity with the opposite sex not involving the vagina. Still others apply the term to any individual who avoids the opposite sex, even though he has no intimate sex activities with members of the same sex. For still others, the term is synonymous with effeminacy, and it is in this sense that it is used most often by the lay public. The term has no specificity or precision in a scientific sense. As a generalization it covers a multitude of behaviors derived from various sources and with various operational meanings. The need for more precision is essential. Perhaps it would be preferable to speak only of homosexual behavior, rather than of homosexuality. "Homosexual behavior" would then take on an operational meaning, even though just what constitutes homosexual behavior would still be open to confusion. From this framework, however, a continuum could be visualized between extreme or less extreme homosexual behavior. It would permit the concept of occasional versus persistent homosexual behavior and would also leave room for the phenomenon of homosexual behavior as a situational problem. A definition in terms of behavior is preferable, for homosexuality is a symptom of underlying personality orientation and not of a single, integrated psychiatric syndrome. Such a broad definition would completely disregard the activities of the individual prior to the maturation of the sexual apparatus on the theory that before he or she is sexual in the adult sense, the label used for adult sexuality cannot be applied. It is clear that such a definition is not only difficult, but inadequate. It might, however, suggest limits and encourage an operational framework within which to explore the phenomenon further. When we recognize the problems inherent in defining homosexuality, we are struck even more by the looseness of the concept of latent homosexuality.

It is obvious that although this concept may have served a useful purpose in the initial development of the psychology of sex behavior, its continued use is detrimental in a scientific and humanistic sense. While it supplied answers to much clinical material in both Freud's experience and that of others, it was based on anatomical and physiological fallacies that have been clarified during the past fifty years. Our knowledge of sex behavior, sexual anatomy, love, and intimacy has advanced our understanding beyond the mere biological or instinctual conception of sex behavior. In this regard the existential psychologists and particularly M. Boss (1949) have been most influential in doing away with the conception of sex as a collection of "partial instincts" and seeing it instead as a total reaction of one human being to another. Disturbances in its function are thus disorders of the total organism rather than of the sexual apparatus alone.

The role of sex in human behavior is a dual one: it serves a biological function in terms of race survival and an extraprocreative or interpersonal role. The interpersonal aspect of the sex function is the role it plays in fulfilling man's need to avoid loneliness and to establish intimate and loving relationships with other human beings. Although this aspect of the sexual function is very intimately related to the biological aspects of sex, it is often extremely difficult to determine in a specific instance whether sexual activity is serving the purpose of procreation, alleviating loneliness or anxiety, proving one's capacity, or forcing some demand on one's partner. Because the procreative function of sex can be (but is not necessarily) so intimately involved in the extraprocreative function, they are often confused. Alexander (1956) expresses this idea in more general terms, stating that what distinguishes man as a personality is what he does with his faculties after he has secured his basic (biological) needs. "What makes man different from all other species is that he uses his creative forces not only for biological growth and propagation, but alloplastically for building different forms of culture which are not solely determined by survival needs. On the contrary, in his playful, nonutilitarian but libidinous, exuberant exercise of his faculties, man makes discoveries, the utility of which is only later discovered" (p. 697).

For survival as integrated and functioning individuals, some people are willing to give up the procreative aspects of sex. This surrender is characteristic of homosexual behavior. Homosexuals still actively use the dramatic integrating power of sex for establishing contact with other human beings. The potentiality for the development of homosexuality is thus present in all of us. This potentiality can be fulfilled or bypassed. In adolescence the final choice must be made. If we accept the bisexual theory of sexual development and the libido theory, then everyone has latent homosexual tendencies. If we view the choice of the sexual object as psychologically determined, then everyone has homosexual potentialities until the final heterosexual mode of sexual intimacy is accomplished. Latent homosexuality is a meaningless term in any new conception of homosexual behavior, for it always characterizes a possibility for behavior when heterosexual intimacy is interfered with—whether in early years by parental injunction or threats or in later years in prisons or under circumstances in which heterosexual behavior is impossible.

The concept of latent homosexuality can be given up only when we are finally prepared to accept the fact that sexual behavior, although dictated by biology, plays many roles in the human being's life. Because the term "homosexuality" carries such derogatory connotations and its application subjects an individual to serious social and occupational difficulties, it should be reserved for instances in which its presence it undoubted. The looseness of the term "latent homosexuality" and its abuse by professionals as well as laymen demands that the validity of the concept be clearly established or else that it be completely abandoned.

REFERENCES

Alexander, F. 1956. Psychoanalysis in Western culture. *American Journal of Psychiatry* 112:692–699.

Beach, F. A., ed. 1965. *Sex and behavior.* New York: J. N. Day & Sons.

Boss, M. 1949. *Meaning and content of sexual perversions.* New York: Grune & Stratton.

Bowman, K. M., and Engle, B. A. 1956. A psychiatric evaluation of laws of homosexuality. *American Journal of Psychiatry* 112:577–83.

Ferenczi, S. 1938. A theory of genitality. *Psychoanalytic Quarterly*

Ford, C. S., and Beach, F. A. 1951. *Patterns of sexual behavior.* New York: Harper & Bros.

Freud, S. 1933. The psychology of women. In *New Introductory Lectures in Psychoanalysis.* New York: W. W. Norton.

———. 1962 (1905). *Three essays on the theory of sexuality.* In J. Strachey, ed., *The standard edition of the complete psychological works of Sigmund Freud* (New York: Basic Books).

Hampson, J. L., and Hampson, J. G. 1961. The ontogenesis of sexual behavior in man. In W. C. Young, ed., *Sex and internal secretions,* vol. 2 (Baltimore: Williams & Wilkins), pp. 1401–32.

Horney, K. 1939. *New ways in psychoanalysis.* New York: W. W. Norton.

Kinsey, A. C., et al. 1948. *Sexual behavior in the human male.* Philadelphia: W. B. Saunders.

———. 1953. *Sexual behavior in the human female.* Philadelphia: W. B. Saunders.

Lillie, F. R. 1939. General biological introduction. In E. Allan, ed., *Sex and Internal Secretions,* 2nd ed. (Baltimore: Williams & Wilkins), pp. 2–14.

Marmor, J. 1954. Some considerations concerning orgasm in the female. *Psychosomatic*

Medicine 16:240–45.

Masters, W. H. 1960. The sexual response cycle of the human female. *Western Journal of Surgery* 68:52–72.

Masters, W. H., and Johnson, V. E. 1960. The human female, anatomy of sexual response. *Minnesota Medicine* 43:31–36.

Ovesey, L. 1954. The homosexual conflict. *Psychiatry* 17:243–50.

Rado, S. 1940. A critical examination of the concept of bisexuality. *Psychosomatic Medicine* 2:459–67.

Robbins, B. S. 1955. The myth of latent emotions. *Psychotherapy* 1 (1):3–30.

Salzman, L. 1954. Premature ejaculation. *International Journal of Sexology* 69–76.

Schlipp, P. A. 1955. *Albert Einstein, philosopher-scientist.* New York: Tudor.

Sherfey, M. J. 1966. The evolution and nature of female sexuality in relation to psychoanalytic theory. *American Psychoanalytic Association Journal* 14:28–128.

Weinstein, E. 1962. *Culture aspects of delusion: a psychiatric study of the Virgin Islands.* Riverside, N.J.: Glencoe Press.

18 / Pseudohomosexuality and Homosexuality in Men: Psychodynamics as a Guide to Treatment

LIONEL OVESEY

SHERWYN M. WOODS

Male patients, heterosexual as well as homosexual, in the course of psychotherapy frequently express wishes to be loved by other men, to be dependent on them, to be protected by them, to dominate or be dominated by them, and to establish physical—especially genital—contact with them. All these fantasies are lumped together in classical Freudian theory under the heading of "latent homosexuality." They are then attributed motivationally to a feminine component in an inherited bisexual constitution striving for gratification through a homosexual instinct. If we dispense with the instinctual frame of reference, these fantasies can be approached from a purely adaptational point of view. The reasons for dropping such Freudian concepts as instincts, instinctual energies, and bisexuality are described in a series of papers delineating the differences between an adaptational frame of reference and the Freudian instinctual frame of reference (Kardiner, Karush, and Ovesey, 1959a, 1959b, 1959c, 1959d).

In terms of the adaptational frame of reference, we can sort out three separate motivations for homosexual behavior: homosexuality, dependency, and power. The homosexual motivation is the only one of the three for which sexual satisfaction is the end goal. The dependency and power motivations, as their names suggest, have completely different, nonsexual goals, although the genital organs may be used to achieve them. The patient usually misconstrues these goals as sexual when in reality they are not. For this reason, the dependency and power motivations are more appropriately designated as pseudohomosexual motivations. The anxiety about being homosexual that accompanies them in heterosexual males is designated as pseudohomosexual anxiety (Ovesey, 1954; Ovesey, 1955a, 1955b).

The concept of pseudohomosexuality was originally devised to facilitate understanding of homosexual anxieties in heterosexual males suffering from dependency and power conflicts. The concept can also be used to reconstruct and understand the psychodynamics of homosexuality during the treatment of male homosexuals. The psychodynamic principles presented with respect to men are equally applicable to problems of a similar nature in women (Ovesey, 1956; Defries, 1976).

Pseudohomosexuality

Pseudohomosexual anxieties may develop in men at times of self-assertive crisis precipitated by failures in the masculine role in any area of behavior—sexual, social, or vocational. In such circumstances a man may unconsciously represent his weakness through a symbolic equation: I am a failure as a man = I am castrated = I am a woman = I am a homosexual. The ideas in this equation are derived from culturally determined attitudes that favor the male. In our society, masculinity represents strength, dominance, superiority; femininity represents weakness, submissiveness, inferiority. For men the former is equated with success, the latter with failure. The equation is a caricature of the social demand that every male fulfill certain "masculine" requirements and of the social judgment that "femininity" and homosexuality are failures for which a man must forfeit all respect from his fellows. Men with inhibitions of assertion who use this equation invariably invoke adaptive techniques either in fantasy or through overt behavior, which make use of dependency or power to repair damage already done or to ward off damage yet to come.

The unconscious wish for infantile dependency in adulthood is a confession of adaptive failure. The person who resorts to this wish is convinced that he lacks the adaptive equipment to satisfy his own needs and to ensure his own survival. The mother-child relationship is the developmental prototype for such a dependency relationship. It is this relationship that the dependent adult seeks to reestablish. To this end, he solicits help, support, protection. In extreme instances, he wants another person to take over all responsibility for his welfare, as his mother did when he was a child. At times of crisis, he may regressively fall back on unconscious fantasies of magical repair (Karush and Ovesey, 1961). The most primitive of such fantasies is incorporation of the maternal breast. However, there is an alternative pseudohomosexual route to dependency which is based on the equation: penis = breast. Its developmental prototype is the father-child relationship. There are two ways in which this equation can be used. In the first, the father's penis appears as a feeding organ similar to the mother's breast, the semen is equated with milk, and the dependency is expressed by the reparative fantasy of sucking the penis. The second involves incorporation of the father's penis, usually by mouth or anus, whereby the dependent male undoes his castration by appropriating the donor's "masculine" strength. These maneuvers are doomed to failure not merely because they are magical, but because the fantasied acts of incorporation are experienced by the patient as if they were truly homosexual in motivation. Paradoxically, they then serve to perpetuate the very anxiety they were designed to alleviate.

The clinical examples that follow demonstrate the psychodynamics of pseudohomosexuality as they emerge in psychotherapy of heterosexual males. In the first example, the patient makes a direct, simple, and obvious equation between the penis and the breast:

The patient was a young man who for weeks had been struggling with his desire to become as successful and powerful as the therapist seemed to be. In the midst of this struggle he suddenly reversed himself and launched a vitriolic attack upon the therapist as not only stupid and inadequate, but also cold and ungiving. He compared him with his hard-driving, ambitious, tyrannical mother, who always found him wanting and treated him with contempt. He began to complain he was getting no better and at the same time reported a rapid deterioration in his relationship with his mother. One day, after a particularly violent quarrel with her, he reported a dream: *He saw a penis and covered it with a handkerchief. Then he performed fellatio. There was an orgasm and a huge gush of milk that looked thin like skimmed milk. Next, he was talking to an analyst, who told him he saw 15 to 30 patients a day. He was amazed at the doctor's capacity and his large income.* The patient compressed a number of motivational and countermotivational ideas into this dream. In the wish to be fed and given his analyst's strength, he identifies the therapist with his mother. The penis functions as a breast and gives him milk, but he dramatizes his dissatisfaction by turning it into skimmed milk from which the richest portion is removed. The underlying envy of the analyst, therefore, continues unappeased. As might be expected the dream aroused intense anxiety about the homosexual implication of the symbolic use of the penis in place of the breast. (Karush and Ovesey, 1961, p. 64)

The next example illustrates anal incorporation of a penis by a patient who symbolically misinterpreted his incapacities as castration:

A dependent male involved in a competitive effort to expand his business became increasingly fearful that he would fail. He repeatedly sought reassurance from the therapist who, of course, did not guarantee his success. The patient thereupon resorted to a magical solution which he revealed in a dream: *He felt ill and went to a hospital. The office of the physician resembled the office of the therapist. The doctor examined him and told him he needed an injection. He was put on a couch face down. The doctor filled a huge syringe and plunged the needle into his buttock. He felt an excruciating pain and then found his penis swelling to an enormous size. He stood up and began to urinate. The stream emerged with such great force and in such gargantuan quantities that it swept everything before it and flooded the whole hospital. He felt immense pride in his power, but awoke in a state of anxiety.* The dream is so obvious it needs no further interpretation except to note that the anxiety was not only a pseudohomosexual anxiety, but also reflected his fear of retaliation for his aggression (Karush and Ovesey, 1961, p. 64)

There are, of course, some heterosexual patients in whom true homosexual desires are "latent" (i.e., are not acted out). However, pseudohomosexual conflicts may coexist, and it is necessary for the therapist to sort out the various motivations in order to make the patient's behavior understandable. This point is illustrated by another example of anal incorporation:

A young man developed an ambidextrous technique for simultaneous genital and anal masturbation. He manipulated his penis with one hand while he pumped a thermometer in and out of his anus with the other. In the fantasy that accompanied this act, he imagined himself sandwiched between his mother and father as they were having intercourse. The father's penis entered the patient's anus, emerged as the patient's penis, and then penetrated the mother's vagina. The incorporative fantasy here had a mixed heterosexual, homosexual, and pseudohomosexual motivation. The patient not only secured sexual gratification of both varieties, but he also incorporated the father's penis and magically made use of its strength to repair his own weakness, not just in sexual situations but in nonsexual situations as well. The homosexual motivation was completely latent, for he had never had any homosexual experiences and engaged exclusively in heterosexual relationships. As one would suspect, however, he had an anxiety about being homosexual, but from the motivational breakdown of his fantasy it was clear that only a part of this anxiety was a true homosexual anxiety; the rest was a pseudohomosexual anxiety. While masturbating the sexual motivations were primary, but on other occasions the pseudohomosexual motivation of dependency took precedence. Nonsexual situations that called for assertion would arouse severe anxiety, and characteristically the patient would retire to the nearest lavatory, give his anus a few quick strokes with a thermometer, and then go out and try to assert himself. He always carried a spare thermometer with him for just such a contingency. Any associated erotic feelings from this act were incidental, for this was not primarily a sexual act; rather it was a magical attempt to achieve strength through a symbolic incorporation of the father's penis. The attempt was temporarily "successful," but the cost was an accentuation of both the homosexual and the pseudohomosexual components of the patient's anxiety. This case is a good example of the motivational complexities of thoughts, feelings, and acts concerned with either actual or symbolic homosexuality. (Ovesey, 1955b, pp. 168–69)

The unassertive male may attempt to deny his weakness by acting out its opposite, a compensatory striving for power. Dependency strivings and power strivings can thus be considered opposite sides of the same coin. The power-driven dependent male is continuously engaged in indiscriminate competition with other men, structuring such relationships in terms of dominance-submission. The relationships are thus symbolically placed in a male-female context in which the weaker male is forced to submit as a woman to the stronger male. This unconscious conception of power struggles between men derives originally from the child's oedipal rivalry with the father and, to a lesser extent, from sibling rivalry with brothers. Unfortunately the unassertive male's conviction of inadequacy is so strong that he concedes defeat in advance. The result is a chronic pseudohomosexual anxiety that flares up acutely in self-assertive crises as a paranoid expectation of homosexual assault, often symbolized in the form of anal rape.

This type of pseudohomosexual anxiety is particularly common in success phobias (Ovesey, 1962) where the patient fears that success will invite retaliative assault, defeat, castration, and humiliation. Often this is based on a projection of the patient's own competitive envy and his wish to steal the other man's strength.

A senior medical student was referred for consultation when he attempted to drop out of medical school three months prior to graduation. Though exclusively heterosexual in behavior, he was panic stricken that he was "becoming gay." With the advent of his senior year he had become increasingly uncertain of his desire to be a physician, and had become phobic of strange or dimly lit places because of fantasies that he would be "attacked from the rear." This had gradually merged into fantasies and dreams of being forced by the attacker to perform fellatio and to submit to anal intercourse which he would, with horror, discover he enjoyed. Subsequent analysis revealed these symptoms to be related not to repressed or latent homosexuality, but to issues of dependency and power derived from unresolved oedipal rivalry with his father, who was a physician. His fears disguised a wish for the very acts he rejected, for by them he would magically incorporate his father's powerful penis. His symptoms had been precipitated by the anticipation of receiving his M.D. degree which was unconsciously experienced as an oedipal attack on his father.

For some patients the fear of homosexual assault in a power struggle may lead to violent acts to ward off the humiliation of masculine pride associated with competitive defeat or dependent longings. Violence, sometimes directed at the therapist, may represent a restorative act to reclaim masculine self-esteem via aggressive demonstrations of power and strength, thus simultaneously denying passive and dependent long ings which are symbolically linked to femininity. The pseudohomosexual equation is thus reversed: I dominate, control, annihilate → therefore I am not castrated → I am not a woman → I am not a homosexual. Avoidance of violence may require the rapid identification of pseudohomosexual versus true homosexual anxiety, and active interpretation of the associated pseudohomosexual conflicts (Woods, 1972).

> A businessman entered treatment because of severe depression precipitated by competitive defeat at the hands of an old business rival. The patient's fantasy of wealth and status were shattered by his rival's completely legal though unethical manipulations which won a coveted contract. In treatment the patient alternated between fits of depression and fits of rage with plots of vengeance and violent destruction. He finally hired someone with instructions to beat and cripple the offender on the anniversary of the incident. The patient defiantly clung to his plan until one day he appeared panic-stricken following a dream. *In the dream he encountered a cripple on the street whose attempts to walk appeared ludicrous and caused the patient to laugh loudly. However, he jumped into the cripple's immensely powerful arms and was promptly stripped naked and impaled upon a huge erection. A crowd gathered and hooted at his humiliation.*
>
> The subsequent dream analysis led to the exposure of longstanding inhibitions in masculine assertiveness dealt with by overcompensatory power strivings. His shame concerned unconscious relief that his rival had rescued him from certain humiliation. His conviction was of gross inability to handle a masculine role of wealth and power, and through violent revenge he hoped to restitute his sense of masculine pride and deny his feeling of castration. Even his attempt at assertion via revenge was doomed, however, and he was shown to the world as preferring to offer himself passively for anal rape rather than face the alienation and destruction associated with masculine potency. No erotic motivations were apparent in this or in subsequent material. With clarification and psychotherapeutic focus upon the true issues, the patient's need for violence decreased and his contract with the underworld was cancelled. (Woods, 1972, p. 257)

Another way in which unconscious pseudohomosexual conflicts can be manifested in heterosexual men is in compulsive, driven, and stereotyped chauvinistic attitudes and behavior with women. Such chauvinism goes beyond that which merely reflects cultural bias. As with violence, it represents an attempt to ward off a sense of failure in masculine gender role adequacy, symbolized as homosexuality, through the depreciation of women. Such men are very vulnerable to anxiety about homosexuality when their defenses fail, or when their chauvinism is challenged as with an encounter with a capable and liberated woman (Woods, 1976).

It is clear from these examples that anxieties about being homosexual need not be motivated by the erotic desire for homosexual gratification but are frequently symbolic reflections of failure in gender-role adequacy—that is, the self-assessed degree to which one matches up to one's self-determined standards of masculinity. Any failure of masculine aspiration or any competitive defeat in power struggles, especially when associated with conscious or unconscious magical reparative fantasies which involve incorporation of a penis, may result in anxiety about homosexuality. Clinically, the great majority of such anxieties in males whose overt sexual behavior is exclusively heterosexual are in fact pseudohomosexual in nature. True homosexual motivation is either minor or, more commonly, absent. The therapist should not be distracted by the patient's preoccupation with homosexuality. He should deal instead with the pseudohomosexual anxiety by directing the patient's attention where it belongs, to the motivations of dependency and power. It is here, particularly, that a classical Freudian constitutional approach, with its insistence on homosexual explanations, can do great damage. The interpretation of overt homosexuality as an expression of inherent bisexuality is discouraging enough to a homosexual patient, but to explain dependency and power striving to a heterosexual patient on the same basis can be catastrophic. How can we expect a human being to come to terms with assumed innate tendencies that cannot be altered and to accept permanent deflation of his self-esteem? Worse yet, he is asked to make this sacrifice for socially unacceptable tendencies that he does not even have. The true problem lies in the integrative failure of self-assertion, not in homosexuality.

Homosexuality

In this section we shall formulate a compact psychodynamic framework within which any homosexual deemed suitable for psychotherapy can be understood and treated. Homosexuals seek genital contact with other men primarily for sexual gratification, that is, for orgastic pleasure. We shall focus, therefore, on the narrow but definitive therapeutic goal of establishing and maintaining pleasurable heterosexual behavior in a homosexual patient who desires to change his sexual orientation. The homosexual motivation, however, does not exist in isolation, but in association with the pseudohomosexual motivations of dependency and power. The latter two operate psychodynamically exactly as they do in the heterosexual, except, of course, that the reparative fantasies are not confined to the imagination but are overtly acted out. They not only enhance the force of the homosexual motivation, but their relative strengths determine the psychosocial structure of the homosexual relationship as well as the physical mechanics of the homosexual act. Pseudohomosexual anxiety is usually absent in confirmed overt homosexuals who have accepted their homosexuality, but may be severe in those who are still conflicted. For the former, anxieties about dependency and power strivings may therefore be experienced directly and need not be symbolically elaborated in the form of pseudohomosexuality. On the other hand, overt heterosexuals with "latent" homosexual desire, like the patient who masturbated anally with a thermometer, suffer from pseudohomosexual anxiety in the same way that totally heterosexual males do, but to an even greater degree.

Let us add now to the earlier descriptions of the dependency and power motivations and trace the developmental history of the homosexual motivation. Adaptationally, homosexuality is viewed as a variant form of sexual behavior into which some persons are driven by the intrusion of fear into the development of normal heterosexual function. The fear arises in response to unconscious fantasies of imagined danger, which, in turn, are generated by unconscious conflict. Developmentally, the fear has two separate and distinct points of origin, one preoedipal and the other oedipal, giving rise to two different types of homosexuality (Ovesey and Person, 1973).

The preoedipal root originates from unresolved separation anxiety during the separation-individuation phase of infantile development. In order to allay the separation anxiety, the infant resorts to unconscious fantasies of symbiotic fusion with the mother. These lead, however, to fears of engulfment and annihilation, which later, in the oedipal period, foreclose a normal resolution of the oedipus complex. Instead, to insure his survival, the boy transfers both his dependent and sexual needs to the father, thus laying down the basis for a homosexual choice of object. His partner's penis is equated with the mother's breast and incorporated orally and anally as a symbolic substitute. In this way he not only preserves his dependency but at the same time gratifies himself sexually.

The separation anxiety in preoedipally-determined homosexuality, because it originates so early in infancy, is never completely resolved and the initial introjective identification with the mother remains intact. For this reason, so-called preoedipal homosexuals inevitably have disturbances of self-identity, gender identity (biological sense of maleness), and gender role (psychological sense of maleness). Thus, their sense of self is fragmented, their gender identity is ambiguous, and their gender role is markedly effeminate. They often become cross-dressers and, under stress, whenever their dependent tie to a man is threatened, may revive the original fantasy of symbiotic fusion with the mother and regress to transsexualism (Person and Ovesey, 1974a, 1974b). Homosexuals of this type fall in the borderline area of psychopathology and comprise a minute segment of the homosexual population. Their homosexuality appears to be obligatory. They are generally totally committed to it and rarely express any wish to change their sexual orientation. Clinically, we doubt they have the capacity to do so, even were they to try, and it is unlikely that they would be amenable to any known treatment.

Homosexuality of oedipal origin differs from its preoedipal counterpart in that the separation-individuation process is essentially completed. The child emerges without undue separation anxiety and both his initial identification with the mother and any concomitant fusion fantasies are for the most part resolved. In consequence, his sense of self is intact and his male gender identity is firmly fixed. Unfortunately, despite the apparently good beginning, he encounters difficulties when he reaches the next phase of development, the oedipal phase. The normal resolution of his oedipus complex is impeded by fears that have been engendered by excessive parental discipline. Such fears may arise directly from implicit or explicit intimidation of sexual behavior, or they may arise indirectly from intimidation that inhibits nonsexual assertion. It makes little difference whether the initial focus of inhibition is sexual or nonsexual; ultimately, function in both areas will be impaired. The impairment occurs because inhibitions do not stay confined to the behavioral areas in which they are originally laid down, but tend to spread to other activities, and new inhibitions appear. The end result of excessive parental prohibition is a generalized inhibition of assertion which undermines the boy's capacity to assume the masculine role.

Under such circumstances, when the boy enters the oedipal period, he may view heterosexuality as a dangerous transgression for which the fantasied punishments are castration and death. He may respond to his oedipal impulses with a fear so great as to force a partial or complete withdrawal from sexual activity. Later, as the child grows, any heterosexual desires revive the earlier fear, and an inhibition of normal sexual behavior is established. Such an inhibition may result in a homosexual choice of object. The person reacts with such intense fear in relation to a heterosexual object that he either fails in performance, or he succeeds mechanically but experiences very little pleasure. His sexual need, however, continues unabated and is diverted to a "safer" homosexual object. The safety presumably derives from the reassuring presence of the penis which allays the homosexual's castration anxiety. Homosexuality of oedipal origin, viewed in this light, may be narrowly seen as a defense against castration anxiety by the phobic avoidance of the female genitals.

In a wider context, the faulty resolution of the oedipus complex not only alters the sexual orientation, but simultaneously inhibits competition with other men and intensifies regressive longings for dependency. As we have indicated, however, the ego integration of the oedipal homosexual is much stronger than that of the preoedipal homosexual in that there is little, if any, unresolved separation anxiety, the sense of self is not fragmented, and male gender identity is intact. Dependency, therefore, in oedipal homosexuality is not based on primitive mechanisms of introjective identification of whole or part objects. These mechanisms are characteristic of the earlier separation–individuation phase. In oedipal homosexuality, the dependency expresses the wich for magical aid at a later stage of development after differentiation between parent and child has been achieved, although the more primitive introjective mechanisms may appear in dreams and may be overtly acted out with homosexual partners. Likewise, neither is effeminacy in oedipal homosexuality based on an introjective identification with the mother; to the contrary, it is mimetic and reflects anxiety about gender role, that is, the sense of masculinity, rather than a disturbance in gender identity. Clinically, many oedipal homosexuals show no stigmata of effeminacy whatsoever, and in those in whom effeminacy exists, it is usually minimal and not present in the exaggerated fashion so characteristic of preoedipal homosexuals, particularly the drag queens. Homosexuals of oedipal origin comprise the great majority of the homosexual population. They all possess some residual heterosexuality, varying only in degree. Their homosexuality is preferential, not obligatory; hence, homosexuals deemed suitable for treatment come from this group. Many have the capacity to change their sexual orientation through psychotherapy, but relatively few are sufficiently motivated to make the attempt.

A theoretical approach to treatment derives logically from an understanding of the motivational basis for the homosexual patient's behavior. Variable combinations of the three motivations involved—sexual, dependency, and power—provide an adaptational formula by means of which the behavior of any overt or latent homosexual patient can be understood. The motivational component in ascendency at any given time can be inferred from the situational and emotional context in which the patient's behavior becomes manifest. It is clinically observable that the three motivations interact one with the other and are mutually reinforcing. Any contact, either actual or fantasied, by a homosexual with another man's body, particularly his genitals, for purposes of heightening dependency or power, usually acts as a sexual stimulant and cannot help but intensify the wish for homosexual gratification. Similarly, in the opposite direction, should the initial contact be for the purpose of achieving homosexual gratification, the homosexual act may weaken the patient's masculine identification, inhibit his assertive capacities, and thereby accentuate either passive strivings for dependency or compensatory strivings for power or some combination of both. The end result in many homosexuals is a vicious circle in which each motivation leads to the other, regardless of the motivational impetus with which the circle may have begun.

The therapeutic task in the preferential homosexual is to break this circle, to reverse the homosexual pattern, and to establish pleasurable heterosexual relations. This can be accomplished by decreasing the intensity of the three motivations that propel the patient toward genital

contact with male objects, while simultaneously enhancing sexual interest in women. The primary focus of the therapy must, of necessity, be
on the homosexual motivation and on the phobic avoidance, when
present, of the female genitals. Ultimately there is only one way that
the homosexual can overcome this phobia and learn to have heterosexual intercourse, and that way is in bed with a woman. In this respect,
psychotherapy of many preferential homosexuals is essentially like that
of any phobia. Sooner or later, the homosexual patient must make the
necessary attempts to have heterosexual intercourse, and he must make
them again and again until he is capable of sustained erection, penetration, and pleasurable intravaginal orgasm. The achievement of these
goals can be facilitated by helping the patient to gain insight into the
unconscious fantasies that convert the vagina into a source of danger.
We must emphasize, however, that such insights are the means to an
end; they are not the end itself.

The secondary focus of the therapy falls on the pseudohomosexual
motivations of dependency and power. In order to decrease the intensity of these motivations, the patient must become more "masculine"
by learning appropriate patterns of assertion and by increasing his
self-sufficiency. Here again the process can be aided by insight into
unconscious ideation. In some cases, a mere increase in nonsexual assertion may prove sufficient to initiate and maintain heterosexual behavior. This change may occur even in a brief therapeutic contact in which
major reliance is placed on support, advice, and guidance, with little
attempt either by the patient or the therapist to explore the unconscious basis of the homosexuality. However, the great majority of homosexuals do not respond to such a superficial approach, nor do they
overcome their difficulties very quickly.

The clinical data in the case that follows have been organized in a
way to demonstrate best the psychodynamics as they emerge in the
course of psychotherapy. Additional examples of successfully treated
homosexuals have been reported elsewhere (Ovesey, Gaylin, and Hendin, 1963). The emphasis falls on the meaning of the patient's behavior
as a basis for therapeutic technique, rather than on the technique itself.
We shall try, however, to indicate at least some of the more important
technical maneuvers, how they relate to the psychodynamics, and why
they are undertaken.

A thirty-year-old, unmarried Jewish man, employed as a junior executive in
an advertising agency, came to treatment because of mounting anxiety in his
work. His difficulties arose from extreme competitiveness with his colleagues, particularly male authorities, which created so much overt hostility
that his job was in jeopardy. The patient casually revealed that he was an
active homosexual, but he did not associate his homosexuality with his problems, nor was it a factor in his seeking treatment.

The patient was short and slightly built but somewhat big of hip. He was dapper, good-looking, and meticulously dressed. His speech, manner, and dress were all studied, and he fitted all the generalizations attributed to Madison Avenue. He was the youngest of three boys from a middle-class family. The father was a moderately successful professional man but weak, inadequate, and totally intimidated by the mother, who was the dominant member of the household. She was sharp-tongued, aggressive, self-willed, and obviously brighter than the father. Despite this severe picture, the patient was much fonder of her than of the father, the implication being that strength at least could be respected. The weakness of his father aroused nothing but contempt.

Throughout his childhood, the patient had had a constant feeling that he was not "manly" like other boys. First, he was small and at a competitive disadvantage physically and second, his mother resented never having had a daughter and attempted to feminize her sons, particularly the patient as he was the youngest. She kept him in girls' clothes until he was three, insisted that he wear his hair long for several years more, and taught him to do feminine chores. He dated girls all through high school, but began to be plagued by homosexual thoughts and feelings that he tried to push out of his mind. At nineteen he was drafted. He was frightened and bewildered and felt "different" from the other men who were generally larger and more aggressive. While feeling particularly unmanly, he had his first homosexual relationship. It followed a specific pattern, which was the prototype for all his subsequent activity. He insists first on satisfying his partner by manual masturbation. He then mounts the partner per anum and performs anal intercourse on him, but does not permit himself to be anally penetrated. He thus plays the dominant masculine role in the relationship, satisfying himself sexually while simultaneously enhancing his deflated masculinity by making a woman out of his partner.

The patient's heterosexual experience was limited to two occasions. In high school, he petted with a girl and gained pleasure from it, but never had an orgasm. His only experience with intercourse occurred reluctantly at the age of twenty-three with a seductive older woman. He performed successfully but mechanically and without pleasure.

The patient was treated psychoanalytically on the couch three times a week for three years for a total of 347 hours. The first major therapeutic maneuver occurred within the first few interviews and arose implicitly from the adaptational concept of homosexuality. The therapist asked why he did not list homosexuality as one of the symptoms he wished to have corrected. The patient was bewildered since it had never occurred to him that homosexuality was a neurotic symptom that might be cured. His brother, a homosexual like himself, was also in psychoanalysis, and his analyst believed that homosexuality was an inherited way of life that could not be altered. The therapist stated unequivocally that he could not agree with this position and that he considered homosexuality a psychiatric disorder treatable by psychotherapeutic means. The patient seemed genuinely confused, anxious, yet delighted.

The assumption by a therapist that homosexuality is a developmental and treatable phenomenon is basic to an adaptational therapy. Such an assumption, when communicated to a patient, can be a powerful therapeutic tool through arousal of hope that the pattern can be altered.

In the second month of therapy, the patient spontaneously began to date girls, although he made no attempt to become sexually involved with them.

The dating was accompanied by constant anxiety, which was invariably associated in the sessions with his father's weakness in the face of his mother's strength. He then became aware that there had been an earlier time in his childhood when he had viewed the father as a superman and when his disillusionment had produced great resentment. The therapist wondered what validity this view of his father's weakness had in his present life as an adult. Why did it still invoke the rage and frustration that it had stirred in his childhood? What possible effect could his father's strength or weakness have on his difficulties with women? Ultimately, such confrontations led the patient to recognize his own fears of standing up to his mother. He needed to enlarge his father, who would then protect him from the mother and by extension from all women. His present fear of women, therefore, not only recapitulated the original fear of his mother but also revived his anger with his father for failing to protect him. This insight led to increased anxiety, a feeling of depression, and a sense that he had "nobody".

He attempted to overcome his fear of women by forcing himself to engage in sex play with his dates. He was chagrined to find that fear so inhibited his aggressiveness that he felt more unmanly than ever. Nevertheless, he persisted and soon began to see a young woman, N., regularly. One night, aware of his failure to carry through sexually with her, even though she obviously was willing, he had the following dream: *He was with N. They were embracing. She petted his forehead and said, "Why don't you pluck your eyebrows?"*

This dream made clear to him for the first time how he equated a lack of "masculine" aggressiveness with feminity. He responded in his characteristic way by attempting to disprove this equation through intercourse with N. He could not sustain an erection, and the attempt proved a failure. Encouraged by the therapist, he continued to try, and finally, one month later, he successfully consummated the act. He exultantly described his success as a "real seduction," in which he took the "masculine, aggressive" role. His triumph ushered in a period of successful sexual relations with N. Except for occasional prematurity, he had no further potency problems, and he experienced increasing pleasure in his orgasms. At the same time, in therapy, he became more and more resistant. He tended to deny homosexual feelings and resisted discussions of those he could not deny. After six months of treatment, he felt that he was cured: he was ready to marry the girl, his problem on the job had disappeared, and he was free of anxiety.

The patient's rapid improvement had all the earmarks of a transference "cure." In his opening dream he had already indicated his magical expectations from therapy. Apparently he had acted on them and,in the transference, had supplanted the original weak father with a stronger one represented by the therapist. Thus magically armed with the latter's strength, he sufficiently overcame his fear of women to embark on his heterosexual adventures, but the fear was hardly resolved, nor were its unconscious origins understood. None of these dynamics was interpreted to the patient during this period. As long as the transference was useful in mobilizing heterosexual activity, it was thought best to leave it alone. With sexual inhibitions of this kind, nothing succeeds like success, and, after his successful involvement, the transference would eventually have to be faced, as indeed it was.

In the period that followed, the patient began increasingly to complain about both his girlfriend and his mother, both of whom were hostile and aggressive. As time went on, the focus of the therapy became the aggressive woman, his involvement with his mother, and his increasing difficulties with

N. All of these themes came to a head with a nightmare: *He was driving his car and skidded on some dog feces. He swirled around and around. N. was seated next to him. She was having a good time and enjoying it. Then he hit a lamp post, which broke in two. The top part fell away, but the bottom part shot up through the floorboard right under him, and he was in danger of being impaled on it.* He woke up in great anxiety.

The dream resulted from a bitter argument the patient had had with his girl, in which she disparaged his manliness and taunted him for being homosexual. That same day, while walking with her, he had stepped into some dog feces on the sidewalk. This dream was a key point in the patient's analysis because it revealed the unconscious fantasies responsible for his fear of women. He associated to the dream for weeks, producing peripheral, confirming dreams, until gradually he understood its meaning. The dream was couched in sexual terms and represented intercourse with a woman as a dirty, potentially dangerous act. It defined not only the penalties for sexual assertion with a woman but also, because it was prompted by a quarrel, for nonsexual aggression against her as well. In either case, the woman can castrate the man, appropriate the penis for herself, and then, as a phallic woman, force the man to submit in feminine fashion to her domination by shafting him per anum with her penis.

The patient felt disenchanted with N. and began to detach himself from her. She protested vehemently and became more abusive than ever. Her behavior stimulated renewed memories of his father's weakness, but now he saw the weakness as a product of his mother's destructiveness. She had castrated the father and usurped his role as a male. He feared that, if he continued his relations with women, the same thing could happen to him. For this reason, he felt ambivalent about becoming a man. Perhaps it was better to remain a homosexual after all. At least it was safer, as another man already had a penis and would not need his.

Up to that point, the patient had struggled mainly to free himself from the crippling distortion that all male-female relationships are duplications of the phallic mother-castrated father and the phallic mother-castrated child prototypes. His competitive difficulties with men had been checked and held in abeyance by his initial rapid success with women, but now, as he began to date again, his pseudohomosexual problem emerged in full force. He dated a great variety of women, seduced them as quickly as he could, and then discarded them. He returned in his sessions to the competition at work, talked of rivalry with his brothers, and of competition with men in general. Gradually, an oedipal trend emerged, in which he saw himself in conflict over women not only with his father but also in transference with the therapist. He had repetitive dreams of rivalry with his father for his mother. The following castration dream was typical of this period in the therapy: *He saw a huge crocodile floating down a river. Suddenly it grabbed hold of a small snake. The next thing he knew he had his hand in a toilet and was pulling out the snake.*

He identified the crocodile as the father (huge penis) and himself as the snake (small penis). The penalty for attempting access to his father's territory, the river (mother's vagina), is castration and death. He saves himself by pulling his penis out of the mother's vagina (the toilet or "dirty hole").

As he examined his oedipal rivalry, the patient began to talk of his father with less hostility and expressed longings for his love. At the same time, he was surprised to find a rise in homosexual desire, despite the fact that he was eminently successful in his heterosexual life. There were several dreams expressing his wishes for dependency on the therapist. Paradoxically, the idea of being dependent on a man, even though he wanted it, was distasteful to him and made him angry. It served only to confirm his sense of inadequacy and made him feel less masculine, more feminine, and, in the end, castrated. The validity of this symbolic sequence was bolstered for him by a number of dreams in which, through fellatio, he sucked strength from a stronger man's penis and so himself became more powerful. It became clear to him that homosexuality was not only a means of sexual gratification but also a magical way of borrowing another man's penis for his own use.

In the next few months, the patient came to grips with his ambivalence toward men—his competitiveness and his dependency. He explored their developmental origins, their dynamic interconnections—with one another and with his homosexuality. He began to understand that his hyperaggressiveness was a compensatory attempt not only to assert his manliness and ward off castration by the father but also to deny his dependency upon him. In essence he learned how the mechanisms we described earlier in our discussion of motivation applied specifically to him. He learned also that he need not look upon all men as his father, any more than he need look upon all women as his mother. Finally, he began to see that his ultimate answers lay neither in compensatory aggression with men nor in passive dependence nor in homosexuality, but in self-sufficiency, equality in relationships, and heterosexuality. Gradually, as he understood these things, he became less competitive with his father, with the therapist, and with other men, and his homosexual urges subsided.

His attention now turned toward his mother's seductive behavior which he had always found disgusting. He recognized that he must also have been attracted by it, or he would never have persisted so long with N. This recognition led into his oedipal feelings toward his mother, which, in turn, revived the oedipal rivalry with his father. He worked through both aspects of his oedipus complex and again terminated the relationship with N., which he had briefly resumed.

The following year brought great changes in the patient's behavior. He became much less competitive at work and also much more successful. He began to date less hysterically. It was no longer important to date and to have intercourse with every attractive woman he met. A marked alleviation of his competitiveness occurred after the interpretation of a particularly revealing dream: *There was a man screaming in anger. He was outraged and frustrated and upset. He was the owner of the Chrysler Building. It was in the midst of construction, and he had just received word that a start had been made on the Empire State Building, which would be bigger. Even before his building was completed, it was going to be only second best.*

The patient recognized that this dream represented his extreme competitiveness, his aspiration always to be the number-one man, the biggest and the best in any competition. As always, he used the penis and its size as the ultimate symbol of masculinity.

Shortly after this dream, the patient met L. and began an affair with her that eventually led to marriage. During the closing months of treatment, sexual relations with L. became extremely pleasurable, and his homosexual impulses abated almost completely. Therapy was terminated just before he married L., and the patient felt quite secure that homosexuality was a thing of the past for him. He was seen in follow-up four years later during a business crisis in which he felt his job was threatened. He had had a mild outbreak of both homosexual and pseudohomosexual fantasies, but he felt that he understood them, and he was certain that they would be transitory, which in fact they were. He was happy in his marriage, more relaxed, much less aggressive in his manner, and enormously successful vocationally. A year later all was still going well, and, in addition, he and his wife had a child. (Ovesey, Gaylin and Hendin, 1963, pp. 22–25)

Conclusion

Some psychodynamic formulations have been described which are useful in the treatment of heterosexual males with anxieties about being homosexual (pseudohomosexual anxieties) and in the treatment of homosexuality in homosexual males. Although we have dealt in this article only with the treatment of homosexuals who wish to become heterosexuals, we would like to emphasize that the pseudohomosexual motivations are equally important in the treatment of homosexual patients who have no interest in change, but whose homosexual relationships are fraught with conflict, instability, and transience. Just as with heterosexuals, it is often the pseudohomosexual components of dependency and power that undermine the formation and maintenance of both mutuality and stability in homosexual relationships. Insight into these areas may enable these individuals to achieve a much higher level of adaptive capacity within the context of their desired homosexual life-style.

REFERENCES

Defries, Z. 1976 Pseudohomosexuality in feminist students. *American Journal of Psychiatry* 133:400–404.

Kardiner, A.; Karush, A.; and Ovesey, L. 1959a. A methodological study of Freudian theory. I. Basic concepts. *Journal of Nervous and Mental Disease* 129:11–19.

———. 1959b. A methodological study of Freudian theory. II. The libido theory. *Journal of Nervous and Mental Disease* 129:133–43.

———. 1959c. A methodological study of Freudian theory. III. Narcissism, bisexuality, and the dual instinct theory. *Journal of Nervous and Mental Disease* 129:207–21.

———. 1959d. A methodological study of Freudian theory. IV. The structural hypothesis, the problem of anxiety, and post-Freudian ego psychology. *Journal of Nervous and Mental Disease* 129:341–56.

Karush, A., and Ovesey, L. 1961. Unconscious mechanisms of magical repair. *Archives of General Psychiatry* 5:55–69.

Ovesey, L. 1954. The homosexual conflict: An adaptational analysis. *Psychiatry* 17:243–50.

———. 1955a. The pseudohomosexual anxiety. *Psychiatry* 18:17–25.

———. 1955b. Pseudohomosexuality, the paranoid mechanism, and paranoia: An adaptational revision of a classical Freudian theory. *Psychiatry* 18:163–73.

———. 1956. Masculine aspirations in women: An adaptational analysis. *Psychiatry* 19:341–51.

———. 1962. Fear of vocational success: A phobic extension of the paranoid reaction. *Archives of General Psychiatry.* 7:82–92.

———. 1969. *Homosexuality and pseudohomosexuality* (a compilation of Ovesey, 1954, 1955a, 1955b, and 1956, and Ovesey, Gaylin, and Hendin, 1963). New York: Jason Aronson.

Ovesey, L.; Gaylin, W.; and Hendin, H. 1963. Psychotherapy of male homosexuality: psychodynamic formulation. *Archives of General Psychiatry* 9:19–31.

Ovesey, L., and Person, E. 1973. Gender identity and sexual psychopathology in men: A psychodynamic analysis of homosexuality, transsexualism and transvestism. *American Academy of Psychoanalysis Journal* 1:53–72.

Person, E., and Ovesey, L. 1974a. The transsexual syndrome in males. I. Primary transsexualism. *American Journal of Psychotherapy* 28:4–20.

———. 1974b. The transsexual syndrome in males. II. Secondary transsexualism. *American Journal of Psychotherapy* 28:174–93.

Woods, S. 1972. Violence: Psychotherapy of pseudohomosexual panic. *Archives of General Psychiatry* 27:255–58.

———. 1976. Some dynamics of male chauvinism. *Archives of General Psychiatry* 33:63–65.

19 / A Psychotherapeutic Approach to Homosexual Men

DAVID S. SANDERS

Treatment of patients who have a history of homosexual behavior has been, over the years, diverse and sometimes bizarre (Weinberg and Bell, 1972). Methods of treatment have included every method used by psychiatrists in managing problems of mental illnesses, including electroshock treatment, lobotomy, aversion therapy, castration, hormone therapy, formal psychoanalysis, psychoanalytic psychotherapy, and group therapies of various types. These methods have had mixed therapeutic results; reported success in changing sexual orientation is from zero to 50 percent. These diverse approaches are the result of individual psychiatrists viewing homosexuality in different ways, but underlying these forms of treatment have been certain common—but doubtful—assumptions, values, and ways of framing the problem that may obscure an appropriate therapeutic approach to the homosexual patient. First, the term "homosexual" has been applied to a wide range of behavior from the single adolescent episode of homosexual behavior to a long-term pattern of homosexual behavior; sometimes men involved in these very different kinds of behavior have been described, in a universal sweep, as homosexuals. Second, a tendency toward generalization, or the notion that all persons who exhibit homosexual behavior fall into a single group, often affects treatment. Schizophrenic, sociopathic, child molesting, and mentally retarded homosexuals are all lumped together, and instead of exploring the diverse aspects of personality functioning, the therapist or the writer discussing homosexuality has focused primarily, sometimes exclusively, on the communality of their homosexual behavior. Third, therapists have too often focused on the homosexual orientation and behavior of a patient as if they caused the personality difficulties the patient has presented; thus homosexual behavior has been seen as the cause, or the result of, depression, anxiety, psychosis, personality disorder, or the patient's being stuck at a particular stage of psychosexual development. All aspects of personality are viewed through the screen of deviant sexuality. This approach would be paralleled, in heterosexual patients, by explaining their psychopathological problems as caused by their heterosexuality. Fourth, most studies of homosexual persons have been studies of patients, that is, people who have come for psychological help. What the patients tell the therapist about the problems of homosexuality is assumed to be true of nonpatient homosexuals. Fifth, societal prejudice against homosexual behavior is strong, and often incorporated by the therapist; hence therapeutic practices often have seemed less designed to help the patient than to enforce the values of the therapist on the patient. The zeal to change the homosexual seems not unrelated to that of the exorcists of the devil in the women at Salem and the nuns at Loudun.

These value-laden, sometimes obscurantist, approaches to therapy have had the approval of the mental health professions. With his customary objectivity, Freud (1951) said in his letter to an American mother, "Homosexuality is assuredly no advantage but it is nothing to be ashamed of, no vice, no degradation. It cannot be classified as an illness; we consider it to be a variation of the sexual functions produced by a certain arrest of sexual development." Nonetheless, until recent years homosexual behavior was diagnosed by the mental health professions as prima facie evidence of mental illness or at least unresolved oedipal difficulties and castration fears. A number of workers (including Bieber et al., 1965, Hatterer, 1970, Socarides, 1968, Hadden, 1958, and Bergler, 1951) took a more extreme position. Believing that the homosexual man had severe psychoneurotic problems and that homosexuality was incompatible with a reasonably happy life, these therapists insisted that treatment should be focused on changing the orientation from homosexuality to heterosexuality. They reported various degrees of success, but little reliable published evidence exists indicating that these results were long-lasting. Such was the range of the prevalent professional opinion until the 1970s, though some eminent psychiatrists such as Marmor (1965) expressed strong dissent. In 1974 the American Psychiatric Association and other professional organizations changed their classification system for mental illness so that homosexual behavior itself was not ipso facto a sign of mental disorder; this change occurred not without considerable debate and difference of opinion within the health professions. These differences and debates continue today.

With this history in mind, I will discuss the issues of evaluation, appraisal, and treatment of men who come for help in which homosexual behavior is part of the presenting symptoms. I will not discuss the problems, or lack of problems, of the 4 percent of the population of the United States—approximately five million homosexual men between the ages of eighteen and sixty-five—who do not seek treatment. Nor will I discuss nonpatient homosexual men, described by Hooker (1965, 1957), Saghir and Robins (1973), and Weinberg and Williams (1974), whose sexual orientation seems to be compatible with a productive, happy, and ethical life, many of whom function quite well. Hence, this chapter is concerned only with homosexual men who seek help.

Patients seek therapy with various motivations and expectations, and the approach to evaluation and treatment will vary with the case. Here are some of the different ways patients may present themselves:

1. A seventeen-year-old boy who is brought by his parents after they came home early one night and walked in on their son having sex with a male friend.
2. An adolescent young man who announces to his parents that he is a homosexual as a climax to a fight they are having.
3. A man in his early twenties who exhibits a panic reaction about the onset of conscious homosexual desires in conjunction with a developing thought disorder and increasing delusional thinking.
4. A quiet twenty-four-year-old man who comes for treatment after having several homosexual experiences and asks, "Which way shall I go?"
5. Men of all ages who seek help following the breakup of a homosexual love relationship and who are depressed and may be suicidal or increasingly alcoholic or may find themselves taking increasing amounts of drugs.
6. A man who may or may not be married who arrives in an acute anxiety state after being arrested in a public toilet or in a public park and is sent by a judge as a condition of probation.
7. A man in his mid-fifties who comes with his wife, after he has announced that he wants to leave her and their three chidlren. He gives a history of increasing impotence and expresses fears of homosexuality. On detailed inquiry it turns out that he has had fleeting homosexual thoughts for the past six months.
8. A man in his early thirties who wants to change his sexual orientation after having lived as a practicing homosexual for the last ten years. He has never been able to have a sustained relationship and has only been able to have homosexual relationships after he has had several alcoholic drinks.
9. A man in his early thirties who has been passed over for a promotion when his employers found out or suspected that he was homosexual and arrives depressed.
10. A forty-year-old man who, living with a homosexual lover, is experiencing impotence or premature ejaculation.

Men who come for treatment can be any age. Some function in the world competently and productively. Others function poorly. Sometimes they are in crisis, sometimes not. They can be divided into a wide number of diagnostic categories. Some are psychotic, some neurotic, and others have severe personality disorders. Some are faced with overwhelming problems. They come at different stages in the life cycle and have all the developmental crises that are appropriate to each life stage. Some are intelligent, some are not. Some have a high ethical standard, some do not. In addition, they often come with experiences of family or societal rejection or both. Since they are members of society, they have often incorporated society's views of homosexuality, causing internal self-hate and low self-esteem.

A rational approach to treatment should be based on etiology, but here a great difficulty appears: the etiology of homosexual behavior remains unclear. Some have suggested genetic, organic, or hormonal causes. Others claim it is a learned pattern of behavior. Among the psychological causes of homosexual behavior are such factors as incest-conflict, identification with the mother, fear of women, a weak or absent father as a model for identification, effeminacy in the father, defects in parenting, mothers who depreciate heterosexuality, and other life experiences that lead to psychodynamic conflicts. However, it is difficult to isolate any one factor inasmuch as heterosexual patients often have the same life experiences and psychodynamic conflicts; there appears to be no single route to homosexual outcome. Even if one or more factors are isolated in an individual case, generalization beyond the individual case must proceed with great caution. Moreover, etiology is complicated because erotic interest in the same sex may vary from a lot to a little. Some men behave as exclusive homosexuals, but some men have histories or interests which combine homosexuality and heterosexuality. As Kinsey, Pomeroy, and Martin (1948, p. 639) have stated, "Males do not represent two discrete populations, heterosexuals and homosexuals. The world is not divided into sheep and goats. It is a fundamental of taxonomy that nature rarely deals with discrete categories."

As with any patient who comes for treatment, a careful evaluation is needed. Relevant initial inquiries include: Why did the patient come at this time? What are the difficulties? What is the patient's motivation for treatment? What does the individual want out of his treatment? What is the life-style of the patient? Most homosexuals come to treatment with the same problems as heterosexuals, that is, difficulty in finding or sustaining relationships, depression after or before the breakup of an important relationship, difficulty in self-realization, various neuroses, depressions, psychotic reactions, and psychophysiologic disorders. Most of these patients are not interested in changing their sexual orientation and should be treated as any other patient. Others are unhappy about their homosexuality and would like to function heterosexually. If they have a wish to change their sexual orientation, they should be given the opportunity to have this possibility evaluated.

Careful study of the patient's psychopathology, life-style, and psychody-namics are essential before a treatment plan can be formulated. Special problems of life-style—including socially or physically dangerous be-havior—need to be evaluated. Special areas in relation to the patient's homosexuality need to be assessed, particularly when the patient comes with a stated goal of making a transition to heterosexuality.

If change to heterosexuality is a desired goal, the following list of factors (a variation and expansion of factors described by C. W. Wahl in 1967) must be examined:

1. *Age.* The older the individual, the less likely that change will take place. If the individual is over thirty, change is difficult.
2. *The length of time a patient has been a practicing homosexual.* The longer the time, the less chance there is of change.
3. *The quality, frequency, and onset of homosexual fantasies.* Are they exclusive or not? What are the preferential fantasies during masturba-tion? Are there homosexual fantasies present during heterosexual inter-course?
4. *Presence of heterosexual experiences, wishes, fantasies, and arousal pat-terns.* Has the patient's experience been exclusively homosexual? Ab-sence of heterosexual experience or arousal gives a poorer prognosis for change.
5. *Feelings about sex with women.* Is there a horror or fear of the female genitals?
6. *Degrees of interest in women.* Is there any interest in friendship with women?
7. *Social life.* What kind of social life does the patient have? Are all of his friends or social relationships with other homosexuals? If so, is this a social pattern that is difficult to change?
8. *Effeminacy.* How effeminate is the patient? If quite effeminate, change is difficult.
9. *Envy.* How much does the patient envy women? If a lot, change is difficult.
10. *Ego-syntonicity of homosexual feelings.* Does the individual feel at home with his homosexual feelings, or are they ego alien? Does he want to get rid of this part of his personality? If the homosexual feelings are ego-syntonic, there is little chance to change.
11. *Other sexual difficulties, such as fetishism or sexual sadomasochism.* Their presence complicates gender reorientation.
12. *If the patient wants to change, why?* Is his picture of his changed life a realistic one?
13. *Love relationships.* The ability to relate to another person in a love relationship over time indicates the capacity to change or adjust to a heterosexual life-style.
14. *Nonsexual uses of sexuality.* How ingrained are the patient's nonsexual uses of sexuality? How does he use sex to handle problems of aggression, control, power, and submission?
15. *Dreams.* Are dreams exclusively homosexual or do they include hetero-sexuality? If exclusively homosexual, change is difficult.
16. *Psychopathology.* If there is a primary disorder such as schizophrenia, the treatment of the disorder takes precedence over change-oriented therapy.

As in most therapies, the goals of therapy change, expanding or contracting, as the therapeutic encounter unfolds. Appropriate treatment of homosexual patients requires a nonjudgmental view which permits the patient to set his own goals, rather than encouraging the patient to move into areas where he has no interest. While there may be no advantage to being homosexual in a homophobic society, a therapist, in order to deal with homosexual patients successfully, must be able to accept the fact that homosexually oriented patients can live respectful, productive, and meaningful lives. Living in a culture that is homophobic, the patient frequently has incorporated the antihomosexual bias of the culture and projects this on the therapist. This frequently becomes one of the early transference manifestations that needs to be handled.

The initial goals of therapy, after a careful, detailed life review, are the restoration of morale and the diminution of the depression and anxiety that usually occur. Viewing the homosexual patient in this way permits the therapist to see him as an individual experiencing the vicissitudes of his own particular development, rather than a stereotyped "homosexual development." If sexual orientation is not the presenting problem, the homosexual patient has the right to be treated for his anxiety, depression, psychosis, and psychophysiologic disorders in the same way as the heterosexual patient is treated, without an attempt being made to change his sexual orientation.

The varied circumstances under which patients present themselves were listed earlier. Sometimes this presenting behavior is a symptom. Sometimes it is pseudohomosexuality, that is, it disguises issues of power and dependence in homosexual guise. Other times it is a massive cortical organization of sexual preference that is resistant to change. The boy having the psychotic breakdown should be treated for his psychosis. Frequently the homosexuality issue then evaporates. The fifty-year-old depressed man who thinks he is a homosexual will be better served by dealing with his depression, middle-age crisis, and impotence than by dealing directly with his homosexual thoughts.

In those patients who are motivated to change their sexual orientation, it is important to clarify what is meant as "cure" or change. In an individual who has the ability to react erotically to both men and women, the patient is helped to clarify his fear of women. He then may become increasingly potent and satisfied in this type of relationship and may be urged to curtail his relationships with men. "Cure" does not necessarily mean the ability to lose the desire or the ability to react erotically to same-sex partners, but means the ability to derive sufficient satisfaction from heterosexuality that the patient does not overtly practice homosexuality. In addition "cure" means to be aware of the nonsexual motivations that trigger homosexual yearnings, so that when they arise, they can be analyzed and are of short duration.

Various outcomes are possible as a result of treatment. Some men who do not have an aversion reaction to the opposite sex can move from sex with a man to a woman, depending on the mood or occasion. Other men can, as a result of treatment, be steered to a basically heterosexual life. "My homosexual period gave pain and pleasure, but I'm glad I made the decision I did. I like my family and don't think I'd have liked to live a homosexual life." Other kinds of adjustment include, "I'm devoted to my wife and children, but every Wednesday night I go out to the baths," and "I only have homosexual thoughts when I masturbate."

While there are those who claim that more significant and enduring changes of sexual orientation are possible, given prolonged psychoanalytic treatment, there are no follow-up studies; many of the reports are anecdotal ones of single case histories.

The psychological approach to those who come for treatment asking for a change varies among different practitioners. Some change-oriented therapists encourage change openly, defining heterosexual performance as the only way to a mentally healthy life. Others, more subtly, analyze everything related to homosexual thoughts or feelings of the patient as bad or neurotic or sick, and everything related to heterosexuality as good. Some of the more influential approaches to change-oriented therapy are summarized here.

Kolb and Johnson (1955) in their early work describe the precipitating factors that lead to the overt eruption of homosexual behavior as the "unconscious permissiveness of one parent with the other parent more or less condoning. . . . It is suggested that overt homosexuality, as well as other aberrant behavior, may be induced or persist through the technique employed by a therapist" (p. 507).

They suggest that the therapist, once he has a grasp of the psychodynamics in the case, prohibit the expression of homosexual behavior and interrupt treatment if the homosexual behavior is resumed "until the patient is willing to give up the behavior and face the consequent frustration anxiety and rage that then ensues." Ovesey (1965) has pointed out that those persons who are exclusively homosexual are phobic of women, and of their genitals in particular, and suggests that while analysis of the phobias is important, this phobia like others is only resolved by the patient's facing the phobic situation, and further suggests that the only way that individuals will ultimately resolve these fears is "in bed with a woman" (p. 222) repeatedly until potency and pleasure are achieved. Bieber et al. (1963) list the following reasons that homosexuals are resistant to treatment, and says that these reasons constitute the core fear complex around which a defensive structure of denial and resistance is organized:

1. Unconscious fear of discovering heterosexual wishes and feelings,
2. Greater fear of acting on them,

3. Fear of discovering the inevitable emotional bankruptcy of homosexuality and
4. Fear of an inability to shift to heterosexuality. (p. 265)

Anna Freud (1949) notes that in her experience men "turn towards the other sex when they realize that the 'strong man' whom they chose as a partner represents their own lost masculinity" (p. 195).

Marmor (1975) noted about types of change-oriented therapy that the common denominator seems to be the discouraging of homosexuality in a context of open and warm acceptance of the patient by the therapist.

While these approaches are helpful in a minority of cases, they are unrewarding in a majority of cases, as they seem to be at least in part based upon society's antihomosexual prejudices and stereotypes. They are also oversimplified, overlooking and discounting the complexity of the etiological factors causing homosexuality and the enormous difficulties and sometimes the impossibility of making a change in sexual orientation.

An important part of any therapy aimed at a change in sexual orientation is the necessity not only to change sexual choices, but to change social patterns as well. Those individuals with significant attachments to the homosexual community will have great difficulty in making the sexual shift from a homosexual to a heterosexual life-style.

The treatment considerations include clarification and working through of family issues, dependency needs, distorted perceptions, and psychodynamic conflicts as well as the problems of transference and resistance. Treatment methods also include patient-therapist collaboration in dream analysis and character analysis as well as the provision of a setting in which the patient can have a "corrective emotional experience." These issues are of therapeutic importance for the homosexual patient whether a change in sexual orientation is desired or not.

There are some homosexual patients who use obsessive personality mechanisms and defenses. In some of them the obsessive rumination is: "Am I homosexual and is it possible to change and how do I go about it?" They spend many years speculating about change, never settling on either a homosexual attachment or a heterosexual one. They frequently describe their treatment as a failure. From their descriptions of treatment, they often seem to have been with change-oriented therapists who continually encouraged them to change their sexual orientation. The therapeutic task with these difficult patients is to identify the obsessive nature of the ruminations and to deal with it. This rumination prevents them from making friends and developing supportive social arrangements and interferes with their sexuality, whether heterosexual or homosexual.

Even the most optimistic psychoanalytic treatment reports suggest that only about 25 to 30 percent of highly motivated men with a history of homosexual behavior can make the gender choice change. How should therapists treat the large majority of homosexual patients for whom a change in sexual orientation is not possible or desired? If these patients are put into the arena of change-oriented therapy, what will be the outcome? As Frank (1974) has often stated, one of the goals of therapy is the restoration of morale. Morale is unlikely to be restored in a setting where the therapist considers a change in sexual orientation to be essential for the successful outcome of treatment.

There are reports in the literature that suggest that aversive therapy has in some highly motivated individuals been able to suppress homosexual feelings, urges, and actions and permit the development and practice of heterosexual behaviors. These reports omit any detailed dynamic descriptions of the subjects and omit detailed follow-up. These workers claim varying degrees of success. The alleged success is not surprising. Aversive therapy is a form of behavior therapy, and as W. H. Auden[1] said, "Of course, Behaviorism 'works.' So does torture. Give me a no-nonsense, down to earth behaviorist, a few drugs, and simple electrical appliances, and in six months I will have him reciting the Athanasian Creed in public."

Little has been written about the tasks and goals of therapy with homosexual patients where sexual preference change is not a central issue. Most reports skim over this matter with comments such as, "supportive therapy was offered." But if the sexual preference of the individual is accepted, major areas are opened up for work in personality change and development. These include analysis of ways in which sex is used for nonsexual aims, such as dependence and aggression. One therapeutic task is to free the patient to use sex for sexual pleasure, recognizing, as Stoller (1976) has recently theorized, that sexual excitement includes more than loving impulses. The homosexual patient is as frequently inhibited sexually and has as many sexual distortions as the heterosexual patient who comes for treatment. Therapy can help with this. Basic issues of self-worth, distortions of body image, sharing, and mutuality can be worked through. The therapist who has a knowledge of successful homosexual life-styles and patterns and their diversity can aid the homosexual patient to see what alternatives are available for him. The therapist then can help him to work toward these alternatives rather than continue with repetitive patterns of deceit and despair that reconfirm his low self-esteem. Therapy can also clarify both the intrapsychic and the societal causes of low self-esteem including societal prejudices incorporated into the patient, and can help him deal with them. Therapeutic work which accepts the patient's sexual orientation permits the therapist and patient to work on disorders of mood, thought,

1. Auden, W. H., *A Certain World, A Commonplace Book* (New York: The Viking Press, 1970), p. 33.

and behavior without relating everything to the patient's homosexuality. In addition, the knowledgeable therapist can help explore the apprehensions that the patient has about homosexuality, such as the inevitability of a lonely old age; homosexuals weather this crisis as well or as poorly as anyone else without children. As Tripp (1970) puts it: "To work toward reachable goals almost instantly lifts depression and opens the door to a stream of small and larger successes" (p. 246). And as Gagnon and Simon (1973) say:

> It is necessary to move away from an obsessive concern with the sexuality of the individual and attempt to see the homosexual in terms of the broader attachments that he must make to live in the world around him. Like the heterosexual, the homosexual must come to terms with the problems that are attendant upon being a member of society: He must find a place to work, live with or without his family, be involved or apathetic to political life, find a group of friends to talk with and be with, fill his leisure time usefully or frivolously, handle all the common and uncommon problems of impulse control and personal gratification and in some manner socialize his sexual interests. . . . Not only are there as many ways of being homosexual as there are of being heterosexual but the individual homosexual, in the course of his everyday life, encounters as many choices and crises as the heterosexual. (p. 142)

In addition to the range of personality problems that homosexual men present, they also come with relationship problems and problems of sexual dysfunction. The relationship problems can sometimes be handled by conjoint therapy with two male partners in which the therapeutic work is directed toward their communication difficulties, clearing up their distorted expectations, and helping them to work out a relationship contract that can meet the needs and desires of both individuals. At other times the conjoint work, as with heterosexual couples, is directed toward helping the couple separate in a way that is not psychologically destructive to either party. Homosexually oriented men also come for help with disorders of sexual functioning such as premature ejaculation and impotence. The techniques of therapy developed by Masters and Johnson (1970) and further elaborated by Kaplan (1974) are applicable in these situations with appropriate modifications applied to the specific psychodynamics of the same-sex couple.

Therapists inexperienced in treating homosexual patients must realize that there are aspects of the homosexual life-style and development that differ from heterosexual life-style and development.

One of the most important of these aspects is "coming out." Coming out is the process in which the young homosexual person labels himself as a homosexual in terms of self-identity and this usually includes an increasing amount of overt homosexual behavior. It is a step in the transition to a homosexual identity. It is not a cause of homosexuality. Coming out is a process in which he finds out that there are others like himself, that not all fit the societal stereotypes of mental illness and degeneracy, and that there are other members of the homosexual sub-culture with whom he can identify and who can become role-models for him. Further, he discovers an existing network of social institutions such as bars, social clubs, baths, newspapers, and peer groups. These can be supportive in this transitional phase of coming to terms with his homosexual identity. The "coming out" process is usually a source of psychological relief of tension and anxiety. This process is somewhat different than that faced by members of other minority groups in that the homosexual usually did not have support and role-models for his homosexuality during his early development.

For some, this coming out is a slow process, and for others, a sudden moment of self-recognition. It usually is experienced as an integrating factor in personality functioning. The homosexually oriented person may come for evaluation and treatment prior to, during, or after this "coming out," and where he is in relation to it will affect his view of himself, his homosexuality, and his future, and it must be taken into consideration in his evaluation and treatment. "Coming out" in the preceding sense does not necessarily mean a public admission of homo-sexuality to family and fellow workers, but is rather a psychological sense of self-identity. Dank's (1971) work suggests that this process is happening progressively earlier in the life cycle of homosexuals because of an increasing public tolerance of homosexuality.

While etiological factors are important in understanding the homo-sexual man's development and personality functioning, the functioning is greatly influenced by the consequences of the establishment of the homosexual life-style. The positive and negative experiences after com-ing out, the friends made thereafter, the difficulties or successes in work, the establishment of a social network, the difficulties with family or the law, the ability to have close relationships, the experiential differ-ences between homosexual and heterosexual life-styles, and the incor-poration of self-hate attitudes all affect personality functioning as much as, if not more than, the original oedipal conflict or the presence of a weak or absent father or a seductive, deprecating mother. The social difficulties in being homosexual depend, in part, on the setting and its openness and acceptance. The difficulties that the homosexual will face living in San Francisco or New York, for example, are different in type and quantity from the difficulties in a small town in Alabama or Iowa.

Classification of homosexual men by preferred specific anatomical role in sexual performance such as "insertor" or "insertee" can be helpful in understanding the psychodynamics of a specific individual as long as it is not used as some summary statement about the functioning of the total personality. Many homosexual men easily change positions and roles during or between sexual encounters. It is a mistake to per-ceive homosexual relationships as simply a copy of male-female rela-tionships with one partner having "masculine" qualities and the other "feminine" qualities, although some men do consistently play one or the other of these roles. Many men have same-sex relationships in which neither man perceives himself in a "woman's role."

As many have noted, most homosexuals do not fit society's stereotype of effeminacy. The range of behavior is from markedly effeminate to hypermasculine. However many homosexuals have some degree of feminine identification, however distorted, and have gone through an early life history of "being a sissy." For some these identifications are egosyntonic and for others, ego alien. They have a variety of symbolic meanings, and their exploration and analysis should be part of the therapeutic process. Some homosexual life-styles permit the overt expressions of these "feminine" characteristics in social settings. They can take the form of "camp" behavior, transient transvestism, or relatively strongly ingrained characterological imperatives. For example, some passive men can only express hostile or aggressive feelings when "camping." Many homosexuals can shift between these different types of behavior with ease.

Many homosexual men are more promiscuous than most heterosexual men. Without the institutions of marriage, the family, and society's other controls, this is not surprising. Without these sanctions many heterosexual men would probably be equally promiscuous. There are however some homosexual patients who use promiscuity as a means to avoid intimate personal relationships, as a means to reinforce their low self-esteem, or as a way of reducing tension, anxiety, depression, or loneliness by constantly looking for impersonal sexual contacts. This issue needs to be clarified and worked on during the treatment process.

While sexual sadomasochism may not be more prevalent among homosexual men than heterosexual men, special sadomasochistic bars, advertisements for sadomasochistic partners in homosexually oriented newspapers, and a plentiful supply of sadomasochistic homosexual pornography are elements of the homosexual scene. Contact with this type of sexual activity is present in the life histories of many homosexuals. Its ready availability may touch the aggressive or self-punishing part of an individual's personality, and it is important in understanding the functioning and adaptation of the individual patient. Since sexual arousal patterns are influenced by cultural directives and individual experience as well as by individual psychodynamics, this type of sexual practice which can be physically dangerous needs to be explored.

Countertransference problems that are evoked by therapeutic work with homosexual patients also require attention. Before treating a homosexual patient, the therapist should have recognized and worked through his or her personal prejudices and derogatory attitudes as well as those of society in general. Knowledge of the homosexual subculture, absence of zeal to change a homosexual to a heterosexual orientation, and a noncoercive professional assessment of motivation are required.

Countertransference issues must not be overlooked. There has recently appeared a substantial body of work by homosexual men who have described their therapeutic experiences where well-trained therapists seemed coercive or prejudiced.

One of the most difficult features of evaluating young homosexuals is dealing with their families. If the families know about the homosexuality and are concerned for their son, they often come asking for change, which is not desired by the patient. They feel as if they have failed and blame themselves and each other as well as their son. They are sometimes only willing to support therapy if the goal is change. A therapist who has a balanced view of the matter can help in these situations by explaining that cause is still unclear, that there is no evidence that homosexuals as a group are unhappier than heterosexuals, that many live productive and full lives, and that while change is possible for some, it is neither possible nor desirable for all. They can help their son by being loving and supportive of his choice of sexual orientation, for after all it is his life to lead. Occasionally family therapy or conjoint or individual therapy for the parents can help. As frequently happens in crisis, forces that lead to resolution can effect more integrated functioning of the family system and can assist in the therapy of the individual patient whether the goal is change or not. It is important also for the family to be informed that not all family relationships between a homosexual man and his family are strained. Different arrangements as to the openness about the homosexual commitment are present, from covert knowledge to nondiscussion to open knowledge and acceptance.

Wives or female lovers of homosexual men need to be taken into consideration. Often a man with a strong preferential homosexual orientation marries in the hope that this will change his sexual orientation. It does not. He continues with a marriage and has extramarital homosexual relationships. Some intrafamilial or external crisis may bring the husband's homosexuality to the wife's attention. Whether to continue the marriage or get a divorce or continue the marriage while the husband is in treatment are among the most difficult clinical problems to be faced. These decisions are particularly difficult in cases in which there are children. If the couple divorces and the man lives as a homosexual, decisions about when, if, and how to convey information about the patient's life-style to the children are issues to be evaluated.

The wives or female lovers of homosexual men often blame themselves for being inadequate because of their inability to aid a homosexually oriented man to become heterosexual. They often need therapeutic help to deal with this frustrated ambition and to help with their conflicted experience of having been sexually and emotionally involved with a homosexual man.

The confusion of gender orientation, the challenging of old psychoanalytic assumptions, and the differences in life-styles can make work with homosexual patients difficult, sometimes confusing, but often gratifying. If the goals are clearly worked out and if the therapist is free of prejudice and ignorance about homosexual life, the therapist can help patients to grow and develop whether the goals include change in sexual orientation or not.

REFERENCES

Bieber, I. 1965. Clinical aspects of male homosexuality. In J. Marmor, ed., *Sexual inversion: The multiple roots of homosexuality* (New York: Basic Books).

Bieber, I., et al. 1963. *Homosexuality: A psychoanalytic study.* New York: Basic Books.

Bergler, E. 1951. *Counterfeit sex.* New York: Grune & Stratton.

Dank, M. J. Coming out in the gay world. *Psychiatry* 34 (May 1971):182.

Feldman, M. P., and MacCulloch, 1965, The application of anticipatory avoidance learning to the treatment of homosexuality. *Behav. Res. Ther.*, 2:165–83; Pergamon Press Ltd., England.

Frank, J. D. 1974. Psychotherapy: The restoration of morale. *American Journal of Psychiatry* 131:271–74.

Freud, A. 1949. Some clinical remarks concerning the treatment of cases of male homosexuality. *International Journal of Psychoanalysis* 30: 195.

Freud, S. 1951. Letter to an American mother. *American Journal of Psychiatry* 107:786.

Gagnon, J., and Simon, W. 1973. *Sexual conduct: The social sources of human sexuality.* Chicago: Aldine.

Hadden, S. B. 1958. Treatment of homosexuality by individual and group psychotherapy. *American Journal of Psychiatry* 114:810.

Hatterer, L. J. 1970. *Changing homosexuality in the male.* New York: McGraw-Hill.

Hooker, E. 1957. The adjustment of the male overt homosexual. *Journal of Projective Techniques* 21:18–31.

———. 1965. Male homosexuals and their "Worlds." In J. Marmor, ed., *Sexual Inversion: The multiple roots of homosexuality.* (New York: Basic Books).

Kallman, F. J. 1952. Comparative twin studies of the genetic aspects of male homosexuality. *Journal of Nervous and Mental Disease* 115:283–98.

Kaplan, H. S. 1974. *The new sex therapy.* New York: Brunner/Mazel.

Kinsey, A. C., et al. 1948. *Sexual behavior in the human male.* Philadelphia: W. B. Saunders.

Kolb, L. C., and Johnson, A. M. 1955. Etiology and therapy of overt homosexuality. *Psychoanalytic Quarterly* 24:506–15.

Marmor, J. 1965. *Sexual inversion: the multiple roots of homosexuality* (New York: Basic Books).

———. 1975. Sexual disorders. In A. Freedman, et al., eds., *Comprehensive textbook of psychiatry,* vol. 2 (Baltimore: Williams & Wilkins), pp. 1510–20.

Masters, W. H., and Johnson V. E. 1970. *Human sexual inadequacy.* Boston: Little, Brown.

Ovesey, L. 1965. Pseudohomosexuality and homosexuality in men: Psychodynamics as a guide to treatment. In J. Marmor, ed., *Sexual inversion: The multiple roots of homosexuality.* (New York: Basic Books).

Saghir, M. R., and Robins, E. 1973. *Male and female homosexuality.* Baltimore: Williams & Wilkins.

Socarides, C. 1968. *The overt homosexual.* New York: Grune & Stratton.

Stoller, R. J. 1976. Sexual excitement. *Archives of General Psychiatry* 33 (August):899–909.

Tripp, C. A. 1970. *The homosexual matrix.* New York: McGraw-Hill.

Wahl, C. W. 1967. The evaluation and treatment of the homosexual patient. In C. W. Wahl, ed., *Sexual Problems* (New York: Free Press).

Weiderman, G. H. 1962. Survey of psychoanalytic literature on overt male homosexuality. *American Psychoanalytic Association Journal* 10:386–490.

Weinberg, M. S., and Bell, A. A. 1972. *Homosexuality: An annotated bibliography.* New York: Harper & Row.

Weinberg, M. S., and Williams, C. F. 1974. *Male homosexuals.* New York: Oxford University Press.

20 / Psychodynamic Psychotherapy of Female Homosexuality

MARTHA KIRKPATRICK
CAROLE MORGAN

Psychodynamic psychotherapy of female homosexuality is a loaded topic. If "psychodynamic" means the involvement of psychological forces beyond one's conscious control which affect and direct feelings and behavior, is there no flexibility and no choice of life-style? If "psychotherapy" means treatment, then treatment for what? If for a disease, then which disease? Guilt? Lack of self-esteem in a prejudiced society? Homosexual feelings or homosexual activity? What is homosexuality? Is it a pathological clinical entity, an infantile fixation, an adaptation, a less-than-optimal adjustment—biologically, personally, legally, socially, or in terms of species survival? What about "female" homosexuality? Is it a mirror image of male homosexuality, or a specifically female sexual style? Is there a sexual continuum for women with heterosexuality and homosexuality representing opposite poles? Is female homosexuality an enhancement of feminine identification, or is it an admiration and envy of males leading to masculine identification or an envy of males leading to a devaluation of men? Is it loving women or hating them—and when: once in a while, all of the time, or only under certain circumstances?

The chaos in which this ill-defined subject resides is further complicated by social prejudice, myth, ignorance, and by a lack of research interest, a lack of clinical experience, and a lack of scientific literature.

Unraveling this tangle of factors is an arduous task. We will first detail some aspects of the historical, as distinct from the psychological, setting which make the subject so murky; then we will struggle with definitions and dynamics so that a discussion of psychotherapy may be more relevant.

History

The psychodynamic understanding of female homosexuality began with the publication of Freud's (1920) paper, "The Psychogenesis of a Case of Homosexuality in a Woman." With Freud's discovery of the infantile roots of adult sexual behavior and the dynamic interplay of forces in personality development, it became possible to understand homosexual feelings as a ubiquitous trend in human psychosexual development. It appeared that homosexual feelings reflected the bisexual or "polymorphously perverse" nature of the infantile origins of sexuality and the infant's experience of being emotionally attached to both parents; homosexuality was found to be part of everyone's sexuality.

Despite the psychodynamic understanding that Freud's work provided, however, condemnatory attitudes still persist in society today. They are reflected in discriminatory laws and practices applied, curiously, almost exclusively to men. Both the attempts to regulate and the attempts to understand homosexuality have only very occasionally been directed towards women.

Kinsey et al. (1953) observed: "Human males throughout history have been most often concerned with the sexual activities of the female when those activities served the males' own purposes, and her solitary and even homosexual activities have often been ignored" (p. 136). Disinterest may have been further supported by the fact that neither the satisfaction of the male partner nor the satisfactory performance of female reproductive function is necessarily dependent on the woman's personal sexual pleasure or her sexual object preference.

While these latter facts are constants in human sexual experience, social attitudes toward them have been undergoing change. Current sexual attitudes emphasize mutuality and satisfaction for both partners. Women have begun to value personal gratification as distinct from, and in addition to, vicarious satisfaction. The reproductive function that formerly defined woman and subsumed her sexual life is no longer a social imperative, nor is it an inevitable consequence of sexual intercourse. Advances in reliable contraception over the last decade have enabled a woman to consider her sexual life separately from the issue of pregnancy and to initiate pregnancy by choice. As a result, there has developed increased concern with the quality rather than quantity of mothering, and with the relationship of that quality to mature female psychological development. In addition, the concern over the population explosion has paralleled a decrease in the social stigma attached to nonreproductive life-styles, including homosexuality. These changes, plus a recent increase in the number of female investigators, are bringing about a wave of interest in understanding female sexual development. Hopefully, we are moving toward a new ERA—Equal Research Attention for women.

Homosexuality in Women's Sexual Development

Until recently, when homosexuality in women was discussed in research, treatment, or theoretical papers, it was frequently limited to a footnote or a short paragraph. Often it was simply assumed that women were either the same as or the reverse of that which was described for men; women's sexuality seemed understandable only by comparison to a male model of sexuality. Although female sexual development and experience remain inadequately investigated, recent research efforts have delineated features of a uniquely female model. These features may help us to understand not only female heterosexuality, but the variations of female homosexuality as well.

In human fetal development, female morphology is primary; it does not require the adventitious influence of hormones as does male development. The female body-form will develop in the absence of female hormones. The male form develops from this basic female form only under the influence of testosterone (Sherfey, 1966). We know that in males the brain as well as the body is altered by fetal testosterone which overrides the cyclic nature of the pituitary gland and enhances the male drive toward aggressive discharge (Money, 1972). Some other possible brain consequences of the sex hormone differences in males and females during fetal development may be the apparently greater neurological maturity in female infants. This greater neurological stability may allow for a longer visual and auditory attention span in infant girls (Cramer, 1971) which, in turn, coupled with the lower motor discharge level, may facilitate early socialization. Early socialization is primarily with mothers or other female caretakers. Thus, an earlier intimacy is possible between girl babies and their mothers compared with boy babies and their mothers (Escalona, 1973; Goldberg and Lewis, 1969). Efforts to document differential handling of infants on the basis of sex suggest a general trend toward gentler body contact and greater vocal interaction with female infants. This different, earlier, and more intense intimacy which may characterize the girl's relationship with her mother may be important in the development of female gender identity.

Stoller (1968, 1975) has suggested that mothers in this culture who provide excessive body contact for male infants may encourage difficulties in male gender identification. The girl is more fortunate in her development of core gender identity in that her first intimate contact is with a same-sexed person. As with morphology, the fundamental sense of humanness and femaleness go together and do not require a later alteration while male gender identity, like physiological maleness, must be forced away from the fundamental female-human style. This may partly account for the counterphobic quality of male gender identity and the existence of many more male than female transexuals. If femaleness is primary, both physiologically and psychologically in human development, this may explain the security of female gender identity, which is thus less vulnerable to distortion or confusion than the harder won male gender identity.

Object choice, however, does not follow simply and directly from gender identity, and since the primary object of love and attachment is usually the mother, heterosexual object choice in females requires a turning away from the original object to the father, and therefore may be less firmly fixed and more flexible or ambiguous than heterosexual object choice in males. This turning to father requires the father's attention and his support of the little girl's developing heterosexual interests (Kleeman, 1971). A reflection of the early mother-daughter relationship is manifest in women's continued need for and ability to benefit from nurturing experiences with other women throughout life. Usually, the sexual quality of this earliest experience is expressed in sublimated form. Men, of course, need the nurturance of women throughout life as well, but nurturing and pregenital needs may be masked by, or are subsumed in, marriage—that is, in the presumption of a heterosexual genital intent.

To recapitulate, current research on female sexual development shows that female gender identity may be more firmly fixed than male by the earliest experiences with mother, while for the same reason sexual object choice may be less firmly fixed, and intimacy with women on some level may be continuous as a natural part of a woman's emotional life. The sexualization of these experiences may not represent as much psychological distortion as in the male. In women, homosexuality and heterosexuality do not appear to be at opposite ends of a continuum as Kinsey et al. (1953) suggested they were. Rather, the two trends might be seen as runninng a parallel course, capable of intermingling and of changing positions of ascendancy in consciousness and behavior under certain circumstances.

This latter view of women's sexual life is presented in the works of popular contemporary feminist authors. A number of works specifically document the lesbian experience, for example: *Lesbian Women* (Martin and Lyon, 1972); *Sappho Was a Right-On Woman* (Abbott and Love, 1972); *The Lesbian Myth* (Wysor, 1974); *Sisterhood Is Powerful* (Morgan, 1970); and the Radical Lesbian Newsletter.

These authors describe lesbian life-styles and a variety of homosexual experiences as well as some sources of social distress. They also present an unexpected and confounding variable: the politicization of lesbianism (Defries, 1975). To some feminist writers, the lesbian is the heroine of the day as women liberate themselves from the male-dominated value system (Raven and Iskin, 1977; Morgan, 1973; Johnston, 1973). They see lesbianism as an essentially feminist experience: the affirmation of woman as lovable, valuable, and complete in herself. They also consider the lesbian experience to be a confirmation of belief in the value of woman's body and mind and a consolidation of feminine psychological identification. A woman may explore lesbian relationships for political reasons and/or to become more confident of her womanhood. While the advent of this political lesbianism further confuses sex researchers, it is interesting to note the similarities between this political position and that of the classical Greeks, who viewed the ritualized homosexual experience of the young man with his meritorious mentor as valuable in promoting and establishing manly pride and virtue.

Kinsey's early statistical studies on nonclinical populations allowed us to discover that homosexual behavior was part of the sexual experience of a number of women (13 percent) at some time in their lives, rather than being the province of a peculiar few. According to the Hite Report (1976), 17 percent of the female respondents had had lesbian experiences. Adolescent crushes are, of course, well known, and even when sexual activity occurs, it is more often in the service of a confirmation of feminine identity than a persistent sexual preference; the potential for sexual attachment between adult women seems not only greater than previously assumed, but even possibly adaptive rather than inevitably fixed by anxiety. For example, Riess (1974) cites a study of California female prisoners convicted of felonies showing that 75 to 80 percent of the confined women engaged in homosexual activity, while only 7 to 10 percent had engaged in similar activity outside of jail. Studies (Balkin, Berger, and Schmidt, 1979; Giallombardo, 1966) have made it clear that these prisoners are not victims of sexual coercion as male prisoners often are, but are seeking emotional relationships which provide social and psychological support as well as sexual pleasure.

The political lesbian and the new visibility of the lesbian mother further demonstrate this flexibility of object choice among women. Lesbian mothers have become mothers by choice as frequently as non-lesbian mothers. The struggles of these mothers to retain custody of their children further suggest that the desire to have and rear children is not tied to heterosexual object choice (Kirkpatrick, 1978). Other investigators have been surprised by the frequency of heterosexual activity, often including orgasm, in the sexual lives of currently homosexual women (Gundlach and Riess, 1968; Saghir and Robins, 1973; Hedbloom, 1973; Wolff, 1971). This flexibility may be facilitated by women's sexual response patterns. Women's sexual satisfaction is never adequately measured by orgasm alone, but depends heavily on a sense of intimacy, tenderness, and mutuality. Such requirements may be met by an intensely loved person (at least temporarily or occasionally) irrespective of the lover's gender.

Definition

The place of homosexuality in women's lives is complex. The vast majority of women go through life without any overt homosexual activity and are committed to and satisfied by heterosexual activity. Is it possible to sort out variant homosexual experiences from homosexuality as a clinical entity? A clinical entity requires a constellation of specific signs and symptoms and a consistent psychological configuration. Recent research and clinical experience provides some direction for this task. Some studies have compared groups of matched homosexually behaving and heterosexually behaving women on projective tests and on personal histories and current adjustment. These studies are discussed elsewhere in greater detail (Riess, chapter 16, this volume). It is important for our discussion to note that when cohorts are divided by one behavioral criterion, namely presence or absence of sexual behavior with members of the same sex, the two groups show few differences which reach a level of significance (Riess, 1974; Gundlach and Riess, 1967; Saghir and Robins, 1973; Oberstone, 1975). Homosexual females are very much like heterosexual females from similar social settings and are quite different from homosexual (or heterosexual) males. The family histories and early sexual experiences of lesbians and heterosexual women are quite similar. Efforts to identify differential responses on psychological tests have also been inconclusive (Siegelman, 1972). Seemingly, when groups are divided only by behavior, i.e., choice of same- or opposite-sexed partner, equally heterogeneous groups of women emerge. Homosexual desire and/or activity is necessary but insufficient to define a clinical entity.

Riess (1974) quotes a psychiatrist with many homosexual patients who defines a lesbian as "a woman who says she is." Ponse (chapter 8, this volume) examined the phenomenon of self-labeling among lesbians and found wide variations within it. She discovered women who had had no sexual experience or only heterosexual experience who defined themselves as lesbians on the basis of fantasies or perceived attractions. Other women, actively engaged in homosexual relationships, labeled themselves as basically heterosexual, considering the current situation to be temporary, expedient, or limited to one special individual. Self-labeling seems useful for the study of self-labeling, but not for the study of homosexuality; it does not define a clinical entity.

Clinical experience also suggests that homosexual behavior in women may have many different meanings: it may be a developmental phase relating to consolidation of feminine identity either in adolescence or in later life when that identity is threatened; it may be reactive as a means of restoring self-esteem and reintrojecting a loving, maternal object in response to loss or disappointment in intimate relationships; it may be adaptive when heterosexual pairing is unavailable; it may be indicative of regression from the competitive anxieties of the oedipal period; or it may be a preoedipal gender disorder with a specific narcissistic defect.

The popular definition of female homosexuality (popular among laymen and numerous therapists) has always included a negative value judgment: that is, female homosexuality is pathological and all female homosexuals are "sick." We believe that homosexual behavior among women represents a variety of psychological and environmental adaptations with and without varying degrees of neurosis. Homosexual behavior by itself is not an indicator of sickness or poor functioning. Freud expressed the same opinion as early as 1905, some fifteen years before he published his case history of a young girl's homosexual interests.

Women with little pathology, i.e., normal neurotics, may experience and enjoy homosexual relationships. Women whose pathology is primarily in a nonsexual area may use homosexuality as a cure for their primary pathology (e.g., anxiety or depression). Some women turn to homosexuality for satisfaction because heterosexual interest revives anxiety from the oedipal period (i.e., a primarily hysterical defense). And a fewer still represent a preoedipal gender disorder. We would like to limit our discussion of female homosexuality as a clinical disorder to this latter group. In women who fall into this group, the conscious (or unconscious) longing for intimate, physical contact with a female producing sexual arousal, which may or may not be put into practice, is accompanied by: (1) an underlying confusion about gender identity, (2) a limitation of the ability to value and enjoy feminine proclivities, (3) an inhibition in experiencing sexual intimacy (not necessarily sexual arousal) with a man. In our ensuing discussion of dynamics we will be particularly interested in understanding the etiology of this particular clinical group.

Dynamics

All human psychological development results from the interplay of (1) the mental processes inherent in the intact human mind, (2) the familial setting, and (3) the cultural surround. No individual develops in a vacuum; in fact, were this possible, there would be no individuality and probably very little development.

We believe that cultural forces play an important role at many points in female development—for example, in the formation of parental role-expectations for female children, in providing or failing to provide peer and cultural support for female competency and autonomy, in delimiting the role of wife and mother, and in forming the patterns of male/-female communication and expectations. Women's acculturation generally has been such as to support male power and protect male possessions—one category of which were the women themselves. Women have adapted to these requirements of male dominated society, but have always had a separate and private culture of their own. While this separate cultural system has provided women with support for self-esteem, it has gone mostly unnoticed by male investigators who believed women's support came from their men and what men gave to them. To the extent that the nuclear family may be found to be pathogenic, this may result from the isolation of the mother and the loss of female-to-female support systems previously available in the extended family.

As mentioned earlier, the old stereotypes of subservience and only vicarious status hampered women's personal individual development. Today, some women are finding a return to the primary source of femininity, represented by intimacy with another woman, to be their way of breaking the hold of cultural stereotypes and of renewing themselves as separate and complete individuals. Rather than an increase in psychopathology, this may represent a healthy growth spurt previously inhibited by a pathogenic aspect of society. The wider visibility and acceptance of female homosexuality makes it possible to differentiate the cultural from the intrapsychic sources of this behavior. Let us now turn to the intrapsychic conditions which may underlie clinically disordered female homosexuality.

Early psychoanalytic writers considered homosexuality in women to be the result of intense castration anxiety in the little girl developing around the age of two to three, with subsequent repudiation of femininity and envious identification with the father and his relationship to the mother. Fenichel (1945) postulated two etiological factors in the psychodynamics of female homosexuality: repulsion to heterosexuality due to penis envy, and a perpetuation of the infantile attachment to the mother. Dynamic considerations of female homosexuality have been dominated by elaborations of these two themes. (For a résumé, see Socarides, 1963, and Romm, 1965.)

Penis envy is a much maligned concept which deserves better understanding. The infantile world is one of physical sensations from which information concerning the body, its boundaries, and its continuity is being processed and organized. Penis envy must be viewed in the context of the infant and young child's appropriate preoccupation with sensual events and its body. Genital arousal can be observed in infants of both sexes and infantile masturbation is well documented (Marcus and Francis, 1975.) However we have no direct access to the psychological processes occurring in the infant's mind. Many emotional states in infancy cause genital excitation. As infants develop emotional attachments to persons, first as part objects by touch, smell, voice, etc., and eventually to the whole person, their relationships become sexualized. Perhaps the emphasis belongs the other way: that is, gradually the early sexualization of many intense emotional states is limited and directed toward fewer and more specific interpersonal events. Remnants of the earliest nonspecific responses and of the early responses to the body parts participate in later individual characteristic sexual responses and preferences. But exactly who and what "turns on" any particular adult is poorly understood. This is true for heterosexual object choice as well as homosexual object choice. ("Object choice" is an unfortunate term. To imply that "choice" exists for a characteristic response whose history begins with the earliest extrauterine experiences is misleading. Some choice may exist in terms of what one does with one's sexual responses, but not in terms of who or what initiates or maintains those responses.)

Early experiences, especially in relationship to mother and feeding, may be sexualized and can remain the idealized source of comfort and sexual satisfaction. Unconscious longing to recreate this experience underlies many addictive states. Alcoholism is found more frequently in homosexual than heterosexual groups in comparison studies (Gundlach and Riess, 1968). For some women homosexuality, like alcoholism, may represent an addiction. The lesbian community recognizes alcoholism as a serious problem. (Women at the Los Angeles Gay Community Center were funded to establish a center for treatment and rehabilitation of alcoholic women in the lesbian community.) An addiction may be seen as an attempt to ward off the pain involved in recognizing separateness (originally from the breast) by replacing the maternal source of comfort which cannot be controlled with a source which can be controlled, possessed, and used. If the original idealized maternal source of comfort and satisfaction does not become integrated into the infant girl's sense of herself but remains outside, she will feel herself to be incomplete, inadequate, and in endless search for the "something missing." Homosexual union may later seem to be the appropriate cure for getting onself together with the missing part. The addictive quality may be revealed by the need to possess and control the lover. In this early state of narcissistic vulnerability, the mother, her body, and her capacities are felt to be awesome, enviable, and unattainable. A distant or devaluing attitude on the part of the mother will increase these feelings. The sense of helplessness over dependency on the mother and her special powers may lead to envious rage, fearful dependency, or a protective reversal, i.e., mother is experienced as dependent on baby rather than the other way around. The little girl who may later become a homosexual woman may feel relieved of her struggle with these feelings by becoming mother's caretaker.

The sense that something is missing may take on new meaning for the little girl with the discovery of sexual differences. Galenson and Roiphe's (1977) observations of early development suggest that manifestations of the awareness of genital differences can be seen in toddlers between fifteen to eighteen months of age. This is the same age at which other observations suggest that the development of gender identity begins (Money and Ehrhardt, 1972). Little girls respond differently than little boys to these differences. Indications of disappointment are seen which seem to turn the girl toward introspection and a temporary depressive mood. However, there is no indication of traumatic loss of body-narcissism or hostile, anxious attitudes except in those girls whose earlier maternal relationships or relationships with their own bodies had been disturbed. Girls who had experienced loss, intensification, or change in the early maternal figure, or who had surgeries or other disruptions to body sensations during the development of body image reacted much more vigorously and painfully to the discovery of genital differences. This "castration anxiety" appears to be a revival of the perceived loss of the fantasied fusion with mother's body which preceded the psychological separation of the infant's own sense of self from mother. In other words, a vulnerable little girl is one who arrives at this phase (during which a sense of herself as a female will include a conscious awareness of genital differences) with a sense of having lost something vital in the past. This "something vital" may now be identified with the penis and its attributes. Male privileges in a male-dominated society provide distressing confirmation for this line of thought, but they do not cause it. The result may be a continuing conflict over one's gender and a lack of pleasure in and esteem for the girl's own body and its sensations.

It is interesting to note that Galenson and Roiphe (1977) believe that the discovery of sexual differences is an impetus for girls to become introspective and spurs the development of symbolic thought, contributing to girls' early speech and social development. Several studies of the psychological characteristics of some female homosexuals have suggested a constricted fantasy life (McDougall, 1970; Deutsch, 1932).

This may be in part a reflection of an early difficulty in acknowledging and making constructive use of the discovery of sexual differences. Later the penis may be envied for its phallic qualities which are felt to provide strength and power against feelings of helplessness and dependency, or it may be resentfully coveted for its ability to interest, satisfy, and control mother. Presumed or actual evidence of preferential treatment for males is experienced as deeply wounding to the vulnerable little girl (Frazier and Sadker, 1975). The little girl's body, so unadorned compared to either mother or father, may continue to be perceived as ugly or unlovable.

Efforts to turn to the father for assurance of the value of being a girl may be rendered useless by (1) the fear that the powerful mother will withdraw or retaliate, (2) the envy or fear of the father, (3) old rage at father for intruding and interrupting the mother/baby couple, and/or (4) unavailability of father's approval. Sexual interest in the father may be experienced as threatening to the necessary bond with mother, or as a betrayal of mother by denying her what she is felt to need from the child, or as dangerous because the father is expected to retaliate for envy, especially envy of his sexual power. An ineffectual or indifferent father deprives the little girl of necessary support for enjoying and enhancing her femininity.

The parental couple are discovered to be providing each other with intimate satisfactions which the child is denied. This may produce such a sense of deprivation and resentment that the sexual act is not seen as loving, but is mentally distorted to be dangerous, painful, humiliating, or forced. The existence of, or pleasure in, heterosexual coupling may be denied while the mother/baby couple is idealized. The sexual act may be feared as destructive to the mother/baby couple, or it may be felt as dangerous to the child's personal integrity; thus a sexual life may seem safer to experience through another woman whose body is like the mother's.

Several writers have considered the major dynamic in this group of lesbians to be painful and frightening hostile feelings which are neutralized by being turned into sexual feelings. Bergler (1958) saw the homosexual woman's love as an attempt to deny, and make up for, a primitive hostile attachment to the mother. Chasseguet-Smirgel (1978) and Etchegoyen (1978) both find sadistic attitudes in their patients. Stoller (1975b) suggests that the essence of perversion is in the psychological modification of infantile hostilities.

These intrapsychic states reflect the idiosyncratic view that the child has of her world. Her world is the world of her family. Her interactions with family members and those of the family members with each other provide part of the raw data for the content of her fantasies. The other part derives from the intensity and quality of her own feelings which color and alter her perceptions. In 1932,

Deutsch described a prototype for the intrafamilial dynamics in female homosexuality: An arbitrary, dominating mother, who shows lack of respect or even contempt for the daughter, and a father who shows manifest weakness and submissiveness to his wife and an inability to relate to his daughter, which leaves the girl in utter helplessness. McDougall (1970) has elaborated on this prototype by examining the details of a specific form of the oedipal constellation. McDougall described a specific constellation of behavioral, historic, and neurotic problems in a small group of very disturbed homosexual women seen in psychoanalysis. She suggests a specific oedipal constellation in those women and believes that their homosexual behavior contributed to maintaining a precarious psychic equilibrium and ego identity. She observed an ambivalent and sexualized attachment to the mother who is idealized at the expense of the little girl's personal narcissism and regard for her own female body. The inner view of the father is as a depleted, sexually unsatisfying figure who fails in his protective role. He does not become a positive sexual object but may be the source of pathological identification.

Silva (1975) suggests that the disturbed pregenital mother-fixation always resides within the interpersonal family relations, and that these relations serve as a nest for pathological fixation but are not the cause of it. Intrafamily dynamics, the "fit" between husband and wife, permits the parents' pathology to be sustained and to create pathology in the children. According to McDougall, the children are caught in the nets of their parents' unconscious desires; the children weave their fantasies out of an amalgam of primitive instinctual drives organized around what they have decoded of their parents' wishes and around what they believe they represent to their parents.

However, it would be a mistake to consider only the intrapsychic structure or the pathology of the mother and father. While it is true that mother, father, and siblings constitute our first contact with reality, they are not the sum total of it. "Our psychological development is also influenced by our genetic endowment, the impact of our society and the social character relevant in our milieu, the geographical site, the historical moment and the ever-present possibility of self determinants" (Silva, 1975, p. 374).

While these early dynamic interactions are essential in determining the direction of sexual interest, they do not determine a whole person, or a whole life. The homosexual woman's capacities and opportunities to make use of her talents, to find social support systems and meaningful approval, and to grow from the interpersonal experiences of later childhood, adolescence, and adult life—all will markedly influence how loving and productive her relationships will be.

We wish to emphasize both that fragments of these dynamics can be found in women who are neither homosexual nor suffering from neurotic problems and that living in or experiencing homosexual relationships is compatible with a high level of psychological functioning and the enjoyment of a loving and productive life.

Psychotherapy

A search of the literature on psychotherapy of female homosexuality (by any definition) revealed the traditional paucity of material. The Chicago Psychoanalytic Index, Weinberg and Bell's (1972) annotated bibliography, and a computer search of the last ten years' work were very disappointing. This is surprising in view of the finding (Saghir and Robins, 1973; Gundlach and Riess, 1968) that the women in homosexual samples had entered psychiatric treatment somewhat more frequently than those in the heterosexual samples. However, Saghir and Robins noted that the duration of treatment tended to be shorter for the homosexual women, and a smaller percentage considered treatment to be successful. It seems likely that psychotherapy of female homosexuality is infrequently described because it is often disappointing to both the patient and the therapist. This may be partly the result of confusion over the aim of treatment. It has repeatedly been questioned whether the reversal of object choice can be an ethical aim of psychotherapy (Acosta, 1975; Stoller et al., 1975). However, patient and therapist may reach a *mutual* decision about the aims of therapy without a miscarriage of ethical considerations.

A patient's intent to change object preference as a therapeutic goal may fluctuate considerably during treatment. As therapy proceeds and anxieties are appropriately reduced, and internal conflicts are separated from contemporary relationships, heterosexuality may become more gratifying or may begin to offer a more fulfilling life. On the other hand, as the impact of social disapproval is lessened through an increase of inner strength and self-esteem, homosexuality may become less guilt-producing and a more satisfying homosexual life may become available.

The possibility of such shifts in focus should warn the therapist that the only invariable goals in such work are increased understanding on the patient's part and an increased capacity to use her mind. When the patient's commitment to change is strong, such behavioral alteration is more likely, but change of the internal psychological state results from increased understanding and not from the therapist's direct attempts to alter behavior. In exploring the possibility of change in sexual object choice, the patient may need to understand that when anxiety is limiting heterosexual pleasure, it may be necessary for the patient to attempt new behavior in order to gain further understanding of the anxiety.

Appropriately, long-term psychotherapy is not aimed directly at behavioral change but at increasing understanding and developing more genuine options and control of one's life. This intent of psychotherapy must not be subrogated to society's need for conformity or to the therapist's political or philosophical ideals. One may believe along with Freud that sexual maturity for humankind is identified by the procreative value of the sexual activity. From this point of view, since reproductive use of genital sexuality insures species survival, it must be the highest level of sexual development. However, at this time in history, it is a moot question whether reproduction by every member of the species insures or endangers species survival. Also, if genitality is considered the highest psychological development, one should remember that heterosexual activity in and of itself is not synonymous with genitality, which is a state of mature object love difficult to reach by any route. However one views sexual maturity, the therapist who approaches the homosexual aspects of the patient as he or she approaches all other aspects of the patient is in the best position to delineate the preoedipal from the reactive or other variant forms of homosexual behavior and to provide responsible treatment.

Treatment consideration must apply to: (1) women with a primary complaint of distress over homosexual experience or conscious homosexual desires who may wish to find primary gratification with a heterosexual partner; (2) women experiencing conflict, guilt and/or fear over homosexual experiences but without a wish to alter their object preference; (3) women who come to treatment for problems which are discovered to relate to unconscious homosexual desires and conflicts; and (4) women who give a history of homosexual relationships but come to treatment for other reasons.

Consideration must also be given in psychotherapy to the homosexual element in the transference of women, since homosexual transference is regularly seen in the course of women's treatment. It may appear in dreams, associations, feelings about other women in the patient's past or contemporary life, and eventually be experienced directly in the transference. These developments occur whether the therapist is male or female, and must be identified as aspects of the sexualization or sexual experiencing of maternal interactions and not as oedipal urges. As well as casting light on the early maternal-infant experience, such reactions in the transference may represent an attempt to avoid reexperiencing the inequality of the infant's need for mother as compared with mother's very different need for the infant. In infancy, survival and growth depend on there being a capable, need-fulfilling, grown-up caretaker, but this inequality can produce envy and rage in the infant who is struggling to hold on to the early misconception of infantile omnipotence. When this struggle is reexperienced as the therapeutic process, one possible unconscious psychic maneuver is to seduce the therapist, irrespective of sex, into a sexual and therefore equally dependent relationship. It can be relieving to explain to the patient that she is afraid of experiencing dependent needs and for that reason she is experiencing the relationship as sexual rather than as therapeutic. This same psychic maneuver may have occurred in infancy, and when the envy and rage have been intense, may have contributed to the development of later homosexuality.

When underlying homosexual conflict is found to be responsible for the presenting symptom, the impulses and defenses must be revealed and explored in the therapeutic relationship with the therapist remaining supportive and allied with the patient as she faces her responsibility for directing her own sexual life.

When a reported homosexual desire or activity represents a symptom of depression—that is, a reaction to loss or disappointment, or an attempt to regain feminine self-esteem, or a means to strengthen a failing sense of inner approval—the exploration of these issues may result in the revival or development of heterosexual interests and satisfactions. Again, the depression or the narcissistic wound is what requires treatment, not the compensatory homosexuality.

The treatment of special problems underlying the small group of female homosexuals with preoedipal characterological disorders requires long and skillful work. (See McDougall, 1970, for clinical examples.) New resolutions may be made available through interpretations of the transference phenomena which allow for a consolidation of gender identity and a repair of the narcissistic defect. To the extent that this is successful, the patient's approval of and pleasure in herself and her own body is enhanced. Relationships may become more loving and mutual and less possessive or addictive. The reduction of ambivalence toward men may result in better understanding and pleasure in relating to them, whether or not sexual relationships with men are preferred.

It is an interesting finding that homosexual women are rarely known to be frigid in their sexual unions (Wolff, 1971). This may result from a fear that admission of such trouble would invalidate the woman's object choice, or perhaps a criterion for sexual satisfaction other than orgasm may have been used. Lesbian couple counseling and lesbian sexual counseling are new therapies growing out of the centers for gay community services. If the work in these settings becomes part of the literature, a deeper and more complete understanding of the sexual experience of the female homosexual may evolve.

There are those homosexual women who abjure appropriate psychiatric treatment for depression, anxiety, alcoholism, etc., because of the fear that the therapist will be primarily interested in the challenge to "convert" them to heterosexuality. A therapist who takes such a position subverts his or her role as therapist into a role as social or moral mentor. Fortunately, such attitudes are becoming less common. A recent survey of psychiatrists' attitudes toward female homosexuality (Gartrell, Kramer, and Brodie, 1974) revealed that 85 percent of the respondents included in their concept of mental health the possibility of a well-adjusted homosexual woman. As the decision of the American Psychiatric Association to remove homosexuality from the diagnostic nomenclature and as studies of psychiatrists' attitudes become more widely known, more/rather than fewer homosexual men and women may feel free to avail themselves of psychotherapy.

Homosexual feelings, whatever else they represent in a particular patient or at a particular time, represent a loving attachment. The therapist's acknowledgment of the authenticity of the patient's loving feelings and of the possibility that they represent a relatively healthy and growing part of the patient can help to reduce the effects of social disapproval. A supportive, empathic, therapeutic relationship can help to reduce the social guilt, reactive defensiveness, and self-hatred that may burden homosexual patients. These latter feelings act as a barrier to genuine exploration of the source and meaning of the patient's individual sexual development, as well as to further development of her other psychological resources. Some of the guilt and self-hatred may stem from the hostile fantasies of infantile psychic life which the homosexual feelings are meant to repair. These cannot be identified and reexperienced therapeutically until self-esteem has been restored. The current gay liberation movement has helped significantly in restoring self-esteem and thus supporting self-inquiry.

Therapy which aims to increase genuine options and which respects the individual's right to make the decisions about those options must allow a patient to continue homosexual relationships despite the possibility of heterosexual satisfactions. The therapist must not, however, be so preoccupied with repairing the damage done by a guilt-producing society that he or she discourages a patient from exploring the intrapsychic sources of anxieties which may be limiting the patient's sexual life, but must rather assist in every way possible when change is desired.

Summary

Political and social changes in the last ten or fifteen years have generated better research opportunities for a more appropriate focus of attention on female sexual development as separate and distinct from male sexual development. Female homosexuality is to be understood as a unique female phenomenon, rather than a state which is either the same as or the reverse of male homosexuality. The debate over pathology versus choice has become more clearly defined, and it seems possible now to separate a specific form of female homosexuality with its particular pathology from the relatively well-adjusted female who has experienced or is experiencing homosexual feelings or relationships.

Female homosexual activity, while rarely studied or reported in clinical papers, is a fairly common experience. Homosexual feelings in women appear to originate in the ubiquitous, early, and specifically female interaction with the mother. As such, they are available in all women's lives and may become conscious and active under a variety of circumstances. Homosexual relationships may be experienced as a revolt against oppressive constraints in heterosexual role-expectations, or valued as a means of reaffirming and expanding one's sense of femaleness and individuality. Women whose pathology is primarily in a nonsexual area may use homosexuality as a cure for their primary pathology (e.g., anxiety or depression). Some women turn to homosexuality for satisfaction because heterosexual interest revives anxiety from the oedipal period. A fewer still represent a preoedipal gender disorder. Only under the impact of certain inner pressures does this latter pathological response develop.

The essential features of this clinical pattern—as opposed to variant and reactive homosexuality—are: (1) the conscious or unconscious longing (which may or may not be put into practice) for intimate, physical contact with a female, with resultant sexual arousal, which must be accompanied by (2) an underlying confusion about gender identity, (3) a limitation of the ability to value and enjoy feminine proclivities, and (4) an inhibition in experiencing sexual intimacy (not necessarily sexual arousal) with a man. In these situations, "choice" is not available.

Etiological features of this clinical pattern most regularly reported include an ambivalent and sexualized attachment to the mother who is idealized at the expense of the little girl's personal narcissism and regard for her own female body. On the other hand, the father is viewed as a depleted, sexually unsatisfying figure who fails in his protective role. He does not become a positive sexual object but may be the source of pathological identification. Family systems may enhance and confirm these fantasies. Lack of cultural support for the development of female competency or constraints on female autonomy further diminish the girl's pleasure in her femininity.

Homosexual patients come to therapy for a variety of reasons. Occasionally a change in object choice is consciously desired. Whatever goals the patient and therapist may agree to pursue, the therapist's goal should be to provide the patient with greater understanding of her mental processes. Exploration of the sources of guilt in a nonjudgmental atmosphere which acknowledges the loving aspect of homosexual feelings may increase self-esteem and make possible the exploration of areas of anxiety. Under these circumstances, heterosexual desires may emerge and may lead to heterosexual relationships as the preferred source of satisfaction. Good and responsible therapy is not defined by this outcome but by relief of distress and increase in personal options for pleasure and for enhancing the quality of life.

REFERENCES

Abbott, S., and Love, B. 1972. *Sappho was a right-on woman.* New York: Stein & Day.

Acosta, F. 1975. Etiology and treatment of homosexuality. *Archives of Sexual Behavior* 4(1):9–29.

Balkin, S.; Berger, R.; and Schmidt, J. 1980 *Crime and deviance in America.* Bellmont, Calif.: Wadsworth Publishing.

Bergler, E. 1958. *Counterfeit sex: Homosexuality, impotence, frigidity.* 2nd rev. ed. New York: Grune & Stratton.

Chasseguet-Smirgel, J. 1978. Reflections on the connexions between perversion and sadism. *International Journal of Psychoanalysis* 59:27–36.

Cramer, B. 1971. Sex differences in early childhood. *Child Psychiatry and Human Development* 1:133–51.

Defries, A. 1975. Pseudohomosexuality in feminist students. In *Scientific Proceedings in Summary Form,* 128th Meeting American Psychological Association.

Deutsch, H. 1932. On female homosexuality. *Psychoanalytic Quarterly* 1:484–510.

Escalona, S. 1973. Basic modes of social interaction: Their emergence and patterning during the first two years of life. *Merrill-Palmer Quarterly* 19:205–32.

Etchegoyen, R. H. 1978. Some thoughts on transference perversion. *International Journal of Psychoanalysis* 59 (part 1):45–54.

Fenichel, O. 1945. *The psychoanalytic theory of neuroses:* New York: W. W. Norton.

Frazier, N., and Sadker, M. 1975. *Sexism in school and society.* New York: Harper & Row.

Freud, S. 1920. The psychogenesis of a case of homosexuality in a woman. In James Strachey, ed., *Standard edition of the complete psychological works of Sigmund Freud* (London: Hogarth Press), 18:147–72.

Galenson, E., and Roiphe, H. 1977. Some suggested revisions concerning early female development. *Journal of American Psychoanalytic Association* 24 (5):29–57.

Gartrell, N.; Kramer, H.; and Brodie, K., 1974. Psychiatrists' attitudes toward female homosexuality. *Journal of Nervous and Mental Disease* 159:141–44.

Giallombardo, R. 1966. *Society of women.* New York: John Wiley.

Goldberg, S., and Lewis, S. 1969. Play behavior in the year-old infant: Early sex differences. *Child Development* 40:21–33.

Gundlach, R., and Riess, B. F. 1967. Birth order and sex of siblings in a sample of lesbians and non-lesbians. *Psychological Reports* 20:61–62.

———. 1968. Self and sexual identity in the female: A study of female homosexuals. In, *New directions in mental health* B. F. Riess, ed. (New York: Grune & Stratton).

Hedbloom, J. 1973. Dimensions of the lesbian sexual experience. *Archives of Sexual Behavior* 2 (4):329–41.

Hite, S. 1976. *The Hite report: A nationwide study of female sexuality.* New York: Macmillan.

Hopkins, J. 1969. The lesbian personality. *British Journal of Psychiatry.* 115(529):1433–36.

Johnston, J. 1973. *Lesbian nation.* New York: Simon & Schuster.

Kinsey, et al. 1953. *Sexual behavior in the human female.* Philadelphia: Saunders.

Kirkpatrick, M. 1978. W. B. Unpublished manuscript.

Kleeman, J. 1971. The establishment of core gender identity in normal girls. *Archives of Sexual Behavior* 1:117–29.

McDougall, J. 1970 Homosexuality in women. In J. Chasseguet-Smirgel, ed., *Female sexuality: New Psychoanalytic views* (Ann Arbor: University of Michigan Press).

Marcus, M., and Francis, J. 1975. *Masturbation from infancy to senescence.* New York: International Universities Press.

Marmor, J., ed. 1965. *Sexual inversion: The multiple roots of homosexuality.* New York: Basic Books.

Martin, D., and Lyon, P. 1972. *Lesbian women.* San Francisco: New Glide.

Money, J., and Erhardt, A. 1972. *Man and woman. Boy and girl.* Baltimore: Johns Hopkins Press.

Morgan, R., ed. 1970. *Sisterhood is powerful.* New York: Vintage Books.

————. 1973. Lesbianism and feminism: Synonyms or contradictions? *Second Wave* 2:4.

Oberstone, A. 1975. Dimensions of psychological adjustment and style of life in single lesbians and single heterosexual women. *Dissertation Abstracts International,* Ann Arbor, Mich.

Raven, A., and Iskin, R. 1977. *Through the peephole: Toward lesbian sensibility in art. Chrysalis* 4.

Riess, B. 1974. New viewpoints on the female homosexual. In, V. Franks and B. Vansanti, eds. *Women in therapy* (New York: Brunner/Mazel).

Riess, B.; Safer, J.; and Yotive, Y. 1974. Psychological test data of female homosexuality: A review of the literature. *Journal of Homosexuality* 1:71–87.

Rodgers, C.; et al. 1976. Group psychotherapy with homosexuals: A review. *International Journal of Group Psychotherapy* 26(1):3–27.

Romm, M. E. 1965. Sexuality and homosexuality in women. In J. Marmor, ed., *Sexual inversion: The multiple roots of homosexuality* (New York: Basic Books).

Rosen, D. 1973. *Lesbianism: A study of female homosexuality.* Springfield, Ill.: Charles C. Thomas.

Saghir, M., and Robins, E. 1973. *Male and female homosexuality.* Baltimore: Williams & Wilkins.

Sherfey, M. D. 1966. The evolution and nature of female sexuality in relation to psychoanalytic theory. *American Psychoanalytic Association Journal* 14:28–128.

Siegelman, N. 1972. Adjustment of homosexual and heterosexual women. *British Journal of Psychiatry* 120:477–81.

————. 1974. Parental background of homosexual and heterosexual women. *British Journal of Psychiatry.* 124:14–21.

Silva, J. G. 1975. Two cases of female homosexuality: A critical study of Sigmund Freud and Helene Deutsch. *Contemporary Psychoanalysis.* 11 (3):357–76.

Socarides, C. W. 1963. The historical development of theoretical and clinical concepts of overt female homosexuality. *American Psychoanalytic Association Journal* 11:386–413.

Stoller, R. J. 1968. *Sex and gender.* New York: Science House.

————. 1972. The "bedrock" of masculinity and feminity: Bisexuality. *Archives of General Psychiatry* 26:207–12.

————. 1975a. *Sex and gender. The transsexual experiment,* Vol. 2. New York: Jason Aronson.

————. 1975b. *Perversion: The erotic game of hatred.* New York: Dell Publishing.

Stoller, R. J., et al. 1975. A symposium: Should homosexuality be in the APA nomenclature? *American Journal of Psychiatry* 130(11):1207–16.

Swanson, D., et al. 1972. Clinical features of the female homosexual patient. *Journal of Nervous and Mental Disease* 155:119–24.

Weinberg, M., and Bell, A. 1972. *Homosexuality: An annotated bibliography.* New York: Harper & Row.

Wolff, C. 1971. *Love between women.* New York: Harper & Row.

Wysor, B. 1974. *The lesbian myth.* New York: Random House.

21 / The Myth of Classical Homosexuality: Views of a Behavioral Psychotherapist

LEE BIRK

There is in fact no such unitary thing as "homosexuality." If there were, the still-controversial scientific and ethical issues regarding its treatability or nontreatability would long since have been resolved. Instead, as this decade of aggressive self-revelation has brought to almost everyone's attention, there are many, many different homosexuals who collectively defy rigid characterization. That fact in itself has necessitated a shift in emphasis for this chapter—away from yet another review of "the behavioral treatment of homosexuality," toward a broader examination of the conditions under which behaviorally based therapies may prove useful to persons who happen to be homosexual. In my experience with a spectrum of patients who are homosexual in their fantasies, sexual urges, and/or their overt sexual behavior, some are "gay males," some are "lesbians," and some do not want to be identified by either of these terms. Not a few adolescents are thoroughly heterosexual in their desires, but are behaviorally homosexual. Many people have lived an exclusively homosexual existence for years, have had one or several enduring relationships, and would describe themselves as satisfied in the most important aspects of their lives. Other homosexuals have experienced their sexual orientation in fantasy only, transiently, anonymously, or remorsefully. Some homosexuals have married and raised children, but remain convinced that for them something is irretrievably missing from the heterosexual relationship. Some married homosexuals have heterosexual intercourse regularly, but find they must rely on homosexual fantasies in order to achieve a complete sexual union. Some homosexuals have sought psychiatric help because they find their sexual needs and impulses painfully distressing; others are not at all distressed, seek no such treatment, and would in fact find the suggestion of therapy unwelcome, even insulting. There are some individuals who are not conflicted about their homosexual orientation but whose impelling feelings of attraction toward members of their own sex are nonetheless thwarted by unremitting sexual dysfunction. There are others who may be sexually functional with partners of the same sex—or with partners of both sexes—but who find themselves troubled by phobias, tension headaches, chronic underassertiveness, obsessive-compulsive symptoms, eating disorders, habit problems, and a myriad of other complaints which are not the exclusive property of a homosexual orientation, but which in fact also trouble many heterosexuals.

Variations of the homosexual adaptation are as diverse as the individuals who find themselves drawn to members of their own sex, and as diverse as variations in heterosexual adaptations. The tendency to make a monolithic concept of homosexuality, as if it effected the same general feelings and behavior in different individuals, has led to the formulation of a variety of unproductive questions about homosexuality: What is *the cause* of homosexuality? Is it a mental disorder? Is it treatable? Should it be treated? If so, what is the best procedure? Any unqualified general answer to questions of this type will be contradicted routinely by much of the population it pretends to cover. There is in short no reliable way to generalize about homosexuality (or for that matter, heterosexuality) or to formalize a standard treatment program, behavioral or other, for persons who are homosexual for the simple reason that homosexuality does not exist as a phenomenon which even approaches uniformity across its dimensions.

What follows then is an overview of the development of behavioral and behaviorally based therapies used or usable with homosexual individuals. The review begins with a critique of the early behavioral work, which in the opinion of this author was for the most part clinically naive and rigid. The review ends with and emphasizes the spectrum of modern behaviorally based techniques which have in fact proved useful under a variety of circumstances with persons who happen to be homosexual or bisexual. These techniques fall naturally into three general categories: (1) behavioral therapies addressing problems not related to sexual orientation; (2) therapies that aim to improve the general and/or sexual adaptation of homosexual persons, without aiming to change, broaden, or "modify" their sexual orientation; and (3) behavioral psychotherapy, designed to help individuals who are homosexual but who want to change or broaden their sexual orientation, or who seek help at least thinking that they do or may want to do this.

Early Behavioral Work

Most of the early work with homosexuals undertaken by behavior therapists was based on what appears to be a uniform a priori assumption to
the effect that homosexuality could be legitimately and exhaustively
reduced to an autonomous and discrete set of "target" behaviors, pre-
dictably elicited by a complementary set of stimulus situations. It followed then that the almost universal goal of these early behavioral
treatment schemes was the elimination, "modification," or reduction of
the so-called target homosexual behaviors, with concomitant reinforcement and enhancement of "more appropriate" heterosexual behaviors.
In essence, the biologically, psychologically, and sociologically complex
and diverse set of phenomena which generally have been lumped together and called "homosexuality" was treated in nearly all of the early
behavioral work as if all the phenomena were reducible simply to
homosexual behaviors, and that such behaviors, in the mode of *res ipsa
loquitur*, were obviously problematic and "maladaptive." Thus it was
all too common for early behavioral therapists to regard all homosexual
behaviors as manifestly undesirable habits, comparable to nail biting or
exhibitionism.

Crucially important issues, such as whether the person in question
liked and felt warmth toward women (or men) or was primarily identified with a man or with a woman, and whether the patient experienced his (or her) homosexual feelings and behavior as ego dys-
tonic or ego syntonic were generally ignored as nonbehavioral and
therefore not relevant. Similar kinds of criticisms could be made of
nearly all the behavioral literature—early and late—for its failure to
acknowledge even the existence, much less the importance, of oedi-
pally based fears of heterosexual feelings and behaviors (Franks and
Wilson, 1973, p. 196). Similarly, to choose one other example among
many, the behavioral literature failed to recognize the fact that some
of the profound, physically experienced yearnings for a man described by some homosexual men seem to represent old unresolved
problems with aloof, maternally proscribed or otherwise alienated,
emotionally unreachable fathers.

Even leaving aside such general clinical criticisms of the early behavioral work dealing with homosexuality (much of the criticism on purely
technical grounds), it must be observed that, like most of the early
behavioral work on alcoholism, it was handicapped by an unbalanced
overreliance on aversive conditioning or avoidance learning methods
of treatment. Moreover, whenever such conditioning was emphasized,
it was typically undermined by poor practical implementation. This
latter defect is illustrated by the widespread early tendency to rely on

chemically mediated nausea-producing aversive stimuli. Such methods are not only unnecessarily unpleasant, but are highly inefficient behaviorally, insofar as they allow no possibility for precise control of the timing of stimulus onset/offset. (Rachman and Teasdale, 1969, pp. 284–85). The seriousness of this latter problem can hardly be overemphasized; using an aversive behavioral technique without precise temporal control of stimulus onset/offset is not just a subtle imperfection; it can be a paralytic shortcoming.

In the interest of a balanced account one should note that there were a number of positive accomplishments by early behavioral therapists. For illustrative purposes the work of two early behavioral therapists will be cited here.

First, there is a paper published almost two decades ago (Stevenson and Wolpe, 1960) employing assertive training for the brief successful treatment of three cases of "sexual deviation"; two of these dealt with men whose behavior patterns were homosexual and who were also markedly underassertive. In the most striking case described (case 2) the patient had been behaviorally homosexual since puberty (for eight years) and his underassertiveness was most pronounced in dealing with his own stepfather. In only ten treatment hours, through psychotherapy not aimed at "de-repression . . . of early traumatic experiences" but instead emphasizing assertive training, this man was able to change the balance of power with his stepfather. With this change came both a considerable personality shift, as well as a heterosexual shift. The man married, "reported far greater pleasure in his sexual relationship with his wife than he had experienced in his homosexual relationships," had a child, and was still stably and happily married at the three-year follow-up. It could be argued that this young man might have been classified as "pseudohomosexual" using the criteria of Ovesey (1965), but this nonetheless remains an early and masterful piece of clinical work, accomplished in an astonishingly few hours of treatment.

Second, there is the work of Feldman and MacCulloch (1964, 1965), whose conditioning therapy represented a serious attempt to base a clinical treatment program on a well-thought-out and carefully implemented behavioral methodology. Although their treatment method did depend heavily on an avoidance learning paradigm, these workers also informally stressed the need to teach the patient new social skills that could serve as competitive responses. Their doing this also probably facilitated identification with the "straight" male therapists. For example, they encouraged their patients to take classes in social dancing, and to try to date women.

Modern Behavioral Work

As stated earlier, it is useful to classify the three major areas of productive behavioral work with people who are homosexual or bisexual as follows:

1. For both men and women, work on target symptoms not related to sexual preference or object choice.
2. Work with homosexual couples where the target symptom is a frank psychogenic sexual dysfunction. For males the important dysfunctions are impotence, inability to ejaculate, or ejaculation that is either partial —without full feeling or pleasure—or premature. In females the salient problems are inability to lubricate, to relax the paravaginal muscles, or to experience a complete orgasmic response. Multiple dysfunctions in a single individual are by no means rare but are generally treatable in short-term therapy.
3. Behavioral psychotherapy work with individuals who have—or think they may have—a wish to broaden their sexual orientation to include heterosexual function, or work with people who have some overt or covert (unconscious) ambivalence about this basic question. Some patients steadfastly present themselves, sometimes over the course of several years, as "wanting simply to be normal and . . . heterosexual," and yet turn out really not to want this at all. A very few other patients initially evince no interest whatsoever in heterosexual matters, yet eventually discover and "work through" previously unconscious or not fully self-acknowledged heterosexual wishes. Some such people over the course of five or more years of weekly behavioral psychotherapy eventually make solid heterosexual shifts, get married, and have children. This situation—confused or ambivalent motives and goals at the beginning of therapy—is not unlike the common one in which a person may enter psychoanalysis ostensibly in order to improve his or her marriage, only to discover that his or her deeper wishes are to end the marriage and work out a new adaptation.

This chapter will concentrate most attention on the third area, behavioral psychotherapy for individuals interested in "change," because unlike the other two areas, which are relatively straightforward and short-term clinically, and which have been or are being written about amply elsewhere, this type of behavioral psychotherapy involves long-term work, amorphous and often controversial issues, a blend of psychodynamic and behavioral principles (Marmor and Woods, 1979), and has been little written about elsewhere.

TREATMENT WHERE THE TARGET SYMPTOM IS NOT RELATED TO SEXUALITY (SHORT-TERM)

If, for example, a person who happens to be homosexual or bisexual comes with a chief complaint of a discrete phobia or with a pattern of habitual meekness (sometimes coupled with periodic episodes of rage) or with frequent tension headaches, then that person should be very efficiently treatable by short-term methods, using systematic desensitization to resolve the phobia, assertive training to reverse the meekness/rage problem, and EMG (electromyograph) biofeedback to cure the headaches. In such cases, the sexual preference of the patient is really a peripheral matter, of demographic interest, but usually otherwise not relevant. References abound on behavior therapy techniques: L. Birk et al., 1973a; Wolpe and Lazarus, 1966; Bandura, 1969; Yates, 1970; Agras, 1972; L. Birk, 1972; Liberman, 1972; L. Birk, 1973; L. Birk, 1973a; Yates, 1975; Goldfried and Davison, 1976; Leitenberg, 1976; A. Birk, 1978.

TREATMENT WHERE THE TARGET SYMPTOM IS A SEXUAL
DYSFUNCTION (SHORT-TERM)

This, of course, is an area originally pioneered primarily by Masters and Johnson with heterosexual couples (1966, 1970) and further advanced and integrated with psychodynamic psychotherapy by Kaplan (1974). In recent years Masters and Johnson have extended their work to include the treatment of homosexual couples (Masters and Johnson, 1979). The present author and his colleagues also use sex therapy techniques with homosexual couples, both in couple therapy and in group therapy where both partners in a homosexual couple happen to be group members. It should be added that sex therapy techniques are fundamentally behavioral in their focus on existing sexual behaviors and the antecedent and consequent conditions which surround these behaviors (A. Birk, 1978).

Sex therapy techniques may on occasion be very useful to patients who do experience a heterosexual shift in the course of their work in therapy but who are troubled by partial or complete sexual dysfunction during initial heterosexual experiences. Especially if the partner involved is a person of importance to the patient, heterosexual sex therapy techniques can be extremely valuable (Brinkley-Birk and Birk, 1975).

BEHAVIORAL PSYCHOTHERAPY WHERE THE PATIENT IS OR
MAY BE INTERESTED IN "HETEROSEXUAL SHIFT"
(LONG-TERM)

Although the vast majority of these individuals who were interested in a heterosexual shift have been male, and so far all such patients treated in group settings have been male, there is obviously a great deal of common ground shared by homosexual women and homosexual men. There are, however, some apparently significant differences, among them, for example, an endocrinological difference (L. Birk et al., 1973b; Gartrell, Lariaux, and Chase, 1977). Another especially prominent difference between homosexual women and homosexual men is reflected in the low frequency with which homosexual women have sought treatment to resolve issues relating partly or wholly to their homosexual feelings, behavior, and/or life-style. Because the bulk of the author's clinical experience with patients interested in a heterosexual shift has involved homosexual men rather than homosexual women, the present section of this chapter will focus on the treatment of men. This should not however be taken to imply the existence of two clinically distinct modes of treatment for male and female homosexuals. There is simply not enough evidence yet to define the psychodynamic and treatment distinctions conclusively.

While our experience with homosexual women interested in "change" has been very limited, over the past twelve years the author has personally seen more than two hundred homosexual men in clinical treatment; of those, approximately one hundred have been treated in long-term therapy, ranging between one and seven years in duration, and averaging about four years. During those twelve years the principal forms of treatment employed have evolved from group therapy combined with a classical behavioral scheme into what is now a well-established treatment format involving weekly behavioral psychotherapy meetings in groups of about nine members led jointly by a male therapist and a female therapist (L. Birk, Miller, and Cohler, 1970; L. Birk, 1974). Depending upon clinical circumstances, this group work is frequently supplemented by family consultation and/or therapy, by homosexual or heterosexual couple therapy, and/or by short-term directive behavioral therapy to alleviate specific sexual dysfunctions of the homosexual couple or of the new heterosexual couple.

In addition, when it is indicated, some group members are referred for concomitant specialized behavioral therapies to deal with important target symptoms not so easily amenable to treatment in a long-term group format. For example, assertive training is recommended more than occasionally. Other kinds of tailor-made recommendations for behavioral treatment are indicated for less common problems; for example, one man with a long-standing socially dysfunctional habit of blinking both eyes, tic-like, whenever he talked with people was successfully treated for this target symptom in two treatment sessions employing EMG biofeedback.[1] Finally, a few patients come to us after a not fully successful analysis, or while still in analysis. In a few other cases, because those particular patients had much to gain professionally from obtaining the best possible education in understanding their feelings in developmental perspective, we have referred alumni of the group experience for classical psychoanalysis. Two men were referred to the group by their analysts—one after maximum benefit from analysis and one early in the analytic process.

Of the homosexual or bisexual men who enter this regular weekly

1. R. Surwit: personal communication, 1974.

therapy, 40 to 50 percent persevere in treatment to the point where significant positive gains become evident enough to both patient and therapists to warrant termination. This typically occurs in three to five years, although for statistical purposes (in evaluating outcome) patients are counted as "persevering" if they remain in treatment for two and one-half years or more, or if they achieve specified goals in less than two and one-half years.

The author's treatment approach with homosexual men interested in "change" borrows from the group techniques of Hadden (1966a, 1966b) and the psychoanalytic concepts of Bieber et al. (1962), Marmor (1965), and Ovesey (1965) but was innovative in terms of its explicit and pre-planned use of a particular therapeutic stratagem—group therapy led jointly by a male and a female therapist. This format was designed to be both behavioral and psychoanalytic in its impact.

Behaviorally, in groups of this kind the patient is in a situation in which he can undergo an in vivo desensitization to having a close, triangular relationship with a woman (the woman therapist) while he simultaneously begins to be able to learn to discriminate between this new woman and his own original female object, his mother. In addition, the patient can eventually learn to discriminate between this new man-woman team (the two group therapists) and his own father and mother. In other words, the patient seems to undergo a "corrective emotional experience" regarding male-female dyads. Most particularly, *and usually quite unlike the situation in his family of origin,* the patient has a new experience in which he can be emotionally close to the man (the male therapist) without experiencing threats, punishment, scorn, or withdrawal from the woman therapist, who, usually unlike the patient's own mother, works cooperatively and respectfully with the man, rather than badly or subtly undermining him and the patient's nascent identification with him.

It is this kind of in vivo desensitization and corrective emotional experience which the author has come to regard as the central and crucial element for success in this approach. For individual patients within the group at particular phases of their therapy, the therapists may use behavioral techniques (primarily operant conditioning) to work toward helping a patient to increase appropriate assertive behaviors, to desensitize himself to his fear of women, or to open up meaningful communication between a patient and his emotionally distant father; in all such cases "insight" is not only welcomed but is assiduously cultivated as an important and sometimes indispensable facilitator of durable behavior change. Moreover, in virtually all such cases the patient and both therapists work together toward these goals in the context of an ongoing relationship and allegiance with the male therapist and with the female therapist. Patients can thrive, grow, and change in this setting because for most of them it is a situation without precedent

to have on their side the persevering interest and unopposed reinforcement of a man and a woman who respect and cooperate with each
other.

A number of things should be said about how these groups function:
the groups are open-ended in that old members terminate as soon as
they are ready, and new members may begin whenever there is a
vacancy. The focus within particular group meetings is also open, and
to a large extent chosen by group process, as is the amount of time
devoted to a particular group member, or to a particular subject or
theme. Because both therapists are interested in how, and from whom,
people learned behavioral patterns, as well as in current behaviors and
the events (stimuli) which punish, set the stage for, and reinforce them,
the group may at times involve itself intensively in explorations of the
history of a feeling; at other times the group may be just as intensively
involved with here-and-now feelings and behaviors occurring within
the group itself. Frequently, patients in these groups, as in other psy-
chotherapies, have intense feelings about one of the therapists that
discussion reveals to be primarily derived from past experiences with
earlier objects; thus transference phenomena, here as elsewhere in
psychiatry, become important bridges between the here-and-now and
the remote past. In many cases these bridges are essential to permit the
development of "insight," and for some patients,* insight may in turn
be necessary to make it possible for them to work cooperatively with
the therapists toward solid behavioral change.

Any description of behavioral psychotherapy would be incomplete
unless it addressed the question of what the therapists actually do. *In
particular, what behaviors do the therapists choose to enhance by social
reinforcement?*[2] What behaviors do they try to promote through modeling and through the progressive process of in vivo operant shaping?
First, like nearly all other experienced therapists, they model and selec-
tively reinforce certain modes of behavior which have widely generalized if not universal adaptive value: honest recognition and conscious
acceptance of feelings (versus unconscious "acting out" of feelings);
genuine façade-free communication with other people; appropriate
assertiveness; coming to be able to see (or remember) one's family of
origin in historical perspective, yet without having to blur any of the
deep and frequently conflicted feelings toward family members; coming to be able to deal with other people in the here and now with

---

*This is true, for example, for some patients who come to treatment thoroughly caught
up in life patterns aimed at "getting even with" or defying their parents, but which in
fact simultaneously serve to insure the defeat of their own stated goals.

2. By social reinforcement, I mean any active participation on the part of the therapist
that serves to encourage or deepen a line of thought or a direction of feeling. Operationally, social reinforcement gestures can be as "simple" as interested looks or nods or as
complicated as evocative interpretations or clarifications (L. Birk, 1968; Ferster, 1972;
L. Birk et al., 1973a, especially pp. 38–39; L. Birk, 1974)

empathy, honesty, and, when possible, generosity. Beyond this, in these groups patients also reinforce particular behaviors that in the author's opinion frequently have special adaptive value for this group. This is not an exhaustive list, but among the behaviors felt to be of special adaptive value, the following would have to be included:

1. Both therapists reinforce attention to the personal side of sexual relationships, male or female. For example, if there is someone with whom the patient is living and/or experiencing sex, or to whom he is attracted, both therapists are immediately and continuingly interested in the personal side of this: "What is his/her name? What is he/she like? Is he/she caring and thoughtful, or impersonal and uninvolved? Or is he/she actually destructive and exploitative?"

2. Both therapists attempt to model a free, open, and nonjudgmental attitude toward sex, whether between people of the same sex or of the opposite sex, and to model and reinforce the attitude that sexual pleasure is in itself good. As a corollary of this, relevant details of sexual interactions, homosexual, heterosexual, or masturbatory, are openly discussed. Nearly all group members are initially at least a little inhibited about some of the details, but with many repetitions, the fears and inhibitions gradually disappear. Many times the therapists elect to reinforce discussion of constructive wholesome homosexual experiences because they represent a shift away from guilt and/or isolation toward pleasure and a real person.

3. Both therapists try to model and reinforce viewing men and women as people first, with good and bad qualities, and as sexual partners second.

4. Both therapists try to help group members to discriminate between exploitative and nonexploitative people and relationships. Obviously, as in psychotherapy with heterosexual people, often this necessarily involves analyzing and working through underlying masochistic wishes.

5. Both therapists try to break down the often false, self-protective black-and-white dichotomizing of self and others into "gay" or "straight." In other words, group members are reinforced for acknowledging fully *all* their conscious sexual feelings and fantasies: more often than not, though not certainly in every case, most group members, even those who are Kinsey 6 behaviorally, have at least some heterosexual feelings concealed within their operating concepts of themselves as purely and simply "gay."

6. Both therapists reinforce patients for trying to analyze what neurotic elements there may be in their homosexual urges and also in their heterosexual behaviors. Some patients learn that they seek an anonymous homosexual outlet when very angry or when afraid of some recent success. Several pedophiles have learned that for them the powerful urge for sex with a young boy has to do with a wholesome though misdirected wish to escape from the stodgy, thoroughly unplayful conservatism of their parents which they generalize onto all adults. Not a few group members who begin therapy zealous "to go straight" or "become normal" need to be prodded into and then reinforced for an examination of the neurotic elements that drive them toward compulsive pseudoheterosexual behaviors.

7. For those group members who do have or discover some genuine ele-

ments of conscious heterosexual interest, both therapists reinforce experimentation in relationships with men *and* women.

8. Both therapists try to reinforce movement toward healthier relationships, with less exploitative human beings, whether those human beings happen to be men or women.

Partly because of the healthy and still-growing sociological trend toward greater cultural acceptance of bisexual and homosexual lifestyles, there are now many more homosexual and bisexual people who want to remain as they are in terms of their sexual orientation. Yet there are still others who do not want to remain exclusively or predominantly homosexual. After extended probing it sometimes becomes clear that some of these people who say that they want to "change" may have neurotic motives underlying this desire. It can mean real progress for such persons to come to terms with this fact and to shift their treatment goals accordingly. There are, however, other homosexual and bisexual people who say that they want to change and who seem to want to do so for nonneurotic reasons. Fortunately, experience indicates that such people can usually achieve heterosexual goals if they are stably and genuinely motivated and willing and able to persevere in treatment.

For statistical clarity, the data to be discussed will be from only a subsample of the total of about one hundred men that the author has personally treated in long-term therapy. Two criteria for inclusion in this subsample were used in order to assess the therapeutic outcome with the most highly motivated, exclusively homosexual patients: (1) only patients who were *exclusively* homosexual and who had never once experienced heterosexual intercourse prior to therapy were included; and (2) only patients who "persevered in therapy" were included—that is, those who remained in therapy two and one-half years or more or else were ready to terminate earlier. Application of these criteria yielded a subsample of twenty-nine patients, of which fourteen came into therapy expressing a clear wish to experience heterosexual feelings and behaviors in a pleasurable way, and fifteen came into therapy with no such well-articulated wish or with only equivocal or ambivalent heterosexual wishes.

Turning now to the data on the therapeutic outcome for this subsample of very highly motivated, exclusively homosexual patients, and looking for the moment only at whether a heterosexual shift took place during extended therapy, I can report the following:

Of the 14 patients who initially expressed a wish to achieve a heterosexual shift:	Of the 15 patients who initially did *not* unequivocally wish to achieve a heterosexual shift:

10 men made heterosexual shifts and are now in stable, apparently happy marriages

11 men remained homosexual

1 man made a heterosexual shift, was married for 3 years, but has recently been divorced

1 man is happily married, enjoying regular heterosexual intercourse, and has 2 children

1 man made a heterosexual shift; he is now unofficially engaged and enjoying regular intercourse with his fianceé

1 man is married and has 2 children, but is currently struggling with a severe marital crisis

2 men made heterosexual shifts, now enjoy heterosexual intercourse, and are dating regularly with a serious interest in "finding a woman to settle down with"

1 man is sporadically dating a very neurotic(narcissistic-hysterical)woman with whom he occasionally has intercourse

total: 10/14 (71%) "Solid" heterosexual shifts

1 man is "engaged" and for many months was having intercourse with this woman; however, since the time of his engagement to her about a year ago, he has not had intercourse with her

total: 1/15 (7%) "Solid heterosexual shifts

Overall Summary of Heterosexual Shifts:

"Solid" 11/29 (38%)
Total 18/29 (62%)

In speaking of heterosexual shifts, I want to make it clear that it is my belief that these represent shifts in a person's salient sexual adaptation to life, not total metamorphosis. Most, if not all, people who have been homosexual continue to have some homosexual feelings, fantasies, and interests. More often than not they also have occasional, or more than occasional, homosexual outlets, even while being "happily married."

It is also worth saying a word about the potential for confusion in attempts to assess the meaningfulness of outcome figures. If the criteria for a heterosexual shift are defined simply as the new emergence of heterosexual behavior, and if one focuses *only* on the fourteen patients treated who persevered in therapy and who initially expressed a strong wish to achieve a heterosexual shift, the outcome figures are fourteen out of fourteen (100 percent). Defining the criteria for heterosexual shift more conservatively however, the outcome figures become ten out of fourteen (71 percent) for patients who began therapy desiring a shift, but only one out of fifteen (7 percent) for those who began therapy without an expressed desire for shift. Finally, if those initially desiring shift and those not expressing this desire are considered together, as I

believe is very often done, the overall results in terms of "solid" heterosexual shifts become eleven out of twenty-nine (38 percent), and eighteen out of twenty-nine (62 percent) for total heterosexual shifts. It
cannot be too strongly emphasized here that those patients who came
into behavioral psychotherapy without a clear wish for a heterosexual
shift and who did not in fact make such a shift are in no way to be
considered treatment failures. Almost all of these people considered
their therapy to have been quite valuable in that they achieved some
personally relevant goals; for the most part of course people who did
not find the therapy valuable did not continue it, and so had dropped
out long before two-and-a-half years.

Three important points can be distilled from these outcome data:

1. Of a total sample of about one hundred male homosexual/bisexual
    patients, approximately 50 percent found weekly behavioral psycho-
    therapy in a group led by male and female cotherapists to be "very
    valuable," enough so that they remained in this treatment for two-
    and-one-half years or more.
2. If we focus on the most highly motivated exclusively, homosexual pa-
    tients (who also said prior to the onset of treatment that they wanted to
    be able to experience sex with a woman), a startling number—(fourteen
    out of fourteen)—were able to do so following extended treatment; ten
    of these fourteen have married and have remained married.
3. For those patients who were highly motivated to attain other goals in
    therapy, not involving heterosexual shift, there were only a small num-
    ber (4/15) who did manifest even transient heterosexual shift in the
    course of treatment, and to date only one man (1/15) clearly has made
    a solid heterosexual shift. This man is now married, has two children,
    and is happy with his new life-style, though he did not explicitly wish
    to "be heterosexual" at the time he entered therapy. Stated as accu-
    rately as possible, he seemed to be vaguely interested in the possibility
    of being heterosexual, and eventually being married, but he certainly
    did not initially hold this as a conscious and unambivalent goal for him-
    self.

Thus, homosexual or bisexual people who might fear "being
changed" without their wishing it might well conclude that they have
little or nothing to fear from behavioral psychotherapy, and potentially
much to gain, in terms of achieving other goals important to them.

Looking Forward

Behaviorally based therapy for homosexual or bisexual people has now
reached the point of development where it offers, or could offer if
enough trained therapists were available, several things of major impor-

tance: homosexual couples (whether composed of two men or two women) in which either partner suffers from a psychogenic sexual dysfunction, can now usually be treated with success in short-term therapy —just as heterosexual couples can be—with full resolution of the dysfunction occurring after five to fifty weekly sessions.

In addition, homosexual or bisexual individuals who have some conflict surrounding their sexual adaptation, and who want to broaden their sexual orientation to include heterosexual function, or who think they might be interested in doing so, now can receive effective treatment at a small fraction of the cost in time and money otherwise required by extensive psychoanalytic treatment, with therapeutic results that compare favorably with treatment via classical psychoanalysis. Unfortunately, however, there is still a dearth of male-female therapist teams trained and experienced in this treatment method.

And finally, homosexual or bisexual men and women who are suffering from some life problem (target symptom) amenable to behavior therapy should now be able to get treatment from experienced general behavior therapists who will work with them toward the achievement of therapeutic goals unrelated to sexual preference without pushing them toward a heterosexual shift.

REFERENCES

Agras, W. S. 1972. *Behavior modification, principles and clinical applications.* Boston: Little, Brown.

Bandura, A. 1969. *Principles of behavior modification.* New York: Holt, Rinehart and Winston.

Bieber, I., et al. 1962. *Homosexuality. A psychoanalytic study of male homosexuals.* New York: Basic Books.

Birk, A. 1978. Sex therapy: A behavioral approach. In A. Nicholi, Jr., ed., *The Harvard guide to modern psychiatry.* (Cambridge, Mass.: Harvard University Press, Belknap Press), pp. 459–70.

Birk, L. 1968. Social reinforcemnt in psychotherapy. *Conditional reflex.* 3(2): 116–123.

Birk, L. 1974. Group psychotherapy for men who are homosexual. *Journal of Sex & Marital Therapy* 1 (1):29–52.

———. 1978. Behavior therapy and behavioral psychotherapy. In *The Harvard guide to modern psychiatry* (Cambridge, Mass.: Harvard University Press, Belknap Press), pp. 433–58.

Birk, L., ed. 1972. Behavior therapy: Achievement, promise, and false promise. *Seminars in Psychiatry* (New York: Grune & Stratton), vol. 4, no. 2, pp. 81–190.

———. 1973. *Biofeedback: Behavioral medicine—The clinical uses of biofeedback in medicine and psychiatry.* New York: Grune & Stratton.

Birk, L., et al. 1973a. Behavior therapy in psychiatry. In American Psychiatric Association Task Force Report no. 5.

———. 1973b. Serum testosterone levels in homosexual men. *New England Journal of Medicine* 289:1236–38.

Birk, L.; Miller, E.; and Cohler, B. 1970. Group psychotherapy for homosexual men by male-female cotherapists. *Acta Psychiatrica Scandavica* special supplement 218.

Brinkley-Birk, A., and Birk, L. 1975. Sex therapy for vaginismus, primary impotence, and ejaculatory incompetence in an unconsummated marriage. *Psychiatric Opinion* 12 (5): 38–42.

Feldman, M. P., and MacCulloch, M. J. 1964. A systematic approach to the treatment of homosexuality by conditioned aversion: Preliminary report. *American Journal of Psychiatry* 121:167–72.

――――. 1965. The application of anticipatory avoidance learning to the treatment of homosexuality. I. Theory, technique, and preliminary results. *The Journal of Behavior Research and Therapy*, ed. H. J. Eysenck, 2:165–83.

Ferster, C. B. Behavior therapy: Achievement, promise, and false promise. In L. Birk, ed., *Clinical reinforcement. Seminars in psychiatry.* 3(2): 101–111.

Franks, C. M., and Wilson, G. T., eds. 1973. *Annual review of behavior therapy theory and practice.* New York: Brunner/Mazel.

Gartrell, N. K.; Lariaux, D. L.; and Chase, T. N. 1977. Plasma testosterone in homosexual and heterosexual women. *American Journal of Psychiatry* 134:10.

Goldfried, M. R., and Davison, G. C. 1976. *Clinical behavior therapy.* New York: Holt, Rinehart and Winston.

Hadden, S. B. 1966a. Treatment of male homosexuals in groups. *International Journal of Group Psychotherapy* 16:13–22.

――――. 1966b. Group psychotherapy of male homosexuals. In J. Masserman, ed., *Current psychiatric therapies,* vol. 6 (New York: Grune & Stratton).

Kaplan, H. S. 1974. *The new sex therapy: Active treatment of sexual dysfunctions.* New York: Brunner/Mazel.

Leitenberg, H. 1976. *Handbook of behavior modification and behavior therapy.* Englewood Cliffs, N.J.: Prentice-Hall.

Liberman, R. P. 1972. *A guide to behavioral analysis and therapy.* New York: Pergamon Press.

Marmor, J., ed. 1965. *Sexual Inversion: The multiple roots of homosexuality.* New York: Basic Books.

Marmor, J., and Woods, S. M. eds. 1979. *The interface between psychodynamic and behavioral therapies.* New York: Plenum.

Masters, W. H., and Johnson, V. E. 1966. *Human sexual response.* Boston: Little, Brown.

――――. 1970. *Human sexual inadequacy.* Boston: Little, Brown.

――――. 1979 *Homosexuality in perspective.* Boston: Little, Brown

Ovesey, L. 1965. Pseudohomosexuality and homosexuality in men: Psychodynamics as a guide to treatment. In J. Marmor, ed., *Sexual inversion: The multiple roots of homosexuality* (New York: Basic Books), pp. 211–33.

Rachman, S. J., and Teasdale, J. 1969. Aversion therapy: An appraisal. In. C. M. Franks, ed., *Behavior therapy: Appraisal and status* (New York: McGraw-Hill), pp. 284–85.

Stevenson, I., and Wolpe, J. 1960. Recovery from sexual deviations through overcoming non-sexual neurotic responses. *American Journal of Psychiatry* 116:737.

Wolpe, J., and Lazarus, A. A. 1966. *Behavior therapy techniques.* Oxford, England: Pergamon Press.

Yates, A. J. 1970. *Behavior therapy.* New York: John Wiley.

――――. 1975. *Theory and practice in behavior therapy.* New York: John Wiley.

Epilogue: Homosexuality and the Issue of Mental Illness

JUDD MARMOR

The issue of whether individuals who manifest homosexual behavior should be regarded as mentally ill continues to be hotly debated, not only in professional mental health circles but also throughout the public. Many psychoanalysts and psychiatrists who consider themselves to be enlightened with regard to discrimination against homosexuals nevertheless feel strongly that homosexuality is a mental disorder.

An extreme example of this attitude is that of Socarides (1970), who asserts that he is against the legal prosecution of individuals for homosexual behavior but, at the same time, insists that they are mentally ill and should be required to undergo psychoanalytic treatment. The following statements by him (Socarides, 1972) about obligatory homosexuals (made in the course of a sworn deposition in a case that resulted in the discharge of a naval civilian employee with an outstanding work record who had accidentally been discovered to be homosexual) are illustrative of his thinking:

> The motivation [of an obligatory homosexual] is to obtain relief [from his unconscious conflict] no matter the price, the danger, putting aside all other considerations of pride, self-esteem, family, friends, relationships to society. The relief can only be obtained in one way, and that is through sexual congress with the person of the same sex. . . . These individuals are driven so overwhelmingly by anxiety that they have to do what they have to do. . . . Such a man is in a sort of psychic disequilibrium. . . . Obligatory homosexu-

als . . . show symptoms and signs upon deep investigation which would probably place them between the borderline neuroses and the psychoses. They are [*sic*] a severe condition.

These remarks of Socarides dramatically illustrate the fact that the issue of psychiatric classification of homosexuals is by no means a harmless or theoretical one. To take a position that homosexuals are seriously mentally ill and compulsively driven by needs over which they have no control and then to say in the same breath that they should not be subject to legal sanctions poses a fundamental contradiction. For if, indeed, all obligatory homosexuals are subject to profound, powerful, and uncontrollable impulses that may even involve the seduction of innocent young people, then certain social and legal consequences inevitably follow. They become subject to discharge from military service just as psychotic or other seriously mentally ill individuals might be, they may be justifiably denied housing, and it becomes reasonable to exclude them from certain occupations such as teaching, where their "sick" behavior might adversely influence young people. In short, psychiatric labeling of homosexuality as a mental disorder lends authoritative weight to those who would discriminate against homosexuals in employment, discharge them from military service without honor, deprive them of various legal rights, and indeed sometimes confine them involuntarily in mental institutions. There is no doubt that such a psychiatric judgment, particularly in these days of computer banks with instantaneously available information about private lives, can have catastrophic consequences for countless homosexuals, both male and female.

It may be argued, however, that regardless of such adverse social and political consequences, if the psychiatric evidence mandates the conclusion that homosexuality is a mental illness, then in terms of scientific integrity, there is no justification for modifying that judgment. Psychiatric opponents of the American Psychiatric Association (APA) Board's decision made precisely this charge when in December 1973 the APA Board of Trustees decided to delete homosexuality from the second edition of the APA *Diagnostic and Statistical Manual for Mental Disorders* (DSM-II). They asserted that the Board had sacrificed scientific integrity on the altar of political expediency and had succumbed to the pressure of gay militancy.

In view of the numerous distortions that have appeared in the popular press concerning this APA decision, it may be of interest to review the facts as they did occur. Early in 1972 the members of the Massachusetts District Branch, a component society of the American Psychiatric Association, acting entirely on their own, passed a resolution expressing their conviction that homosexual behavior in and of itself was not a mental illness and requesting the APA to remove it from the DSM-II. This resolution was sent through normal channels to the Reference

Committee, made up largely of the chairpersons of the various APA Councils and chaired by the president-elect of the APA. The Reference Committee, following normal procedure, referred the resolution to the Council on Research and Development, which in turn sent the matter to one of its component committees, the Committee on Nomenclature, for study of the scientific issues involved.[1] None of these steps involved or was motivated by pressure from gay activists but reflected the normal way in which the APA handles any such emerging issue.

In the fall of 1973 the Committee on Nomenclature, after studying the matter intensively for almost a full year, concluded that homosexuality in and of itself did not constitute a mental illness and recommended to the Council on Research and Development that it be removed from DSM-II. This decision was approved by the Reference Committee and brought to the Board of Trustees of the APA in December for a final decision. The Board ratified the recommendation and unanimously (two abstentions) passed the following resolution:

> Whereas homosexuality per se implies no impairment in judgment, stability, reliability, or general social or vocational capabilities, therefore, be it resolved that the American Psychiatric Association deplores all public and private discrimination against homosexuals in such areas as employment, housing, public accommodation, and licensing and declares that no burden of proof of such judgment, capacity, or reliability shall be placed upon homosexuals greater than that imposed on any other persons. Further, the American Psychiatric Association supports and urges the enactment of civil rights legislation at the local, state, and federal level that would offer homosexual citizens the same protections now guaranteed to others on the basis of race, creed, color, etc. Further, the American Psychiatric Association supports and urges the repeal of all discriminatory legislation singling out homosexual acts by consenting adults in private.

Under normal circumstances a decision of the Board of Trustees does not have to be ratified by the membership. Opponents of the decision, however, quickly marshaled the necessary two hundred signatures to compel a referendum of the entire membership of the APA. The referendum was voted upon in the spring of 1974 coincidentally with a national election for new officers of the APA, during which all three candidates for the presidency expressed themselves as being strongly in favor of the Board's decision. The decision of the Board of Trustees was upheld by a substantial majority, with 5,854 (58 percent) in favor, and 3,810 (37.8 percent) opposed; 367 (3.6 percent) abstained.

Contrary to the impression given by the popular press, this decision has *never* been reversed by the members of the American Psychiatric

1. Coincidentally, the issue became public and was the subject of considerable debate at various meetings of the American Psychiatric Association. At the May 1973 APA meeting in Honolulu, an animated panel discussion took place on the issue between representatives of various points of view, including a member of the Gay Liberation Front (Stoller et al., 1973).

Association or by its Board of Trustees. In 1977 the journal *Medical Aspects of Human Sexuality* sent a survey questionnaire to twenty-five hundred members of the American Medical Association who identified themselves as psychiatrists but who may or may not have been members of the APA; this survey showed that a majority of the respondents believed that homosexuals were "less responsible" than heterosexuals. This has been eagerly seized upon by opponents of the APA resolution as indicating that the "APA membership" had reversed its position on the original vote. Such a conclusion is without foundation.[2]

Moving away from such "political" considerations, however, let us examine the *scientific* issues involved in the question of whether or not a homosexual orientation should be considered in the realm of psychopathology. It is ironic that the strongest proponents of the psychopathology concept of homosexuality are psychoanalysts, and yet the founder of psychoanalysis, Sigmund Freud, did not himself consider it an illness. In *Three Essays on the Theory of Sexuality* (1905), he wrote that homosexuality "is found in people who exhibit no other serious deviations from the normal . . . whose efficiency is unimpaired, and who are indeed distinguished by specially high intellectual development and ethical culture." Also, in an interview reported in a Vienna newspaper (Freud, 1903), Freud is quoted as saying, "I am . . . of the firm conviction that homosexuals must not be treated as sick people, for a perverse orientation is far from being a sickness. Wouldn't that oblige us to characterize as sick many great thinkers and scholars of all time, whose perverse orientation we know for a fact and whom we admire precisely because of their mental health? Homosexual persons are not sick." Similarly, in his famous "Letter to an American Mother" Freud wrote: "Homosexuality is assuredly no advantage, but it is nothing to be ashamed of, no vice, no degradation, it cannot be classified as an illness" (Freud, 1951).

Freud's lifelong consistency in this matter was revealed in a recently discovered correspondence with Ernest Jones in 1921, wherein Jones expressed the conviction that it was improper to accept a doctor known to be manifestly homosexual into membership in the psychoanalytic

---

2. Still another popular misconception is that the APA has taken the position that all homosexuals are "normal." Nothing can be further from the truth. Such a position would be no less absurd than the analogous one that all heterosexuals are "normal." All that the Board's resolution implies is that the mere fact of being homosexual *in and of itself* does not warrant labeling a person as neurotic or as suffering from a mental disorder. It merely requires that the presence or absence of a mental disorder be adduced on the basis of the same criteria as it would be in heterosexual persons, and not just on the basis of a same-sex object preference. It in no way negates the fact that many homosexuals are indeed mentally ill, just as many heterosexuals are. In fact, although no accurate data on this point are available, it would not at all surprise me to find a higher incidence of emotional disturbance among homosexuals, as compared to heterosexuals, considering the widespread opprobrium and social antagonism with which they have to cope in the course of their development.

association, but asked for Freud's opinion. On 11 December of that year Freud and Otto Rank jointly replied: "Your query, dear Ernest, concerning prospective membership of homosexuals has been considered by us and we disagree with you. In effect we cannot exclude such persons without other sufficient reasons, as we cannot agree with their legal prosecution. We feel that a decision in such cases should depend upon a thorough examination of the other qualities of the candidate" (Freud and Rank, 1921).

Nevertheless, many contemporary psychoanalysts continue to consider homosexuality per se as a form of psychopathology incompatible with a reasonably happy life. What is overlooked in such a conclusion is the fact that even if it were true that it is difficult for most homosexual individuals to have a reasonably happy life in contemporary society, it does not necessarily follow that this is an indication of psychopathology *intrinsic* to their homosexuality. One could with equal justification argue that being a Jew or a black person in some societies is "incompatible with a reasonably happy life," but it would not follow that being Jewish or black in and of itself constitutes psychopathology.

The fact is that most practicing analysts have arrived at their opinions about homosexual psychopathology from the patients they see in their offices, who have come to them with mental problems. Socarides' lurid views of the homosexual personality are obviously derived from seriously neurotic, compulsively cruising homosexuals who have consulted him. These views have no validity in relation to the many thousands of homosexuals in the world who have never found it necessary to seek psychotherapeutic help and who live quiet, dignified, and responsible lives. If psychiatrists drew similar generalizations about heterosexuals, based only on their experience with heterosexual patients, they would arrive at equally skewed impressions about the psychopathology inherent in being heterosexual!

The "scientific" arguments concerning the abnormality of homosexuality rest on three major premises: (1) that homosexual behavior is a disorder of sexual development resulting from disturbed family relationships, (2) that it represents an obvious deviation from the biological norm, and (3) that when homosexuals are studied psychodynamically they are found to be emotionally disturbed and unhappy people. Let us examine these three points in detail.

The argument that homosexuality is a form of disordered sexual development due to faulty parenting actually says nothing other than that the outcome of the sexual development is not considered to be normal. Strongly religious people might argue that all atheism is a form of disordered moral development and political conservatives might insist that radicalism is an example of disordered social development. Indeed, there *was* a time in the psychoanalytic literature when all radicals were considered to be neurotics who were rebelling against their fathers. Similarly, women who aspired to what were then considered masculine professions were all assumed to be suffering from "neurotic" penis envy. In recent years the free world has been justifiably distressed because in some nations the very act of political dissent has been made a basis for a diagnosis of psychiatric illness. Yet are we not doing the same thing with those whose sexual preferences differ from those of the majority?

As we have seen (see Overview, this volume), homosexuals may come from quite diverse family backgrounds and may differ just as widely in styles of living and in personality as do heterosexuals. The fact is that *all personality differences are the results of individual variations in developmental background.* Excluding genetic factors, the idiosyncratic way in which every person lives and acts can almost always be plausibly "explained" by a careful psychoanalytic reconstruction of his or her life history and family background. In the final analysis, psychiatric categorization of the development of homosexual preference as a form of "disordered" sexual development is simply a reflection of our society's disapproval of such behavior, and psychiatrists, whether they realize it or not, are acting as agents of social control in putting the label of psychopathology upon it (Marmor, 1972). Psychiatric textbooks of the late nineteenth century, on the same basis, authoritatively labeled the tendency to masturbate as indicative of serious mental disturbance.

Behavioral scientists should have grave reservations about the propriety of attaching a deviant label to variant behavioral patterns simply because they differ from those favored by the majority. As a matter of fact, they do not ordinarily do this, except where they are unwittingly reflecting the culture's prejudice toward a particular variety of behavior. For example, psychiatrists do not usually classify adherents of astrology, numerology, spiritualism, or various unusual religious sects as being mentally ill. In this regard, psychiatrists, like other citizens in open democratic societies, recognize the rights of individuals to adhere to widely diverse ideological or religious patterns without being labeled as mentally "deviant." The labeling of homosexual behavior as a psychopathological disorder, or "perversion," however honestly believed, is an example of defining normality in terms of adjustment to social conventions.

Cultures other than our own have had and do have widely varying attitudes toward homosexual behavior (Ford and Beach, 1952). Moreover, history reveals that sexual mores are constantly changing. Some patterns of sexual behavior that were considered quite deviant only a decade ago are now widely accepted as being within normal limits, e.g., young unmarried couples living together quite openly. Thus it would be a mistake to assume that our society's current reaction to homosexual behavior is either eternal or sacrosanct. As an example, there is already a discernible trend in the mores of the current younger generation toward tolerance of patterns of bisexuality.

The second major argument for the pathology of homosexual behavior is that it is contrary to the biological norm and therefore "unnatural." It is asserted that all mammalian species are clearly heterosexual and that, were this not so, the survival of the species would not be possible. Does it not follow, therefore, that homosexual behavior is contrary to the "laws of nature"?

It is true that exclusive and obligatory homosexuality is rarely seen in lower animals except under extreme and unusual environmental conditions. *It is equally true, however, that exclusive and obligatory heterosexuality is also most unusual.* The widespread occurrence both of obligatory homosexuality and obligatory heterosexuality is unique to human society. All lower animals, including infrahuman primates (see Denniston, chapter 1, this volume), display obvious patterns of homosexual behavior from time to time, even though heterosexual reactions are predominant. Homosexual behavior in primates has been shown to occur even in the presence of available heterosexual partners. It has been observed between females as well as between males, but more often among the latter. Both autoerotic and homoerotic practices tend to be more varied and extensive the higher an animal is on the evolutionary scale.

Proponents of the thesis that homosexual behavior is biologically abnormal argue that the homosexual reactions that are observed in lower mammals are manifestations of dominance and have nothing to do with sexuality. They assert, moreover, that when apparent copulatory behavior takes place between such males there is no anal penetration and ejaculation never occurs. These assertions, however, are simply contrary to fact. Every cattle breeder knows that a young bull can be used as a teaser to induce not only mounting but also ejaculation in a breeding bull, and this teasing is a method that is used to obtain semen for artificial insemination in cattle. Indeed, breeders have learned that if such teasing is done too often the bull may begin to react more readily to his own sex than to a female! Penetration and ejaculation have also been observed in subhuman primates (Chevalier-Skolnikoff, 1974; Erwin and Maple, 1976). In any event, the argument about anal penetration is a specious one. Human homosexual behavior does not necessarily involve anal penetration, and the erotic exchanges that have been observed between same-sex primates and other animals would certainly be regarded as unequivocally homosexual if they occurred between human beings of the same sex. On the basis of all the evidence from comparative zoology, Beach (1948) concluded, "Human homosexuality reflects the essential bisexual character of our mammalian inheritance. The extreme modifiability of man's sex life makes possible the conversion of this essential bisexuality into a form of unisexuality with the result that a member of the same sex eventually becomes the only acceptable stimulus to arousal" (p. 276).

The argument that homosexuality is biologically unnatural becomes even more specious when one considers that all civilized human behavior from the cooking of food to the wearing of clothes is a departure from the strictly "natural." We do not label vegetarianism or sexual celibacy as automatic evidences of psychopathology, even though these behavioral patterns do not follow "natural" biological expectations. Actually, one of the most distinctive characteristics of human beings is their extraordinary capacity to modify and transform their "natural" biological drives into widely diverse patterns of behavior, whether this be in terms of sexuality, eating, devising shelters, worshiping gods, or developing the mathematical precision that enables them to land a man on the moon or fire intercontinental missiles with pinpoint accuracy.

The biological argument dovetails with the "abnormal sexual development" argument in its assumption that, in the absence of a disordered family background, all people would "naturally" become exclusively heterosexual. This not only goes counter to the evidence from comparative zoology, but also completely ignores the fact that human beings arrive at homosexual behavior by widely diverse paths. As has been shown, there is a considerable likelihood that at least some individuals may be born with a propensity towards homosexual behavior as a result of variations in the degree of androgenic sensitization of hypothalamic brain centers during intrauterine development (Dörner, 1967; see also chapter 3, this volume). In others, there may be some hormonal variations that lead to such propensities (see chapter 2, this volume). Still others come from family backgrounds not significantly different in any particular from those of heterosexual individuals (Siegelman, 1974). Clearly, the biological argument is but another rationalization for our society's moral disapproval of homosexual behavior. It is not accidental that the most frequent characterization of homosexual behavior as a "crime against nature" has come from religious sources, not from scientific ones.

The possibility, as formulated by Money (1967), that there may be a "hidden genetic predisposition" to homosexuality, at least in some homosexuals, makes it analogous in such instances to left-handedness. Left-handedness, also due to a genetic factor, involves problems of adaptation in a predominantly right-handed society, but we do not therefore label this "deviant" pattern as an illness. Indeed, we do not even try any more to force left-handed children to change their handedness, recognizing that such efforts may do more harm than good.

The third argument "justifying" the labeling of homosexual behavior as psychopathological is that in-depth psychodynamic studies of homosexual individuals reveal them all to be deeply disturbed and neurotic individuals. Some of the psychoanalytic hypotheses derived from such studies are: (1) that all homosexuals suffer from a deep-seated castration anxiety which makes them afraid to approach women because women as "castrated" people arouse their phobic fears. Thus they turn to persons with penises as a reassurance against the fear of castration. Obviously, this theory has no validity for the millions of individuals who are bisexual or even preferentially homosexual (groups 2, 3, and 4 on the Kinsey scale) and yet are still able to enjoy heterosexual relations; (2) that all homosexuals are deeply narcissistic and are therefore seeking an object like themselves and, in fact, are "in love with themselves." Such a formulation obviously does not explain why *most* individuals diagnosed as narcissistic personalities are nevertheless *heterosexual* in orientation; (3) that homosexuals suffer from a tremendous fear and hatred of women based on a relationship with a possessive, controlling, "castrating" mother, symbolically represented by the devouring, dentate vagina. The only trouble with this formulation is that fantasies and symbols of dentate vaginas also appear in the dreams and fantasies of heterosexual men; (4) that the male homosexual pattern derives from an identification with the mother, either because she was the more loving and important parent, or because she was the stronger, more dominant one (identification with the aggressor). This would presumably explain why some homosexual men have profound feminine identifications, and why they predominate in "effeminate" occupations such as ballet, hairdressing, interior decorating, etc., as well as why they seek relations with very masculine men toward whom they can relate as female counterparts. Such a formulation, however, does not account for the countless homosexuals who do not fit the effeminate stereotype in any way and who operate effectively in "nonfeminine" occupations, nor does it account for those who are attracted to effeminate partners.[3]

It must be recognized that there are very few individuals indeed, heterosexual or homosexual, in whom deep psychoanalytic probing would not elicit *some* evidences of deviance from ideal normality. No

3. Kirkpatrick and Morgan (chapter 20, this volume) attempt to define under what circumstances "female homosexuality" is pathological and to separate out a small group who "represent a preoedipal gender disorder." It seems to me that in so doing they have fallen into the trap of defining the psychopathology in these women in terms of their sexuality instead of seeing them as females who suffer from certain characterologic problems which are reflected in their patterns of sexuality also. Preoedipal characterologic disorders with narcissistic defects of the kind described by Kirkpatrick and Morgan are not limited to lesbians. They are seen with considerable frequency among heterosexual females also. If homosexuality in women is a nonpathological variant in most lesbians as these authors assert, why label it as a "gender disorder" in this group of lesbians? I wish to emphasize that I do not disagree that there exist lesbians in whom the psychodynamics elucidated by Kirkpatrick and Morgan can be demonstrated by psychoanalytic investigation. But as these authors themselves recognize, "fragments of these dynamics can be found in women who are neither homosexual nor suffering from neurotic problems." Under these circumstances, to carve out a separate clinical grouping or entity for lesbian women with such problems and then label it as a clinical *disorder* called "female homosexuality" seems to me to be a regressive step.

one is *perfectly* healthy, psychologically, in an absolute sense. This is just as true for heterosexuals as it is for homosexuals. The four basic psychoanalytic hypotheses about male homosexuality described above (some of which are obviously mutually contradictory, and none of which are pathognomonic for all homosexuals) are based on therapeutic experience with *neurotic* homosexual patients. To attribute them to all homosexuals is just as unwarranted as similar generalizations about heterosexuals based only on analytic work with *neurotic* heterosexuals would be. Countless objective psychological tests have been done by now on nonpatient groups of homosexuals with matched groups of heterosexuals, beginning with Evelyn Hooker's classic study (1957). With surprising uniformity, the vast majority of these studies have shown few, if any, significant differences in personality structure between the two groups and no greater psychopathology among nonpatient homosexuals than among matched heterosexual controls (see chapter 16, this volume).

The basic issue, however, is not whether some or many homosexuals can be found to be neurotically disturbed. In a society like ours where homosexuals are uniformly treated with disparagement or contempt—to say nothing about outright hostility—it would be surprising indeed if substantial numbers of them did *not* suffer from an impaired self-image and some degree of unhappiness with their stigmatized status (see chapter 6, this volume). It is manifestly unwarranted and inaccurate, however, to attribute such neuroticism, when it exists, to intrinsic aspects of homosexuality itself. Even if only a minority of homosexuals are found not to be neurotic by ordinary standards, it would be scientifically incorrect to stereotype them all as suffering from psychopathology. In actual fact many homosexuals, both male and female, function responsibly and honorably in positions of the highest trust and live emotionally stable, mature, and well-adjusted lives that are indistinguishable from those of well-adjusted heterosexuals, except for their different sexual preferences.

The issue of homosexual object choice should be regarded as essentially irrelevant, therefore, to the issue of mental illness. Any diagnostic judgments about homosexuals should be made, like those about heterosexuals, on the basis of the existence of specific underlying mental disorders. I am hopeful that ultimately this is what will happen. In DSM-I, the first *Diagnostic and Statistical Manual* of the American Psychiatric Association, homosexuality was listed under the category of "psychopathic personality with pathological sexuality." A decade or so later, in DSM-II, it was categorized as a "sociopathic personality disturbance" until it was removed from this category by the APA's December 1973 decision. In the new DSM-III homosexuality per se is not listed as a mental disturbance, but there is a category called "egodystonic homosexuality" referring to homosexuals who are unhappy with their homosexual object choice and seek help to change it. There is no doubt that such homosexual individuals exist, but, in my opinion, to create a separate category for them still constitutes a relic of ancient prejudice and a tendency to deal with them differently from heterosexuals. Psychiatrists see "egodystonic celibacy," "egodystonic states of being unmarried," and "egodystonic states of being divorced" all the time, yet no one would think of creating separate diagnostic categories for such reactions. Only when we totally free ourselves from the tendency to put psychiatric labels on homosexuals that singularly differentiate them from heterosexuals with analogous problems will psychiatrists finally become free from the age-old prejudice in this area.

REFERENCES

Beach, F. A. 1948. Sexual behavior in animals and men. Harvey Lecture Series 43:-254–80.

Chevalier-Skolnikoff, S. 1974. Male-female, female-female, and male-male sexual behavior in the stumptail monkey. *Archives of Sexual Behavior* 3:95–116.

Dörner, G. 1967. Tierexperimentalle untersuchungen zur frage einer hormonellen pathogenese der homosexualitet. *Acta Biologica et Medica Germanica* 19:569–84.

Erwin, J., and Maple, T. 1976. Ambisexual behavior with male-male anal penetration in male rhesus monkeys. *Archives of Sexual Behavior* 5:9–14.

Ford, C. S., and Beach, F. A. 1952. *Patterns of sexual behavior.* New York: Harper & Bros.

Freud, S. 1903. Quoted in an interview in *Die Zeit,* Vienna, 27 October, p. 5.

———. 1905. Three essays on the theory of sexuality. In J. Strachey, ed., *The standard edition of the complete psychological works of Sigmund Freud,* vol. 7 (London: Hogarth Press), pp. 135–243.

———. 1951. Letter to an American mother. *American Journal of Psychiatry* 102:786.

Freud, S., and Rank, O. 1921. Circular letter dated 11 December, Vienna. The correspondence with Jones was discovered by J. D. Steakley, in the course of research into the early European gay rights struggle, and was published in *Body Politic* (May 1977, p. 9), a Canadian gay liberation journal.

Hooker, E. 1957. The adjustment of the male overt homosexual. *Journal of Projective Techniques* 21:18–31.

Marmor, J. 1972. Homosexuality: Mental illness or moral dilemma? *International Journal of Psychiatry* 10 (1):114–17.

Money, J. 1967. Sexual dimorphism and homosexual gender identity. Working paper prepared for the National Institute of Mental Health's Task Force on Homosexuality.

Siegelman, M. 1974. Parental background of male homosexuals and heterosexuals. *Archives of Sexual Behavior* 3:3–18.

Socarides, C. 1970. Homosexuality and medicine. *Journal of the American Medical Association* 212:1199–1202.

———. 1972. In a sworn deposition taken on 21 September 1972.

Stoller, R. J., et al. 1973. A symposium: Should homosexuality be in the APA nomenclature? *American Journal of Psychiatry* 130:11, 1207–16.

INDEX